THE THESSALONIANS DEBATE

THE THESSALONIANS DEBATE

Methodological Discord or Methodological Synthesis?

Edited by

Karl P. Donfried and Johannes Beutler

WILLIAM B. EERDMANS PUBLISHING COMPANY
GRAND RAPIDS, MICHIGAN / CAMBRIDGE, U.K.

© 2000 Wm. B. Eerdmans Publishing Co.
255 Jefferson Ave. S.E., Grand Rapids, Michigan 49503 /
P.O. Box 163, Cambridge CB3 9PU U.K.

Printed in the United States of America

05 04 03 02 01 00   7 6 5 4 3 2 1

ISBN 0-8028-4374-3

This book is respectfully dedicated to

John Cardinal O'Connor
devoted servant of the church

and

the members of
the Thessalonians Correspondence Seminar
Studiorum Novi Testamenti Societas
with gratitude for their creative insights,
vast learning and generous collaboration

Contents

CONTENTS

PART 2
1 THESSALONIANS:
THE METHODOLOGICAL DEBATE

Contents

Is Synthesis Possible?

Acknowledgments

The papers collected here are revised — substantially revised — and translated versions of seminar papers or responses given in meetings of the *Studiorum Novi Testamenti Societas* (SNTS). It was our privilege to co-chair the Seminar on "The Thessalonian Correspondence," and we are grateful to the SNTS for providing the opportunity to participate in its work in this way. In the first two years of the Seminar (1995-96) we focused on 1 Thess 2:1-12 and the methodological issues involved in the interpretation of 1 Thessalonians, which are the subjects of the papers gathered here. To the contributors we owe a special debt of thanks for participating in this collective work, for accepting a variety of suggestions, and for expanding or contracting their work so that the result would be more comprehensive and less repetitive. More participants and respondents were involved in the ongoing work of the Seminar than are represented here; all have made helpful contributions to our common work, shaping the discussion in important ways. It is with pleasure and gratitude that we also acknowledge these colleagues.

SNTS Seminar on "The Thessalonian Correspondence"

Prague (1995)

Jan Lambrecht, "A Structural Analysis of 1 Thessalonians 4–5"

Johannes Schoon-Janßen, "On the Use of Elements of Ancient Epistolography in 1 Thessalonians"

Frank Hughes, "The Rhetoric of Letters and the Social Situations Implied by Rhetoric"

Edgar Krentz, "1 Thessalonians: Rhetorical Flourishes and Formal Constraints"

Raymond Collins, "'I Command That This Letter Be Read': Writing as a Manner of Speaking"

Charles Wanamaker, "Epistolary vs. Rhetorical Analysis: Is a Synthesis Possible?"

Strasbourg (1996)

Karl P. Donfried, "The Epistolary and Rhetorical Context of 1 Thessalonians 2:1-12"

Rudolf Hoppe, respondent

Traugott Holtz, "On the Background of 1 Thessalonians 2:1-12"

Johan S. Vos, respondent

Otto Merk, "1 Thessalonians 2:1-12: An Exegetical-Theological Study"

Jeffrey Weima, respondent

Birmingham (1997)

Rudolf Hoppe, "Apostel ohne Gemeinde — Gemeinde ohne Apostel. Zur kompositorischen und theologischen Stellung von 1 Thess 2.17–3,10"

Seyoon Kim, respondent

Birger A. Pearson, "Once Again: 1 Thessalonians 2:13-16 as a Deutero-Pauline Interpolation"

Rudolf Hoppe, respondent

John C. Hurd, "1 Thessalonians 3:11-13: A Pivotal Example of Prayer in the Structure of Paul's Letters"

Chrys C. Caragounis, respondent

Copenhagen (1998)

Raymond F. Collins, "The Function of Paraenesis in 1 Thessalonians 4:1-12 and 5:12-22"

Wiard Popkes, respondent

ACKNOWLEDGMENTS

Abraham Malherbe, respondent
Günther Haufe, respondent
Chrys C. Caragounis, respondent
Jeffrey Weima, respondent

We acknowledge the permission of Sheffield Academic Press to reprint in revised form Frank W. Hughes's "The Rhetoric of Letters," which first appeared as chapter 2 in *Early Christian Rhetoric and 2 Thessalonians* (JSNTSup 30; Sheffield: JSOT, 1989), 19-50, and of Peeters Publishers to reprint, in slightly revised form, Jan Lambrecht, "Thanksgivings in 1 Thessalonians 1–3," which first appeared in *The Thessalonian Correspondence* (ed. R. F. Collins; BETL 87; Leuven: Leuven University Press–Peeters, 1990), 183-205.

It has been a pleasure and an enormous learning experience to collaborate with such knowledgeable and creative colleagues.

Karl P. Donfried
Johannes Beutler

Acronyms and Abbreviations for Journals and Book Series

AASF	Annales Academiae Scientiarum Fennicae
AB	The Anchor Bible (commentary series; Garden City, N.Y.: Doubleday)
AJP	*American Journal of Philology*
ANRW	*Aufstieg und Niedergang der römischen Welt* (ed. Hildegard Temporini; Berlin: W. de Gruyter, 1972-)
Arctos	*Arctos. Acta historica, philologica, philosophica Fennica*
ASGW.PH	Abhandlungen der (K.) Sächsischen Gesellschaft der Wissenschaften — Philologisch-historische Klasse
ATR	*Anglican Theological Review*
AusBR	*Australian Biblical Review*
BETL	Bibliotheca Ephemeridum Theologicarum Lovaniensium
BFChTh	*Beiträge zur Förderung christlicher Theologie*
BHT	Beiträge zur historischen Theologie
Bib	*Biblica*
Bijdr	*Bijdragen*
BiLe	*Bibel und Leben*
BKAW	Bibliothek der klassischen Altertumswissenschaften
BNTC	Black's New Testament Commentaries
BPAA	Bibliotheca Pontificii Athenaei Antoniani
BPTF	*Bijdragen van de philosophische en theologische faculteiten der nederlandsche Jezuiten*
BR	*Biblical Research*

BSGRT	Bibliotheca Scriptorum Graecorum et Romanorum Teubneriana
BTN	Bibliotheca theologica Norvegica
BulBR	*Bulletin for Biblical Research*
BWANT	Beiträge zur Wissenschaft vom Alten und Neuen Testament
BZ	*Biblische Zeitschrift*
BZNW	Beihefte der Zeitschrift für die neutestamentliche Wissenschaft
CBQ	*Catholic Biblical Quarterly*
CJ	*Classical Journal*
CLR	*Classical Review*
ConBNT	Coniectanea biblica, New Testament
CQ	*Classical Quarterly*
CThM.BW	Calwer theologische Monographien, Bibelwissenschaft
DBAT	Dielheimer Blätter zum Alten Testament
EDNT	*Exegetical Dictionary of the New Testament* (3 vols.; ed. Horst Balz and Gerhard Schneider; Grand Rapids: Eerdmans, 1990-93).
EKK	Evangelische Kirchenkunde
EKKNT	Evangelisch-katholischer Kommentar zum Neuen Testament
EtB	Études bibliques
ETL	*Ephemerides Theologicae Lovanienses*
EvTh	*Evangelische Theologie*
EWNT	*Exegetisches Wörterbuch zum Neuen Testament* (3 vols.; ed. Horst Balz and Gerhard Schneider; Stuttgart: Kohlhammer, 1980-83).
FFNT	Foundations and Facets, New Testament
FRLANT	Forschungen zur Religion und Literatur des Alten und Neuen Testaments
FS	*Franziskanische Studien*
FS.B	Franziskanische Studien, Beiheft
GBSNT	Guides to Biblical Scholarship, New Testament
GNS	Good News Studies
GSThR	Gießener Schriften zur Theologie und Religionspädagogik
GTA	Göttinger theologische Arbeiten
HAW	Handbuch der Altertumswissenschaft
HNT	Handbuch zum Neuen Testament
HThK	Herders theologischer Kommentar zum Neuen Testament
HTR	*Harvard Theological Review*
Hyp	Hypomnemata
HUTh	Hermeneutische Untersuchungen zur Theologie
IBC	Interpretation Biblical Commentary
ICC	International Critical Commentary
Int	*Interpretation*

JBL	*Journal of Biblical Literature*
JRH	*Journal of Religious History*
JSNT	*Journal for the Study of New Testament*
JSNTSup	Journal for the Study of the New Testament, Supplement Series
JSOT	*Journal for the Study of the Old Testament*
JSOTSup	Journal for the Study of the Old Testament, Supplement Series
JTS	*Journal of Theological Studies*
KEK	Kritisches-exegetischer Kommentar über das Neue Testament
LCL	Loeb Classical Library
LD	Lectio Divina
LEC	Library of Early Christianity
LS	*Louvain Studies*
MeyerK	H. A. W. Meyer, Kritisch-exegetischer Kommentar über das Neue Testament
MThS	Münchener theologische Studien
MThSt	Marburger theologische Studien
NCBC	New Century Bible Commentary
NClarBC	New Clarendon Bible Commentary
NICNT	New International Commentary on the New Testament
NIGTC	New International Greek Testament Commentary
NovT	*Novum Testamentum*
NovTSup	Novum Testamentum, Leiden — Supplements
NT	New Testament
NTD	Das Neue Testament Deutsch
NTS	*New Testament Studies*
NTTS	New Testament Tools and Studies
OJRS	*Ohio Journal of Religious Studies*
RGG	*Religion in Geschichte und Gegenwart* (6 vols.; ed. K. Galling; 3rd ed.; Tübingen: J. C. B. Mohr, 1957-62)
RMP	Rheinisches Museum für Philologie
RSRev	*Religious Studies Review*
RTR	*Reformed Theological Review*
SBL	Society of Biblical Literature
SBLDS	SBL Dissertation Series
SBLMS	SBL Monograph Series
SBLPS	SBL Texts and Translations: Pseudepigrapha Series
SBLRBS	SBL Resources for Biblical Study
SBLSBS	SBL Sources for Biblical Literature
SBLSP	*SBL Seminar Papers*
SBLSS	SBL Semeia Series
SBS	Stuttgarter Bibelstudien

SemSup	Semeia Supplements
SHCT	Studies in the History of Christian Thought
SN	*Studia Neotestamentica*
SN.S	Studia Neotestamentica. Subsidia
SNTSMS	Society for New Testament Studies Monograph Series
SP	Sacra Pagina
StTDJ	Studies on the Texts of the Desert of Judah
StUNT	Studien zur Umwelt des Neuen Testaments
TAPA	*Transactions of the American Philological Association*
TD	*The Thessalonians Debate*
TDNT	*Theological Dictionary of the New Testament* (10 vols.; ed. G. Kittel and G. Friedrich; Grand Rapids: Eerdmans, 1964-76)
ThF	Theologische Forschung
ThH	Théologie Historique
ThR	*Theologische Rundschau*
ThStKr	*Theologische Studien und Kritiken*
TynB	*Tyndale Bulletin*
UB	Urban-(Taschen-) Bücher
UTB	Uni-Taschenbücher
WBC	Word Biblical Commentary
WUNT	Wissenschaftliche Untersuchungen zum Neuen Testament
ZBK.NT	Zürcher Bibelkommentare. NT
Zet	*Zetemata*
ZNW	*Zeitschrift für die Neutestamentliche Wissenschaft*
ZWKB	Zürcher Werkkommentar zur Bibel

INTRODUCTION

The Scope and Nature of the Debate:
An Introduction and Some Questions

Karl P. Donfried

1. Overview

The renewed interest in 1 Thessalonians during the last two decades has been extraordinary.[1] While the exegetical labors have been intense, little consensus has been reached with regard to the purpose and intention of this writing, Paul's first letter and thus the earliest extant Christian document. The Thessalonians Correspondence Seminar of the *Studiorum Novi Testamenti Societas* (SNTS) began its work in Prague in 1995 under the leadership of Professors Johannes Beutler, a German Roman Catholic, and Karl P. Donfried, an American Lutheran; the majority of the essays collected in this volume were given at either the Prague (1995) or Strasbourg (1996) meetings of the Seminar.[2] The continuing dialogue among the members of the Seminar at subsequent meetings (Birmingham, 1997, and

---

1. See Jeffrey A. D. Weima and Stanley Porter, *An Annotated Bibliography of 1 and 2 Thessalonians* (NTTS 26; Leiden: Brill, 1998).

2. We are also pleased to add two other essays, one by Frank Hughes and the other by Jan Lambrecht. Frank Hughes did deliver a paper entitled "The Rhetoric of Letters," but this has been expanded to contain a substantial part of the second chapter of his book, *Early Christian Rhetoric and 2 Thessalonians* (JSNTSup30; Sheffield: JSOT, 1989), 19-50. When Jan Lambrecht delivered his paper, "A Structural Analysis of 1 Thessalonians 4–5," the Seminar members were asked to read his previous article, "Thanksgivings in 1 Thessalonians 1–3," as preparation. The original essay is found in R. F. Collins, ed., *The Thessalonian Correspondence* (BETL 87; Leuven: University Press–Peeters, 1990), 183-205.

Copenhagen, 1998) has also influenced the final shape and format of this volume.

The goal of the editors is not simply to present the essays in the order in which they were delivered, but rather to frame them in such a way that they will help the reader both to understand the exegetical challenges that 1 Thessalonians presents and to illustrate the diverse methodological approaches that are put to use in the interpretation of this letter. This volume will not only illustrate different methods, such as epistolary and rhetorical analysis, but will also show how these methods themselves can be used in significantly different, if not incompatible, ways. Thus, one's overall understanding of 1 Thessalonians will depend largely on which methodological approach one gives priority and how one applies it.

This volume will not provide easy answers to these wide-ranging challenges, but it will try to illustrate and bring to the fore the nature of these differences in a critical way. Only in such a manner can one hope to move toward the goal of increased consensus in the understanding of 1 Thessalonians among scholars. In order to achieve that end, *The Thessalonians Debate* approaches the contested issues from two different perspectives. The first group of essays (Part 1) concentrates on and discusses a specific text, 1 Thess 2:1-12, in light of different starting points and divergent interpretations; the second set of papers (Part 2) focuses on the larger methodological issues that are raised by these dissimilar, if not incompatible, interpretations of the selected text and, further, consciously ponders whether a synthetic approach using different methodologies, with clearer definitions of what these methodologies imply, is possible.

2. Part 1: 1 Thessalonians 2:1-12 as Symptomatic of the Exegetical Debate

One of the considerable areas of dispute is whether 1 Thess 2:1-12 should be considered an apology, that is, whether Paul is specifically defending himself against some kind of accusations. With this in mind Karl Donfried's essay, "The Epistolary and Rhetorical Context of 1 Thessalonians 2:1-12,"[3] begins with a review of those scholars who hold that 2:1-

3. *TD*, 31-60.

12 is an apology, and he comments on the diverse ways in which those who so describe the text understand its purpose. Then he turns to the epistolary context of these verses. While appreciating the importance of identifying epistolary components, he remains hesitant that an epistolary analysis[4] of 1 Thessalonians, *by itself,* can determine the intention, especially the intention of this letter as a "speech-act,"[5] because of its inability to identify with any degree of clarity or precision the parameters of the letter "body."[6]

Since 1 Thess 5:27 ("I solemnly command you by the Lord that this letter be read to all of them") contains a specific Pauline indication that he understands this letter as a "speech-act," that it is something that must be *read* before the entire congregation, Donfried turns to the contributions of classical rhetorical criticism and, in light of it, indicates that 1 Thessalonians has certain affinities with epideictic rhetoric. In judicial rhetoric, for example, 1 Thess 2:1-12 would have been taken up in the *probatio,* which is exactly what does not happen here. Within the general framework of epideictic, this pericope is placed within the context of the larger *narratio* of the communication (2:1–3:10). The first part of the *narratio* (2:1-16) is neither apologetic nor polemic. Rather, it recounts the relationship of friendship established between Paul and the Thessalonians during the time of his founding visit; it serves to distinguish Paul's gospel and *ethos* from the error and delusion surrounding the Thessalonian Christians, specifically from the idolatry of the pagans; and it presents characteristics of Paul's *ethos* that the apostle wishes to remind his congregation about in the *probatio,* especially in 4:1, "Finally, brothers, we ask you and urge you in the Lord Jesus that, as you learned from us how you ought to live and to please God (as, in fact, you are doing), you should do so more and more." In light of this, the apostle's antithetical style serves not as a defense against hypothetical accusations but rather, as in Hellenistic Judaism, as an attempt to distance himself and the Thessalonians from both pagan thought and practice by using this stylistic technique. Donfried urges that one should neither define 1 Thess 2:1-12 as an apology nor read this text in a mirror fashion as if Paul were countering specific charges that had been leveled against him.

Rudolf Hoppe, responding to Donfried's paper, is cautiously positive

---

4. See Charles Wanamaker, "Epistolary vs. Rhetorical Analysis," in *TD,* 283-86, for his understanding of this terminology.

5. I am primarily indebted to Raymond Collins for this term.

6. Wanamaker, "Epistolary vs. Rhetorical Analysis," in *TD,* 268-69.

about the use of a rhetorical approach in the analysis of the Pauline letters, although he warns that one should not impose rhetorical systems upon the Pauline correspondence. Hoppe proceeds to make the following observations:

1. 1 Thess 5:27 alone does not allow one to identify this letter as a speech. (One should note that Raymond Collins takes up this theme at some length in the concluding essay of this volume.)

2. Is the relationship of the *exordium,* the *narratio,* and the *probatio* as immediate in 1 Thessalonians as ancient rhetoric would suggest? If so, might one not have expected the triad "faith, hope, love" to be found more extensively in the rhetorical composition of the letter? The work of Frank Hughes, followed by Donfried, does attempt to speak to this valid concern.

3. Although he accepts the position that 1 Thess 2:1-12 is not an apology, and acknowledges that the antitheses in 2:3-8 cannot be used as an argument that Paul was clashing with actual opponents, he questions whether this conclusion is the result of Donfried's having identified this pericope as epideictic speech or whether, in fact, a similar conclusion could not be reached by the use of "tradition and motif-historical reflections."[7] This is a particularly critical observation because it brings to the fore an important methodological issue: Can one analytic approach more effectively analyze the purpose of a given textual unit than another? As we will quickly observe, the essays by Traugott Holtz and Jeffrey Weima do, in fact, make use of epistolary analysis and, as a result, they reach quite different conclusions from Donfried.

4. Concerning Donfried's epistolary classification of 1 Thessalonians, is the genre "friendship letter" adequate and what methodologies are at play in making such a determination? Given his further arguments for the prophetic context of 1 Thess 2:1-12, might not the letter more accurately be described as an "apostolic" letter? The reader will wish to consult further the extended discussion of these themes in the essay by Schoon-Janßen as well as Edgar Krentz's presentation of Thomas Olbricht's suggestion that 1 Thessalonians might be referred to as an example of "church rhetoric." In light of these and other discussions in this volume, the interpreter will want to consider the likelihood that since epistolary and rhetorical analyses are different but potentially complementary — at least for some — there is not necessarily any contradiction in specifying

---

7. Rudolf Hoppe, "A Response to Karl P. Donfried," in *TD,* 65.

different genres once one recognizes the dual character of the document: as oral communication in the form of a letter.

5. For the purpose of further discussion, one should ask whether, in rhetorical terms, it is not the theme of "the reliability of the divine *logos/gospel*" that holds the *exordium* and the *narratio* together. A positive response to such a query can be found not only in the work of Karl Donfried but also of Otto Merk. Hoppe's conclusion is significant:

> To achieve this overarching goal of rendering plausible the effective power of the gospel, Paul begins in 2:1-12 to present the evidence that his personal behavior serves precisely the purpose of his proclamation, namely, that it is radically subordinated to God's Word and informed by faith, that this gospel is capable of succeeding, and that its validity is diminished neither by repressive measures against his person nor against the church. Paul's task is to convince — a task that he must achieve from the distance imposed on him. The fact that he can do this constructively and without any polemic against the church or its individual representatives is indicative of his ongoing good relationship with the Macedonian Christians.[8]

Traugott Holtz in his contribution, "On the Background of 1 Thessalonians 2:1-12," finds unacceptable Johannes Schoon-Janßen's conclusion that 1 Thess 2:1-12 should not be classified as an apology both because of the letter's proximity to the genres of friendship letters (epistolary analysis) and to epideictic (rhetorical analysis).[9] A primary concern for Holtz is that too often both methodologies are applied with insufficient attention to the context of the letter and its specific background.

Particularly in his discussion of "The Situation of the Text," Holtz places emphasis on the historical context of 1 Thessalonians in general and 2:1-12 specifically. He writes:

> It is likely, then, that behind the differentiating characterizations that Paul presents concerning his initial role in the founding of the church in 1 Thess 2:1-12, concrete suspicions about his person, contingent on an actual situation, become visible. Recently, there has been a proper caution against the widespread tendency that assumes that behind every negation or differentiation in Paul's letters a mirror-like image must be re-

8. Hoppe, "A Response to Karl P. Donfried," in *TD*, 67-68.
9. Johannes Schoon-Janßen, "On the Use of Elements of Ancient Epistolography in 1 Thessalonians," in *TD*, 192-93.

flected. Nevertheless, by exercising cautious judgment at crucial points, one can certainly make conclusions on the basis of a configuration of ideas in which Paul sees it necessary to refute what others are saying.

The concrete historical situation is described in some detail as "persecution" understood as "social discrimination."[10] It is essentially a mirror-reading of 2:1-12 that leads to this hypothesis. While some will wish to distance themselves from both this approach and this conclusion, one must recognize that Holtz has brought to the fore a very urgent question: What is the relationship of the historical-critical method to the rhetorical and epistolary approaches?

Our understanding would suggest that the term "historical-critical method" is the broadest of categories that is willing to use any and all critical methodologies that would hope to shed light on the given document being examined. By way of a brief reminder concerning the intention of this historical-critical method, it will be useful to listen to these words of Edgar Krentz:

> The first task of the historian . . . is simply to hear the texts with which he is working. He uses every linguistic tool at his disposal to determine the sense the text had for its writer and first audience (the *sensus literalis sive historicus*). He seeks to hear the text apart from the mass of biblical interpretation that has been laid over it in the history of its use. This basic respect for the historical integrity of a text is inherent in all historical criticism.[11]

So, for example, both rhetorical and epistolary analyses would be useful to a historical-critical investigation, as would textual criticism, other literary, historical, philosophical, and religious sources, as well as archaeological artifacts and resources. The careful reader must inquire whether Holtz's hesitation with regard to epistolary and rhetorical methodologies is supplemented in specific and detailed ways by the other tools or methods that one normally associates with the historical-critical method.

This is not to say that Holtz does not recognize the influences of rhetorical features in 1 Thessalonians, although their contributions to under-

10. Traugott Holtz, "On the Background of 1 Thessalonians 2:1-12," in *TD,* 77.
11. Edgar Krentz, *The Historical-Critical Method* (GBS; Philadelphia: Fortress, 1975), 39. See also Karl P. Donfried, *The Dynamic Word: New Testament Insights for Contemporary Christians* (San Francisco: Harper & Row, 1981).

standing the letter seem limited at best because of their constant association with the claims of the philosophical rhetoricians themselves. Even though he finds the contributions of Malherbe helpful, for Holtz there is a very sharp demarcation between the apostle and the wandering Cynics. "In distinction to the rhetorician, Paul did not represent himself or his own view — even if it was an inspired one — but only the gospel of God entrusted to him and to which his own person was intimately bound."[12] This leads to his further assertion that "Paul, however, did not need to fear, as did Dio Chrysostom, similar confusion with pagan preachers wandering the countryside, because the apostle did not view his proclamation nor his authority as belonging to himself."[13] Even though Paul's self-understanding is clear, many Jews and pagans in Thessalonica were intent on invalidating Paul's proclamation by placing it in the context of the common phenomenon of wandering philosophers. As a result, in 1 Thess 2:1-12 the apostle is refuting the misgivings and allegations that are being launched against him by the predominantly non-Christian members of the city. Thus, 1 Thess 2:1-12, correctly understood, serves an apologetic function.

By way of summary, "On the Background of 1 Thessalonians 2:1-12" raises a number of issues that are critical to the interpretation of Paul's first letter and require further debate. Although the first of these has very broad implications, the second and third, while being more limited in scope, nevertheless have important implications for the interpretation of 1 Thessalonians as a whole:

- whether rhetoric, understood as the art of persuasion, should be so closely linked with certain schools of philosophical thought and rhetorical practice that, at least implicitly, they are dismissed as a valuable tool available to the practitioner of historical-criticism. Cannot similar language and methods of persuasion be used by radically different persons?
- whether the correct reading of 1 Thess 2:7 is that of Nestle-Aland[26/27], νήπιοι, or that of Nestle-Aland[25], ἤπιοι. Holtz prefers ἤπιοι, and Otto Merk,[14] as we will observe, holds to νήπιοι.

---

12. Holtz, "On the Background of 1 Thessalonians 2:1-12," in *TD*, 74.
13. Holtz, "On the Background of 1 Thessalonians 2:1-12," in *TD*, 76.
14. Otto Merk, "1 Thessalonians 2:1-12: An Exegetical-Theological Study," in *TD*, 106.

• whether the term τροφός should be understood as a nurse, wet-nurse, or mother. Holtz, Donfried, and Merk, to cite only a few examples from the essays collected here, understand this term in substantially different ways.

Johan Vos, in his response to Traugott Holtz, expresses hesitancy with any argument that suggests that the reconstruction of unverifiable data behind a text can have precedence over those that are dependent on the information explicitly offered by the text. There simply is not enough precise information in the letter to validate the position that Paul is referring to actual complaints made by pagan and Jewish residents of Thessalonica who desired to undermine the absolute claims made by Paul in his proclamation. As a result Vos does not accept the view that 1 Thess 2:1-12 can be described as an apology or that its purpose is paraenetic.

What prompts Paul to write this letter is the situation described in 2:17–3:10, namely, the apostle's unexpected absence from the church and his deep concern about their welfare in the midst of persecutions and other social pressures. Vos proceeds to suggest that the first three chapters stand under "the sign of *strengthening*" and the final two chapters under "the sign of *encouragement*."[15] If this is indeed the case, then 2:1-12 might better be described as a "self-recommendation" rather than as an apology.

Vos's perspective with regard to the antitheses is also quite different from that of Holtz. The primary thesis of the text that the Seminar selected is to be derived from 2:1 and 2:13; Paul's visit in Thessalonica was not in vain, but, as they themselves have experienced, it involved the proclamation of a divine word that was truly the word of God. And so by appealing to their experience with him, "Paul allows the church to write a good recommendation about him."[16] Thus there is nothing "unusual" in the antitheses, which are found not only here but elsewhere in the letter, for example, in 4:4-8 and 5:4-10. These antitheses, together with the subtheses, serve to support the main thesis, namely, "that the Thessalonians rightly accepted the apostle as a genuine messenger of God."[17] This is exactly the function of the antitheses, to support the main thesis that the Thessalonians were correct in accepting Paul as a genuine messenger of God. "If

---

15. Johan Vos, "A Response to Traugott Holtz," in *TD*, 83.

16. Vos, "A Response to Traugott Holtz," in *TD*, 84.

17. Vos, "A Response to Traugott Holtz," in *TD*, 87.

one links the antitheses with the main thesis and its subtheses . . . , one can say neither that the passage contains unusual elements nor that the antitheses are not logically derived from the theses."[18] This positive image of Paul that the antitheses convey has parallels not only in Hellenistic rhetoric and popular philosophy but also in the writings of biblical and early Christian pneumatics and prophets.

Critical for Otto Merk's essay, "1 Thessalonians 2:1-12: An Exegetical-Theological Study," is that this textual unit must be seen within its larger context. There is, for example, a close connection to 1:4-10, where Paul speaks about the original founding of this congregation. The passage in question is also closely linked with 2:13-16. Further, 2:17 provides the reason why the letter is written: Paul's forced separation from the congregation that he had only recently founded. While 1 Thess 2:17–3:10 marks something new, it still relates to the founding of this church. Both the conventional views concerning the division of the letter and the new contributions of rhetorical criticism agree that 2:1-12 must be seen as a unit functioning within a larger context. Already it is evident that for Merk there must be an interrelationship between situation, background, and rhetoric in the interpretation of the theology of this letter. Given the methodological concerns of the Seminar, he notes "that the rhetorical elements elucidate the theological concern in Paul's writing and thus have a hermeneutical function, but they do not supply the basis for what is said in this passage."[19]

At best this pericope is a "potential apologia." But it is manifest that Paul "does not defend nor need to defend."[20] Basing his reflections on the work of J. L. Hill, Merk explains that "Pauline proclamation (which includes admonition and instruction) pushes open the door, so to speak, for a critical evaluation of the credibility of diverse itinerant preachers of the most varied provenance. This allows the concerns of Paul, as the congregation's founder who is distinct from such people, to come to the fore without there being an immediate reason for this in the specific situation."[21]

Let us now single out only a handful of rich exegetical and theological insights that Merk presents:

---

18. Vos, "A Response to Traugott Holtz," in *TD*, 87.
19. Merk, "1 Thessalonians 2:1-12," in *TD*, 98.
20. Merk, "1 Thessalonians 2:1-12," in *TD*, 96.
21. Merk, "1 Thessalonians 2:1-12," in *TD*, 95.

- what does Paul mean that his entrance in 2:1 was "not in vain"? Donfried has already suggested that οὐ κενή refers to "the character" of the apostle's labors in Thessalonica and recommended that this phrase be translated as "has not been found empty." Building on E. Reinmuth's suggestion that "not in vain" refers to the "coming to the goal of God's election, the outward form of which is the church,"[22] Merk urges consideration that "God's ἐκλογή unites the Thessalonians and the founder of their church, and Paul represents this 'not in vain' in his missionary service, with his proclamation and with his very being. This last connection is necessary to understand why Paul continues in 2:2 with ἀλλά."[23]

- with regard to the terminology and language of the itinerant preachers, it must always be remembered that when Paul extracts such terminology to both differentiate and integrate, it is "hermeneutically transposed so that it serves the gospel, thus corroborating the comprehensive power and might of the gospel in both word and deed within the churches established by Paul."[24]

- with regard to the (ν)ήπιοι problem, Merk prefers the better-documented and more difficult reading of νήπιοι, and so "Paul himself has become a νήπιος in that he does not allow himself to be financially dependent as do the itinerant pagan preachers."[25]

- concerning the translation of ὁμείρεσθαι, Merk endorses Baumert's derivation of this verb from ὁμείρομαι, in the sense of "being separated from," "being kept apart from."[26]

Finally, if a congregation is to be truly established, then the gospel entrusted to Paul — for which he himself becomes a model to be emulated by the Christians in Thessalonica — must be understood both as an "initial proclamation" and as a continuing "supportive proclamation." It is to that latter situation that 1 Thessalonians responds, and it as well, Merk reminds us, "is part of his theological activity."[27]

In his response to Otto Merk, Jeffrey Weima is intent on showing

22. As cited by Merk, "1 Thesssalonians 2:1-12," in *TD*, 99.
23. Merk, "1 Thesssalonians 2:1-12," in *TD*, 99.
24. Merk, "1 Thesssalonians 2:1-12," in *TD*, 102.
25. Merk, "1 Thesssalonians 2:1-12," in *TD*, 106.
26. Merk, "1 Thessalonians 2:1-12," in *TD*, 108.
27. Merk, "1 Thessalonians 2:1-12," in *TD*, 113.

that both Merk's rejection of the apology thesis and his use of rhetorical criticism are incorrect. The shift toward understanding 1 Thess 2:1-12 as paraenetic rather than as an apology is attributed to the work of Abraham Malherbe. The reader may wish to consider whether this narration is sufficiently comprehensive. Wolfgang Stegemann and Karl Donfried, both of whom stand in opposition to any form of apology hypothesis, are comprehensive in their criticism of a variety of Malherbe's theses. The former rejects the cultural analogies that are developed, and the latter rejects the thesis that the apostle serves primarily as a model for paraenetic purposes.[28] Thus, many who reject the apology thesis can be found on different sides of the paraenesis/paraclesis dispute.[29]

Weima does exactly what a skilled respondent should do: generate lively discussion! So let us single out some of the areas where he advances the dialogue:

- 1 Thess 1:2-10 is described as the "thanksgiving section," but it is unique among the Pauline letters because it focuses on Paul and not on his readers. Does this separation accurately describe Paul's intention, or is Merk closer to the mark in his assertion that "ἐκλογή unites the Thessalonians and the founder of their church . . ."?[30]
- for Weima 2:17–3:10 is an "apostolic *parousia*" that serves as "a defense of Paul's *present* absence from the Thessalonians . . ." in the same way that 2:1-12 "is a defense of Paul's *past* ministry among them."[31] Aside from the hesitation that Lambrecht[32] and others have with the categorization "apostolic *parousia*," has Weima presented exegetical evidence to contest Merk's exegesis in both of these sections in which Merk places the emphasis on Paul's "loving attention

---

28. See K. P. Donfried, "The Theology of 1 Thessalonians as a Reflection of Its Purpose," in *To Touch the Text* (Festschrift J. A. Fitzmyer; ed. M. P. Horgan and P. J. Kobelski; New York: Crossroad, 1989), 243-60, and the emphasis there on paraclesis rather than on paraenesis.

29. See K. P. Donfried, "The Theology of 1 Thessalonians," in *The Theology of the Shorter Pauline Letters* (ed. K. P. Donfried and I. H. Marshall; New Testament Theology; Cambridge: Cambridge University Press, 1993), 28-63.

30. Merk, "1 Thesssalonians 2:1-12," in *TD*, 99.

31. Jeffrey Weima, "The Function of 1 Thesssalonians 2:1-12 and the Use of Rhetorical Criticism," in *TD*, 118.

32. Jan Lambrecht, "A Structural Analysis of 1 Thessalonians 4–5," in *TD*, 164.

to the church . . ."[33] and in which he accepts Baumert's translation of 2:8: "So we are determined, while we are kept apart from you, to share with you not only God's gospel but our own life because you have become very dear to us"?[34] When dealing with 2:17–3:10, Merk suggests that Paul is explaining to the Thessalonians that he "has been orphaned through no fault of its own" and that the purpose of this is to link "the orphaned Paul to his congregation just as the church's geographically distant founder is linked to them 'in heart.'"[35] So the careful student of this letter will need to discern, in light of these two different evaluations, whether it is adequate to describe 2:1-12 as a "defense" of Paul's previous ministry among them?

- in his exegesis of 2:1-12 Weima makes a number of keen observations that result in the conclusion that "the widespread claim that 2:1-12 is exclusively paraenetic . . . would appear to be an exaggeration."[36] This, our respondent asserts, "confirms my contention that the traditional view of this passage has been too quickly abandoned and that the primary function of 2:1-12 is an apologetic one . . . ," and it "plays an important role in reestablishing the trust and confidence of Paul's readers such that they will obey the instructions that he will yet give them in this letter."[37] Here one must ask, however, whether the alternatives, either paraenetic or apologetic, are the proper ones, and whether or not the church in Thessalonica "will obey the instructions that he will yet give them in this letter" is really the key issue in the remainder of 1 Thessalonians. Is it accurate to describe the contents of 4:13-18, for example, as "instructions" and is the primary issue one of "obedience"?

With regard to method, this response to Otto Merk urges the position that rhetorical and epistolary analysis must supplement, not supersede, the "traditional exegetical analysis of the text."[38] But will one not need to have greater clarity with regard to the phrase "traditional exegetical analysis of the text" if the discussion is to proceed in a produc-

---

33. Merk, "1 Thesssalonians 2:1-12," in *TD*, 107.
34. Merk, "1 Thesssalonians 2:1-12," in *TD*, 108.
35. Merk, "1 Thesssalonians 2:1-12," in *TD*, 91.
36. Weima, "The Function of 1 Thesssalonians 2:1-12," in *TD*, 122.
37. Weima, "The Function of 1 Thesssalonians 2:1-12," in *TD*, 123.
38. Weima, "The Function of 1 Thesssalonians 2:1-12," in *TD*, 124.

tive manner? Still, Weima's intention is unambiguous: it is illegitimate to engage in the rhetorical analysis of the Pauline letters as well as to apply the conventions of ancient rhetoric to these letters. Following a series of arguments about the applicability of classical rhetoric to Pauline letters (many of which will be discussed in detail in the following essays), Weima cannot accept the premise that rhetorical analysis, presumably of any sort, "holds the hermeneutical key that will unlock the true meaning of the apostle's writing."[39] While one can certainly entertain such a position, it would have been invaluable to have had some discussion of how Weima would interpret 1 Thess 5:27: "I solemnly command you by the Lord that this letter be *read* to all of them."[40]

Our discussion up to this point makes evident that interpreters of 1 Thessalonians not only give priority to different methodologies in their analysis of the letter as a whole and 1 Thess 2:1-12 in particular, but also that, with some frequency, they sharply disagree with certain approaches that their colleagues utilize. Therefore, the second part of this volume will be less concerned with this specific text (1 Thess 2:1-12) per se, which in micro form is a sample of the larger issues confronting the interpreter of any of the Pauline letters, but will move on to broader questions concerning, for example, the appropriateness of a variety of exegetical methods, how they are defined, and the degree to which they might be integrated with each other.

3. Part 2: 1 Thessalonians: The Methodological Debate

Epistolary Analysis

One of the factors that leads to considerable confusion is the fact that when scholars use the designation "epistolary" or "rhetorical" they are not always using these terms equivalently. The nomenclature "epistolary analysis" is used in quite different ways not only in the articles in this section but also in the final section of this collection, "Is Synthesis Possible?" The reader should be alerted to the fact that the two sections to follow (dealing with "Epistolary Analysis" and "Rhetorical Analysis") are further ex-

---

39. Weima, "The Function of 1 Thesssalonians 2:1-12," in *TD*, 131.
40. Italics mine.

panded and analyzed in relationship to each other in this final section just referred to.

If for just a moment we preview an aspect of Charles Wanamaker's essay in this final part of *The Thessalonians Debate*, we note that, based on a review of other relevant secondary literature, he would separate three distinct, but related, subunits when speaking of "Epistolary Analysis": formal literary analysis, thematic analysis, and form criticism. *Formal literary analysis* is most concerned with structure and the examination of such formulaic features as the opening and closing forms of the letter itself as well as the main body. *Thematic analysis* concerns itself with epistolary *topoi* and themes, such as friendship, consolation, or exhortation. *Form-critical analysis* is primarily interested in *oral* forms, such as liturgical and paraenetic formulae, that have been become incorporated in letters as written forms. The essays that follow include aspects of all three of these subunits of epistolary criticism, with Jan Lambrecht emphasizing formal literary analysis and Johannes Schoon-Janßen engaging primarily in a thematic analysis of 1 Thessalonians.

The contributions of Jan Lambrecht can best be appreciated by viewing his two essays together. His first essay, "Thanksgivings in 1 Thessalonians 1–3," originally published in 1990,[41] is foundational for his subsequent contribution to the SNTS Seminar entitled "A Structural Analysis of 1 Thessalonians 4–5." Lambrecht's approach is revealed by the title of the latter paper. Structural analysis, an analysis of the "surface" structure of a letter, involves a combination of epistolary and thematic criteria and is thus *eclectic* by definition. As a result it is self-evident that rhetorical impact must be considered by the very fact that Paul writes a letter that is "to be read to all the brethren" (1 Thess 5:27) as well as by the fact that epistolary analysis reveals important insights in a variety of ways. But often, Lambrecht laments, the practitioners of these methods are driven to an extreme, a phenomenon described by Lambrecht as "inventive speciousness." This concern is underscored by the assertion that even "to attribute to Paul a more or less spontaneous, subconscious following of preexisting patterns may constitute here an unwarranted postulate."[42]

To understand the structure of the first three chapters of 1 Thessalonians, we need to see them within the broad context of Paul giving

---

41. In Collins, ed., *The Thessalonian Correspondence*, 183-205.
42. Lambrecht, "A Structural Analysis of 1 Thessalonians 4–5," in *TD*, 164.

thanks in the present, past, and future as well as a repeated double focus on the addressees and writer in their mutual relationship to God and Jesus Christ. In his essay on 1 Thessalonians 4–5, Lambrecht finds a structure of striking similarity to the first three chapters, also with five internally related units. However, this structural similarity should not disguise the notably different content that is to be found in 1–3 in contrast to 4–5.

This results in the following outline for the entire letter:[43]

1:1: salutation
    a. 1:2-10: thanksgiving
        b. 2:1-12: apologetical report
    a. 2:13-16: thanksgiving
        b. 2:17–3:8: report on the intervening period
    a. 3:9-10: thanksgiving
3:11-13: eschatological wish-prayer
4:1-2: introductory paraenesis
    a. 4:3-12: paraenesis
        b. 4:13-18: final destiny of Christians
    a. 5:1-8: paraenesis
        b. 5:9-11: final destiny of Christians
    a. 5:12-22: paraenesis
5:23-24: eschatological wish-prayer

Since content considerations are of great importance to these contributions and since it is they that seem to regulate if and when epistolary and rhetorical considerations are appropriate, it is important to turn our attention to the content of 1 Thessalonians. At the most fundamental level, this letter is divided into two major parts: (1) 1 Thessalonians 1–3, giving emphasis to thanksgiving and apology; (2) 1 Thessalonians 4–5, articulating exhortations and instructions.

In the analysis of the first part, Lambrecht makes known his significant reservations with regard to Paul Schubert's *Form and Function of the Pauline Thanksgiving*. For Schubert, the thanksgiving is the body of the letter (1–3) and chapters 4–5 simply form the conclusion. Rather than accepting such a broad, generalized thanksgiving pattern of which the di-

---

43. Lambrecht, "Thanksgivings in 1 Thessalonians 1–3," in *TD*, 157, and Lambrecht, "A Structural Analysis of 1 Thessalonians 4–5," in *TD*, 172.

gressions are a part, Lambrecht acknowledges the presence of three really separate thanksgivings, with the material between them as genuine digressions. Further, since the final two chapters contain not only paraenesis but also "dogmatic" information, these two dimensions also belong to the body of the letter.

The content of 1 Thessalonians 1–3 is described under three primary categories: how one should understand Paul's prayerful thanksgivings in relation to the Christians in Thessalonica; how Paul's apostolic existence explains 2:1-12 as an *apologia pro vita sua;* and how God is the source and energizer of the irresistible gospel, which is commandingly active among the believers in Thessalonica and through them to the whole world. With regard to 1 Thessalonians 4–5, Lambrecht sees the content primarily in terms of paraenesis and eschatology. There are two paraenetic sections, 4:1-12 and 5:12-22, and eschatology is located in a central eschatological section, 4:13–5:11, which has three units, with the third corresponding to the first: a, 4:13-18; b, 5:1-8; a′, 5:9-11.

What is significant for Lambrecht is a structural analysis in which form and content are held together and in which the thematic structure includes formal criteria. Many of his warnings are cogent and his insights keen. Yet some scholars would surely raise a number of methodological questions. Lambrecht, for example, urges that before one give "compulsory obedience to given genres . . . one should always first try a more natural procedure,"[44] a procedure also referred to as "commonsense reflections."[45] Yet, without other criteria at work, why should one accept the designation of 2:1-10 as an "apology" that is "presumably a reply to personal attacks"?[46] Along the same lines one might ask how convincing it is to designate virtually the entire writing as the letter "body," based on the argument that Paul employs a unique letter-style?

Johannes Schoon-Janßen values ancient epistolography for several reasons. In his "On the Use of Elements of Ancient Epistolography in 1 Thessalonians" he maintains that the examination of epistolary themes allows the interpreter to make assertions about the situation of a letter, in particular the kind of relationship that the author has with the addressees at the time the letter is written. A close examination of the "letter of

---

44. Lambrecht, "Thanksgivings in 1 Thessalonians 1–3," in *TD,* 155.
45. Lambrecht, "Thanksgivings in 1 Thessalonians 1–3," in *TD,* 155.
46. Lambrecht, "Thanksgivings in 1 Thessalonians 1–3," in *TD,* 155.

friendship" in antiquity reveals four primary characteristics of such a φιλικός-type letter: (a) the letter as a conversation; (b) the ἄπων/πάρων or the παρουσία or the μνεία motif, all of which could evolve in broader contexts; (c) the "present in the spirit" motif, alternatively referred to as the παρουσία motif, and (d) the thematization of consolation and longing.[47] All of these are found throughout 1 Thessalonians, and it is thus fair to argue that the most appropriate epistolary genre from antiquity for 1 Thessalonians is that of the "letter of friendship."

Although Paul's first letter is predominantly philophronetic, there are some important nonphilophronetic sections that move toward exhortation and instruction particularly with regard to the fate of the dead prior to the time of the *parousia*. Does this weaken Schoon-Janßen's fundamental thesis? Not at all, because "Paul approaches the Thessalonians rather in the manner of a parent (see 2:7, 11), as an intimate and trusted friend who, at the same time, as role model, consoles and admonishes."[48] Thus 1 Thessalonians portrays Paul primarily as a "pastoral friend." In terms of epistolary theory he rejects the thesis that the intention of this letter is paraenetic in favor of a primarily friendly/pastoral purpose; in terms of rhetorical theory he declines the designation of the letter as symbouleutic in favor of epideictic as the most likely genre.

Schoon-Janßen's methodological considerations lead him to the conclusion that it is impossible to classify 1 Thess 2:1-12 as an apology in which the apostle is specifically responding to criticisms that have been made against him by the church in Thessalonica.

Rhetorical Analysis

As the essays in this and the final section will make evident, and to which Jeffrey Weima has already alluded in one of his footnotes,[49] when scholars today refer to "rhetorical analysis" they may be using that descriptor in any of three major ways. Perhaps the most widely practiced form of rhetorical analysis employed by New Testament exegetes is what is frequently re-

---

47. Schoon-Janßen, "Ancient Epistolography in 1 Thessalonians," in *TD*, 184.
48. See Schoon-Janßen, "Ancient Epistolography in 1 Thessalonians," in *TD*, 189, n. 67.
49. Weima, "The Function of 1 Thessalonians 2:1-12," in *TD*, 124, n. 29.

ferred to as "ancient rhetoric," that is, a rhetoric that is derived from the speeches and categories found in the classical rhetorical handbooks and compositions. What is not uncommonly referred to as the "new rhetoric" is a rhetorical analysis influenced by contemporary rhetorical categories that are not necessarily related to or derived from ancient rhetorical conventions. It is a more "philosophically based approach that concentrates on argumentation: its structure, premises, and techniques."[50] A third type of rhetorical analysis is also practiced today: a hybrid that combines features of both the "ancient rhetoric" and the "new rhetoric." The essays of Frank Hughes are based on ancient rhetorical analysis. Within this context of ancient rhetorical analysis, Edgar Krentz's essay will raise the issue whether for those interpreting New Testament texts the ancient rhetorical canon should be limited to Aristotle and the Greeks or whether it can also legitimately include the manifold materials written in Latin. Both Krentz and Charles Wanamaker are in dialogue with the other types of rhetorical analysis just described.

Frank Hughes begins his discussion in "The Rhetoric of Letters"[51] with the observation that both the rhetorical and epistolary handbooks are remarkably silent concerning rhetorical *dispositio,* no doubt because it was not considered advisable to persuade by letters. Letters lacked the final two parts, memory and delivery, essential to rhetorical theory since the time of Aristotle, thus making use only of invention, arrangement, and style. This, in effect, would have teachers of rhetoric suggesting to their students that two of their subjects were irrelevant, thus in essence making declamation nonmaterial to their rhetorical instruction. However, Hughes points out that in an imaginary dialogue between Antonius and Catulus in *De oratore* 2.49, Cicero represents Catulus as suggesting that letters could take up and employ rhetorical characteristics taken from speeches. Further, Hughes's own analysis of Demosthenes' *Epistle 1* confirms that letters could use rhetoric even if the handbooks from antiquity remain silent. Although the precise relationship between rhetorical and epistolary analysis remains open, Hughes is confident that a methodological synthesis between the two can be actualized. A most helpful review of the relevant literature from antiquity through the Middle Ages to the contemporary period, as well as a most useful analysis of

---

50. Weima, "The Function of 1 Thesssalonians 2:1-12," in *TD,* 124, n. 29.
51. Hughes, "The Rhetoric of Letters," in *TD,* 194-215.

genera and *partes orationis* (the parts of rhetorical discourses) rhetoric, strives to intensify this conviction.

Although Hughes makes extensive use of the Greek and Latin rhetorical traditions, he would have no difficulty with Krentz's observations as starting points. In his essay, "The Social Situations Implied by Rhetoric,"[52] Hughes is convinced that even if rhetorical theory and instruction did not include letters, the practice of rhetoric was essential for official communications in distant places. Further, Hughes also shares some of Krentz's reservations by insisting that rhetorical criticism, properly understood, has the "potential" for becoming a valuable tool that may help the biblical exegete in understanding the significance of difficult texts and making intelligible authorial intentions. Rhetorical criticism is *one* of several methods, and it needs to be *correlated* with the insights gained from other approaches. Clearly, despite Hughes's high regard for the advantages of classical rhetorical criticism for the interpretation of the New Testament, his very cautious approach certainly allows him to steer clear of what some critics of this methodology have labeled "rhetorical imperialism."

Rhetorical criticism, understood primarily as including "strategies of persuasion," has as its aim the more precise understanding of the author, his audience, and his purpose in wishing to communicate with a particular audience. Thus, rhetorical analysis can be useful in reconstructing the historical provenance of letters. Yet Hughes is quite correct in observing that such a rhetorical analysis does not move *directly* from the rhetorical text to the historical or social situation of the audience. Serving as an intermediary between the two is the "rhetorical situation." The historical situation and the rhetorical situation are not identical! The situation implied by "a rhetorical discourse and the historical situation observable by others can be understood to be related, but not identical."[53] One must, therefore, recognize the difference between *what a text says* about a situation and *the situation itself.* While rhetorical criticism can assist in determining the social/historical situation of the audience, and Hughes demonstrates this quite convincingly with regard to 1 Thessalonians, a comprehensive evaluation of *all* the determinative factors will require additional methods of analysis.

---

52. Hughes, "The Social Situations Implied by Rhetoric," in *TD*, 241-54.
53. Hughes, "Social Situations," in *TD*, 254.

Is Synthesis Possible?

Especially over the last two decades, there has been an intense renewed emphasis on understanding 1 Thessalonians. Increasingly this and other letters are not being read only or primarily as historical and theological documents but rather for their *quality as letters*. As a result, the question of methodology has come to the fore, a phenomenon witnessed throughout the discussion of this SNTS Seminar on "The Thessalonian Correspondence." Over and over, one observes, we have noted this critical question: What are the appropriate methods that should be applied to this, and, for that matter, any New Testament letter? Of the varied approaches, two in particular have been especially dominant in the essays contained in this volume: epistolary and rhetorical analysis. Charles Wanamaker was asked to elucidate and evaluate these two specific methodological approaches and to consider whether they are fundamentally discordant or whether a synthesis between the two is possible. Thus the title of his essay: "Epistolary vs. Rhetorical Analysis: Is a Synthesis Possible?"

At the outset of his essay Wanamaker asks most appropriate question, namely, what exactly is meant by the term "form-critical/epistolary analysis"? We have already reviewed the components of this phrase: formal literary analysis, thematic analysis, and form criticism. In light of these distinctions Wanamaker prefers to understand "form-critical/epistolary analysis" as including only formal literary and thematic analysis. For the purposes of the wider discussion, one should raise the question whether the inclusion of the category "form criticism" under the category "epistolary" might not have been appropriate as well as profitable? To have included this technique of analysis would not in any way have weakened Wanamaker's review; in fact, its inclusion would have enhanced the strength of his instructive essay.

Informative is the choice of the "introductory thanksgiving" as a way to point out both the strengths and limitations of a formal analysis of 1 Thessalonians. Paul Schubert's recommendation that the thanksgiving period extended from 1:2–3:13 set off a subsequent debate concerning the structure of this letter (formal literary analysis) as well as a search for characteristic *topoi*, themes, and formulaic features. Referring to a wide range of studies, Wanamaker concludes that such epistolary analyses have not led to consensus in terms of structure and that analysis of the letter in detail has led to a reductionism that is unable to explain the relationships between these individual components and the letter as a whole. Such an enterprise fragments the narrative structure into "obliteration."[54] Schubert's attempt to see the threefold thanksgiving of 1 Thessalonians 1–3 as the effective body of the letter has failed, and subsequent epistolary studies have not been able to overcome this fixation with the thanksgiving formulae. One result has been the inability to hold 1 Thessalonians 1–3 and 4–5 together as a cohesive whole.

In the transition to his review of the potential of rhetorical analysis as a helpful tool for the study of 1 Thessalonians, Wanamaker cites one of the foremost of the epistolary critics, John White. Formal literary analysis, for example, cannot adequately assess carefully the larger intermediate part of the body of the letter. Since Paul expected his letters to represent his spoken presence, the letter's body resonates with patterns of oral proclamation. This has led White himself to turn toward classical rhetoric as a means to examine the letter-body more adequately. In so doing White accepts a form of analysis that has been applied anew to the Pauline letters only within the last two decades. Wanamaker cites the pioneering work of Betz, Wuellner and Kennedy, and Wanamaker affirms Kennedy's observation that the ultimate goal of rhetorical analysis "is the discovery of the author's intent and of how that is transmitted through a text to an audience."[55]

Hughes and Olbricht give much attention to the classical rhetorical analysis of 1 Thessalonians. Whereas Hughes uses a more eclectic type of classical analysis that employs both Aristotle and such Latin rhetoricians as Cicero and Quintilian, Olbricht employs a very strictly Aristotelian form of analysis. Both are concerned with attempting to understand this first Pauline letter both with regard to Paul's intention in writing and how, where possible, the original recipients would have understood it in their specific sociohistorical context. Wuellner, who tries to integrate both classical Graeco-Roman and contemporary European and North American rhetorical approaches, distinguishes a quite different rhetorical situation operative at the time of writing and the time of reading. In fact, Wuellner seems to suggest that the contemporary reader of 1 Thessalonians is unable to read it in the same way as its original readers. Although these diverse rhetorical approaches lead to quite dissimilar results, they do under-

---

54. Wanamaker, "Epistolary vs. Rhetorical Analysis," in *TD*, 268.
55. Wanamaker, "Epistolary vs. Rhetorical Analysis," in *TD*, 270.

score Aristotle's comments that rhetoric is an art and a skill. As a result, Wanamaker urges, some attempts will be more successful than others in illuminating the rhetorical situation and the rhetorical strategies that are encountered in the text. Nevertheless, the rhetorical approach has the definite potential of enabling the unitary and persuasive message of 1 Thessalonians to emerge with clarity.

The final question that Wanamaker addresses is whether these quite disparate approaches, epistolary and rhetorical, can be utilized in a complementary fashion. One example of the differing approaches of these two methods can be seen in their strikingly different way of handling the thanksgivings in 1 Thessalonians. His evaluation assumes that classical rhetoric had influenced Paul and his writings, and thus rhetorical analysis has the advantage of approaching Paul within a framework that he was not only familiar with but also practiced in his correspondence. Whereas epistolary analysis concentrates on small, formal units and thus has great difficulty in viewing the entire narrative whole, rhetorical analysis can do both. As a result it can help to understand both why the text has been constructed as it has and to demonstrate the persuasive strategies that help to reveal the author's intentionality in particular historical and rhetorical situations; thus it has a greater capacity and potential to uncover the purpose and meaning of an entire text.

Epistolary analysis can be useful in designating and characterizing the opening and closing formulae as well as the introductory and concluding conventions of the body-middle of the Pauline letters. It is precisely the inability of the epistolary approach to adequately elucidate the body-middle and to sufficiently discern that these letters are literary productions in their own right that limits its useful interpretative function. While recognizing that rhetorical criticism can be charged with a certain arbitrariness in the identification and interpretation of certain units, Wanamaker nevertheless concludes: "Rhetorical analysis, both of the ancient and the modern varieties, takes us far closer to the issues that really matter: meaning and significance, intention and strategy."[56] There can be a synthesis between epistolary and rhetorical analysis, yet, ultimately, it is a "marriage of unequal partners."

Also concerned with the relationship of epistolary ("formal") and rhetorical analysis is Edgar Krentz's essay, "1 Thessalonians: Rhetorical

---

56. Wanamaker, "Epistolary vs. Rhetorical Analysis," in *TD*, 286.

Flourishes and Formal Constraints." Do these different methods "intersect, conflict, or supplement" each other? Porter, Classen, Reed, and Anderson are among those scholars cited who are disinclined to give positive value to the rhetorical analysis of the Pauline letters.[57] Although Anderson argues against using Aristotle's *Ars rhetorica* as an appropriate resource for evaluating 1 Thessalonians, it is precisely Aristotle whom Krentz will use in his attempt to evaluate the usefulness of rhetorical analysis.

According to Aristotle's taxonomy, speeches are divided into three genres (deliberative, forensic, and epideictic). Although a given speech may use more than one genre, normally one will be dominant. Given this taxonomy, is consensus given to the classification of 1 Thessalonians? Kennedy was one of the first to classify 1 Thessalonians as deliberative speech, an argument that Krentz finds less than compelling. Jewett, Hughes, Wanamaker, and Donfried are among those who classify the letter as epideictic. This, too, is not persuasive since Hughes, especially, is too dependent on a wide chronological range of texts that for the most part are Latin. With regard to the latter, namely, the use of the Latin rhetoricians, Anderson urges, against Krentz, the appropriateness of their incorporation. Nevertheless, Krentz faults these four scholars for failing to adequately consider the "vocabulary, style, or ornamentation" suited to the epideictic genre. The judicious student of 1 Thessalonians will want to study in some detail the extensive work of Hughes,[58] for example, to determine whether or not he or she would come to the same conclusion.

Relying exclusively on Aristotle, but utilizing the flexibility inherent in *Ars rhetorica* to incorporate other situations, Thomas Olbricht argues that none of the Aristotelian categories fits 1 Thessalonians; thus he urges the use of a new genre, "church rhetoric," and understands this first Pauline letter to be involved in "reconfirmational church rhetoric."[59] While viewing this designation as a possibility, Krentz prefers to see the letter as deliberative and to understand that rhetorical and epistolary analysis are complementary modes of inquiry that cohere with each other. In making such a statement, however, Krentz agrees neither that epistolary forms

---

57. Krentz, "1 Thessalonians," *TD,* 289-94.

58. Especially "The Rhetoric of 1 Thessalonians," in *The Thessalonian Correspondence,* 94-116.

59. As cited by Krentz, "1 Thessalonians," *TD,* 301.

25

drive toward fragmentation nor that it is profitable to depend on a rhetorical method that is overly dependent on Latin handbooks. To follow such a rhetorical approach, citing with approval the words of W. Rhys Roberts, is to overlook the fact that Paul, as well as others among early Christians, "knew and appreciated ancient Greek literature, though concerning themselves little with formal rhetoric and literary criticism."[60] Krentz's conclusions, then, affirm the coherence of the two methods and approve "the value of rhetorical analysis. . . ."[61]

Arguing for a synthesis of rhetorical analysis with epistolary, Raymond F. Collins understands that such an application of methods must take place simultaneously. The very title of his essay, "'I Command That This Letter Be Read': Writing as a Manner of Speaking," describes 1 Thessalonians as a "speech act," that is, Paul by his absence from Thessalonica uses the medium of the letter as a form of dialogue that he expects to be publicly read before the church in Thessalonica (1 Thess 5:27). What we have before us as a letter is in reality an ongoing conversation between the apostle and the congregation that he founded; although forged in written words, it is in reality an oral composition both prior to its sending, in the sense that Paul dictated it to a secretary, and as a result of its sending, insofar as its intention is to become an oral act before the gathered congregation.

Since for Collins a speech act is, in effect, a rhetorical act, one finds a wide diversity of clues revealing the orality of 1 Thessalonians. Thus, Paul can use the verbs "to write" and "to speak" quite interchangeably and synonymously. The former is found in 4:9 and 5:1, while the latter is used in 1:8; 2:2, 4, 16. Noteworthy in this connection is the introductory phrase used to introduce the word of the Lord in 4:15-17: "for this we declare to you (ὑμῖν λέγομεν) by the word of the Lord" (v 15). Here, as with a variety of preteritional formulae found elsewhere in the letter, the exegete is forced to recognize that Paul speaks through and by means of his written word. As a result the emphasis of scholarship need not be so much to discover rhetorical devices in his letter or to find the use of parallel expressions among the ancient rhetoricians, but rather to recognize that Paul actually conceives "his speech acts to be rhetorical exercises."[62]

---

60. Krentz, "1 Thessalonians," *TD*, 317.
61. Krentz, "1 Thessalonians," *TD*, 318.
62. Raymond Collins, "'I Command That This Letter Be Read,'" *TD*, 323.

Epistolary analysis suggests that 1 Thessalonians is intended, much along the lines described by Pseudo-Demetrius, as a personal, friendly letter. Indications in this direction are given both by the epistolary salutation and the closing conventions, as well as by expressions throughout the letter that make evident the close relationship that existed between the writer and the audience. Not insignificant in this regard is the fact that the apostle addresses his hearers some fourteen times as ἀδελφοί. Affectionate language, whether kinship or familial, characterizes the positive tone of the communication.

Had Paul studied Pseudo-Demetrius or other epistolary handbooks, or had he read Aristotle or formally studied rhetoric? While not answering this question in the affirmative, Collins sees the situation as one in which Paul "learned letter-recognition and letter-writing from the cultural situation in which he lived."[63] As a first-century Hellenistic production, it was written in a society that considered letter-writing an exercise in rhetoric. Thus, given the nature of the composition at hand, it is necessary to apply epistolary and rhetorical approaches simultaneously in order to properly understand the purpose of 1 Thessalonians.

Concluding Comment

A volume such as this can only be a starting point for further study. The serious student of 1 Thessalonians will want to pursue some of the areas discussed in these essays even more completely and thoroughly. One should therefore pay careful attention to the footnotes and the many references to other significant studies that are mentioned there. May I commend two particularly significant starting points for such further study: (1) Jeffrey A. D. Weima and Stanley Porter, *An Annotated Bibliography of 1 and 2 Thessalonians;*[64] and (2) Duane Watson and Alan J. Houser, *Rhetorical Criticism of the Bible: A Comprehensive Bibliography with Notes on History and Method.*[65] And, of course, the most important resource of all should not be overlooked: *the text of 1 Thessalonians!*

63. Collins, "'I Command That This Letter Be Read,'" in *TD*, 339.

64. Weima and Porter, *An Annotated Bibliography of 1 and 2 Thessalonians.*

65. Duane Watson and Alan J. Houser, *Rhetorical Criticism of the Bible: A Comprehensive Bibliography with Notes on History and Method* (Biblical Interpretation Series, 4; Leiden: E. J. Brill, 1994).

PART 1

1 THESSALONIANS 2:1-12
AS SYMPTOMATIC OF
THE EXEGETICAL DEBATE

The Epistolary and Rhetorical Context
of 1 Thessalonians 2:1-12

Karl P. Donfried

1. The Problem

One of the specific problems that this Seminar has set out to examine is how 1 Thess 2:1-12 functions within the letter and in what ways epistolary and rhetorical criticism might assist us in addressing this question.

Since many scholars have argued that this text functions as an *apology*, it will be useful to give a definition of this term so that we might attempt to avoid unnecessary ambiguity in our discussions: "A work can be called an apology provided its content throughout aims at presenting a defense in answer to accusations against a certain person or group of persons or at overcoming or preventing opinions adverse to them."[1]

A review of the literature suggests at least three major ways in which 1 Thess 2:1-12 has been understood as an apology.

1. as an apology against specific opponents and concrete attacks. Some further specify it as an apology:
   a. against a Jewish attack;[2]

---

1. J. A. Goldstein, *The Letters of Demosthenes* (New York: Columbia, 1968), 98.
2. Richard Adelbert Lipsius, "Über Zweck und Veranlassung des ersten Thessalonicherbrief," *ThStKr* 27 (1854): 905-34; James E. Frame, *A Critical and Exegetical Commentary on the Epistles of St. Paul to the Thessalonians* (ICC; New York: Scribner's,

b. against libertinists and gnostics who deny the resurrection;[3]
2. as an apology determined by Paul's inner feelings;[4]
3. as an apology influenced by its Hellenistic culture:
   a. determined by the milieu of wandering Cynic-Stoic philosophers, although there may not be a specific challenge that prompts the apology, or[5]
   b. determined by the established rhetorical *topos* of the serious Cynic who wishes actually to dissociate his message from those of other wandering preachers.[6]

The last position (3b) has been especially argued by Abraham Malherbe in his now well-known essay "Gentle as a Nurse." He lists a number of terms that are shared by Dio Chrysostom and Paul, such as ἀγών, παρρησία, κενός, ἤπιος, and βάρος. The real question is whether these terms share a similar field of meaning in the two different contexts. With

---

1912); William Neil, *The Epistle of Paul to the Thessalonians* (Naperville: Allenson, 1957); Béda Rigaux, *Saint Paul. Les Épîtres aux Thessaloniciens* (EtB; Paris: Gabalda and Gembloux: Duculot, 1956).

3. Wilhelm Lütgert, "Die Volkommenen im Philipperbrief und die Enthusiasten in Thessalonich," *BFChTh* 13 (1909): 547-654; W. Hadorn, "Die Abfassung der Thessalonicherbriefe auf der dritten Missionsreise und der Kanons des Marcion," *ZNW* 19 (1919-20): 67-72; W. Hadorn, "Die Abfassung der Thessalonicherbriefe auf der dritten Missionsreise des Paulus," *BFChTh* 24 (1919): 157-284; Bo Reicke, "Thessalonicherbriefe," in *RGG*[3], 6.851-53; Walter Schmithals, "The Historical Situation of the Thessalonian Epistles," in *Paul and the Gnostics* (Nashville: Abingdon, 1972), 128-318.

4. Ernst von Dobschütz, *Die Thessalonicher-Briefe* (Nachdruck der Ausgabe von 1909. Mit einem Literaturverzeichnis von Otto Merk; ed. Ferdinand Hahn; Göttingen: Vandenhoeck & Ruprecht, 1974).

5. Martin Dibelius, *Die Briefe des Apostels Paulus. II. Die Neuen Kleinen Briefe* (HNT; Tübingen: Mohr, 1913); also speaking against a specific attack are von Dobschütz, *Die Thessalonicher-Briefe,* and Albrecht Oepke, *Die Briefe an die Thessalonicher* (NTD 8; repr. of 1933 ed.; Göttingen: Vandenhoeck & Ruprecht, 1970).

6. Abraham Malherbe, "'Gentle as a Nurse': The Cynic Background to 1 Thess ii," in Abraham J. Malherbe, *Paul and the Popular Philosophers* (Minneapolis: Fortress, 1989), 35-48 (originally in *NovT* 12 [1970], 203-17), followed by Willi Marxsen, *Der erste Brief an die Thessalonicher* (ZB; Zürich: Theologischer Verlag, 1979); Gerhard Friedrich, "1-2 Thessalonians," in J. Becker, H. Conzelmann, and G. Friedrich, *Die Briefe an die Galater, Epheser, Philipper, Kolosser, Thessalonicher und Philemon* (NTD; Göttingen: Vandenhoeck & Ruprecht, 1981); Hans-Heinrich Schade, *Apokalyptische Christologie bei Paulus* (GTA 18; Göttingen: Vandenhoeck & Ruprecht, 1981).

regard to βάρος, for example, Malherbe comments that a "special complaint is that the transients were sometimes brutally harsh rather than seeking to benefit their hearers."[7] Further on we will suggest that Paul is using this phrase in a markedly different way. While Malherbe's essay provides much useful comparative material, it does not directly help us assess whether, based on these parallels, 1 Thess 2:1-12 is an apology or not. For, on the one hand, he appears to suggest that Dio is contrasting his own philosophical ethos with specific "hucksters in mind"[8] and that "there is no question of his having to defend himself against specific charges that he was a charlatan."[9] But, then, on the other hand, he proceeds to say that in "view of the different types of Cynics who were about, it had become desirable, when describing oneself as a philosopher, to do so in negative and antithetic terms. This is the context within which Paul describes his activity in Thessalonica. We cannot determine from his description that he is making a personal apology."[10]

In the subsequent literature there have been several criticisms of Malherbe's proposal both by those who agree and those who disagree that 1 Thess 2:1-12 is an apology. Wolfgang Stegemann, who stands in opposition to any form of the apology hypothesis, is extensive in his criticism of both Dibelius and Malherbe. Understanding Dibelius as drawing a vague relationship between Paul and the Cynics[11] and Malherbe a more specific one,[12] he criticizes both: "Eine sprachliche Nähe zum kynischen Wortschatz muß also auch hier nicht zwangsläufig auf denselben Topos apologetischer Rhetorik verweisen."[13] Traugott Holtz, who vigorously defends the apology position, is, however, in agreement: "Indessen ist die Analogie deshalb nicht überzeugend, weil Dio tatsächlich popularphilosophischer Wanderprediger war und das natürlich auch wußte,

---

7. Malherbe, "Gentle as a Nurse," 45.
8. Malherbe, "Gentle as a Nurse," 46.
9. Malherbe, "Gentle as a Nurse," 37.
10. Malherbe, "Gentle as a Nurse," 48.
11. Wolfgang Stegemann, "Anlaß und Hintergrund der Abfassung von 1 Th 2,1-12," in *Theologische Brosamen für Lothar Steiger* (ed. Gerhard Freund and Ekkehard Stegemann; DBAT 5; Heidelberg, 1985), 398: "Er rechnet also mit einer durch das 'Milieu' bedingten Apologie, die durchaus keines aktuellen Anlasses bedurft habe."
12. Stegemann, "Anlaß und Hintergrund," 399: "Jedenfalls läßt sich für die von MALHERBE herangezogenen Beispiele nich ausschließen, daß sie auf reale, konkrete Vorwürfe reagieren."
13. Stegemann, "Anlaß und Hintergrund," 399.

während Paulus das nicht war und das ebenfalls wußte."[14] Stegemann insists that one must inquire about a "spezifische Anlaß in den Verhältnissen der Gemeinde in Thessalonich diesen Text des 1. Thessalonicherbriefes motiviert haben könnte."[15] Once again Holtz agrees with this, although he and Stegemann see the situation very differently: "So muß seine Abgrenzung einen aktuellen Anlaß haben."[16]

Can one read 1 Thess 2:1-12 in a mirror fashion so that the antithetical formulations are indications that Paul is countering charges made against him by opponents either within or outside of the church in Thessalonica? Lyons, seeing this text more broadly as an "autobiography," indicates that any attempt to go beyond the current impasse must take into account that how "an author approached his autobiography depended upon his relationship with his audience, the social setting of which and for which he wrote, and, most importantly, his intention (τέλος/causa) in writing."[17] We now turn to the question whether epistolary criticism is able to assist in determining this causa?

2. The Epistolary Context

Particularly since Paul Schubert's study, *Form and Function of the Pauline Thanksgivings*,[18] the phrase "form-critical analysis" has been used in a broad way. Charles Wanamaker reminds us that this phrase contains three originally distinct components:[19]

1. *Formal literary analysis* is primarily concerned with the study of "formulaic features of ancient letters" such as the forms occurring at the

14. Traugott Holtz, *Der erste Brief an die Thessalonicher* (EKK XIII; Zürich: Benzinger, 1986), 93, n. 422.

15. Stegemann, "Anlaß und Hintergrund," 401

16. Holtz, *An die Thessalonicher*, 93, n. 422. Similar is the criticism of Jan Lambrecht, "Thanksgivings in 1 Thessalonians 1–3," in *The Thessalonian Correspondence* (ed. Raymond F. Collins; BETL 87; Leuven: Leuven University Press, 1990), 203-4, and 135-62 (in this volume).

17. George Lyons, *Pauline Autobiography: Toward a New Understanding* (SBLDS 73; Atlanta: Scholars, 1985), 61.

18. Paul Schubert, *Form and Function of the Pauline Thanksgivings* (BZNW 20; Berlin: Töpelmann, 1939).

19. Charles A. Wanamaker, "Epistolary vs. Rhetorical Analysis: Is a Synthesis Possible?" 255-86 (in this volume).

opening and closing of an ancient letter, and other formulae involved either within the letter-body or at its beginning and ending. Stowers refers to this as "studies of structure and form."[20]

2. *Thematic analysis* refers to the study of "epistolary *topoi* or commonplace themes such as friendship and paraenesis, and the stock motifs that were used in relation to these themes."[21]

3. *Form-critical analysis* attempts to isolate primary oral forms such as doxological units and paraenetic formulae that have been incorporated in the letters as written forms, but that received their shape in other, more oral contexts, such as the liturgy and the instruction of baptismal candidates. "The fact that letters functioned in part as surrogates for oral communication encouraged the preservation of these traditions."[22]

These various dimensions of the epistolary analysis of New Testament, Graeco-Roman, Hebrew, and Aramaic letters are invaluable for the understanding of these writings in many respects. John L. White, to cite one example, summarizes the components isolated by formal literary analysis:[23]

Opening

Address: Paul, an apostle of Jesus Christ, to the church of God at
————, sanctified (beloved, called, etc.) in Christ.

Grace greeting: Grace to you and peace from God our Father and the
Lord Jesus Christ.

Thanksgiving prayer: I thank God (always) for (all of) you, because
of . . . , and I pray that the Lord may make you increase (mature)
in such activity so that you may be pure and blameless when
Christ returns.

Body

Introductory formula: I want you to know, brethren, that . . . (I/we do
not want you to be ignorant, brethren, that/of . . .). Or: I appeal to
you, brethren, that . . .

---

20. Wanamaker, "Epistolary vs. Rhetorical Analysis," 256-57.

21. Wanamaker, "Epistolary vs. Rhetorical Analysis," 257.

22. David Aune, *The New Testament in Its Literary Environment* (LEC 8; Philadelphia: Westminster, 1987), 192.

23. John L. White, "Ancient Greek Letters," in *Graeco-Roman Literature and the New Testament* (ed. David E. Aune; SBLRBS 21; Atlanta: Scholars Press, 1988), 97.

Transitional formulae: Often indicated by Paul's use of the vocative, "brethren," and with request/disclosure phrases.

Concluding section/Paul's apostolic presence section

1. Autobiographical (authoritative) reference to the letter and expression of confidence in the recipients' willingness to comply with Paul's instruction.
2. Identification/recommendation of Paul's messenger.
3. Announcement of Paul's anticipated (hoped for) visit.
4. Paraenetic section: Reminder of Paul's instruction, reference to Paul's/the congregation's former conduct, and appeal to the example of Christ.
5. Prayer of peace.

Closing

Closing greetings: from (to) third parties.

The holy kiss greeting.

Grace benediction: The grace of our (the) Lord Jesus Christ be with you (your spirit).

While valuing highly the many helpful letter components that have been identified, one must still inquire whether epistolary analysis can help us discern, with substantial precision, the specific intentions, particularly the oral intentions, of the letter.[24] Such ambiguity, when it exists, can be attributed to the inability of this methodology to properly identify the parameters of the "body" of the letter.

Such inexactitude with regard to the letter-"body" is highlighted in Paul Schubert's monograph, *Form and Function of the Pauline Thanksgivings.* The thanksgiving is a formal section in most of Paul's letters, normally concluding the letter-opening and setting forth themes that will be taken up in the remainder of the letter. Simultaneously, Schubert concludes that "the thanksgiving itself constitutes the main body of 1 Thessalonians. It contains all the primary information that Paul wished to convey." In fact, he continues, "the thanksgiving *is* the letter."[25] Jan Lam-

---

24. Klaus Berger, "Hellenistische Gattungen im Neuen Testament," in *ANRW* II, Principat 25.2, 1291, reminds us: "Wie für die Briefe des Demosthenes, so gilt schließlich auch für die des Paulus: Sie sind Reden in Brieffform."

25. Schubert, *Form and Function,* 26.

brecht takes issue with what he considers to be Schubert's arbitrary classification of the pattern of the Pauline thanksgivings and the exclusion of
1 Thessalonians 4 and 5 from the "body" of the letter. A similar concern is
raised by David Aune in his suggestion that 1 Thessalonians "is the only
Pauline letter in which the 'concluding' hortatory section (4:1–5:22) constitutes the main part."[26] Lambrecht issues a warning that needs to be
heeded: "The danger, however, lies in exaggeration, in increasingly inventive speciousness, in too much, often far-fetched and strained, genre hunting. One might wonder whether Paul consciously starts the body of his letter in 2:1, deliberately composes an apostolic *parousia* in 2:17–3:13, or
really intends a twofold epistolary recommendation in 2:1-12 and 2:17–
3:8."[27]

As is evident from John Hurd's analysis of 1 Thessalonians, a too precise application of these identifiable components can lead to an overconfi-
dence with regard to the structure of the letter. He suggests that this first
letter of Paul "has the *normal structure* [italics mine!!] of a Pauline letter:
sender(s), recipient(s), greeting (1:1), thanksgiving (1:2-10), body (with
renewed thanksgiving, 2:1-16), apostolic visitation (2:17–3:13), paraenesis
(4:1–5:22), blessing (5:23-24), and autograph coda (5:25-28)."[28] The concept of a "normal" letter with regard to the "body" has not been demonstrated, as can be seen from the vastly divergent views of what the parameters of the "body" are in 1 Thessalonians![29]

John White recognizes the limitations of epistolary analysis of the Pauline letters when he writes: "Regarding the body portion of Paul's letters,
common features are less evident than in the opening and closing. The re-

---

26. Aune, *The New Testament in Its Literary Environment*, 206.

27. Lambrecht, "Thanksgivings in 1 Thessalonians 1–3," 135-62 (in this volume).
Note also I. Howard Marshall, *1 and 2 Thessalonians* (NCBC; Grand Rapids: Eerdmans,
1983), 8: "This characterisation of both sections of the letter [apostolic apology and apostolic *parousia*] is justified in terms of their content and the parallels detected with similar
material in other letters. However, a closer analysis of the parallels suggests that it is over-
precise and perhaps misleading to think of these as two specific 'formal' parts of Pauline
epistles which constitute structural elements in them. It would appear rather to be the case
that here we have two themes which recur — for good contextual reasons — in various of
Paul's letters in which he naturally expresses himself in similar ways."

28. John C. Hurd, Jr. "Thessalonians, First Letter to the," in *Interpreter's Dictionary of
the Bible* (ed. K. Crim; Nashville: Abingdon, 1976), 4.900.

29. See the chart in Robert Jewett, *The Thessalonian Correspondence: Pauline Rhetoric
and Millenarian Piety* (FFNT; Philadelphia: Fortress, 1986), 220.

currence of major motifs, and of an identifiable structure, seems to be limited to the closing section of the body." When he continues that as far as "the introductory part of the body is concerned, Paul introduces the message with conventional epistolary phrases: a disclosure formula in five cases (Romans, 2 Corinthians, Galatians, Philippians, and 1 Thessalonians) and a request formula in the two remaining letters (1 Corinthians and Philemon)," two immediate questions come to mind: (1) whether to mark the beginning of the "body" purely on the basis of conventional epistolary phrases is accurate; and, (2) whether the category "body" is sufficiently vague and abstract to not only be not helpful but perhaps misleading as well.

White moves in the right direction when he recognizes that the "theological body is characterized by dialogical and argumentative features that are especially influenced by oral rhetorical traditions. The individual letters, or certain parts of them, reflect the influence of one or another type of argumentation." Still, the limitations of this approach become evident when, without the benefit of a formal rhetorical analysis, White urges that "hortatory reminder, and a paraenetic style, characterizes 1 Thessalonians."[30]

Given the inability of epistolary criticism to provide a formal and structural analysis of the "main body" of the letter, it can provide little assistance in solving the conundrum related to 2:1-12. Thus, we must ascertain whether a more sustained application of rhetorical criticism will help illuminate the function of 1 Thess 2:1-12 within the letter.

3. The Rhetorical Context

It is a major contention of this analysis that an awareness of the social situation in Thessalonica and a consideration of the structure of the letter itself will greatly assist the task of understanding the theology of 1 Thessalonians. The structure of a letter can be analyzed by employing the methodologies commonly referred to as epistolary and rhetorical criticism, analytical tools that can help determine Paul's intentions in writing this letter. The former explains how parts of letters are constructed; the latter, that is, Graeco-Roman rhetorical criticism, allows us to see more vividly why the letter is constructed the way it is as well as giving us further

---

30. White, "Ancient Greek Letters," 99.

insight into the lived situation of the letter.[31] As we have resisted the imposition of existing epistolary categories on 1 Thessalonians, so we must be equally cautious to avoid a similar situation in the application of rhetorical criticism, especially when we are alert to the fact that this letter is a first attempt in Christian letter-writing.

Theology, structure, and social situation are closely interwoven in 1 Thessalonians and other Pauline letters. Thus rhetorical criticism can, by using its analytical tools, alert us not only to distinct emphases in a given letter but also to certain dimensions in the rhetorical situation, which gives suggestions about the larger social situation, that might otherwise have been overlooked. To recognize, for example, which of the three types *(genera)* of rhetoric, deliberative, judicial, or epideictic, a document is tending toward already gives important clues as to its social situation as well as its intention. While being sensitive to the fact that there may be overlap between these *genera,* it is useful to know that the proper time for deliberative rhetoric is the future, that the appropriate time for epideictic rhetoric is primarily the present, though often with reference to both the past and the future, and that the appropriate time for judicial rhetoric is the past. To be precise in identifying the different types of rhetoric, it is critical to note the standard topics that are common to each. For epideictic rhetoric these are primarily praise (e.g., 1 Thess 2:1-12) and blame (e.g., 1 Thess 2:14-16), and in deliberative rhetoric these standard topics are advantage and honor, namely, that which is expedient and/or harmful to the intended recipients. Thus the identification of these and other "strategies of persuasion" will allow us to gain "greater understanding of the author, the audience, and the author's purpose in communicating with the audience."[32]

Understanding 1 Thessalonians as primarily an epideictic letter allows for some significant conclusions both about what Paul intended and what he did not intend to communicate:

1. On the one hand, recognizing 1 Thessalonians as belonging to the epideictic genus of rhetoric allows us to see that the Thessalonian Christians have become the object of Paul's praise. Hughes summarizes the matter well:

31. For a further discussion see Frank W. Hughes, *Early Christian Rhetoric and 2 Thessalonians* (JSNTSup 30; Sheffield: JSOT Press, 1989), 19-50; and Stanley K. Stowers, *Letter Writing in Greco-Roman Antiquity* (Philadelphia: Westminster, 1986).

32. Frank W. Hughes, "The Social Situations Implied by Rhetoric," 243 (in this volume).

In fact, the strong use of epideictic rhetoric, as compared with deliberative and judicial rhetoric, reveals a great deal about the intention of the author in writing the letter. Epideictic rhetoric classically focused on the development of persuasive writing based on values held in common between the rhetor and the audience. Although Paul, like other persuasive writers, was quite capable of using features drawn from all the *genera* of persuasion, the fact that he did not do so in 1 Thessalonians would recommend the centrality of the epideictic topics of praise and blame to what he was trying to accomplish in the letter. Instead of praising the beauty of a mountain or river or of some honorific dead person, the apostle chose to modify this *genus* of rhetoric slightly, so that the recipients of the letter themselves were the object of Paul's praise. Paul's emphasis on praise reinforced the joyful relationship between the Thessalonians and their founder that had existed for some time — though the relationship was troubled by Paul's non-presence in Thessalonica during the congregation's recent difficulties, characterized by the deaths of some in the Thessalonian church. Paul's persuasive response to this bereaved congregation is to praise their faithfulness and love, to explain in an affective manner the reasons for his absence from the city (2:17–3:10), to confirm the teaching that he had given (the first two proofs: 4:1-8 and 4:9-12), and to add instruction that he had not conveyed previously (such as the material in 4:13–5:3). This additional direction is specifically not identified by the apostle as prior teaching but rather as revelation, as a "word of the Lord" (4:15).

Such a persuasive response, coupled with the skillfully crafted triad of virtues in 1:3, the listing of the *propositiones* in the *partitio* (3:11-13), including their careful and subtle recapitulation in the *peroratio* (5:4-11), all suggest that Paul either learned rhetoric in school or had developed an extraordinary gift for the subject in which he grasped the appropriateness of various rhetorical precepts for his letter without ever having formally learned them.[33]

2. On the other hand, since 1 Thess 2:1-12 does not contain any explicit and sustained charges against Paul, this letter cannot be categorized as belonging to the judicial genus of rhetoric. In judicial rhetoric such charges would have to be taken up and defended in the *probatio* (proof), which is exactly what does not happen. While 1 Thess 2:17–3:10 may pos-

---

33. Hughes, "Social Situations," 252-53 (in this volume).

sibly suggest some concerns about Paul's premature departure from Thessalonica, certainly one cannot, as a result of this understandable worry, conclude that Paul is arguing against opponents in this letter.

Although Graeco-Roman rhetorical theory does not focus significantly on letters, the actual practice of rhetoric did include letters. Therefore one can speak of a "rhetorical letter" and, perhaps, add that in terms of epistolary genre 1 Thessalonians approximates, but is not identical with, ancient letters of consolation. In terms of rhetorical genus there is a clear connection with epideictic rhetoric. Not unimportant for this particular linkage is the fact that among the two most important categories of the epideictic genus of rhetoric is the funeral speech (ἐπιτάφιος) and consolatory speech (παραμυθητικός). Paul's intention in writing 1 Thessalonians is, as we have urged,[34] to console a Christian community suffering the effects of persecution and death, to encourage the discouraged.

What follows is an abridgment and slight modification of the rhetorical structure of 1 Thessalonians proposed by Frank W. Hughes:[35]

I. *Exordium* (Introduction) (1:1-10)
   A. Epistolary prescript (1:1)
   B. Thanksgiving prayer (1:2-10)
II. *Narratio* (Narrative[36]) (2:1–3:10)
   A. Introduction to *narratio* (address) (2:1)
   B. A description of Paul's first visit to the Thessalonians (2:1-16)
   C. Paul's desire for a second visit (2:17–3:10)
III. *Partitio* (Statement of Propositions[37]) (stated as an intercessory prayer; 3:11-13)

---

34. See the discussion in Karl P. Donfried, "The Cults of Thessalonica and the Thessalonian Correspondence," *NTS* 31 (1985): 336-56 and, further, in Karl P. Donfried and I. Howard Marshall, *The Theology of the Shorter Pauline Letters* (Cambridge: Cambridge University Press, 1993).

35. Hughes, "The Rhetoric of 1 Thessalonians," in *The Thessalonian Correspondence*, 94-116.

36. Cicero in *De inventione* 1.27 defines the *narratio* in this way: "The narrative is an exposition of events that have occurred or are supposed to have occurred."

37. In *Rhetorica ad Herennium* 1.17 it is explained that this exposition or statement of proposition "consists in setting forth briefly and completely, the points we intend to discuss."

   A. First petition (transition from *narratio*): the topic of Paul's desired journey to the Thessalonians (3:11)

   B. Second petition: the topics of the three-part *probatio* introduced (3:12-13)

     1. First topic: "increase in love" (3:12-13)

     2. Second and third topics: "being preserved at the *parousia*" (3:13)

       a. Second topic: "to establish your hearts blameless in holiness"

       b. Third topic: "at the coming of our Lord Jesus Christ with all his saints"

IV. *Probatio* (Proof) (4:1–5:3)

   A. First proof: "how it is necessary to walk and to please God" (4:1-8)

   B. Second proof: "concerning brotherly love" (4:9-12)

   C. Third proof: "concerning those who have fallen asleep" (4:13–5:3)

V. *Peroratio* (Epilogue) (5:4-11)

   A. Transition from previous section (5:4)

   B. Honorific description of Thessalonians (5:5)

   C. First consequence of description: wakefulness (5:6)

   D. Reasons for consequence: association of sleeping and drunkenness with night (5:7)

   E. Second consequence of argument: preparation for action (5:8-10)

   F. Third consequence of argument: console one another (5:11)

VI. Exhortation (5:12-22)

   A. Introduction of exhortation (5:12)

   B. First exhortation: concerning church order (5:12)

   C. Second exhortation: concerning church discipline (5:14-22)

VII. Final Prayers and Greetings (Epistolary Conclusion) (5:23-28)

   A. Intercessory prayer (5:23-24)

   B. A request for prayer (5:25)

   C. Final greetings (5:26-27)

   D. Final prayer (5:28)

a. 1 Thessalonians 2:1–3:10 as Narratio

2:1   A. Introduction to *narratio* (address): "For you know, brothers, our εἴσοδος to you" (see 1:9).

2:1-16   B. A description of Paul's first εἴσοδος to the Thessalonians

2:1   1. Negatively: "not in vain"

2:2-16   2. Positively

2:2a   a. The prehistory of the visit: Paul's disaster in Philippi
                i) "we had suffered"
                ii) "we were shamefully treated"
                iii) The readers' relationship to the Philippi incident: "you know"

2:2b   b. The visit to Thessalonica itself
                i) Statement of Paul's activity
                   A) Summary: "we had courage in our God to declare to you the gospel of God in the face of great opposition"

2:3-8   B) Concerning Paul's activity in Thessalonica

2:3   1) Stated negatively (concerning Paul's παράκλησις)

2:4   2) Stated positively (concerning Paul's apostolic office)

2:5   3) Stated negatively (concerning Paul's rhetorical methods)

2:6   4) Stated negatively (concerning Paul's motivations)

2:6   5) Stated positively (concerning Paul's right as an apostle)

2:7   6) Stated positively (concerning Paul's activity as a pastor)

2:8   7) Summary of Paul's activity
                     a) Statement: "we were ready to share with you not only the gospel of God but also our own selves"
                     b) Reason for activity: (relationship with readers) "because you had become very dear to us"

2:9-12	C) Concerning Paul's behavior at Thessalonica (description of the ἦθος of Paul)
2:9	1) Paul as hardworking
	a) Calling of witnesses: "For you remember, brethren"
	b) Statement of description: "we worked night and day"
	c) Motive of Paul: "that we might not burden any of you"
2:10	2) Paul as moral
	a) Calling of witnesses
	(A) "you"
	(B) "God also"
	b) Statement of description: "how holily and righteously and blamelessly"
2:11-12	3) Paul as fatherly
2:11	a) Calling of witnesses: "For you know how"
2:11-12	b) Statement of description: "like a father with his children, we exhorted each one of you"
2:13-16	D) Concerning the Thessalonians' behavior
2:13	1) In regard to reception of the gospel . . .
2:14-16	2) In regard to suffering . . .
2:17–3:10	C. Paul's desire for a second εἴσοδος

1. An Overview of the *Narratio*

According to Quintilian, the *narratio* "consists in the persuasive exposition of that which either has been done, or is supposed to have been done. . . ."[38] He and other rhetoricians urge that "it should be lucid (*lucidam*), brief (*brevem*), and plausible (*verisimilem*)."[39] Aristotle allows that the speaker may introduce himself and his adversary as being "of a certain moral character."[40] He also observes that the function of the *narratio* in epideictic rhetoric pertains "most appropriately to the present, for it is the existing conditions of things that all those who praise or blame

---

38. *Institutio oratoria* 4.2.31.
39. *Institutio oratoria* 4.2.31-32.
40. *Ars rhetorica* 3.16.10.

44

have in view. It is not uncommon, however, for epideictic speakers to avail themselves of other times, of the past by way of recalling it, or of the future by way of anticipating it."[41]

The *narratio* builds upon the *exordium*, and the latter functions both as a *captatio benevolentiae* and to introduce themes that will be expanded further on in the discourse. Several themes mentioned in the *exordium* (Paul's behavior [1:5], the sufferings of Paul [1:6], the sufferings of the Thessalonians [1:6], and Paul's missionary intention [1:9]) are elaborated further in the *narratio*. As the *narratio* is dependent on the *exordium*, so is the *probatio* dependent on the foundation laid by the *exordium*, *narratio*, and *partitio*.

In studying the relationship between the *exordium* and the *narratio*, one observes that the integrity of Paul's past behavior is both a significant factor that led to the gospel's being accepted with full assurance (1:5; see 2:13) during his first visit and that that same integrity will also allow his current paraclesis to be accepted with the same full assurance. The power and effectiveness of the Word is intimately linked with the credibility of the messenger; the truth of the divine *logos* is demonstrated by his ethos, that is, by Paul's embodiment of the gospel, and by his divine authorization (2:4, δεδοκιμάσμεθα).[42] For these reasons, what is said in 1 Thessalonians, and especially, as we shall see, in the prophetic word announced by him in 4:15, is to be acknowledged as valid and authoritative.

It will be our contention that the first part of the *narratio* (2:1-16) of 1 Thessalonians is neither apologetic nor polemic, a fact that is confirmed by the absence of any charges or suspicions against Paul in the *probatio*. This first part of the *narratio* functions in the following three ways:

a. It recounts the relationship of friendship established between Paul and the Thessalonians during the time of his founding visit (εἴσοδος, 1:9; 2:1), whereas the second part of the *narratio*, 2:17–3:13, concerns their relationship since Paul's departure (ἔξοδος) from Thessalonica and their separation (ἀπορφανισθέντες, 2:17).

b. The first part of the *narratio* serves to distinguish Paul's gospel and ethos from the error and delusion surrounding the Thessalonian Chris-

---

41. *Ars rhetorica* 1.3.4.

42. Bartholomäus Henneken, *Verkündigung und Prophetie im 1. Thessalonicherbrief* (SBS 29; Stuttgart: Katholisches Bibelwerk, 1969), 101 and 105, citing A.-M. Denis, "L'Apotre Paul, prophete 'messianique' des Gentils. Etude thématique de 1 Thess., II,1-6," *ETL* 33 (1957): 245-318.

tians, specifically from the idolatry of the heathen, namely, their false or nonexistent understanding of God (4:5, τὰ ἔθνη τὰ μὴ εἰδότα τὸν θεόν). As a result these pagans have no hope and succumb to grief (4:13). It is this non-knowledge of God that leads to what Denis has called *l'erreur eschatologique*,[43] an error to which Paul must address his prophetic word in 4:15. One can understand much of 1 Thessalonians as a consistent clarification and application of what had taken place during Paul's first εἴσοδος, when he reminds them that ἐπεστρέψατε πρὸς τὸν θεὸν ἀπὸ τῶν εἰδώλων δουλεύειν θεῷ ζῶντι καὶ ἀληθινῷ (1:9).

c. The *narratio* also presents characteristics of Paul's ethos that the apostle will develop further in the *probatio,* especially in 4:1, "Finally, brothers, we ask you and urge you in the Lord Jesus that, as you learned from us how you ought to live and to please God (as, in fact, you are doing), you should do so more and more." Schoon-Janßen comments appropriately: "1 Thess 2,1-12 ist im Sinne unserer Definition keine Apologie, sondern die Beschreibung eine vorbildlichen Verhaltens, das die Gemeinde zur Nachahmung ermuntern soll."[44]

2. Selected Exegetical Observations within Part I of the *Narratio*

(a) Concerning Paul's εἴσοδος (2:1-2)

The *narratio* begins in 2:1: Αὐτοὶ γὰρ οἴδατε, ἀδελφοί, τὴν εἴσοδον ἡμῶν τὴν πρὸς ὑμᾶς ὅτι οὐ κενὴ γέγονεν. Three matters call for comment.

1. As in other literature of antiquity, the possible offensiveness of autobiographical comments is reduced by using "we" or "our," where "I" or "my" might have been expected. "In this way," suggests Lyons, "the corpo-

---

43. Denis, "L'Apotre Paul, prophete 'messianique' des Gentils," 274-75.

44. Johannes Schoon-Janßen, *Umstrittene 'Apologien' in den Paulusbriefen: Studien zur rhetorischen Situation des 1. Thessalonicherbriefes, des Galaterbriefes und des Philipperbriefes* (GTA 45; Göttingen: Vandenhoeck & Ruprecht, 1991), 64. In principal, Klaus Berger, "Hellenistische Gattungen," 1287, evaluates this dimension of the text correctly, although the term "Mahnrede" is an overstatement of Paul's intent and has the potential of misunderstanding 1 Thessalonians as primarily a paraenetic letter: "Auch in 1 Thess 2,1-12 sind weder Anklage vor Gericht noch auch überhaupt ein bereits erfolgter persönlicher Angriff vorauszusetzen. Der Text ist — angesichts der Bedeutung des Motivs der Nachahmung des Lehrers in philosophischen Lehrbriefen — auch bereits voll verständlich als Mahnrede an 'Schüler', die Paulus, ihr persönliches Vorbild, nachahmen sollen."

rateness and mutuality rather than the uniqueness of a claim appear to be emphasized."[45]

2. The strong relationship between the meaning of εἴσοδος in 2:1 and the content of the εἴσοδος referred to in 1:9, ἐπεστρέψατε πρὸς τὸν θεὸν ἀπὸ τῶν εἰδώλων δουλεύειν θεῷ ζῶντι καὶ ἀληθινῷ. Although he does not use this exact term again, the apostle in 3:10 is very much hoping for another εἴσοδος among the Thessalonians; however, since that is not immediately possible, his letter must, in effect, be, at least, a temporary substitute until that new εἴσοδος may be possible. He very much hopes that the reception of this speech act will be as positive as the first reception of the Word among them (e.g., 1:9; 2:13).

3. What does Paul mean when he describes his εἴσοδος in 2:1 as οὐ κενή? How is one to translate οὐ κενή? As "in vain" with the NRSV, as "fruitless" with the REB, as "without effect" with the NAB, or as "pointless" with the NJB? The use of οὐ κενή here in 2:1 is different from its use in 3:5, where the concern is with "the fruit of his labors"; here the concern is with "the character" of his labors in Thessalonica.[46] A translation of οὐ κενή as "has not been found empty" is to be recommended. The emphasis, then, is placed on the content of Paul's preaching and life rather than on its result. Rather than being "empty," Paul's εἴσοδος had these characteristics:

- it was preceded by suffering;
- it was distinguished by boldness of utterance;
- it was identified by absence of deceit, of uncleanness, and of guile;
- it was identified by fidelity, by gentleness, and by disinterested self-denying love;
- it was marked by continuous and affectionate labor and toil.

That all of this had results, that it bore fruit, as suggested in 2:13, is not to be denied; but one must recognize that this is not the primary point being made in 2:1. "Das Adjektive κενή bezeichnet also in diesem Kontext einen Mangel an Authentizität, die fehlende Übereinstimmung von Verkündigung und Existenzweise des Verkündigers selbst."[47] Precisely because this

---

45. George Lyons, *Pauline Autobiography,* 69.

46. John Eadie, *Commentary on the Greek Text of the Epistles of Paul to the Thessalonians* (New York: Macmillan, 1877), 55.

47. Stegemann, "Anlaß und Hintergrund," 403.

is not the case Paul negates the adjective κενή and emphasizes the οὐ κενή, that is, the *character* of his work in Thessalonica.

Paul wishes to stress the character and fullness of his entrance, as opposed to its vacuity, by reminding his readers about the prehistory of his visit, namely, the distress he experienced in Philippi: "we had suffered," "we were shamefully treated." Following this he incorporates the reader's relationship to these events by adding "you know." Yet, despite this state of affairs, he reminds his audience in 2:2b that ἐπαρρησιασάμεθα ἐν τῷ θεῷ ἡμῶν λαλῆσαι πρὸς ὑμᾶς τὸ εὐαγγέλιον τοῦ θεοῦ ἐν πολλῷ ἀγῶνι. As we will suggest, this narrative is preparing for the words of encouragement that will be expanded in the *probatio*.

Not only does ἐπαρρησιασάμεθα play a significant role here, but also the insistent emphasis on ἐν τῷ θεῷ ἡμῶν. Despite having suffered cruelty and indignity in Philippi, Paul had the courage to preach the gospel in Thessalonica. Clearly his ability to proceed with assurance to this capital city of Macedonia despite these obstacles comes from God; it is part of the divine purpose of election (τὴν ἐκλογὴν ὑμῶν) (1:4), and that is why the apostle's message during his original εἴσοδος was received with πληροφορίᾳ πολλῇ. In this narrative section Paul is laying a foundation for his paraclesis, for a new form of εἴσοδος that is being communicated to this community. The intention of his encouragement is taking shape: just as hardships and persecutions had not deterred him, so, too, should similar exigencies not deter the believers in Thessalonica from their fidelity to God.

(b) Concerning Paul's Activity in Thessalonica (2:3-8)

In verse 3 Paul states negatively that his παράκλησις did originate ἐκ πλάνης οὐδὲ ἐξ ἀκαθαρσίας οὐδὲ ἐν δόλῳ. Two items require our consideration: παράκλησις and ἐκ πλάνης.

1. παράκλησις. In addition to the noun παράκλησις, the verb παρακαλέω is used eight times in this brief letter.[48] Thus, in 1 Thess 5:9-11 Paul can write: "For God has not destined us for wrath, but to obtain salvation through our Lord Jesus Christ, who died for us so that whether we wake or sleep we might live with him. Therefore encourage [παρακαλεῖτε] one another and build one another up, just as you are doing."

---

48. 2:12; 3:2, 7; 4:1, 10, 18; 5:11, 14.

The concentration on this word group is not unusual given the fact that 1 Thessalonians has much in common with a λόγος παραμυθητικός, a word of consolation and encouragement to a Christian church suffering the effects of persecution.[49] Παραμυθέομαι is used only in 1 Thess 2:12 and 5:14 within the Pauline corpus. In fact, the advice given in 5:14, "encourage [παραμυθεῖσθε] the fainthearted," is not far from the mark in describing the intention of the letter as one of encouragement to the discouraged. They are discouraged precisely because "hope" has become disengaged from their faith as a result of unexpected deaths in their midst. The preservation of 1 Thessalonians in the canon is a testimony to its effectiveness in correcting, through encouragement, this atmosphere of hopelessness among some in the church of Thessalonica. Paul's intention in writing 1 Thessalonians resembles Second Isaiah's announced intention in 40:1: "Comfort [παρακαλεῖτε], comfort [παρακαλεῖτε] my people, says your God."

The use of παράκλησις coheres with the interpretation of 1 Thessalonians as a λόγος παραμυθητικός. When Paul refers to ἡ γὰρ παράκλησις ἡμῶν in 2:2 he means not only "the words but also the disposition of the one who proclaimed them — his freedom won through persecution and his complete devotion to the readers and to the ministry (verses 1-12), whose fruit is a purer faith, made stronger by suffering (verses 13-14) and — retroactively — the comfort of the one who made the proclamation (3:7)." 1 Thess 4:1 does not introduce "an ethical appendix to the letter, but the contemporary renewal of the appeal with increase as its goal." Containing a further important insight is this observation by Johannes Thomas: "The paraclesis embeds the contemporary . . . in the traditional on five separate occasions . . . and consequently always aims at mutual comfort in the congregation. . . ."[50] That is exactly why five of the occurrences of παρακαλέω are found in chapters 4 and 5.

2. ἐκ πλάνης. The antithetical style that begins here "should not be interpreted as Paul's defense of hypothetical accusations. Rather," Aune wisely reminds us, "it is a technique that *amplifies* thought by contrasting ideas using negation, antonyms, and other devices."[51] In fact, Paul

---

49. See Donfried, "The Cults of Thessalonica."

50. Johannes Thomas, "παρακαλέω," *EDNT* 3.26.

51. Aune, *The New Testament in Its Literary Environment*, 206. Aune cites Aristotle, *Rhetoric* 1409b-10a; Pseudo-Aristotle, *Rhetoric to Alexander* 1435b; Hermogenes, *On Invention* 4.2.

employs the rhetorical device of antithesis throughout 1 Thessalonians as a way of expressing himself. Further, both antithetical parallelism and similar terminology as found here are used by Hellenistic Judaism in its rejection of heathen idolatry, especially in texts such as the Wisdom of Solomon 11–15.

Paul's παράκλησις is not ἐκ πλάνης, not from error, but ἐκ τοῦ θεοῦ. The Thessalonians were converted to the true and living God (1:9); as a result they have been freed from the idolatry of the heathen and from the error of those who do not know God (4:5, μὴ ἐν πάθει ἐπιθυμίας καθάπερ καὶ τὰ ἔθνη τὰ μὴ εἰδότα τὸν θεόν). Similarly, Paul's gospel does not have its origin in such error or delusion. Here in the same verse (2:3), another sign of pagan error and delusion with regard to God is referred to as ἀκαθαρσία. It occurs again in 4:7, where it is explicitly connected to the conduct of "τὰ ἔθνη who do not know God." The correspondence to the language and thought world of the Wisdom of Solomon is remarkable, as is evident, for example, in 14:22: Εἶτ᾽ οὐκ ἤρκεσεν τὸ πλανᾶσθαι περὶ τὴν τοῦ θεοῦ γνῶσιν, ἀλλὰ καὶ ἐν μεγάλῳ ζῶντες ἀγνοίας πολέμῳ τὰ τοσαῦτα κακὰ εἰρήνην προσαγορεύουσιν.

In passing it should be added that the circumstances to which the apostle is addressing his paraclesis in 1 Thessalonians is far more similar to the situation described by the author of the Wisdom of Solomon than to that portrayed by the Cynic preachers. These brief comments suggest, then, that Paul's παράκλησις, in terms of both content and demeanor, is not related to paganism but originates with God. Thus, the entire first part of the *narratio* is an attempt by the apostle to distance himself and the Thessalonians from both pagan thought and practice.

In 1 Thess 2:4 Paul turns to make positive statements about his God-given task: ἀλλὰ καθὼς δεδοκιμάσμεθα ὑπὸ τοῦ θεοῦ πιστευθῆναι τὸ εὐαγγέλιον, οὕτως λαλοῦμεν, οὐχ ὡς ἀνθρώποις ἀρέσκοντες ἀλλὰ θεῷ τῷ δοκιμάζοντι τὰς καρδίας ἡμῶν. With regard to δεδοκιμάσμεθα the general intent is clear: Paul has been tested and approved by God prior to the initiation of his ministry, and this accountability before the forum of God alone continues. That is why the word of God that he has proclaimed and continues to proclaim (literally, "to speak") is, in fact, truly word of God, a fact that the Thessalonian Christians themselves acknowledge (2:13) and will hopefully also continue to acknowledge as a result of this speech-act known as 1 Thessalonians.

In Jer 11:20 one finds a similar use of the verb δοκιμάζω: κύριε κρίνων δίκαια δοκιμάζων νεφροὺς καὶ καρδίας, ἴδοιμι τὴν παρὰ σοῦ ἐκδίκησιν ἐξ αὐτῶν, ὅτι πρὸς σὲ ἀπεκάλυψα τὸ δικαίωμά μου. God is here described as the one who "tests/assays the kidneys and the heart. . . ." Given the parallel in 12:3 (καὶ σύ, κύριε, γινώσκεις με, δεδοκίμακας τὴν καρδίαν μου ἐναντίον σου), it is probable that Jeremiah himself is being tested. The prophet is confident that as a result of God's definitive and conclusive "test" he will not be found wanting. Because Jeremiah has been examined and validated by God, God can pronounce to Jeremiah: "I have made you a tester and refiner among my people so that you may know and test their ways" (6:27, δοκιμαστὴν δέδωκά σε ἐν λαοῖς δεδοκιμασμένοις, καὶ γνώσῃ με ἐν τῷ δοκιμάσαι με τὴν ὁδὸν αὐτῶν). This is precisely what Paul intends with the sending of his surrogate, Timothy, and the assessment given upon his coworker's return from Thessalonica (3:6-10). As a result of the effective reception of Paul's paraclesis, now referred to as 1 Thessalonians, those "in Christ" are expected to do their own "testing" (5:20).

The relationship of this material in Jeremiah to this earliest Pauline letter is strengthened even further when one recalls the nature of the prophet's call in 1:5: Πρὸ τοῦ με πλάσαι σε ἐν κοιλίᾳ ἐπίσταμαί σε καὶ πρὸ τοῦ σε ἐξελθεῖν ἐκ μήτρας ἡγίακά σε, προφήτην εἰς ἔθνη τέθεικά σε. What we have here is a "true internationalizing of the prophetic office."[52] Recognizing a close relationship between the *narratio* of 1 Thessalonians and Jeremiah, Albert-Marie Denis proceeds to emphasize Paul "comme un prophète messianique" and that the apostle stands at "la charierne des deux plans: prophète messianique, il est apôtre des Gentils."[53] Henneken's insightful monograph reaches a similar conclusion with regard to 2:1-4: "Das Selbstverständnis des Apostel Paulus ist in ganz eigentümlicher Weise prophetisch geprägt."[54] In addition, as we have seen and will continue to observe, many of the expressions found in 1 Thessalonians cohere quite precisely with Paul's definition of prophecy in 1 Cor 14:3: ὁ δὲ προφητεύων ἀνθρώποις λαλεῖ οἰκοδομὴν [see 1 Thess 5:11] καὶ παράκλησιν [see 1 Thess 2:3, 12; 3:2, 7; 4:1, 10, 18; 5:11, 14] καὶ παραμυθίαν [see 1 Thess 2:12; 5:14].

1 Thess 2:7 makes two positive assertions, the first concerning Paul's right as an apostle (δυνάμενοι ἐν βάρει εἶναι ὡς Χριστοῦ ἀπόστολοι) and

---

52. William L. Holladay, *Jeremiah 1* (Hermeneia; Philadelphia: Fortress, 1986), 34.
53. Denis, "L'Apotre Paul, prophete 'messianique' des Gentils," 316-17.
54. Henneken, *Verkündigung und Prophetie*, 98.

the second concerning Paul's activity as a pastor (ἀλλὰ ἐγενήθημεν ἤπιοι ἐν μέσῳ ὑμῶν, ὡς ἐὰν τροφὸς θάλπῃ τὰ ἑαυτῆς τέκνα). Difficult exegetically is the phrase ἐν βάρει εἶναι. Does it refer to being burdensome with regard to the apostles' right to be supported financially or does it point to the honor that they might have expected to receive from the Thessalonians? The two meanings are not incongruous, although the first is to be given more weight. Drawing attention to what follows in this same verse, Stegemann writes: "Diese *clementia*/ηπιοι hat der Apostel Paulus walten lassen, indem er darauf verzichtete, seinen Unterhaltsanspruch als Apostel Christi einzufordern."[55] Perhaps Paul is exploiting rhetorically the double sense of the phrase ἐν βάρει εἶναι, much like the Latin proverb: "Honos propter onus."[56]

With regard to the final part of 2:7, it must be emphasized that Paul is not talking about a "mother"; rather, τροφός explicitly refers to a "nurse."[57] Understood in this way, this metaphor coheres exactly with the proposed understanding of ἐν βάρει. Stegemann has it quite right: "Doch Paulus sagt eben nicht, wie eine Mutter ihre Kinder hegt, sondern: wie eine Amme ihre eigenen Kinder hegt. . . . D.h. da Bild von der liebevollen Hingabe einer Amme an ihre eigenen Kinder muß auf dem Hintergrund ihre normalerweise für Entgelt geschehenden Pflege eines fremden Kindes verstanden werden."[58]

(c) Concerning Paul's Behavior (2:9-12)

In 1 Thess 2:9-12 correlations between the *narratio* and the *probatio* continue by means of a detailed description of Paul's ἦθος. Already in the summary of Paul's activity in 2:8 (οὕτως ὁμειρόμενοι ὑμῶν εὐδοκοῦμεν μεταδοῦναι ὑμῖν οὐ μόνον τὸ εὐαγγέλιον τοῦ θεοῦ ἀλλὰ καὶ τὰς ἑαυτῶν ψυχάς, διότι ἀγαπητοὶ ἡμῖν ἐγενήθητε) reference is made to the theme of

---

55. Stegemann, "Anlaß und Hintergrund," 408; similarly Wolfgang Schrage, *Der erste Brief an die Korinther* (1 Kor 1,1–6,11) (EKK VII/1; Zürich: Benzinger, 1991), 346-47: "Paulus hat gearbeitet, um niemandem zur Last zur Fallen (1 Thess 2,9 u.ö.), um so deutlich zu machen, daß er nicht das Ihre, sondern sie selbst sucht (2 Kor 12,14; vgl. auch 1 Kor 9,19)."

56. George Milligan, *St Paul's Epistles to the Thessalonians* (London: Macmillan, 1908), 21.

57. See Donfried, "The Cults of Thessalonica," 338.

58. Stegemann, "Anlaß und Hintergrund," 409.

love: he is willing not to burden them as an apostle of Christ because they are beloved. Here and elsewhere in the *narratio* intentional links are made with themes that will be taken up in the *probatio* (e.g., love, in 4:9-12).[59]

Paul as hardworking in 2:9 (μνημονεύετε γάρ, ἀδελφοί, τὸν κόπον ἡμῶν καὶ τὸν μόχθον: νυκτὸς καὶ ἡμέρας ἐργαζόμενοι πρὸς τὸ μὴ ἐπιβαρῆσαί τινα ὑμῶν ἐκηρύξαμεν εἰς ὑμᾶς τὸ εὐαγγέλιον τοῦ θεοῦ) picks up the theme of verse 6 (ἐν βάρει) and provides a model for what will be said in 4:11 (καὶ ἐργάζεσθαι ταῖς [ἰδίαις] χερσὶν ὑμῶν, καθὼς ὑμῖν παρηγγείλαμεν). Hock's sociological evaluation that for Paul work "was also the source of much personal hardship and social humiliation . . ." and, further, that he "viewed his working at a trade none too positively as toil, slavery, and humiliation,"[60] coheres with Gordon Fee's theological insight that the apostle lists work as part of his apostolic hardships in 1 Cor 4:6-13 in order to indicate to this church that "'depriving' them of the privilege of helping him was . . . in keeping with his overall stance as a disciple of the crucified one."[61] For Paul, Fee continues, "discipleship meant 'sharing in the sufferings of Christ,' not in its expiatory sense but in its *imitatio* sense (v. 16) — being in the world as Christ was in the world. Christ was really like this; those who would follow him must expect that they, too, will be like this."[62]

The description of Paul as moral (2:10, ὁσίως καὶ δικαίως καὶ ἀμέμπτως), with the invocation of God and the Thessalonian Christians as witnesses, is undoubtedly intended to portray Paul as an example of the new life in Christ and to anticipate the *probatio*.

Verses 11-12 portray Paul as fatherly (ὡς ἕνα ἕκαστον ὑμῶν ὡς πατὴρ τέκνα ἑαυτοῦ). In the ancient world the father was responsible for the behavior of his children. Conversion requires socialization into a new lifestyle, and that is precisely what Paul is attempting to do through his proclamation of the gospel, through the example of his own behavior, and through this speech-act known as 1 Thessalonians. Through these means he is "appealing, encouraging, and testifying" (παρακαλοῦντες ὑμας καὶ

---

59. Schrage, *Der erste Brief an die Korinther,* 346: "1 Thess 4,9 stellt sie unter das Stichwort der Agape bzw. Philadelphia."

60. Ronald F. Hock, *The Social Context of Paul's Ministry: Tentmaking and Apostleship* (Philadelphia: Fortress, 1980), 67.

61. Gordon D. Fee, *The First Epistle to the Corinthians* (NICNT; Grand Rapids: Eerdmans, 1987), 179.

62. Fee, *The First Epistle to the Corinthians,* 181.

παραμυθούμενοι καὶ μαρτυρόμενοι) that they "lead a life worthy of God, who calls you into his own kingdom and glory." This strongly eschatological note is found throughout the letter and reaches its climax in 4:13-18. Eschatology and ethics are inextricably linked.[63]

(d) Concerning the Thessalonians' behavior (2:13-16)

These verses are an integral part of the letter, and with Wuellner we understand them as a digression within the *narratio*.[64] Such digressions often provide the basis for subsequent discussion, as, for example, in 4:13-18, where the suffering Thessalonians need once again to be comforted. In speaking so harshly about the persecutors of the Jewish Christians, Paul "makes a thinly veiled statement promising divine condemnation."[65] Do we see here echoes of Jer 11:20, where the testing and approval of the prophet leads to the condemnation of the opposition?

5. Paul, An "Eschatologic Person"[66]

In our review of the problem of whether or not to understand 2:1-12 as an apology, we have already had opportunity to touch on the issue of Paul's self-identification, especially with regard to Malherbe's attempt to link these verses with the world of the Cynic wandering preachers. In light of our examination of the first part of the *narratio*, let us examine the text of this first extant Christian letter for additional clues that might help us understand something more about Paul's self-understanding and function.

---

63. K. P. Donfried, "The Kingdom of God in Paul," in *The Kingdom of God in 20th Century Interpretation* (ed. W. Willis; Peabody, Mass.: Hendrickson, 1987), 175-90, especially 181-82.

64. Wilhelm Wuellner, "Greek Rhetoric and Pauline Argumentation," in *Early Christian Literature and the Classical Intellectual Tradition* (Festschrift Robert M. Grant; ed. William R. Schoedel and Robert L. Wilken; Théologie Historique 54; Paris: Beauchesne, 1979), 177-88.

65. Charles A. Wanamaker, *Commentary on 1 & 2 Thessalonians* (NIGTC; Grand Rapids: Eerdmans, 1990), 110.

66. Anton Fridrichsen, *The Apostle and His Message* (Uppsala: Almqvist-Wiksells, 1947), 3.

a. The Spirit-Filled Word: 1 Thessalonians 1:6, 8; 2:13

In 1:8 Paul writes: "For not only has the word of the Lord sounded forth from you in Macedonia and Achaia, but your faith in God has gone forth everywhere, so that we need not say anything." The phrase "the word of the Lord" is used synonymously with "the gospel" (see 2:9), a term that Paul can also describe as "the word of God" in 2:13. Since Paul had referred to the Thessalonians' imitation of Paul and the Lord in suffering just a few verses before (1:6), he again uses the term "Lord" not only as a reference to the risen One to whom the church is responsible now and on the last day but also as a reminder that he whom they declare as Lord is also the One who was despised and suffered at the hands of human beings. Despite the difficulty of their situation, the gospel, especially because it is the word of the suffering and risen Lord, has burst forth from Thessalonica in such a powerful way that they have become an example (τύπος, 1:7) to all the believers in Macedonia and Achaia. Perhaps Paul is wishing to suggest that they were not only a model in suffering but also, precisely because of their willingness to suffer, an example, an embodiment, even if imperfectly, of that hope which is present in their midst now, although its consummation still lies in the future.

Given the brevity of 1 Thessalonians, it is at first surprising to realize that the term εὐαγγέλιον is used six times (1:5; 2:2, 4, 8, 9; 3:2) and its synonym, "word" (λόγος), is used at least four times (1:6, 8; 2:13; 4:15),[67] a rather high percentage when compared with, for example, Romans.[68] This is largely due to Paul's emphatic attempt in the *narratio* to distinguish his gospel and ethos from that of the pagan context of Thessalonica. As a result he makes the following assertions about the gospel as the word of God in 1 Thessalonians:

1. The gospel was proclaimed in Thessalonica, not only in word, but also in power and in the Holy Spirit and in full conviction (1:5), that is, it is a performative word and it is actively at work (ἐνεργεῖται) in and among the believers (2:13); as a generating center it is foundational for the existence of the church.

2. The Thessalonian Christians received the word in the midst of af-

---

67. See also 1 Thess 1:5 and 4:18.
68. εὐαγγέλιον occurs nine times in Romans (1:1, 9, 16; 2:16; 10:16; 11:28; 15:16, 19; 16:25), and λόγος, specifically as "word of God," appears only once (9:6).

fliction (1:6). In so doing they became imitators of Paul and his associates, as well as of the Lord. In addition, by receiving the word in the midst of affliction they received it with joy inspired by the Holy Spirit (1:6); this is itself a sign of hope even if the Thessalonians Christians had not fully recognized it as such. Paul also acknowledges this existential situation when he asserts in 2:2 that he declared to them "the gospel of God in the face of great opposition."

3. The word has proceeded out from Thessalonica to all the believers in Macedonia and in Achaia. As a result, whether intentionally or not, the Thessalonian church became a missionary base for the gospel (1:8).

4. This gospel has been entrusted to Paul in a special way by God (2:4).

5. This gospel is something that is "shared" by Paul with the Thessalonians, and it is proclaimed without burden to them because Paul "worked night and day" (2:8-9).

6. Timothy is God's servant and Paul's coworker in the gospel of Christ. It is Paul's hope that when the Christian community in Thessalonica is more thoroughly rooted in the gospel the result will be a firmer establishment, encouragement, and stabilization of their faith in the midst of their current afflictions.

b. The Spirit-Filled Word: 1 Thessalonians 4:15

Paul's frequent description of his message as an effective, Spirit-filled, divine *logos* together with his emphasis on the repetition and new application of his previous proclamation and teaching, paves the way for the unprecedented and decisive information and consolation that he is about to share with this church in 4:13-18. Thus, the *narratio* and the *probatio* are closely linked; the former prepares the way for the latter. At the heart of the pronouncement stands a "word of the Lord" (ἐν λόγῳ κυρίου). This new information attempts to console the Thessalonian Christians at a most neuralgic point: some of them have died, and now some are about to abandon a critical dimension of their faith, namely, hope. Paul's word of consolation would be ineffectual if he had not first attempted to demonstrate the efficacy of the word of God that he had preached previously. Only then can this word of the Lord, presented here as new information, that is, information not shared during his original visit in Thessalonica, be considered as a convincing intervention in response to the problem of death caused by persecution.

The first problem that needs to be resolved with regard to the phrase ἐν λόγῳ κυρίου in 4:15 is whether the contents of this "word of the Lord" are limited to verse 15, verses 15-16, or verses 15-17. The second problem is the origin of this material. Options suggested are that it is a lost saying of Jesus, that Paul has freely adopted a saying of the historical Jesus, that the apostle has modified a word proclaimed by the risen Lord in the post-resurrectional period, or that we have here a prophetic announcement from the risen Lord through the prophet Paul.

Our proposal is that Paul is an ecstatic prophet, thoroughly shaped and influenced by the milieu of Jewish mystical-apocalypticism. Factors supporting this perspective of the apostle include a charismatic under-standing of apostleship dependent on a vision of the risen Christ (Gal 1:11-17); his attestation of mystical ascensions to the heavenly worlds (2 Cor 12:1-10); and his frequent use of Jewish mystical vocabulary, such as σύμμορφος (e.g., Phil 3:21), to describe the transformation experienced by those who are in Christ. Using such an evaluation of Paul, we would un-derstand this "word of the Lord" as one transmitted by the heavenly Lord to the prophet Paul. We are dealing, then, with a prophetic expression, not one stemming from the historical Jesus but from the risen Lord.

One should note in passing that the phrase ἐν λόγῳ κυρίου is situated in a similar context in the Septuagint. The "man of God" speaks in 1 Kings 13:9, "For thus I was commanded by the word of the Lord (ὅτι οὕτως ἐνετείλατό μοι ἐν λόγῳ κύριος λέγων): You shall not eat food, or drink wa-ter, or return by the way that you came." In our present context we must defer a more detailed treatment of this phrase to Henneken's instructive examination.[69]

According to the recent study by Helmut Merklein,[70] it is likely that the prophetic utterance is to be limited to 1 Thess 4:15b: "We who are alive, who are left until the coming of the Lord, shall not precede those who have fallen asleep." Verses 16-17 are further elaborations of the pro-phetic declaration using a variety of traditional, apocalyptic motifs. By means of an instructive comparison of 1 Thess 4:13-18 with 1 Cor 15:50-

---

69. Henneken, *Verkündigung und Prophetie,* 92-93.

70. "Der Theologe als Prophet: zur Funktion prophetischen Redens im theologischen Diskurs," *NTS* 38 (1992): 402-29.

58, Merklein has discovered a number of parallels between these two chapters that give further support to limiting the prophetic word to verse 15b as well as allowing us to better comprehend it and its interpretation. With regard to 1 Thessalonians we note the following unfolding of the pattern: (a) in 4:14a dimensions of the gospel, already familiar to the recipients, are expressed; (b) in 4:14b an introductory and transitional thesis is presented that must be confirmed and expanded by the yet-to-be announced prophetic word and its further elaboration; (c) in 4:15b a hitherto unknown eschatological mystery is disclosed, although such prophetic revelation does not stand in contradiction to the gospel to which it is always subordinate; (d) in 4:16-17 the interpretation of the prophetic word seeks to clarify matters not immediately evident from the gospel itself as a result of issues prompted by local, contingent situations, and it is not, therefore, intended as a further dogmatic expansion of the gospel; (e) in 4:18, the concluding part of this prophetic discourse, the theme of *consolatio* is unmistakable: "Therefore comfort one another with these words (ἐν τοῖς λόγοις τούτοις)." The prophetic word of verse 15 is foundational for this paraclesis.

Our analysis of 1 Thess 4:15-17, then, discloses that embedded in verse 15b is a prophetic word transmitted by the heavenly Lord to the prophet Paul, with verses 16-17 providing a further interpretation of this eschatological mystery. We have no evidence that this is a word from the historical Jesus, and Merklein's study goes far to eliminate this as a serious option.

c. The Words of Prophets: 1 Thessalonians 5:19-21

"Der Apostel Paulus ist Prophet der mit Christus hereingebrochenen geisterfüllten (1 Thess 4,8) Heils- und Endzeit, einer Zeit darum auch voller Bedrängnis, die er den Thessalonichern angesagt und vorausgesagt (vgl. 1 Thess 3,4) hat. Das alles gibt seiner gesamten apostolischen Verkündigung eine prophetische Grundlegung und Färbung. Daneben ist Paulus auch Prophet im engeren Sinne der Weissagung, wie die Analyse von 1 Thess 4,15-17 gezeigt hat."[71] If one were to agree with Henneken's profile of Paul, does 1 Thess 5:19-21 ([19] τὸ πνεῦμα μὴ σβέννυτε,

---

71. Henneken, *Verkündigung und Prophetie*, 103.

προφητείας μὴ ἐξουθενεῖτε, [20] πάντα δὲ δοκιμάζετε, [21] τὸ καλὸν κατέχετε) have any relevance to our earlier discussion of the *narratio* of 1 Thessalonians?

Does προφητεία in this context refer to the gift of prophecy or to the words spoken by the person prophesying? The accusative plural of the noun suggests the latter. Perhaps the two different references in 5:19 and 5:20 suggest a differentiation between the gospel as the Word of God handed on by the church but made alive by the Spirit and prophetic utterance as a Spirit-driven revelation of hidden mysteries that is primarily concerned with the encouragement of God's people. The first would be "quenched" by refusing to listen to God's word and will, and the latter would be "despised" by treating it/them as irrelevant to the life of the congregation. The former is concerned with the announcement of the eschatological moment of salvation in the form of human weakness and frailty and thus as the embodiment of the suffering God, as incarnation in the present moment, whereas the latter is the dynamic announcement of God for the upbuilding, encouragement, and consolation of the desolate. Such a differentiation would cohere well with our previous interpretation of paraclesis, namely, that it embraces the past and incorporates it into the present.

Therefore, it is possible that 1 Thess 5:19 and 20 are not referring to some general, abstract situation in the midst of the Thessalonian congregation or to some aspect of conventional ethics, but are, rather, explicitly referring both to the gospel and the new word from the risen Lord that has been the central focus of this new speech-act itself. πάντα δὲ δοκιμάζετε would then refer to the testing of all dimensions of their lives by the will of God as revealed in the gospel and word of the Lord, in the same way that Paul was tested by God and found acceptable.[72] Thus, according to verse 22, they are not to follow the path of pagan culture (ἀπὸ παντὸς εἴδους πονηροῦ ἀπέχεσθε) but to follow the revealed will of God (τὸ καλὸν κατέχετε). Consequently, πάντα relates to what follows and not to what precedes.[73] It is not a testing of the prophecies; rather, all dimensions of life (πάντα) are to be tested by the gospel and by the prophetic word (προφητείας).

What, very briefly, is the relationship between Paul as prophet and

---

72. See above for our previous discussion of Jeremiah.
73. Against Wanamaker, *Commentary on 1 & 2 Thessalonians*, 203.

Paul as apostle? The latter term appears only once in 1 Thessalonians (2:7) and in a plural form. It is obvious that this designation per se is not intended to be given major attention in this letter; consequently one needs to be careful not to import discussions about the epistolary *intitulatio* from Paul's later letters. To be an apostle is to proclaim the prophetic gospel to the Gentiles; but that can only be accomplished by the prophet who has been so authorized by God.

6. Conclusions

1. 1 Thess 2:1-12 is not an apology of any sort, specific or general, and one should not read this passage in a mirror fashion so that it could be argued that Paul is countering charges made against him.

2. Epistolary criticism does not assist us in a substantial way to interpret the intention of especially 1 Thess 2:1-12 within the letter.

3. The identification of this text by rhetorical criticism as belonging to the *narratio* opens new possibilities for understanding its more precise function within the total act of communication. The *narratio* in 1 Thessalonians serves: (a) to recount the relationship of friendship established between Paul and the Thessalonians; (b) to distinguish Paul's gospel and ethos from the error and delusion from the idolatry of the heathen, and (c) to utilize the ethos of Paul as a model within the remainder of the paraclesis. This opens up the possibility of better understanding certain components of the first part of the *narratio* in relationship to the remainder of the letter. On the one hand, we have noted how the *narratio* advances further what has been said in the *exordium,* and, on the other hand, we have seen how many of the themes developed in the *narratio* anticipate new actualization and elaboration in the *probatio.*

The Epistolary and Rhetorical Context
of 1 Thessalonians 2:1-12:
A Response to Karl P. Donfried

Rudolf Hoppe

In 1993 Karl P. Donfried presented a study of 1 Thessalonians that was as philologically thorough as it was theologically significant, including a review of current scholarship.[1] An equally constructive project was presented by the author in his contribution "The Epistolary and Rhetorical Context of 1 Thessalonians 2:1-12." I am grateful for the opportunity to direct a few questions to this excellent study and to make some suggestions with regard to a few matters. The significance of a study is evident in the number of questions it answers as well as in the new questions it raises. My response paper is to be understood in this positive sense.

1. The Use of Rhetorical Analysis

Since the appearance of Hans-Dieter Betz's commentary on Galatians,[2] the rhetorical analysis of the Pauline epistles has become a widespread

---

1. Karl P. Donfried, "The Theology of 1 Thessalonians," in *The Theology of the Shorter Pauline Letters* (ed. Karl P. Donfried and I. Howard Marshall; New Testament Theology; Cambridge: Cambridge University Press, 1993), 1-79.

2. *Galatians* (Hermeneia; Philadelphia: Fortress, 1979); see also Hans-Dieter Betz, "The Literary Composition and Function of Paul's Letter to the Galatians," *NTS* 21 (1975): 353-79.

methodological approach to determine a given author's intention and his relationship to the addressees. Soon after George Kennedy dedicated a chapter in his book, *New Testament Interpretation through Rhetorical Criticism*,[3] to 1 Thessalonians, additional studies followed.[4] These works are instructive inasmuch as they pointedly ask about the relationship between the speaker and the addressee; in so doing they give attention to the structure of the text and to specific aspects of particular verses, factors that otherwise might tend to remain in the background or be considered in too summary a fashion.[5]

With regard to the passage under consideration in 1 Thessalonians 2, rhetorical analysis presses for a more precise definition of the concept "apology" in all of its complexity. Admittedly, by remaining within the context of its approach, the rhetorical perspective can attempt only a partial explanation of this concept; nevertheless, it can assist in the formulation of such questions. In the classical sense, 1 Thess 2:1-12 would be apologetic only if Paul were obliged to defend himself against so-called opponents, either external or internal;[6] but, as far as the text is concerned, that would surely have to be differentiated, as the discussion of the individual contributions found in the present volume demonstrates.

Also in a positive manner, rhetorical analysis is capable of recognizing and overcoming the imprecise divisions of previous approaches.[7] Yet to this day the rhetorical approach has not led to consensus in questions of structure. Despite this situation, rhetorical analysis can at least be *one* of several steps toward analyzing the text. To attempt more than this would mean that rhetorical criticism would risk both overextending itself and, perhaps, even abandoning its ultimate task, at least if one follows the pos-

---

3. George Kennedy, *New Testament Interpretation through Rhetorical Criticism* (Chapel Hill: The University of North Carolina Press, 1984), 141-44.

4. The following list of works does not claim to be definitive: Robert Jewett, *The Thessalonian Correspondence* (FFNT; Philadelphia: Fortress Press, 1986); Frank W. Hughes, "The Rhetoric of 1 Thessalonians," in *The Thessalonian Correspondence* (ed. Raymond F. Collins; BETL 87; Leuven: Leuven University Press–Peeters, 1990), 94-116; Charles A. Wanamaker *The Epistles to the Thessalonians* (NIGTC; Grand Rapids: Eerdmans, 1990); Steve Walton, "What Has Aristotle to Do with Paul? — Rhetorical Criticism and 1 Thessalonians," *TynB* 46 (1995): 229-50; see also the contributions in this volume.

5. See the division suggested by Hughes, "The Rhetoric of 1 Thessalonians," 10-11.

6. See, e.g., W. Lütgert, "Die Volkommenen im Philipperbrief und die Enthusiasten in Thessalonich," *BFChTh* 13 (1909): 547-654.

7. Traugott Holtz rightly recognizes this in his contribution in *TD*, 69-70.

tulate of Kennedy: "The ultimate goal of rhetorical analysis, briefly put, is the discovery of the author's intent and of how that is transmitted through text to audience."[8] Further, the rhetorical approach should emphasize that a speech not only makes the author's intention clear, but, above all, that it makes evident what motivates the intended statement and/or influences the attitudes expressed; and, further, to which situation of the addressees the speech is reacting, thus allowing conclusions to be drawn with regard to such a situation. The question, therefore, is whether rhetorical analysis can, consonant with its inherent characteristics, perform that which, according to Kennedy's definition, it has defined as its task.

In "dialogue" with epistolary theory and classical form criticism, rhetorical analysis can undoubtedly contribute constructive insights and even modifications to these different methods. But we must proceed with caution. We cannot begin with a rhetorical "system" and then transfer this, as a fixed form, to the text. Rather, one must recognize that each text must be made the starting point and that its individuality must be taken seriously; only then, if appropriate, can it be compared with the rules of rhetoric. I remind the reader here of Classen's article and agree, at this point, with Traugott Holtz.[9] It may well be that a letter contains rhetorical figures and that it employs rhetorical means in the interest of its intention. This does not necessarily mean, however, that it ought to be classified as a speech. Thus, for example, 1 Thess 5:27 by itself does not allow us to identify this letter as a speech in the classical sense.

2. The Analysis of Karl Donfried

Following a careful consideration of the pros and cons of adopting both a rhetorical and epistolographical analysis of 1 Thessalonians, Donfried makes the decision to utilize the potential of ancient rhetoric in the study of this letter. He applies rhetorical categories to our text and, within this context, attempts in particular to determine the function of 2:1-12. Given the perspectives already mentioned in the first part of my reflections — points that, in my opinion, should make us cautious — the following questions are appropriate:

8. Kennedy, *New Testament Interpretation*, 12.
9. See C. J. Classen, "Paulus und die antike Rhetorik," *ZNW* 82 (1991): 1-33, and the contribution of Traugott Holtz in *TD*, 69-80.

a. Speech divisions of ancient rhetoric allow the *narratio* and the *probatio* to develop the substantial points of argumentation that are introduced in the *exordium* as in a musical overture, and, in this manner, link the thematic material of the *exordium* with that of the following parts of the speech. The application of this approach to 1 Thessalonians presupposes that this scheme may be verified by the *narratio* or the *probatio*. This point may be illuminated by an example from the world of music. In the overture to W. A. Mozart's *Don Giovanni* one can hear a theme that, at the end of the second act, is performed very horribly during Don Giovanni's descent into hell. The theme is sounded in the overture but receives its full force in the course of the composition. But back to our text. Do we also find these tendencies in 1 Thessalonians? Surely one can presuppose that the sections Donfried considers the *exordium*, the *narratio*, and the *probatio* are linked together by transitional materials.[10] But this does not yet correspond to the presentation of the rhetorician, who *develops the basic thematic materials* of the *exordium* in the *narratio*.

This statement may be clarified by an illustration of the triad "faith, hope, love." It is true that, with respect to substance, parts of the triad are taken up in 2:9-12 and again in 5:12-18.[11] The point, however, is that the references to the triad, which come later in the letter, are clearly less developed than the triad itself.[12] The weight of the statements rests on the triad in 1:3, but not in the later references. The connections of the motifs probably allow us to claim the literary uniformity of the letter; but in his writing Paul does not proceed according to the rhetorical system, in which, incidentally, the declaration of the theme can be completely absent.[13]

b. Donfried's evidence for the prophetic perspective underlying

10. Donfried rightly refers to the connection between 1:5 and 2:13. It is also correct to see that the theme of suffering, which emerges in the *exordium*, is taken up later in chap. 2 (thus in the *narratio*), as specified by Donfried, "Epistolary and Rhetorical Context," in *TD*, 45.

11. See Jewett, *The Thessalonian Correspondence*, 76, who sees in 4:1-8, 4:9-12, and 5:12-22 a correspondence to the term ἀγάπη in 1:3; and a further development of the term ἐλπίς in the eschatological section, 4:13–5:11.

12. To be sure, one would still need to examine where the actual linkages are; 4:13–5:11, e.g., can hardly be considered to be connected with the motif of hope in 1:3. See, however, Jewett, *The Thessalonian Correspondence*, 76.

13. See H. J. Klauck, "Hellenistische Rhetorik im Diasporajudentum. Das Exordium des vierten Makkabäerbuches (4 Makk 1,1-12)," *NTS* 35 (1989): 451-65, here 455.

1 Thessalonians is convincing. That both Johan Vos, in his response to Traugott Holtz,[14] and Donfried come to this conclusion independently of each other is, objectively speaking, well founded; even more could be added to the evidence presented.[15] Likewise, the observations regarding the text itself are quite instructive and suggestive.[16] But, as a result, questions about the role of the rhetorical approach become even more pressing. Certainly, the hesitation in classifying the section as an "apology," which results from considering it as a kind of prophetic speech, is fully plausible, but it does not result from the rhetorical description of epideictic speech — as the letter is classified by Donfried — but rather from tradition and motif-historical reflections. The results are to be emphasized, but they do not result from rhetorical analysis.

3. Is 1 Thessalonians a "Friendship Letter"?

Donfried claims that rhetorical analysis makes it possible to describe more precisely the communication between Paul and the Thessalonians. The *narratio,* he says, functions to emphasize the friendly relationship of the apostle to the Macedonian church and to distinguish the gospel of Paul from pagan religiosity, and, thereby, to render it a model for the addressees. This is also the point of departure for understanding the paraclesis in 1 Thessalonians.[17] My question is, again, whether the classification of the letter as a "friendship letter" is the result of the methodological means of rhetoric, or whether it is in fact reached by other means. Still, ever since K. Thraede's study of ancient letter categories, at the latest, this classification of 1 Thessalonians has been proposed,[18] as is evident in the work of

14. For further detail, see both contributions in this volume.

15. It should only be mentioned that Philo can interpret the παρρησία motif prophetically; see also Philo *Joseph 77;* here 5-29, especially 27. Additional LXX and extrabiblical, Jewish evidence could also be cited; see, e.g., the contribution of Johan Vos in *TD,* 81-88.

16. For example, the fact that the context of ἀκαθαρσία in both 2:3 and 4:7 has to do with the contrast to the pagans (Donfried, "Epistolary and Rhetorical Context," in *TD,* 50).

17. See Donfried, "Epistolary and Rhetorical Context," in *TD,* 60: "to distinguish Paul's gospel and ethos from the error and delusion surrounding the Thessalonian Christians, specifically from the idolatry of the heathen. . . ."

18. K. Thraede, *Grundzüge griechisch-römischer Brieftopik* (*Zet* 48; Munich: Beck, 1970).

Johannes Schoon-Janßen.[19] Whether this is an adequate classification of 1 Thessalonians requires further discussion.

As already mentioned above, Donfried convincingly describes the prophetic frame of reference from which 1 Thess 2:1-12 is to be understood. If Paul, however, imparts his instruction with a prophetic claim (2:12), the classification "friendship letter" seems inadequate. The letter should more nearly be called an "apostolic" letter, if one does not narrow this concept too drastically. Paul is concerned with his responsibility to the church. Separated from it, he tries to stabilize it; he seeks to get news about their condition from Timothy, whom he had sent; he sends his coworker to them; he answers their fundamental questions in order to ensure their identity with the gospel (4:13-18).

Does 1 Thess 2:1-12 have as its intent "to distinguish Paul's gospel and *ethos* from the error and delusion surrounding the Thessalonian Christians, specifically from the idolatry of the heathen . . ."?[20] If Donfried successfully presents the inner textual point of contact between 2:3 and 4:7, it is nevertheless clear that Paul assures the Thessalonians that they have already forsaken the idols and turned to the one God (1:9-10). The pragmatic intention of Paul appears, then, not to lie in the admonition to forsake the idols. For this reason I should like to propose for discussion an aspect — in my opinion, an instructive one — that is linked to Donfried's observations regarding the concepts εὐαγγέλιον and λόγος — terms that appear surprisingly often in 1 Thessalonians.[21]

In 1:2-10 Paul expresses his gratitude for the exemplary Christian behavior practiced by the church members in Thessalonica, which is demonstrated in their faith, hope, and love. Embedded in 1:4-5 is an appeal to the foundation of the present status of the church as being anchored in its election, its ἐκλογή. Therefore, these Christians now have the responsibility to stress the *effective power of the gospel*, "not only ἐν λόγῳ, but also ἐν δυνάμει and in ἐν πνεύματι ἁγίῳ" — which is given to them in their election — as well as to emphasize its correlation with their θλῖψις experience in 1:6. That the concern here is primarily the *effectiveness* of the gospel is demonstrated by the sequence ἐγενήθη — ἐγενήθημεν ("the gospel came to

19. See his *Umstrittene "Apologien" in den Paulusbriefen* (GTA 45; Göttingen, 1991), 39-65, as well as Schoon-Janßen's contribution in *TD*, 179-93.

20. Donfried, "Epistolary and Rhetorical Context," in *TD*, 45-46.

21. Donfried, "Epistolary and Rhetorical Context," in *TD*, 55-56.

you not in word only — just as you know what kind of persons we proved to be among you," 1:5), which draws attention, *first of all,* to the fact of the gospel itself and, *only then,* to the successful missionary activity of the apostle. Paul is concerned with proving the power of the gospel precisely in the midst of the experienced incongruity between salvation message, church praxis (faith, hope, love), and the reality of past and present persecution, which manifests itself particularly in the coerced absence of the apostle.

At this point Paul makes a connection with the antitheses in 2:3-8. The οὐκ — ἀλλά opposition hardly allows us to conclude that there was a clash with competing opponents. The elaborate reference to his personal behavior should rather be understood *functionally.* It has the function of presenting this behavior as one appropriate to the gospel, with the proclamation of which he, Paul, is entrusted (2:4). Appropriate conduct expresses an important dimension of the gospel: it prevails against all outward appearances. As in 1:5, the concern is basically the *gospel.* Indeed, this line of thought corresponds with the structure of the *exordium* and the *narratio* in rhetorical works.

Paul is concerned with the assurance of the reliability of the divine *logos*/gospel and with the future confirmation of the Christians in Thessalonica at the *parousia.* Paul finds it necessary to strengthen this process of persuasion which he himself initiated when he first founded the congregation. In order to assure the church of this, but also to assure *himself* of like-mindedness with the church he had founded, Paul sends Timothy. Paul writes this letter to convince the church of the effectiveness of the gospel, specifically its validity and sustaining power in an alien environment and within the experience of contradiction, and, thereby, he also attempts to respond to its internal crisis. In 2:15, he takes up a Jewish tradition that had already helped overcome the most serious of crises in postexilic Judaism: an interpretative model of Jesus' death rooted in Deuteronomy's view of history.

To achieve this overarching goal of rendering plausible the effective power of the gospel, Paul begins in 2:1-12 to present the evidence that his personal behavior serves precisely the purpose of his proclamation, namely, that it is radically subordinated to God's Word and informed by faith, that this gospel is capable of succeeding, and that its validity is diminished neither by repressive measures against his person nor against the church. Paul's task is to convince — a task that he must achieve from the distance imposed on him. That he can do this constructively and without any polemic against the church or its individual representatives is indicative of his ongoing good relationship with the Macedonian Christians.

On the Background of 1 Thessalonians 2:1-12

Traugott Holtz

1. On Rhetorical Analysis

As the previous work of this Seminar has shown, the analysis of the Pauline letters according to the rules of ancient classical rhetoric plays a significant role in current scholarly work. This is true of the work done in America, as well as that influenced by it. This scholarship has been so forceful that, on occasion, it appears as if interpretations of Paul's letters that are not based on rhetorical analysis may be considered essentially unproductive.

It is an indisputable contribution of this methodological approach that it clearly calls attention to the unity of the Pauline letters in the midst of varied individual sections, each with their polymorphic structure. Not only does each thematically defined section intend to serve as an instrument of communication claiming authority but also the apostolic letter itself. Indeed, each individual and unique letter also communicates a specific message, yet only in its entirety. This observation has significance for all sections of a single, entire letter, since these sections should be interpreted with this latter perspective in mind. That the message itself (its statement and its function within the whole letter) can only be ascertained with the help of a previous analysis of the individual sections does not delegitimize this methodological process, but rather only places it within the hermeneutical circle of all intellectual interpretations. The particular must be understood within the whole, which, in turn, can only be presented in particulars.

However, one can and must ask — if one wants to achieve a sufficiently differentiated picture — whether the way of rhetorical analysis according to the intellectual understandings of antiquity is, in fact, the royal road to the discovery of the "essential message." The application of rhetorical theory to letters stands, methodologically, on shaky ground. At least as problematic, however, is the presupposition that intellectual theories can, without any questioning or attention to context, be applied to literary products that, as a rule, have each originated in circumstances that were anything but transparent. The owls of Athens, as is well known, fly at night![1]

2. On Epistolographical Analysis

What has just been said is also true with regard to attempts to classify Pauline letters with respect to their form and structure, and then, subsequently, to determine their content on the basis of ancient epistolography. Epistolographical categories are, of course, quite relevant to the Pauline correspondence, since the apostle truly wants to write real letters to his churches, as the greetings, the prescript, and the closing, the *eschatokoll,* clearly demonstrate. The completely different types of letter in which these parts are used show with what complete freedom he was able to utilize the epistolary form. That the thematic emphases of a single letter can also be very different, if not in opposition, is demonstrated clearly in 2 Corinthians. Nevertheless, contemporary research, correctly in my view, is once again tending to understand this letter as having had an original unity (with the possible exception of 6:14–7:1). But even if we should be dealing with a secondary redaction, the editor (and all of his readers) must still have considered a work like 2 Corinthians, as we now have it before us, as a possible letter by Paul.

---

1. On Dio Chrysostom of Prusa, see W. von Christ, W. Schmid, and O. Stählin, *Geschichte der griechischen Literatur* (ed. Wilhelm Schmid and Otto Stahlin; 6th ed.; 5 vols.; HAW 7.1; Munich: Beck, 1920), II.1.366: "His speeches are usually not carefully constructed; one finds misunderstandings between the separate parts, especially overly long introductions, repetitions, long-windedness, unexplained conclusions." See also the recent work by R. G. Hall, "Arguing like an Apocalypse: Galatians and an Ancient Topos outside the Greco-Roman Rhetorical Tradition," *NTS* 42 (1996): 434-53, especially p. 435 (opposing an over-emphasis on the rhetorical theory: this "did not simply replace native rhetoric").

The conclusion resulting from these reflections with regard to the epistolographical evaluation of the Pauline letters is that the purpose of an entire text, such as 1 Thessalonians, does not require that we see all of its individual parts determined in the same manner and thereby deduce from them conclusions regarding their intended message. Johannes Schoon-Janßen has demonstrated in this Seminar that 1 Thessalonians can be located in the genre of friendship letters. Further, his suggestion that the section 2:1-12 reminds us of the topic in friendship letters designated "unity in friendship" is undoubtedly correct and is further impressively supported by Schoon-Janßen's reference to Cicero's work, *Laelius de Amicitia*.[2] However, despite his overall correct classification of the letter, the conclusion that he draws from the designation of the letter as "*more nearly* friendly/pastoral [epistolary theory!] and epideictic [rhetorical theory!]," namely, that in "light of these negative results [referring to the 'more nearly'] the thesis that 1 Thess 2:1-12 is an apology in which Paul reacted to criticisms made against him can be eliminated . . ."[3] is simply not justified.

3. The Appeal Character of the Text

One can naturally ask whether it is correct to consider the distinguishing characteristic of this entire section as an "apology." Its central function in the letter as a whole is surely to strengthen the credibility of Paul's message, that is, the gospel, by reminding the listeners of the experiences they had had with him when he appeared as its messenger. The text does not indicate that his message is being questioned by those who received it; nevertheless, he evidently considers it necessary to make his readers conscious once again of their own certainty.

In a striking way, they are reminded of their own knowledge. Verse 1 points them to their own recollections of his "successful entrance" among them when he first came both to proclaim faith and to establish the congregation; verse 2 recalls the knowledge of his prior fate of suffering in Philippi; verse 5 appeals to their certainty regarding his integrity, for which also God is a witness; verse 9 makes them aware of the blameless conduct he made evi-

2. Johannes Schoon-Janßen, "On the Use of Elements of Ancient Epistolography in 1 Thessalonians," in *TD*, 188.

3. Schoon-Janßen, "Ancient Epistolography in 1 Thessalonians," in *TD*, 192.

dent among them; verse 10 speaks again of their being witnesses to his righteous apostolic work among them, and to which, in like manner, even God, but also they themselves, are witnesses; finally, verse 11 recalls their knowledge of his devotion to each of them. The intensity of the appeal to the church's own experience with their apostle is singular. It lends to this section a special urgency that goes beyond purely grateful recollections.

4. Antithesis I: The Position

The assumption that such an urgent recollection of his initial visit and work has a specific background is strengthened by the fact that the entire passage is arranged antithetically. Now it is evident that antithesis is chiefly a rhetorical-stylistic mannerism, by means of which the positively intended message should be emphasized. If we are not, however, dealing with a purely rhetorical-stylistic exercise, then the antithesis simultaneously shapes the thesis in a specific way. If the antithesis is not simply derived from the thesis as its logical negation, then it reveals against which, among several other possibilities, the actual reality is argued.

That Paul utilized antithetical speech here simply as rhetorical decoration may be discounted. The positive statements are not simply repetitions of standard rhetorical formulations, nor are the antitheses of these statements — in any case, in their essential parts — logically developed out of the reality presented by their negation. The actual manner of Paul's "entrance" to Thessalonica is rooted in his special apostolic mission to proclaim the gospel.

In Paul's description of his entrance, there are certainly remarkable points of contact with the way in which the rhetorician Dio Chrysostom, approximately half a century later, presents himself to his audience. παρρησία (openness/frankness) is an essential virtue of the speaker. Boldness of speech is the sign of its truth (especially *Orationes* 32.5, 11; 3.2: Trajan expects of Dio Chrysostom ἀληθείᾳ καὶ παρρησίᾳ ἢ θωπείᾳ καὶ ἀπάτῃ). Paul indeed does make use of the verb παρρησιάζομαι here in 1 Thess 2:2 (in distinction from the noun; the verb is not otherwise used by him), but in a much more formal manner than one can observe in Dio Chrysostom. Speaking with sincerity, in and of itself, is not yet the truth; that is reserved for the gospel alone. It is, however, part of his responsibility as an apostle to proclaim this gospel openly, despite his prior negative experiences. This particular direction of his thinking is also demonstrated by Paul's use of the noun: 2 Cor 3:12; 7:4; Phil 1:20; Philem 8.[4] Despite the different way in which the term is used, one cannot rule out the fact that Paul intentionally wished to evoke a positive description of the trustworthy messenger of truth, especially as he brings to remembrance his church-founding proclamation.

In addition, the concluding mention of his conduct over and against the Thessalonians in verse 7 ("we were gentle among you," ἐγενήθημεν ἤπιοι ἐν μέσῳ ὑμῶν) makes use of ἤπιος, a term that is almost completely missing in the most closely related Jewish literature (LXX, *T. 12 Patriarchs, Joseph and Aseneth*),[5] but that, rather interestingly, is quite at home in the rhetoric of approximately the same era.[6]

It is not possible here to go into the philological difficulties of the passage; in distinction from Nestle-Aland[26], ἤπιοι is presupposed as the original text; the end of the sentence, which begins with ἀλλά, is ἐν μέσῳ ὑμῶν. The image that follows, introduced with ὡς, is particularly characteristic of Paul's way of thinking. The reflections on the wet-nurse, τροφός, have evidently been conditioned by the reception of the rhetorical tradition, as seems likely in the previous section. Paul, however, immediately shifts these thoughts in the direction of his specific view of his apostolic mission, namely, that through him the members of his church become his children. This is expressed in verse 11 both by his use of the father image and his reference to each individual person. Thus for Paul the word τροφός took on the meaning of "mother," which it does not inherently have. He nevertheless uses it primarily because it is conventional rhetoric, although he takes for granted its other established meaning as well. The image of the mother is evidently presupposed also by Gal 4:19; otherwise, however, Paul

---

4. See W. C. van Unnik, "The Christian's Freedom of Speech in the New Testament," in W. C. van Unnik, *Sparsa Collecta* (2 vols.; Leiden: Brill, 1980), 2.269-89.

5. In the literature compiled in A.-M. Denis, *Concordance Grecque des Pseud-épigraphes d'Ancien Testament* (Louvain-la-Neuve: Université Catholique de Louvain, 1987), only in Pseudo-Phocylides 207 (on the education of children) and in Aristobulus, *Fragmenta* 4 (13.12.6; a citation from Aratus that speaks about God). In the New Testament, 2 Tim 2:24; in the Apostolic Fathers, 1 Clem. 23.1 (adverb; referring to God, compare Aristobulus, *Fragmenta* 4).

6. See Abraham J. Malherbe, "'Gentle as a Nurse': The Cynic Background to I Thess. ii," *NovT* 12 (1970): 203-17; now also in A. J. Malherbe, *Paul and the Popular Philosophers* (Minneapolis: Fortress, 1989), 35-48.

presents himself — as in verse 11 — as a "father" to his church (1 Cor 4:14-21; [2 Cor 6:13; 12:14]; Philem 10; compare also Phil 2:22). Our passage is concerned with the parental devotion that has become integrated with the presentation of the gospel.

Thus, admittedly, aspects of Paul's preaching become visible that are otherwise unusual for him and that remind us of other preachers of philosophical-religious messages of salvation. These elements are, however, immediately turned in a direction that points the way to a radically different path from the one the philosophical rhetorician claims for himself. In distinction from the rhetorician, Paul did not represent himself or his own view — even if it was an inspired one — but only the gospel of God entrusted to him and to which he was intimately bound.

5. Antithesis II: Negation

The image of the contemporary philosophical teacher, who lives in order to bring salvific guidelines to the public, confronts us much more clearly and consistently in the negations of the antitheses than in these characteristically transformed positive expressions of one's calling. This corresponds completely with that which was current in ancient literature, whether in polemical exaggeration or satirical pointedness.

This is particularly clear in Dio Chrysostom. He sets himself emphatically apart from so-called philosophers (τοὺς καλουμένους φιλοσόφους), some of whom do not appear in public at all and do not want to expose themselves to argument (οὐδὲ θέλουσι διακινδυνεύειν); others hold forth in so-called lecture halls (ἐν τοῖς καλουμένοις ἀκροατηρίοις φωνασκοῦσιν) before listeners loyal to them (*Orationes* 32.8). Above all, however, he sets himself apart from those called Cynics (τῶν Κυνικῶν λεγομένων; *Orationes* 32.9), of whom there are a rather large number in residence at Alexandria (ἐν τῇ πόλει πλῆθος οὐκ ὀλίγον). They are of the worst type; in truth they know nothing; they are only interested in earning a living. "On the street corners, in the narrow alleyways and temple doorways, these people congregate and deceitfully sweet-talk childish persons, sailors, and other such people."[7] "They do nothing good;

---

7. Dio Chrysostom, *Orationes* 32.9: οὗτοι δὲ ἔν τε τριόδοις καὶ στενωποῖς καὶ πυλῶσιν ἱερέων ἁγνίζουσι καὶ ἀπατῶσι παιδάρια καὶ ναύτας καὶ τοιοῦτον ὄχλον.

rather they do the greatest evil possible, by accustoming the brainless to ridicule the philosophers."[8] It is not so easy to encounter one who speaks candidly and sincerely, without evil disposition and intention (καθαρῶς καὶ ἀδόλως παρρησιαζόμενον; *Orationes* 32.11), without thought of fame or the acquisition of money (μήτε δόξης χάριν μήτ' ἐπ' ἀργυρίῳ προσποιούμενον; *Orationes* 32.11); rather, a surplus of flatterers, deceivers, and braggarts dominates (ἀφθονίᾳ κολάκων καὶ γοήτων καὶ σοφιστῶν; *Orationes* 32.11).

One can find additional references in Dio Chrysostom, in some cases many, for the negations found in 1 Thess 2:1-12. In the interest of greater clarity, I have presented above all a cohesive and coherent text. Individual features of the portrait appear scattered randomly. It is in this way that the speaker of wisdom and the messenger of life presents himself in the ancient city; one recognizes him in the typical manner of his appearance, simultaneously verifiable through personal experience. Admittedly, one is dealing here with more or less standard characterizations that, therefore, cannot be linked to concrete, individual cases. This fact is accentuated by the rhetorical order in which they appear. However, it does not suggest that, with regard to the antitheses as a whole, one is dealing here with sheer rhetoric.

This has been suspected again and again. Thus Martin Dibelius believed that the text offers formulae shaped by rhetoric that Paul used when remembering the missionary era — "and probably instinctively . . . since such popular topics were treated without particular necessity."[9] Even Abraham J. Malherbe, who has so admirably and convincingly demonstrated the formal analogy between Paul and the ancient rhetoricians, concludes from the observation, which, incidentally, is not obvious from Dio Chrysostom, that, as Dio is not responding to personal attacks, so too, Paul's statements do not presuppose any personal suspicions with regard to his appearance.[10]

---

8. Dio Chrysostom, *Orationes* 32.9: Τοιγαροῦν ἀγαθὸν μὲν οὐδὲν ἐργάζονται, κακὸν δ' ὡς οἷόν τε τὸ μέγιστον, καταγελᾶν ἐθίζοντες τοὺς ἀγνοήτους τῶν φιλοσόφων.

9. Martin Dibelius, *An die Thessalonicher I, II. An die Philipper* (3rd ed.; HNT 11; Tübingen: Mohr, 1937), 11. See also O. Kuß, *Paulus. Die Rolle des Apostels in der theologischen Entwicklung der Urkirche* (Regensburg: Pustet, 1971), 88, n. 5: "The reproaches evident in 1 Thess 2:3-12 belong to standard polemics and their refutation, therefore, to standard apologetics as well."

10. Malherbe, "Gentle as a Nurse," 217.

Nevertheless, it is not unimportant to recognize that decisive differ-ences remain between Dio Chrysostom and Paul, and that these are deci-sive in determining whether 1 Thessalonians 2 has to do with merely rou-tine matters, or whether one is dealing with an actual confrontation rooted in concrete reproaches. Dio Chrysostom, on the one hand, was fully cogni-zant of the fact that he was a popular philosophical speaker who traveled around and earned his living from this activity. Paul, on the other hand, had an entirely different style. His apostolic self-understanding, in spite of the absence of the term ἀπόστολος in the letter opening of 1 Thessalo-nians, was characterized by his missionary work in Thessalonica, and it is this dimension of Paul that, appropriately, stands behind our text, as is evi-dent especially from 1 Thess 2:7.

A particularly crucial point of comparison with these wandering professionals, whom Dio Chrysostom represents very positively, is the de-cisive and undoubtedly historically accurate assertion of the apostle that he worked day and night so that his support would not be a financial bur-den to the church. Paul's course of action is presumably influenced by the behavior of the (ordained) scribes of the Pharisees, who made their living as artisans rather than teachers,[11] and it is this that signals the direction of Paul's professional life as a preacher.

In spite of Dio Chrysostom's declaration that his is not a self-appointed but rather a divinely given responsibility (ἐγὼ μὲν γὰρ οὐκ ἀπ' ἐμαυτοῦ μοι δοκῶ προελέσθαι τοῦτο, ἀλλ' ὑπὸ δαιμονίου γνώμης; *Orationes* 32.12), he must nevertheless employ means of persuasion and reason (διὰ πειθοῦς καὶ λόγου; *Orationes* 32.18). Ultimately, Dio Chry-sostom claims to speak by his own authority; as a result he must begin by legitimizing himself over against those who presented themselves to the public in like fashion. Paul, however, did not need to fear, as did Dio Chrysostom, similar confusion with pagan preachers wandering the coun-tryside, because the apostle did not view his proclamation nor his author-ity as belonging to himself. Nor was this his usual practice. When Paul is forced to defend his appearance as an authorized messenger of the gospel, as in 1 and 2 Corinthians, he does this in a completely different way than is the case here in 1 Thessalonians.

11. See Traugott Holtz, *Der erste Brief an die Thessalonicher* (2nd ed.; EKK 13; Zürich: Benziger; Neukirchen: Neukirchener Verlag, 1990), 86-68, together with n. 376.

6. The Situation of the Text

It is likely, then, that behind the differentiating characterizations that Paul presents concerning his initial role in the founding of the church in 1 Thess 2:1-12, concrete suspicions about his person, contingent on an actual situation, become visible. Recently, there has been a proper caution against the widespread tendency that assumes that behind every negation or differentiation in Paul's letters a mirror-like image must be reflected.[12] Nevertheless, by exercising cautious judgment at crucial points, one can certainly come to conclusions on the basis of a configuration of ideas in which Paul finds it necessary to refute what others are saying.[13] This is apparently the case in this text.

That the statements in question reflect the view of the recipients of the letter is excluded by the overall perspective of the author. In the very next sentence, 1 Thess 2:13, Paul expresses his thanks to God that the Thessalonians received (ἐδέξασθε) the message preached by him (παρ' ἡμῶν) not as human words, but rather as that which it truly is, God's word. Thus the apostle probably had in mind suspicions and slander regarding his own person that people from the outside are trying to impose on the church and its members. As the explanatory γάρ (2:14) indicates, the effectiveness of God's word is evident among those who believe in it, even when they experience suffering at the hands of the community in which they live, in the same way that, earlier, Jewish churches had suffered at the hands of their compatriots, the Jews. Essentially, the situation here is one of social discrimination. Entrance into the Christian community was accompanied by acute social isolation, since all of public and private life was permeated with religion. The painful consequences would have been felt above all in family circles. The situation of suffering present in the church is primarily such social persecution, which Paul both anticipated and presupposed in the case of Thessalonica — and beyond as well.

It is understandable that precisely such persecution provided the first stage in the well-intentioned attempt to bring back into the previous social community those fellow countrymen and family members who had

---

12. See G. Lyons, *Pauline Autobiography: Toward a New Understanding* (SBLDS 73; Atlanta: Scholars Press, 1985).

13. See in this regard J. M. G. Barclay, "Mirror-Reading a Polemical Letter: Galatians as a Test Case," *JSNT* 31 (1987): 73-93.

become Christians. N. Walter has shown how foreign the notion must have been, especially to anyone bound to Greek-Hellenistic thought, that the εὐαγγέλιον, the good news, is necessarily and meaningfully tied to suffering and that it receives its confirmation precisely in such a negative experience.[14] To submit oneself to such a message, with all of its consequences, even with respect to the conduct and experience of one's life, was, for the most part, incomprehensible to the ordinary Greek.

Yet such a misunderstanding by friends and relatives was difficult for the members of the Thessalonian church to comprehend, especially because the nonmembers placed the Christian message where they thought it belonged: among the manifold and assorted group of promises about salvation that were repeatedly offered for sale by wandering rhetoricians. By placing Paul alongside the group of familiar wandering philosophers, his proclamation could be classed with a number of other proclamations of redemption and, as a result, its claim to absoluteness could be undermined from the outset. One enjoyed listening to such people, and probably occasionally allowed oneself to be impressed by their rhetoric, but, so it was argued, one should certainly not surrender to them the totality of one's life.

7. The Public Context

That wandering Christian preachers could in actuality appear to pagan observers to be interchangeable with popular philosophical Sophists is verified in the presentation of Peregrinus Proteus by Lucian in *De morte Peregrini*. It was, admittedly, written more than a century after Paul's appearance in Thessalonica[15] and, additionally, with satirical exaggeration. Nevertheless, it verifies how easily a wandering Cynic preacher could be transformed into an itinerant Christian messenger — and then back again. And, of course, for Lucian, Peregrinus is untrustworthy in all of his manifestations, even when he professes to be a Christian, and those who are taken in by him are equally inane.

It is not difficult to imagine how, even a good hundred years earlier,

---

14. N. Walter, "Die Philipper und das Leiden," in *Die Kirche des Anfangs* (Festschrift H. Schürmann; ed. R. Schnackenburg et al.; Leipzig: St. Benno, 1977), 417-34.

15. According to von Christ, Schmid, and Stählin, *Geschichte der griechischen Literatur*, II.2.734, it was written shortly after 167 C.E.

angry relatives and friends opposed those who had let themselves be misled into baptism through the proclamations of Paul and his coworkers with the same arguments, if not with the same pointedness and eloquence. At the time of Lucian there were established Christian churches that had existed for some time and that could be distinguished from the usual philosophical-religious groups around them (groups that they would eventually "neutralize" in the not-too-distant future).

Furthermore, Christian preachers were not very different from philosophical rhetoricians with regard to their background: Paul is a Hellenized Jew, though apparently a natural-born Roman citizen who came from Tarsus in Cilicia; Silas/Silvanus is a bilingual Jew from Palestine/Jerusalem; and Timothy, son of a Greek father and a Jewish mother, though uncircumcised, comes from Lycaonia (Lystra). Dio Chrysostom of Prusa comes from Bithynia in the northern part of Asia Minor, and he owes his Roman citizenship, as we may presume from his nickname Cocceianus, to Emperor Nerva; Lucian, whose roots were in Samosata (Kommagene), came from a simple family and had to learn (proper) Greek.[16] All of these "backwoodsmen" were active at the intellectual, cultural, and political centers of their world, and those who have just been referred to, quite successfully! In addition to them, one may presume that a multitude of similar figures were active — people who were perhaps concerned to some degree with the cause they represented, but whose primary interest was to secure their livelihood.

Paul can have been personally active in Thessalonica only for a short period of time, the exact length of which we really do not know but which certainly could not have been longer than a few months; then he abruptly left the city and the congregation as well. As a result he had to reckon with the fact that a negative propaganda campaign that aimed to destroy his work by attacking his person could have grave consequences.

If the presentation of Paul's εἴσοδος in Athens is accurate (Acts 17:16-21), he may have experienced there how his proclamation was labeled as belonging to the company of σπερμολόγοι (v 18) and how the core of his message was scorned (v 32). Although this description is probably

---

16. Lucian, Δὶς κατηγορούμενος *(Bis accusatus sive tribunalia),* 27: κομιδῇ μειράκιον ὄντα, βάρβαρον ἔτι τὴν φωνὴν καὶ μονονουχὶ κάνδυν ἐς τὸν Ἀσσύριον τρόπον περὶ τὴν Ἰωνίαν . . . πλαζόμενον ("a man still young, the language still barbaric, clad almost still in a kaftan of Assyrian type, wandering around in Ionia").

the work of Luke,[17] it nevertheless shows how such an evaluation of Paul was possible within the context of Hellenistic culture. It is negative propaganda of this sort that, from the apostle's perspective, presented a grave danger to his young church in Thessalonica, and 1 Thess 2:1-12 demonstrates how he responds to precisely such a threat.

---

17. See Jürgen Roloff, *Die Apostelgeschichte* (NTD 5; Göttingen: Vandenhoeck & Ruprecht, 1981), 254ff.; R. Pesch, *Die Apostelgeschichte* (EKK V/2; Zürich: Benziger; Neukirchen: Neukirchener Verlag, 1986), 2.129-42, presupposes a source that leads back to the "historical Paul" (142).

On the Background of 1 Thessalonians 2:1-12: A Response to Traugott Holtz

Johan S. Vos

1. The Thesis of Traugott Holtz

Traugott Holtz defends the thesis that 1 Thess 2:1-12 can best be understood against the background of specific complaints about Paul. The apostle is not referring to complaints from the Christians in Thessalonica, but rather to suspicions and accusations from the larger society of which the Thessalonian Christians are a part. Concretely, he imagines the situation thus: both pagan and Jewish members of society wanted to undermine the absolute claims of Paul's proclamation when they placed the apostle with the familiar company of wandering philosophers. Paul's answer in 2:1-12, according to Holtz, specifically addresses these complaints and therefore has the character of an apology.[1]

---

1. See also his article "Der Apostel des Christus. Die paulinische 'Apologie' 1. Thess. 2,1-12," in *Als Boten des gekreuzigten Herrn* (Festschrift W. Krusche; ed. H. Falcke et al.; Berlin: Evangelische Verlagsanstalt, 1982), 101-16, especially 109-10; and his commentary, *Der erste Brief an die Thessalonicher* (2nd ed.; EKK XIII; Zürich: Benziger; Neukirchen-Vluyn: Neukirchener Verlag, 1990), 92-94. Regarding the place of this view in the history of interpretation, see Ernst von Dobschütz, *Die Thessalonicher-Briefe* (7th ed.; KEK [1909]; Göttingen: Vandenhoeck & Ruprecht, 1974), 106-7; B. Rigaux, *Saint Paul. Les Épitres aux Thessaloniciens* (EtB; Paris: Gabalda; Gembloux: Duculot, 1956), 58-62; W. Schmithals, *Paulus und die Gnostiker* (ThF 35; Hamburg-Bergstedt: Reich, 1965), 109-11; G. Lyons, *Pauline Autobiography* (SBLDS 73; Atlanta: Scholars Press, 1985), 182-84; W. Stegemann, "Anlaß

Holtz gives two reasons for his view: (1) The strength of the appeal to the church members' own experience with the apostle is, in his opinion, unique. It lends to the passage a "special urgency which goes beyond purely grateful recollections."[2] (2) The antitheses are not employed as mere rhetorical decoration since they cannot be derived from the thesis alone, nor do they merely articulate its logical negation. Several unusual elements in the antitheses remind one of the appearance of other proclaimers of philosophical-religious doctrines of salvation.

2. Clues in the Text

I question whether these arguments are compelling. An interpretation that can explain the argumentation of a passage with the help of data explicitly offered by the text deserves, in my view, precedence over an interpretation that must resort to a reconstruction of unverifiable data behind the text. The question in this concrete case is whether the argumentation of Paul in 1 Thess 2:1-12 can be sufficiently explained with the help of explicit information about the situation. In the letter there is not a single explicit sign that suggests that the contrasts pictured in 2:1-12 are referring to *actual* complaints, from either the church or fellow citizens. As I hope to show in the following discussion, there are nevertheless clues that suggest that, in this section, Paul has a *potential* denial of the divine nature of his gospel in view.

3. The Situation of the Letter

The situation from which the letter was born is unambiguously described by Paul in 2:17–3:10: During his absence, he feared that the church would lose faith and subsequently reject his proclamation as untrue, due to "persecutions" or pressure from the surrounding society. The belief or unbelief of the church is for Paul a matter of life and death: if the church rejects his gospel, his work is all in vain (3:5); if, on the other hand, it remains faith-

---

und Hintergrund der Abfassung von 1 Th 2,1-12," in *Theologische Brosamen für Lothar Steiger* (ed. G. Freund and E. Stegemann; DBAT 5; Heidelberg: Esprint, 1985), 397-416, especially 397-99.

2. See Traugott Holtz, "On the Background of 1 Thessalonians 2:1-12," in *TD*, 72.

ful, it will be his "crown" and his "glory" at the *parousia* of the Lord (2:19-20).[3] Twice the apostle emphasizes that the tension was so great that he could not stand it any longer. Since Satan prevented him from coming personally, he sent Timothy both to strengthen (στηρίξαι) the Thessalonians and to encourage (παρακαλέσαι) them in their faith "so that no one would be shaken by these persecutions" (3:2-3). After Timothy had reported that the Thessalonians were still believers and that they had good memories of the apostle, Paul himself assumes this latter perspective in his letter. There is no talk about the persecution being over (see 3:7); the danger of falling away is a constant one, and in his letter Paul strengthens and encourages the church "so that no one would be shaken by these persecutions." Under the sign of *strengthening* stand the first three chapters (see 3:13); under the sign of *encouragement* stand the final two chapters (see 4:1, 10, 18).

4. Self-Recommendation

If one reads 2:1-12 against this background, the passage is more a self-recommendation[4] than an apology. An apology responds to complaints that are actually expressed; a self-recommendation may contain apologetic elements (e.g., 2 Cor 10:12-18) but does not necessarily have to; it can also anticipate potential reservations or reflections (e.g., Acts 20:18-21). An apology is oriented toward the past, a self-recommendation toward the future. A self-recommendation can be used either to introduce oneself to persons with whom one is unknown or to strengthen an already established reputation. In the letters of Paul, a self-recommendation always has the latter function. In 1 Thessalonians 2, Paul takes up his initial acceptance by the church and uses the experiences that the church has had with him to insure that their acceptance of him will endure.

5. The Appeal to the Experiences of the Church

Within the framework of a self-recommendation, Paul's repeated appeal to the church's own experience has a clear function. The apostle wants to

---

3. See Phil 2:16 and 2 Cor 1:14.

4. See K. Berger, *Formgeschichte des Neuen Testaments* (Heidelberg: Quelle & Meyer, 1984), 265-67.

confirm and strengthen the agreement between himself and the church.[5] Agreeing with another person's opinion is easiest when the other person says what you yourself think or believe. By repeatedly appealing to the church's own experience, Paul gives the impression that he is not attempting to force something strange upon them, but only confirming what they already know. The appeal to their own experience is a system-strengthening device that has the function of winning the Thessalonians over to Paul in a lasting way. Against the opinion that this device is linked with complaints against the apostle is, above all else, the fact that Paul utilizes it just as intensively in chapters 4 and 5 (4:1-2, 9-10; 5:1-2).

What Paul does in 1 Thess 2:1-2 has a clear parallel in 2 Cor 2:14-17. He asserts there that, in accordance with his mission, he is fulfilling his role as an apostle, and he compares himself with others who are not doing that. In conclusion, he asks the question: "Are we beginning to commend ourselves again? Surely we do not need, as some others do, letters of recommendation to you or from you, do we? You yourselves are our letter, written on our hearts, to be known and read by all" (3:1-2). When Paul calls the church's existence his letter of recommendation, he combines two types of recommendations: a self-recommendation and a recommendation issued by a church, namely, the life of the congregation, which he characterizes as a letter of recommendation. In 1 Thessalonians 2 he does the same thing: by appealing to the experience that the church had with him, Paul allows the church to write a good recommendation about him.

6. The Antitheses

Can one also understand the antitheses in 2:1-12 from this perspective? The question of whether the antitheses are the logical negation of the thesis is linked with the question of what the thesis of the passage is. The main thesis of 2:1-12 is to be derived from 2:1 and 2:13: Paul's visit with the Thessalonians was "not in vain" since the church received the apostle's proclamation not as a human, but as a divine, word, and, as such, it is working in them. In 2:1-12 Paul proves from his ἦθος (character) as an

---

5. See Berger, *Formgeschichte*, 267: "Paul understands the decisive recommendation for himself to be the *I-you relationship* of the apostle to his church."

apostle that his proclamation is truly the word of God. He emphasizes his faithfulness to his calling, in both word and deed. He proclaimed the gospel in keeping with his divine mission, and his behavior corresponded in every respect to the divine norm (2:2-4, 10).

From this standpoint I see no "unusual" elements in the apostle's argumentation or antitheses that would not be a logical negation of the main thesis and its sub-theses. The positive image Paul gives to his range of activity, as well as the antitheses that belong to it, are paralleled not only in Hellenistic rhetoric and popular philosophy — as Holtz, following Malherbe and others, has correctly demonstrated — but also in biblical and early Christian pneumatics and prophets. For practically every aspect found in 2:1-12, one can cite parallels, either literal or substantial, from this area of literature. At this point I will give only a few parallels to each of Paul's statements; the material, however, could be expanded at will.[6]

2:1   Paul's visit to the Thessalonians was "not in vain" (οὐ κενή). See Isa 49:4: the prophetic servant of God fears that his work is in vain (κενῶς);[7] Herm. *Man.* XI.3, 13-16: the false prophet is himself empty (κενός) and can answer empty human beings (κενοῖς) only with something empty (κενά).

2:2   "But though we had already suffered and been shamefully mistreated at Philippi. . . ." See 2:14-15; Acts 7:52: persecution means following in the footsteps of the prophets.

2:2   ". . . we had courage in our God . . ." (ἐπαρρησιασάμεθα ἐν τῷ θεῷ). See 2 Cor 3:4-18: the boldness (παρρησία) of the apostle is characteristic of the service of the Spirit and is the opposite of the appear-

---

6. See A-M. Denis, "L'Apôtre Paul, prophète 'messianique' des Gentils," *ETL* 33 (1957): 245-318; W. Horbury, "I Thessalonians ii.3 as Rebutting the Charge of False Prophecy," *JTS* 33 (1982): 492-508; K. O. Sandnes, *Paul — One of the Prophets?* (WUNT 2/43; Tübingen: Mohr, 1991), 195-223.

7. According to C. J. Bjerkelund, "'Vergeblich' als Missionsergebnis bei Paulus," in *God's Christ and His People* (Festschrift N. A. Dahl; ed. J. Jervell and W. A. Meeks; Oslo: Universitetsforlaget, 1977), 175-91, especially p. 180, εἰς κενόν in the Septuagint functions to indicate the difference between what comes from God and what does not. See also W. Radl, "Alle Mühe umsonst? Paulus und der Gottesknecht," in *L'apôtre Paul. Personnalité, style et conception du Ministère* (ed. A. Vanhoye; BETL 73; Leuven: Peeters, 1986), 144-49; E. Reinmuth, "'Nicht vergeblich' bei Paulus und Pseudo-Philo, Liber Antiquitatum Biblicarum," *NovT* 33 (1991): 97-123.

ance of Moses; Acts 4:23-31: boldness is the sign of the spiritual person within the context of persecution.

2:3 "For our appeal does not spring from deceit or impure motives or trickery" (οὐκ ἐκ πλάνης οὐδὲ ἐξ ἀκαθαρσίας οὐδὲ ἐν δόλῳ). See Matt 24:24: false prophets will lead people astray (πλανῆσαι); Rev 16:13: from the mouths of false prophets come foul (ἀκάθαρτα) spirits; Acts 13:10: the false prophet Bar-Jesus is full of deceit and villainy (πλήρης παντὸς δόλου).

2:4 "We speak, not to please mortals, but to please God." See 1 Kings 22: false prophets say what pleases people; the true prophet speaks in accordance with his divine calling; similarly Herm. *Man.* XI.1-2, 6, 13.

2:4 "God who tests our hearts" (θεῷ τῷ δοκιμάζοντι τὰς καρδίας ἡμῶν). See Jer 11:20; 12:3: God tests the heart (δοκιμάζων . . . καρδίας) of the prophet.

2:5 ". . . or with a pretext for greed" (οὔτε ἐν προφάσει πλεονεξίας). See 2 Pet 2:3: false prophets and false teachers act out of greed (ἐν πλεονεξίᾳ); similarly Isa 28:8 (LXX); Mic 3:5.

2:6 "nor did we seek praise from mortals." See Herm. *Man.* XI.12: the false prophet always wants to rank first.

2:7 ". . . we were gentle (ἤπιοι) among you. . . ." See Herm. *Man.* XI.8: the true prophet is gentle, quiet, and humble.

2:9 ". . . we worked night and day, so that we might not burden any of you." See Mic 3:11; Herm. *Man.* XI.12: false prophets prophesy for money.

2:10 ". . . how pure, upright, and blameless our conduct was toward you believers." See Matt 7:15-23: true and false prophets will be known by their fruits.

From this perspective, the next section (2:13-16) continues without a break. Here Paul takes up again the theme of 1:6 (and 2:1-2): the Thessalonians received the gospel as the Word of God "under great persecution." If, on the negative side, suffering contains the danger of the church's apostasy, on the positive side, it places Paul and the church in the line of the true prophets. Successively persecuted were the prophets, the Lord, Paul, the churches in

Judea, and the church of the Thessalonians. The function of 2:13-16 in this context is primarily to present the church as successor to the true prophets and the messenger of God in a world hostile to them.

If one links the antitheses with the main thesis and its subtheses with this perspective in mind, one can say neither that the passage contains unusual elements nor that the antitheses are not logically derived from the theses. The subtheses and their antitheses serve to strengthen the main thesis, namely, that the Thessalonians rightly accepted the apostle as a genuine messenger of God.

Added to this is the fact that the antithetical manner of argumentation in this passage is no more pronounced than in the paraenetic sections 4:4-8 or 5:4-10. From the tone and style of the passage, one cannot, in any case, conclude that it is polemical in nature. Holtz thinks that the work is "much too engaged and harsh"[8] to be considered "Standardpolemik." Against this position, Martin Dibelius writes that the particular stylistic characteristics of 1 and 2 Corinthians — "the mark of agitation, passionate, ironic, or authoritative diction"[9] — are completely missing in our passage. Similarly, P. Vielhauer writes: "1 Thess 2:1-12 shows no sign of passion, anger or sarcasm, no sign of the polemical traits that, in 2 Corinthians and Galatians, characterize the apostle's reaction to attacks on his personal integrity; the passage rather preserves a completely peaceful tone and is consistently structured rhetorically."[10]

The question of why Paul must stress, in detailed fashion, that the gospel that the Thessalonians received was not from mortals but rather from God, corresponds in its intensity to his previous fear that the Thessalonians had turned away from him and his proclamation. The elaborate confirmation of the divine origin of his gospel serves to strengthen the faith of the church.

7. The Intention of the Passage

Interpreters who challenge the view that Paul in 1 Thess 2:1-12 is defending himself against concrete criticism often emphasize the paraenetic aim

---

8. Holtz, "Der Apostel des Christus," 102.

9. *An die Thessalonicher I.II. An die Philipper* (HNT 11; Tübingen: Mohr, 1937), 10.

10. *Geschichte der urchristlichen Literatur* (Berlin/New York: de Gruyter, 1975), 86.

of the passage.[11] Now one can hardly deny that paraenetic intentions exist. For example, in verses 10-12 Paul explicitly links his own behavior with that of the church, and some elements from 2:1-12 are repeated in the paraenetic passage 4:1-12 (see 4:6-7, 11). The primary intention of the self-recommendation of 2:1-12, however, is not *paraenesis,* but rather the strengthening of the faith of the church in a situation where it was being persecuted by its compatriots. The main emphasis of the passage is on the fact that the Thessalonians received Paul's proclamation as God's Word and thereby they have affirmed his apostolic mission.[12]

11. For example, K. Berger, "Hellenistische Gattungen im Neuen Testament," in *ANRW* II.25.2 (Berlin/New York: de Gruyter, 1984): 1031-32, especially 1290; G. Lyons, *Pauline Autobiography: Toward a New Understanding* (SBLDS 73; Atlanta: Scholars Press, 1985), 182-201, 218-21; A. J. Malherbe, *Paul and the Thessalonians: The Philosophic Tradition of Pastoral Care* (2nd ed.; Philadelphia: Fortress, 1988), 54-60.

12. Along the same lines, Stegemann, "Anlaß und Hintergrund," especially p. 415.

1 Thessalonians 2:1-12:
An Exegetical-Theological Study

Otto Merk

Almost a hundred years ago, in an essay that is still worth looking at today when discussing 1 Thess 2:1-12, Friedrich Zimmer (1855-1919) wrote: "A rich, as yet unharvested, field has grown from the study of the letters to the Thessalonians." Concerning the passage under consideration here, he declared: "It is very far from being properly understood."[1] These comments of Zimmer teach us modesty and are relevant to almost all the exegetical problems in these verses, which continue to be a cause of contention today. An exegetical-theological survey obviously cannot ignore epistolary or rhetorical aspects, or the background of 1 Thess 2:1-12, even though the papers immediately preceding my own, presented by my esteemed colleagues Donfried and Holtz, leave only a few further comments for me to make.

1. Introduction to the Topic

In the first place, the scope must be somewhat widened. Paul is apparently compelled to leave the congregation unexpectedly (2:17). Worried about

---

1. F. Zimmer, "I Thess. 2,3-8 erklärt," in *Theologische Studien* (Festschrift Bernhard Weiss; ed. C. R. Gregory; Göttingen: Vandenhoeck & Ruprecht, 1897), 248-73, see pp. 248-49.

them, he sends his coworker (and later cosender of the letter), Timothy, to Thessalonica, while he himself apparently journeys on by way of Athens to Corinth (as there are grounds for concluding; see 3:1-5). After Timothy's return and his reassuring news about the situation of the congregation (3:5-10), Paul composes 1 Thessalonians, whereby their good standing in the faith may have enhanced his recollection of the time the church was founded. A plausible reconstruction of Paul's missionary activity dates 1 Thessalonians to 50 C.E., with the founding of the congregation in Thessalonica about a year earlier (49 C.E.).[2] This view is not without evidence, but — as is all too seldom taken into account — one must bear in mind that the Jerusalem Council preceded this, so that an agreement on the law-free gospel, which Paul preached and practiced, had already been reached.[3] The establishment of the church in Thessalonica and Paul's presumably earliest letter must be viewed in light of this decision.

For the purpose of our deliberations I presume the literary unity of 1 Thessalonians and do not consider 1 Thess 1:2–2:16; 3:2b-5a (and further sections from chaps. 3–5) as post-Pauline additions inserted into a genuine Pauline letter to the Thessalonians;[4] here, too, I am in agreement

2. For an overview of the extensive agreement as well as divergent opinions see, e.g., W. G. Kümmel, *Introduction to the New Testament* (Nashville: Abingdon, 1986), § 14, 255-62; U. Schnelle, *Einleitung in das Neue Testament* (UTB 1830; Göttingen: Vandenhoeck & Ruprecht, 1994), 62-64, especially 63, n. 82; somewhat uncritically exaggerated in W. Schmithals, "Methodische Erwägungen zur Literarkritik der Paulusbriefe," *ZNW* 87 (1996): 51-82, 57, n. 2: "Without further critical examination of the arguments, the consensus persists that 1 Thessalonians was written during Paul's second missionary journey. This emphasis is primarily due to the desire to have at least *one* example of a Pauline letter written during this time frame and, thus, to avoid the fact that the letters were written within a very limited period of time."

3. For an overview see T. Holtz, "Die Bedeutung des Apostelkonzils für Paulus," in *Geschichte und Theologie des Urchristentums. Gesammelte Aufsätze* (ed. E. Reinmuth and C. Wolff; WUNT 57; Tübingen: Mohr, 1991), 140-70; T. Holtz, "Paulus, Jerusalem und die Wahrheit des Evangeliums. Beobachtungen zu Gal 1 und 2," in *Nach den Anfängen Fragen* (Festschrift G. Dautzenberg; ed. C. Mayer, K. Müller, and G. Schmalenberg; GSThR 8; Gießen: Selbstverlag des Fachbereichs Evangelische Theologie und Katholische Theologie und deren Didaktik, 1994), 327-40.

4. Thus C. Demke, "Theologie und Literarkritik im 1. Thessalonicherbrief," in *Festschrift für Ernst Fuchs* (ed. G. Ebeling, E. Jüngel, and G. Schunack; Tübingen: Mohr, 1973), 103-24, especially 115-23; with regard to the literary criticism of Thessalonians, see W. Schmithals, *Die Briefe des Paulus in ihrer ursprünglichen Form* (ZWKB; Zürich: Theologischer Verlag, 1984), 111-24, especially 119-24, and his article, "Methodische

with the prevailing perspectives. Even so, an exegetical-theological survey of 1 Thess 2:1-12 is not so predetermined by these two assumptions as to make false judgments virtually assured in everything that follows. One can and must, in any case, begin with the final form of our letter — that is, with the synchronic level — and argue exegetically from that assumption.

2. The Contemporary Position
with Regard to 1 Thessalonians 2:1-12

(a) To understand 2:1-12 properly, one must also examine 2:17(-20). Paul begins a new section, as is shown by the introductory words ἡμεῖς δέ, ἀδελφοί, yet he continues on the same theme. He explains in 2:17, using metaphorical language, that he was compelled to leave the congregation on short notice. The passive form of ἀπορφανισθέντες ἀφ' ὑμῶν[5] expresses the orphaned state as one that has been forced upon him, and his mode of expression also shows that he has been orphaned through no fault of his own.[6] The plural form (see 2:18) refers to Paul himself; he has been orphaned, separated from his congregation. He himself was not the cause of this action; he did not forsake the congregation willingly. His many fervent attempts to see them again have been thwarted. No explicit grounds are given (2:18). The result: his congregation in Thessalonica has also been orphaned through no fault of its own. This links the orphaned Paul to his congregation just as the church's geographically distant founder is linked to them "in heart" — that is, in spirit (see 1 Cor 5:3). Eschatological expectation, as he views it, is intimately rooted in and with the life of this congregation (2:19b, 20). The immediate reason for the letter is linked to the establishment of the church. This suggests that the "beginnings" must be made present and actualized by reminding them of the close bonds and the fellowship that have existed, and the importance of these factors not

---

Erwägungen," which in my judgment is too sweeping; see p. 77, n. 92; p. 81, n. 105: "Whoever wishes to explain the literary composition of 1 Thessalonians . . . as due to the idiosyncrasy of Paul the letter writer must then reckon with the fact that they have then created in Paul an author to whom one may no longer apply the usual literary criteria."

5. See O. Seesemann, "ὀρφανός," *TDNT* 5.487-88; B. Rigaux, *Saint Paul. Les Épîtres aux Thessaloniciens* (EtB; Paris: Gabalda; Gembloux: Duculot, 1956), 457-58.

6. See H. Schlier's far-reaching exegesis: *Der Apostel und seine Gemeinde. Auslegung des Ersten Briefes an die Thessalonicher* (Freiburg, Basel, Wien: Herder, 1972), 42-48.

only existentially but also with regard to the future of both the congregation and its founder.

(b) The external boundaries and internal structure of 2:1-12 are intertwined, yet one should begin by looking at the parameters of the passage. It is current practice to treat 1 Thess 2:1-12 as a section complete in itself. But it is connected to the preceding chapter in content and substance, belonging with the thanksgiving in 1:2, and it gains a closer connection to the establishment of the congregation through what is written in 1:4-10. Likewise this passage is linked to 2:13-16.[7] It is true that 2:13 marks a new beginning within the thanksgiving of 1:2–3:13, but this verse is connected to 1:5 and is even more closely related to 2:4. It can also be seen as a significant summary of many comments in 2:1-2, 5-6 (and, *cum grano salis,* of 2:1-12), while 2:14 (2:15-16) is more closely connected to 2:2 (1:6) and is, moreover, intended to give an example for and comparison between the situation of the young church in Thessalonica and the Christian congregations in Judaea. Hence it is only in 2:17 that one can see a more clearly defined new beginning that, as previously stated, still relates to the situation of the founding of the Thessalonian church. Precisely in view of this situation, however, our literary demarcation requires further differentiation.

If one surveys the research done on the structure of 1 Thessalonians, it becomes evident that 2:1-12 is widely considered as a complete unit within a larger section. This holds true both for those who do not employ the principles of rhetorical criticism — such as the majority of earlier exegetes — and for those who do. It becomes apparent, however, that not only the conventional but also the rhetorical method of dividing the text frequently take 2:1-12 and 2:13-16 as being connected within a single structure of meaning, and this is also emphasized by the division of the text. Representatives of those following a traditional approach who take 2:1-16 as a unit include W. Bornemann,[8] B. Rigaux,[9] Willi Marxsen ("Apologie

---

7. U. Schnelle, *Einleitung,* 65, stresses a clearer separation of 2:1-12 as belonging to the "introduction to the letter" (1:1–2:12) from 2:13-16, which belongs to the "body of the letter" (2:13–5:11). J. L. Hill offers a similar division in "Establishing the Church in Thessalonica" (Unpub. Ph.D. diss., Duke University, 1990), 7-9, but she makes special reference to the particularly close connection of 2:13–3:10 to what has gone before (9-10; see also pp. 11-17).

8. W. Bornemann, *Die Thessalonicherbriefe* (KEK X; Göttingen: Vandenhoeck & Ruprecht, 1894), 71-119.

9. Rigaux, *Thessaloniciens,* 397-434, 434-56.

des Evangeliums [2,1-16]"),[10] and Traugott Holtz (who concludes emphatically: "The textual coherence of 2:1-12 turns out to be determined entirely by one theme").[11]

As representative of those who divide the letter according to rhetorical categories I would mention Frank W. Hughes, who, from the section entitled *"Narratio"* (2:1–3:10), extracts the subsection "2:1-16b: A Description of Paul's First εἴσοδος to the Thessalonians,"[12] a conclusion that Karl P. Donfried endorses.[13] Linguistic and rhetorical analysis in particular corroborates the conventional view that 2:1-12 can be better understood from its own evidence as a self-contained section within a larger framework (see especially B. C. Johanson[14] and the excellent survey by Robert Jewett[15]). Consequently, one is justified in interpreting 2:1-12 as a unit, but must keep its larger context in view throughout the analysis[16] and exegesis of this section.

But this still does not entirely answer the questions of the outer limits and subdivisions of the passage. Let me give two examples. First, Traugott Holtz has correctly shown that 2:13 cannot be connected to 2:10-12

10. W. Marxsen, *Der erste Brief an die Thessalonicher* (ZBK.NT 11.1; Zürich: Theologischer Verlag, 1979), 28; see also pp. 42-51.

11. T. Holtz, *Der erste Brief an die Thessalonicher* (EKK XIII; Zürich, Einsiedeln, Köln: Benziger; Neukirchen: Neukirchener Verlag, 1986), ix, 32, 92 (quotation).

12. F. W. Hughes, "The Rhetoric of 1 Thessalonians," in *The Thessalonian Correspondence* (ed. R. F. Collins; BETL 87; Leuven: Leuven University Press–Peeters, 1990), 94-116 (110 quotation).

13. K. P. Donfried, "The Theology of I Thessalonians," in K. P. Donfried and I. H. Marshall, *The Theology of the Shorter Pauline Letters* (New Testament Theology; Cambridge: Cambridge University Press, 1993), 5-7.

14. B. C. Johanson, *To All the Brethren: A Text-Linguistic and Rhetorical Approach to I Thessalonians* (ConBNT 16; Stockholm: Almquist & Wiksells, 1987), 89-93, 99, 157, 164-68.

15. See R. Jewett, *The Thessalonian Correspondence: Pauline Rhetoric and Millenarian Piety* (Philadelphia: Fortress Press, 1986), 216, 218, 220; for Jewett's own view, 71-87 (especially 73). Also informative for the state of research is C. A. Wanamaker, *The Epistles to the Thessalonians: A Commentary on the Greek Text* (NIGTC; Grand Rapids: Eerdmans; Exeter, U.K.: Paternoster 1990), 90-108 and — with its own particular emphases — D. Patte, *Paul's Faith and the Power of the Gospel: A Structural Introduction to the Pauline Letters* (Philadelphia: Fortress, 1983), 140-44: "Paul's Relationship to the Thessalonians (2:1-12)."

16. See also most recently S. Schreiber, *Paulus als Wundertäter: Redaktionsgeschichtliche Untersuchungen zur Apostelgeschichte und den authentischen Paulusbriefen* (BZNW 79; Berlin and New York: Walter de Gruyter, 1996), 252-66.

— as Ernst von Dobschütz once held — to form a "subunit."[17] Consequently, 2:1-13 does not form a closed unit with verse 13 as "the last trump in his [Paul's] apologia," no matter how certain it may be, as von Dobschütz maintains, that 2:13 takes up the central content of what was said from 2:1 on.[18]

Second, Rudolf Bultmann, in hand-written notes on 1 Thessalonians, which were penned during his early years as a lecturer, understood 2:1-12 as a section complete in itself but embedded in a larger thanksgiving and interpreted it in part in this wider connection.[19] Decades later (1946/47), as has only recently become known from other manuscripts, he identified the following configuration: "1:4–2:4, recollection of the mission in Thessalonica, of the attitude of the congregation and of the success of the apostle's work"; "2:5-12, apologia for the blamelessness of Paul's character."[20] Bultmann clearly sees this — and this is taken into account in the division of the text — as a broader, unified recollection by Paul of his sojourn at the founding of the church; the division of the text interprets it in the framework of an extended thanksgiving 1:2–3:13 ("extended *prooemium* with subdivisions").[21]

(c) The internal structure compels us to take account of the situation, background, and rhetorical data, since structure and content interlock. Here, however, it is necessary to address only briefly the methodological requirements, since the results of research are currently well known and the history-of-religions parallels are being taken comprehensively into consideration.

17. Holtz, *1 Thessalonicher,* 65 and n. 223.

18. E. von Dobschütz, *Die Thessalonicher-Briefe* (KEK X; Göttingen: Vandenhoeck & Ruprecht [1909]; repr. 1974), 82, 103 (quotation).

19. See O. Merk, "Zu Rudolf Bultmanns Auslegung des 1. Thessalonicherbriefes," *Glaube und Eschatologie* (Festschrift W. G. Kümmel; Tübingen: Mohr, 1985), 189-98, especially pp. 192-95.

20. See the evidence in B. Jaspert, *Sachgemässe Exegese: Die Protokolle aus Rudolf Bultmanns Neutestamentlichen Seminaren 1921-1951* (MThS 43; Marburg: Elwert, 1996), 116; here one can also observe how he divided the remaining part of 1 Thessalonians: "2:13-16, return once again to the thanksgiving motif: Thanks to God for the steadfastness of the congregation"; "2:17–3:10, confirmation of perspective: The reason for sending Timothy is grounded in the apostle's longing to visit the congregation again"; "3:11-13, theme of intercession, and with that the conclusion of the expanded *prooemium*." How Bultmann divided the remainder of 1 Thessalonians (and 2 Thessalonians) is not relevant in this context.

21. Jaspert, *Die Protokolle,* 116.

Even before the publication of his commentary, T. Holtz put forward a forceful and instructive analysis that took account of the sentence construction, method of argumentation, and background of the statements in 1 Thess 2:1-12.[22] The numerous contributions on the classification of the genre of the letter also led to conclusions about the content of this section, and analyses of the letter's rhetoric became normative for understanding its content.

The most far-reaching summary and discussion that takes account of the theoretical aspects of communication is that put forward by J. L. Hill in her doctoral dissertation, "Establishing the Church in Thessalonica" (1990).[23] She shows how in 2:1-12 "nonverbal communication," namely, through "accommodations" in Paul's activity and in his person, coincides with "verbal communication." Further, after the introductory verse 1 Thess 2:1, one encounters both "a series of contrasts" in 2:2-8 and "a series of positive" statements in 2:9-12[24] that acquire their decisive depth of meaning through "Paul's verbal communication."[25] This is so because Pauline proclamation (which includes admonition and instruction) pushes open the door, so to speak, for a critical evaluation of the credibility of diverse itinerant preachers of the most varied provenance. This allows the concerns of Paul, as the congregation's founder who is distinct from such people, to come to the fore without there being an immediate reason for this in the specific situation.[26] Hill's important and illuminating deductions are reinforced on several occasions by calling into play the whole of 1 Thessalonians, even if much is overinterpreted. Although her dissertation was intended to give a sociohistorical assessment of the congregation at Thessalonica, she has nevertheless made an important contribution to the understanding of 1 Thess 2:1-12 and has put forward suggestions that have been discussed almost simultaneously in various European studies.

In a paper presented to our Seminar, Johannes Schoon-Janßen gave examples of various "echoes of the rhetoric of the ancient letter of friend-

---

22. T. Holtz, "Der Apostel des Christus. Die paulinische 'Apologie' 1. Thess 2,1-12," in *Als Boten des gekreuzigten Herrn* (Festschrift W. Krusche; ed. H. Falcke, M. Omnasch, and H. Schultze; Berlin: Evangelische Verlagsanstalt, 1982), 101-16. Now also in Holtz, *Geschichte und Theologie des Urchristentums*, 297-312.

23. Hill, *Establishing the Church*, 71-141.

24. Hill, *Establishing the Church*, 83-119; see also Johanson, *To All the Brethren*, 87-93.

25. Hill, *Establishing the Church*, 119-41.

26. Hill, *Establishing the Church*, 83-119.

ship" important to 1 Thessalonians and characterized its literary genre "as primarily epideictic . . . on the basis of the *topos* of praise (and, to a lesser degree, rebuke), together with the governing sentiment of love."[27] In so doing he judiciously differentiates and assesses the "element(s) of diatribe" in 1 Thessalonians as a whole and comes to the conclusion that in 1 Thess 2:1-12 there is a "potential apologia" — namely, that upon closer examination of this section it becomes evident that Paul does not defend nor need to defend.[28] In other words, according to 1 Thess 2:1-12 Paul is portrayed "as a Christian who offers himself to the congregation at Thessalonica, while generally in good condition, as an encouraging example in a time of oppression and distress."[29] Schoon-Janßen divides the text in a way quite similar to that of Hill. After understanding 2:1 as a general introduction to 2:2-12, he subdivides this section into three parts: 2:2-4 (the divinely guided mission); 2:5-8 ("retrospective . . . and more concrete statements," especially in v 5b); and 2:9-12 (an emphatic restatement of the most important points in 2:1-8).[30] Here, too, he is in agreement with Hill's interpretation that the absolutely fundamental dissociation of Paul from contemporary itinerant preachers of any kind becomes clear through the comparison with religio-historical parallels.[31]

R. Reck analyzed the structure and content of 1 Thess 2:3-8 from the perspective of "Communication and the Emergence of Congregations,"[32] to which Hill already referred; thus this study complements the two above-mentioned contributions with their convergent concerns. Reck draws attention to what characterizes the section — a factor already observed by

27. J. Schoon-Janßen, *Umstrittene "Apologien" in den Paulusbriefen. Studien zur rhetorischen Situation des 1. Thessalonicherbriefes, des Galaterbriefes und des Philipperbriefes* (GTA 45; Göttingen: Vandenhoeck & Ruprecht, 1991), 52; see also p. 63.

28. Schoon-Janßen, *Umstrittene "Apologien,"* 39-65.

29. Schoon-Janßen, *Umstrittene "Apologien,"* 63.

30. Schoon-Janßen, *Umstrittene "Apologien,"* 56-57.

31. In both dissertations the significance of A. J. Malherbe's observations, originally published in 1970, is evident: "'Gentle as a Nurse': The Cynic Background to I Thessalonians 2," in *Paul and the Popular Philosophers* (Minneapolis: Fortress, 1989), 35-48, as well as the careful examination of 1 Thess 2:1-12 by G. Lyons in his work *Pauline Autobiography: Toward a New Understanding* (SBLDS 73; Atlanta: Scholars Press, 1985), 177-201.

32. R. Reck, *Kommunikation und Gemeindeaufbau. Eine Studie zur Entstehung, Leben und Wachstum paulinischer Gemeinden in den Kommunikationsstrukturen der Antike* (SBS 22; Stuttgart: Verlag Katholisches Bibelwerk, 1991). For closer attention to the linguistic analysis of 1 Thess 2:3-8, see also Zimmer, "I Thess. 2,3-8 erklärt."

previous research[33] — namely, "the opposition of οὐκ — ἀλλά . . . even into the subordinate clauses, whereby with rhetorical finesse the position to be rejected is always placed first. Paul dissociates himself from deception and impurity as the background (ἐκ/ἐξ) of his work, from cunning, flattery and display of apostolic power as his methods (ἐν), and from the praise and flattery of his fellows (2:3, 5, 6). On the contrary, he stresses his position as custodian" (2:4), "his responsibility before God, which expresses itself in practice in a maternal, solicitous love" (2:7). The result of this is that "love as a sustentative attitude" is shown to be "a basis for the fact that the communication of the gospel does not take place merely on a cognitive level but remains bound to the communication of life" (2:8). To this Reck appends the following decisive conclusion: "Such an intimate and consequently defenseless manner of proclamation . . . is so in keeping with the essence of the gospel that the method itself in this way becomes part of the message and, vice versa, the message takes shape in the method; *the method communicates analogously/non-verbally what the message contains digitally/verbally in words.* It is fully in accord with this that the apostle passes on the gospel with full commitment and defends it with determination."[34]

R. Gebauer also points in this general direction.[35] Like Schoon-Janßen he sees a "potential apologia" in 2:1-12. 2:1 makes a connection with 1:9-10. Through 2:3 (with direct reference to 2:2, 4) "the preaching of the gospel" "as the realization of the apostolic παράκλησις" is paraphrased as "the proclamation of the missionary message," whereby the "unique choice of words" allows us to "infer a style of communication which was particularly encouraging and shows to advantage the 'relevant claim' of the gospel." This becomes clear at various points — for example, in 2:7-8 — and develops into pastoral "care" and "support" in 2:11-12. "Just as he [Paul] in 1:9-10 alludes to the conversion of the Thessalonians (with the repetition of the missionary message), so he allows the section 2:1-12 with its closing reference to his fatherly admonition (verses 11-12) to develop into the apostolic paraclesis which reinforces that conversion. For it is in

33. See Holtz, "Der Apostel des Christus," 300-306 and those referred to there.

34. Reck, *Kommunikation,* 165-98, especially 174-75 (quotation underlined in the original); see also the central section: "Das Evangelium als initiative Kraft der urchristlichen Kommunikation" (162-64 and frequently elsewhere; relating to the whole, 318-23).

35. R. Gebauer, *Paulus als Seelsorger: Ein exegetischer Beitrag zur praktischen Theologie* (CThM.BW 18; Stuttgart: Calwer Verlag, 1997).

this that we see the fundamental difference in 'decisive elements'[36] of his activity between the methods of itinerant philosophers and orators."[37]

Even these few recent positions (since 1990) on the internal division of 2:1-12, although they have their differences and each has its own particular concerns, confirm that the structure of this passage was carefully thought out. The initially problematic methodological interest in the interrelationship of situation, background, and rhetoric has chiefly led to the result that the rhetorical elements elucidate the theological concern in Paul's writing and thus have a hermeneutical function, but they do not supply the basis for what is said in this passage.

3. Exegetical-Theological Survey of 1 Thessalonians 2:1-12

2:1

Emphasizing the knowledge of the Thessalonians[38] — which is recalled so as to make this remembrance contemporary — Paul reminds them of the foundation of the church and consequently of his εἴσοδος among them. With the use of γάρ Paul establishes the connection with what he has written immediately before. He points back, as does εἴσοδος, to 1:9 and from there through further connections to 1:4, which is explained in 1:5-8.[39] Paul is writing to people loved by God who are aware of their divine election. Their election and the founding of their church belong together, for they are chosen in the Word, through God's saving action in Christ proclaimed in the gospel. This is confirmed by the many references to the gospel in connection with the recollection of the founding of the congregation (1:5; 2:2, 4, 9).[40]

---

36. Refer to Holtz, *1 Thessalonicher*, 89, as cited by Gebauer, *Paulinische Seelsorge*, 96, n. 21.

37. Gebauer, *Paulinische Seelsorge*, 94-96 (quotation).

38. On particular details see Holtz, *1 Thessalonicher*, 66; Rigaux, *Thessaloniciens*, 399-400.

39. See also A.-M. Denis's deliberations in "L'Apôtre Paul, prophète 'messianique' des Gentils. Étude thématique de 1. Thess. II,1-6," *ETL* 33 (1957): 245-318, especially 247-50.

40. See J. Becker, "Die Erwählung der Völker durch das Evangelium: Theologie-geschichtliche Erwägungen zum 1 Thessalonikerbrief," in *Studien zum Text und zur Ethik des Neuen Testaments* (Festschrift H. Greeven; ed. W. Schrage; BZNW 47; Berlin and New York: Walter de Gruyter, 1986), 82-101. Now also available in J. Becker, *Annäherungen: Zur*

Perhaps the connection of 2:1 to 1:4 is even more far-reaching. E. Reinmuth has suggested — although I personally think that this is demonstrable only in 1 Thessalonians — that "not in vain" (which comes into play in 2:1) refers to the "coming to the goal of God's election, the outward form of which is the church." The divine election "is realized" in "Paul's preaching Christ"; indeed, "for the sake of God's identity his works of election and salvation cannot be in vain."[41] God's ἐκλογή unites the Thessalonians and the founder of their church, and Paul represents this "not in vain" in his missionary service, with his proclamation and with his very being. This last connection is necessary to understand why Paul continues in 2:2 with ἀλλά.

But here one should pause for a moment, since the obvious connection to chapter 1 allows for a further observation. The initial missionary events that led to the founding of the church indubitably form a unit, but it may perhaps still be divided into two phases that are very closely connected. The first phase or contact with the Thessalonians is recorded in 1:9-10: their turning away from the idols, for which stock phrases of such an initial proclamation are mentioned in 1:10, in order to announce the new faith. But this beginning is immediately followed by the second phase, which Paul characterizes as the proclamation (2:9, κηρύσσειν) of the gospel (of God) (1:5; 2:2, 4, 8, 9) to those who have just become Christians. It is the expounding of the Good News, the effect of which in the newly established congregation in Thessalonica is clear (1:6-8). It is *this* phase, which undoubtedly required several weeks (months), that makes it possible to discern and establish with certain knowledge that Paul, as a missionary, is clearly different from itinerant preachers, peripatetic philosophers, or representatives of diverse religious cults.

But this fact has a twofold implication:

a. It is important to recognize that the conversion that leads to the founding of a church is a very elaborate process, even if Paul gives relatively few direct references to this in his letters.

---

urchristlichen Theologiegeschichte und zum Umgang mit ihren Quellen (BZNW 76; Berlin and New York: Walter de Gruyter, 1995), 79-98; see also J. Becker, *Paulus: Der Apostel der Völker* (Tübingen: Mohr, 1989), 138-48; O. Merk, "Nachahmung Christi: Zu ethischen Perspektiven in der paulinischen Theologie," in *Neues Testament und Ethik* (Festschrift Rudolf Schnackenburg; ed. H. Merklein; Freiburg, Basel, Wien: Herder, 1989), 172-206, especially 193-96.

41. E. Reinmuth, "'Nicht vergeblich' bei Paulus und Pseudo-Philo, Liber Antiquitatum Biblicarum," *NovT* 33 (1991), 97-123 (quotation 123).

OTTO MERK

b. The message of the gospel is not restricted to the points mentioned in 1:10; it has a broader range. That is also why the recollection of the founding of the church is not simply nostalgic information about earlier times but is to be seen as having contemporary relevance in its consequences for the church and for its (worried) founder: as "steadfastness in faith" and "existence in the Lord" (3:1-8, especially 6-8), particularly in times of temptation and affliction (1:6; 3:3).

2:2

Paul came from Philippi, where, in proclaiming the gospel, he had endured the sufferings of a missionary. As the Thessalonians are aware, he persevered in spite of suffering (and expulsion). The Thessalonians, who themselves are now ἐν θλίψεσιν, have, in becoming Christians, encountered a missionary who understands what it means to bear the consequences of the gospel. The events in Philippi had not intimidated Paul, but instead preserved his inner freedom, a freedom that derives from God and that comes to expression in the gospel, specifically in the proclamation of this message among the Thessalonians. The metaphorical use of ἀγών does not necessarily imply that the initial situation in Thessalonica was particularly difficult for the missionary or that it should be compared to a "conflict," since the word was often used in a metaphorical way in pagan Hellenism as well as in Hellenistic Judaism.[42] Ἐν πολλῷ ἀγῶνι rather expresses the unceasing, total commitment of the missionary Paul. Even if the expression is used metaphorically here and there is no evidence of a conflict-situation occasioned by the establishment of the church, one is still faced with the following question: Did Paul, now "orphaned" (2:17) and having been forced to leave the congregation through no fault of his own, look back to his time in Thessalonica as a time of conflict? This question appears in a new light since the contemporary Hellenistic background of the meaning of almost all the concepts in 1 Thess 2:2b-7c has been uncovered, and since it has been recognized that Paul appropriated the terminology of the Cynics and itinerant preachers to highlight his own missionary work and to show what was decisively different in the proclamation of the gospel. The wealth of evi-

42. See the evidence in G. Dautzenberg, "ἀγών," *EDNT* 1.25-27.

dence from the "Old" and the "New Wettstein,"[43] the important reappraisal of the material in the work of Martin Dibelius[44] and Abraham Malherbe,[45] and the collection made by M. Adinolfi[46] — which must be used with discrimination — only gain their full impact as relevant analogies and references when the exegete recognizes the reason why Paul included these phrases. As for the material itself, the following needs to be emphasized: Paul falls back on individual ideas/concepts selectively. One must also remember that in his reports Paul is not transmitting rhetorical themes and argumentation in the form of a unified speech or train of thought, and, moreover, "it is questionable whether the confrontations of certain orators in their public debates with other philosophers (that is, from other schools) were intended to serve as *apologiae*."[47]

Consequently Wolfgang Stegemann concludes — and here his position comes very close to those mentioned above, although reached by a different route: "In my opinion the understanding of 1 Thess 2:1-12 as a — real or rhetorical — *apologia* cannot be sustained." He holds that the main concern is *not* to deliver an *apologia* relating to the person of Paul but, as the context of thanksgiving shows, has to do with the Thessalo-

---

43. *Neuer Wettstein: Texte zum Neuen Testament aus Griechentum und Hellenismus,* Vol. II: *Texte zur Briefliteratur und zur Johannesapokalypse* (ed. G. Strecker and U. Schnelle, with the participation of G. Seelig, Part 1; Berlin and New York: Walter de Gruyter, 1996), 771-74.

44. M. Dibelius, *An die Thessalonicher I.II. An die Philipper* (3rd ed.; HNT 11; Tübingen: Mohr, 1937), 7-13.

45. Malherbe, "Gentle as a Nurse," 35-43. See also H.-W. Kuhn, "Die Bedeutung der Qumrantexte für das Verständnis des Ersten Thessalonicherbriefes. Vorstellung des Münchener Projekts: Qumran und das Neue Testament. — The Impact of the Qumran-Scrolls on the Understanding of Paul's First Letter to the Thessalonians. Presentation of the Munich Project on Qumran and the New Testament," in *The Madrid Qumran Congress: Proceedings of the International Congress on the Dead Sea Scrolls (Madrid, 18-21 March 1991)* (ed. Julio Trebolle Barrera and Luis Vegas Montaner; StTDJ XI,1; Leiden: Brill, 1992), 1.339-53, 344: "In this regard, the parallels of both of these images ['Father' and 'Nurse'] to Qumran might well be more significant, although for the passage as a whole, one should properly assume Paul's dependence on the popular philosophers." See also p. 341.

46. M. Adinolfi, *La prima lettera ai Tessalonicesi nel mondo greco-romano* (BPAA 31; Roma: Editrice 'Antonianum', 1990), 60-91.

47. Thus W. Stegemann, "Anlaß und Hintergrund der Abfassung von 1 Th 2,1-12," in *Theologische Brosamen für Lothar Steiger, zu seinem fünfzigsten Geburtstag* (ed. G. Freund and E. Stegemann; DBAT 5; Heidelberg: Selbstverlag, 1985), 397-416, 401 (quotation).

nians, who, as emulators of Paul, have "now become his μιμηταί in a special way." For Paul's "coming" to them, following his "mistreatment" in Philippi, "prefigures in a concise way their experience."[48]

This suggestion deserves serious consideration. It is limited, however, to a premise that can be questioned: in 1 Thess 2:1-12 Paul comes to terms with "the congregation's traumatic experiences (for example, the fact that the acceptance of the gospel has become a source of tribulation for the Thessalonians)," and this would explain "the paraenetic undertone" of "affliction and sorrow" in the section under discussion.[49] If this interpretation is followed, there is no way of explaining how it was that Paul was compelled to leave the congregation. Furthermore, it is not clear why gospel and suffering are causally related in the context of a message that is oriented toward deliverance and salvation (1 Thess 1:19; 2:12; 5:9, 23-24).

Paul has no need to remind the young church in Thessalonica that, if they accept the gospel, they must be prepared to suffer. It is perhaps no accident that the word θλῖψις is missing in 2:1-12. The "comparative material" that Paul brings in serves to emphasize his irreproachable work in founding the church. But a second stratum can be inferred from this causal one: it is itinerant preachers, wailers of every kind, "missionaries" of pagan religions and representatives of the indigenous cults, who are putting pressure on the young Christian congregation in Thessalonica, and thereby on their fellow countrymen.

To what extent and in what way was Paul himself "persecuted"? Paul used the terminology and language of these itinerant preachers and others both to differentiate and to integrate, but always utilizing their concepts in the service of Christian mission. Mission and gospel reach into the multi-layered religiosity of the world. The terminology of this religiosity is extracted — at least partly — from it and hermeneutically transposed so that it serves the gospel, thus corroborating the comprehensive power and might of the gospel in both word and deed within the churches established by Paul. What Paul frequently does in his later letters, namely, to take over the concepts of his opponents and use them in his own sense, is a result of his missionary concerns and action.[50] This is what creates enemies. It is his

---

48. Stegemann, "Anlaß und Hintergrund," 401, 415.

49. Stegemann, "Anlaß und Hintergrund," 415.

50. See O. Merk, *Handeln aus Glauben. Die Motivierungen der paulinischen Ethik* (MThSt 5; Marburg: Elwert, 1968); see also the survey in K. P. Donfried, "The Cults of

missionary use of such terms that brings religious opposition into the arena. For, according to Paul, the Christian faith does not stand alongside the numerous quasi-religions of the time as yet another offering, but penetrates them for the purpose of the world's salvation (see also 1 Thess 5:9-10). It is not only the connection with the synagogue but also the contacts with the pagan religions, for which the Thessalonian church is a prime example, that arouses the opposition of the Gentiles. Nevertheless, Paul considers such associations to be of vital importance, even though he is forced to leave Thessalonica through such a collision with the pagan world. While it is impossible for us to reconstruct this incident in detail, it was certainly known to the church in Thessalonica. What happened to Paul can occur in any missionary activity, just as suffering on the part of the congregation and its founder is potentially and existentially inherent in the acceptance of the gospel message and standing firm in faith. The specific case illuminates the fundamental principle: Paul is separated from his church, innocently orphaned, because the contradiction inherent between the saving gospel and a world filled with religiosity had taken concrete shape as a result of his activity in Thessalonica.

In this way παρρησιάζεσθαι (2:2), taken from the linguistic stock of the itinerant philosophers,[51] achieves its fundamental significance in the gospel. It expresses an openness to God and humankind[52] that reflects for the preacher of the message the eschatological dimension of the gospel that allows one to make a free decision for faith.[53] Once this principle is made evident, only a few additional comments will be necessary in what follows.

Thessalonica and the Thessalonian Correspondence," *NTS* 31 (1985): 336-56; K. P. Donfried, "The Assembly of the Thessalonians: Reflections on the Ecclesiology of the Earliest Christian Letter," in *Ekklesiologie des Neuen Testaments* (Festschrift Karl Kertelge; ed. R. Kampling and T. Söding; Freiburg, Basel, Wien: Herder, 1996), 390-408; P. Perkins, "1 Thessalonians and Hellenistic Religious Practices," in *To Touch the Text* (Festschrift J. Fitzmyer; ed. M. P. Horgan and P. J. Kobelski; New York: Crossroad, 1989), 325-34, 329; sometimes critically against earlier research H. Koester, "Archäologie und Paulus in Thessalonike," in *Religious Propaganda and Missionary Competition in the New Testament World* (Festschrift D. Georgi; ed. L. Bormann, K. Del Tredici, and A. Standhartinger; NTS 74; Leiden: Brill, 1994), 393-404.

51. On the Cynic use of the expression see Malherbe, "Gentle as a Nurse," 39-40.

52. See H. Schlier, "παρρησία," *TDNT* 5.871-86, especially 874 and 883.

53. See also Denis, *L'Apôtre Paul*, 256-58; H. R. Balz, "παρρησία," *EDNT* 3.105-12, 110; Schlier, *Der Apostel und seine Gemeinde*, 30.

2:3

παράκλησις, as R. Gebauer has shown,[54] is a philosophical term used by itinerant preachers and teachers of ethics;[55] here, however, it is reinterpreted as an expression for "the proclamation of the missionary message" that, as such, also includes admonition and advice. Three characteristic negatives are also derived from the Cynic background: πλάνη, ἀκαθαρσία, and δόλος.[56] Paul clearly dissociates himself from these terms by comparing them antithetically in 2:4 with his own mandate to preach the gospel — a gospel that is not of human origin but divinely entrusted and answerable to God alone. G. Schunack draws attention to the fact that δοκιμάζειν in Paul "involves the critical-practical understanding and response of faith in the Kyrios, the knowledge of God in Christ, and that this act is to be accomplished by the believer himself and recognized by the Church."[57] The God who tests hearts supports the credibility of Paul as a messenger of the gospel, and the effect of such credibility is that it is appropriated "and recognized by the Church."[58] Just as he takes over concepts from itinerant philosophers/teachers and transforms them for the purpose of the gospel, so it is with his behavior as opposed to theirs. The new, transforming effect of the gospel has corresponding results in the life and work of the messenger.

2:5, 6

These verses with their concepts (and allusion to 2:3b) are likewise clearly to be understood in light of the milieu of the itinerant preachers, but connected here with two striking elements. First, there is the phrase "God is witness." Precisely where contemporary pagan references are adopted,[59] Paul's primary concern emerges with great clarity: the God of the gospel is

---

54. Gebauer, *Paulinische Seelsorge,* 95.

55. See Malherbe, "Exhortation in 1 Thessalonians," 49-51, especially p. 51 (documentation).

56. Schoon-Janßen, *Umstrittene "Apologien,"* 58, accurately evaluates the facts: "From the context we can neither infer real accusations levelled at Paul in this area nor insinuations by Paul of sexual outrages in the congregation."

57. G. Schunack, "δοκιμάζω," *EDNT* 1.341-43, 342 (quotation).

58. Schunack, "δοκιμάζω," 342.

59. Adinolfi, *Tessalonicesi,* 71.

witness — here not within the framework of an apology but as the one who opens the eyes (see also 2:4) and reveals the standard. Of this Paul is sure and can call God as witness. Second, the enumeration of the *negativa* as a mirror-image of the itinerant preachers' and philosophers' activity that could be seen daily even in Thessalonica provides the young church there with information that enables them to make distinctions on the basis of the gospel and thus to assess their founder's behavior to them in relationship to it.

2:7

This verse causes several problems but not with regard to pagan references.[60] Points of contention are the punctuation of the verse, the interpretation of verse 7a, the reading (ν)ήπιοι, and how this metaphor relates to the context. Contrary to Nestle-Aland, *Novum Testamentum Graece*[27], a comma should be put after ἀπόστολοι and a full stop after ἐν μέσῳ ὑμῶν.[61] "On the one hand, a repeated οὔτε demands an ἀλλά in the *same* complex sentence, and, on the other hand, ὡς in verse 7c belongs with οὕτως in verse 8."[62] In any case, the three statements connected with οὔτε are dependent on ἐγενήθημεν in such a way that the ἀλλά contrasts Paul's position to them. But then verse 7a becomes a parenthesis to be resolved grammatically as a concessive clause.[63] Heinrich Schlier takes a different view: "Verse 7a only makes sense as an antithesis to 7b. This would mean taking δυνάμενοι as a finite verb, but this causes no difficulty in Paul."[64] If it is decided to follow the first punctuation, then the meaning of the verse must be made clear.

The phrase ἐν βάρει εἶναι is generally interpreted as "to have prestige," "power," or "honor." While there is clear evidence for τὸ βάρος[65] hav-

---

60. Malherbe, "Gentle as a Nurse" (see n. 32 above), 47-48; Adinolfi, *Tessalonicesi*, 79-80.

61. So already Dibelius, *An die Thessalonicher* (see his translation, 8); Stegemann, "Anlaß und Hintergrund," 405-6; N. Baumert, "Ὁμειρόμενοι in 1 Thess 2,8," *Bib* 68 (1987): 552-63 (561).

62. Stegemann, "Anlaß und Hintergrund," 406.

63. See also Rigaux, *Thessaloniciens*, 411, 416; T. Holtz, *1 Thessalonicher*, 75.

64. Schlier, *Der Apostel und seine Gemeinde*, 112, n. 45; so also Merk, "Zu Rudolf Bultmanns Auslegung," 17.

65. See Holtz, *1 Thessalonicher*, 78, n. 316.

ing such a meaning, there is no other evidence of Paul using the phrase in this sense. With this difficulty in mind, Bultmann urged that verse 7a should be understood as leading toward 2:9.[66] Similarly, Wolfgang Stegemann declares: "I believe that in the participial parenthesis of 1 Thess 2:7a, Paul is thinking of his special prerogative as apostle — the right to be maintained by the congregation."[67] But even if the more proper interpretation of 2:7a is to take it as a reference to the apostle's right to maintenance by the congregation, it is still necessary to consider the background. An acceptance of financial support would have made Paul appear like one of the itinerant pagan preachers. The participial statement in the concessive form is related in its tenor to the statements of 2:6 — and yet so far removed that the "apostle of Christ" (the plural form refers to Paul alone) could have asserted his apostolic right.

In verse 7b, contrary to what is today clearly the better-attested reading, and following the earlier Nestle editions (up to and including the 25th edition) as supported by widespread pagan parallels, ἤπιοι is generally read rather than νήπιοι. This decision is no doubt influenced by the metaphorical mode of expression that follows in verse 8. The choice of this reading is at first sight reasonable,[68] almost too plausible.

Nevertheless, it is proper to emphasize that, just as ἀπόστολοι (the first instance in a Pauline letter) refers to the apostle Paul himself, so νήπιοι (ἤπιοι) also refers to him. If this is accepted and νήπιοι, which is better documented, is read, then Paul himself has become a νήπιος in that he does not allow himself to be financially dependent as do the itinerant pagan

---

66. Merk, "Zu Rudolf Bultmanns Auslegung," 192-93 [R. Bultmann, Ms 1 Thess, 17-18]. See also J. G. Strelan, "Burden-Bearing and the Law of Christ: A Re-Examination of Galatians 6:2," *JBL* 94 (1975): 266-76, especially 273; the balanced discussions in Holtz, *1 Thessalonicher,* and Wanamaker, *The Epistles to the Thessalonians,* should also be taken into consideration with regard to this passage.

67. Stegemann, "Anlaß und Hintergrund," 408.

68. Of the more recent commentaries, plus Malherbe, *Paul and the Popular Philosophers,* 6, 35-48, 53; Schoon-Janßen, *Umstrittene "Apologien,"* 59-60; Stegemann, "Anlaß und Hintergrund," 408-9; *Griechisch-deutsches Wörterbuch zu den Schriften des Neuen Testaments und der frühchristlichen Literatur* (ed. K. Aland and B. Aland; 6th ed.; Berlin and New York: Walter de Gruyter, 1988), 1088: "1 Thess 2:7 has not infrequently been read as ἤπιοι instead of νήπιοι, which has been the preference of interpreters from Origen to the present. . . ." The assumption of dittography — ἐγενήθημεν νήπιοι — is also considered questionable. Baumert, "Ὁμειρόμενοι in 1 Thess 2,8," 561: "Richtiger ist es, mit Aland in 2,7 νήπιοι zu lesen."

preachers. Possibly, indeed probably, Paul is taking up a description or characterization of himself prevalent in the milieu of the itinerant preachers that was intended to belittle him. The Christian congregation in Thessalonica was very well aware of this caricature and was well able to evaluate it. The description of Paul's conduct as presented in the following verses is his answer to this insinuation. Our interpretation of the text would give preference to that reading which is better attested and more difficult *(lectio difficilior)*.

How Paul in fact nurtured his newly founded church in Thessalonica is shown through a metaphorical comparison in the new sentence beginning at 2:7c. The attitude of the apostle to his congregation, which is emphasized here, corresponds to pagan parallels.[69] And yet the picture Paul employs, for all the apostle's use of metaphor, is not altogether successful. Given the shared conceptuality, it is necessary to differentiate between the position of Paul and his loving attention to the church expressed pictorially (like a foster-mother caring for her children) and its usage in the pagan world, namely, the foster-mother is paid for her work, while the apostle is not.[70]

2:8

As already indicated above, the ὡς in 2:7c must be related to the οὕτως in verse 8, and this has contributed to the popular understanding of what this verse means: Paul's loving attitude, which includes the proclamation of the gospel and his personal concern for the congregation, also expresses his yearning for them. As a rule ὁμείρεσθαι is equated with ἱμείρεσθαι, although, according to Blass/Debrunner/Rehkopf, "an etymological connection of the two (verbs) is impossible,"[71] as Bultmann already observed in his remarks on 1 Thessalonians.[72] For this reason one should give careful

---

69. See Malherbe, *Paul and the Popular Philosophers* 6, 35-48, 53; Schoon-Janßen, *Umstrittene "Apologien,"* 59-60; *Neuer Wettstein,* 771-72.

70. See the important evidence in Stegemann, "Anlaß und Hintergrund," 409. Whether ἡ τροφός can also mean "mother" is hard to envisage in the pagan usage and is controversial.

71. F. Blass and A. Debrunner, *Grammatik des Neutestamentlichen Griechisch* (14th ed.; rev. F. Rehkopf; Göttingen: Vandenhoeck & Ruprecht, 1976), § 101; 78, n. 59.

72. Merk, "Zu Rudolf Bultmanns Auslegung," 192-93 [R. Bultmann, Ms 1 Thess, 18-19].

thought to N. Baumert's recently published derivation of the word from ὁμείρομαι, in the sense of "being separated from," "being kept apart from," and his resulting new translation: "So we are determined, while we are kept apart from you, to share with you not only God's gospel but our own life because you have become very dear to us."[73] It makes good sense: just as a foster-mother nourishes her children, so we, although separated from you, give you the gospel and ourselves because you have become beloved to us. Here, too, the apostle refers to himself when using the first person plural. For Paul the letter's occasion (2:17) and the time of the church's foundation interlock like two connected planes. Exegesis must take into account the basic meaning of the word ὁμείρεσθαι as it has now been established.

In 2:9-12 what has gone before is taken up and corroborated in various ways, since these verses recall for the Thessalonians their experience with the apostle (note also the knowledge and witness of the congregation in 2:10-12).

2:9

Paul has earned his living with the work of his own hands, and in the course of this work he has proclaimed the gospel. There is a modal sense in the participle ἐργαζόμενοι.[74] The more specific train of thought concerning Paul's self-support has been rounded off with verse 9.[75] But the verse also belongs with verses 10-12, and thus it has a connecting function.

2:10

A way of life in accordance with the gospel is defined as follows: "pure, upright, and blameless." God and the believing congregation are witnesses to it. For Paul, too, the gospel of God he proclaimed (2:9) and God's "witness" for this way of life go hand in hand like root and branch. Without be-

---

73. See Baumert, "'Ομειρόμενοι in 1 Thess 2,8," 552-63, 561 (quotation).

74. See R. F. Hock, "The Workshop as a Social Setting for Paul's Missionary Preaching," *CBQ* 41 (1979): 438-50 and the discussion in the more recent commentaries.

75. Merk, "Zu Rudolf Bultmanns Auslegung," 192-93 [R. Bultmann, Ms 1 Thess, 24].

ing expressly mentioned, the "indicative" and "imperative" also apply to the apostolic existence, or, to be more specific, to the founder of the church.

2:11

Just as verse 7c uses the picture of the foster-mother caring for her children, 2:11, using similar metaphorical language, now depicts Paul as a father in his affectionate relationship to each individual in the congregation. This is pastorally and paraenetically developed in 2:12 to encourage them to a way of life worthy before God, "who calls you into his own kingdom and glory."[76] This last statement, however, has recently been a matter of debate.

The few and diverse occurrences of βασιλεία in Paul belong, according to G. Haufe, to the "baptismal paraclesis."[77] P. Wolff carries this view further,[78] while Karl P. Donfried takes a more critical attitude. They believe that it contains both prebaptismal kerygmatic and postbaptismal paraenetic aspects. Donfried concludes *inter alia* that 1 Thess 2:11-12 (along with 1 Cor 4:20 and Rom 14:17) is not eschatological but refers to the βασιλεία as already present.[79] Counter to this, Ki-Seong Lee has shown, with extensive documentation, that kerygma and paraenesis overlap in the context of becoming/having become Christian. As he sees it, according to 1 Thess 2:12 their "divine calling" (namely, in the present) "obliges" the Thessalonians "to maintain their existence in the faith, particularly in their active lifestyle."[80] This associates them, according to

76. See Gebauer, *Paulinische Seelsorge*, 98-99; O. Merk, "Miteinander: Zur Sorge um den Menschen im Ersten Thessalonicherbrief," in *"Daß allen Menschen geholfen werde . . ."* (Festschrift M. Seitz; ed. R. Landau and G. R. Schmidt; Stuttgart: Calwer Verlag, 1993), 125-33.

77. G. Haufe, "Reich Gottes bei Paulus und in der Jesustradition," *NTS* 31 (1985): 467-72.

78. P. Wolff, *Die frühe nachösterliche Verkündigung des Reiches Gottes* (Unpubl. Theol. diss.; Greifswald, 1987).

79. K. P. Donfried, "The Kingdom of God in Paul," in *The Kingdom of God in 20th Century Interpretation* (ed. W. Willis; Peabody, Mass.: Hendrickson, 1987), 175-90, especially 181-82.

80. Ki-Seong Lee, *Die Basileia Gottes bei Paulus* (Unpubl. Theol. Mag. thesis; Erlangen 1993), 9-14, 13.

Lee, with the "eschatological reality," which should be taken "strictly in the future sense," for which βασιλεία and δόξα are synonymous. In the same way the eschatological future reciprocally connects with the present. "Their relationship to/connection with the present consists solely in the sovereign, salvific καλεῖν of the true God by which he has always acted. This means that God calls people into his community of healing, where he constantly confronts them with his abiding claim and ultimately leads them to his eschatological goal, his βασιλεία and δόξα"[81] (see 1 Thess 5:24 and Phil 1:6).

While dependent only indirectly upon previous research, W. Kraus[82] would like to give a new interpretation to 1 Thess 2:12 based on the following premise: "We must ascertain precisely what Paul means when he affirms that, against the background of Jewish opposition (namely, in 2:12), the Thessalonians are called to βασιλεία καὶ δόξα." This should be viewed in relation to 1 Thess 5:9, since 2 Thess 2:14 "appears to be a combination of both verses." Emphasizing the present participle καλοῦντος and taking into consideration a primarily present understanding of βασιλεία (though not excluding eschatological aspects) found closely connected to ἡ δόξα in the Sabbath Hymns of Qumran, Kraus concludes: "The expression 'to be called to the βασιλεία' in fact means the same as 'to belong to the people of the βασιλεία.' By using this expression Paul places the Gentiles who have come to the faith on the same level with the members of God's people. The calling of the Gentiles who have become believers to the βασιλεία in 1 Thess 2:12 is unmediated. It means nothing less than that the Thessalonians who have come to faith in Jesus are equated with the people of God."[83]

If 1 Thessalonians is to be grasped theologically in the coordinating co-network of decisive statements on election,[84] and election understood as something fundamentally new in the Christ-event in such a way that Paul intentionally designates the Thessalonians as church, then 1 Thess 2:12 must certainly be considered in this light. But there is no evidence of a "Jewish opposition" to the church and Paul in the letter itself, nor does the reference to 2 Thess 2:14 permit more precise conclusions, since a loose

---

81. Lee, *Die Basileia Gottes*, 14.

82. W. Kraus, *Das Volk Gottes. Zur Grundlegung der Ekklesiologie bei Paulus* (WUNT 85; Tübingen: Mohr, 1996), 130-38, 134 (following quotation).

83. Kraus, *Das Volk Gottes*, 138 (partially italicized in the original citation).

84. See n. 41.

collection of statements from 1 Thessalonians is not uncommon in that letter. Consequently, further-reaching theological conclusions for 1 Thessalonians are possible only in part and with reservations.[85] The interpretation brought in from the Sabbath Hymns of Qumran, even if it lay in the distant background, would hardly have been understood by the Christians in Thessalonica, who came from a Gentile environment.

In their relevant publications on βασιλεία, Martin Hengel and A. M. Schwemer do not admit this particular reference in relation to 1 Thess 2:12 and emphasize that here the eschatological rather than the "present" sense is definitive.[86] Furthermore, Schwemer, whose work has significantly extended the history-of-religions background with regard to "present" and "future" in the understanding of βασιλεία, rightly stresses that the leading themes in 1 Thess 2:12 are in substance eschatological and would also be understood by the congregation as paraenetic.[87]

In 1 Thess 2:12 βασιλεία and δόξα are to be taken as more distinctly eschatological, just as is δόξα in 2:19 and God's calling in 5:24 (in connection with 5:23). To have used the phrase "to be placed on the same level" with regard to the pagans and the people of God, unless explained by Paul, would have remained beyond the comprehension of the originally pagan Thessalonian Christians. The thanksgiving continues in 1 Thess 2:13, where it functions both to summarize the proclamation of the gospel (2:1-12) as correctly understood by the Thessalonians and to permit the thought of the letter from 1:4 onward to come to the fore again.[88]

---

85. This is corroborated by W. Trilling in *Der Zweite Brief an die Thessalonicher* (EKK XIV; Zürich, Einsiedeln, Köln: Benziger; Neukirchen: Neukirchener Verlag, 1980), 118, 123 in his interpretation of 2 Thess 2:14; further, O. Merk, "Überlegungen zu 2 Thess 2,13-17," in *Nach den Anfängen Fragen* (Festschrift G. Dautzenberg; ed. C. Mayer, K. Müller, and G. Schmalenberg; GSThR 8; Gießen: Selbstverlag des Fachbereichs Evangelische Theologie und Katholische Theologie und deren Didaktik, 1994), 405-14, especially 408-10.

86. *Königsherrschaft Gottes und himmlischer Kult im Judentum, Urchristentum und in der hellenistischen Welt* (ed. M. Hengel and A. M. Schwemer; WUNT 55; Tübingen: Mohr, 1991), 18 (Preface).

87. A. M. Schwemer, "Gott als König und seine Königsherrschaft in den Sabbatliedern aus Qumran," in *Königsherrschaft Gottes und himmlischer Kult*, 45-118, 117-18; on the fundamental question, see also H.-W. Kuhn, *Enderwartung und gegenwärtiges Heil: Untersuchungen zu den Gemeindeliedern von Qumran, mit einem Anhang über Eschatologie und Gegenwart in der Verkündigung Jesu* (StUNT 4; Göttingen: Vandenhoeck & Ruprecht, 1966).

88. See recently Schreiber, *Paulus als Wundertäter*, 264-66.

4. Assessment and Conclusion

Our rapid exegetical-theological exploration of 1 Thess 2:1-12 has only touched upon a few of the larger problems. Still the following conclusion can be reached: it is possible to speak of a "potential apologia,"[89] but one must be careful to make distinctions. Paul exposes the basic elements of the situation encountered by the Christian missionary and congregation-founder in such a way that his own missionary proclamation and behavior are brought into play in a positive way, with the specific being displayed in the general. Reconstruction and interpretation allow us hypothetically to derive the circumstances and the specific situation resulting from contact and contradiction in the course of missionary activity. Further, such critical analysis makes one aware of the consequences of the gospel entrusted to Paul, up to and including his own apostolic life, as a model to be emulated by the congregation. Also, in the context of the "thanksgiving," 2:1-12 gains further precision of meaning.

The situation was not that of Acts 17:1-10,[90] in which "Luke" describes the founding of the church at Thessalonica in stereotyped fashion, but rather that of Acts 17:16-34, which "Luke" reserved for Paul in Athens. Perhaps the author of Acts was aware of the reality of the Thessalonian situation but deliberately reserved Paul's encounter with the pagan world and its religions for the city of the philosophers. Here, however, specific questions of Lucan composition cannot be considered. At any rate, Paul, according to this letter, was not forced to leave Thessalonica because of Jewish or Jewish-Christian attacks or agitations but, as far as can be determined, because of a pagan, probably cultically motivated, eviction.

Paul's primary theme in this letter is the gospel and, consequently, the God to whom the Thessalonians have been converted. But he also deals

---

89. See also Schoon-Janßen, *Umstrittene "Apologien,"* 65, on his methodological procedure, which would admittedly benefit from a more precise exegesis.

90. See the open and frequently controversial discussion in the commentaries on 1 Thessalonians; the list of research in G. Schneider, *Die Apostelgeschichte* (HThK V/2; Freiburg, Basel, Wien: Herder, 1982), 220; further K. P. Donfried, "1 Thessalonians, Acts and the Early Paul," *The Thessalonian Correspondence*, 3-26; D. Lührmann, "The Beginnings of the Church at Thessalonica," in *Greeks, Romans and Christians* (Festschrift Abraham J. Malherbe; ed. D. L. Balch, E. Ferguson, and W. A. Meeks; Minneapolis: Fortress Press, 1990), 237-49.

with the consequences of the gospel for this congregation who, as a result of their faith, have had to experience ongoing tribulations.

If it is correct, as has been previously suggested, that both an initial proclamation and a supportive proclamation of the gospel are necessary for the establishment of a congregation, this leads to a further problem to which only passing reference can be made in this context. In 1 Thess 2:1-12 the phrase "gospel of God" is mentioned four times (see also 1:5; 2:13 [word of God]; 3:2). When Paul uses the term "gospel," does he refer to the gospel in its entirety, even if he does not mention every dimension of it in 1 Thessalonians? Is it, perhaps, an "early Pauline" version of the gospel[91] corresponding to an "early Pauline" understanding of faith and manner of believing (see 1:3, 8; 3:2, 5, 6, 8, 10; for πιστεύειν, see 1:7; 2:10, 13; 4:14)? However, neither the Christology and the understanding of σωτηρία, nor the allusions inherent in them, correspond to such a view. In addition, the use of the terms "faith" and "gospel" in 1 Thessalonians do not permit far-reaching conclusions about a development from an early Pauline phase to a later one.[92] The letter reflects in its own way, rather, the particular situation in which Paul is writing — for the very first time, as far as can be ascertained. He contributes theologically what the situation demands, namely, the subject matter that responds to the specificity of the moment. That, too, is part of his theological activity.

---

91. This is the moderate and well-considered suggestion put forward by T. Söding in "Der Erste Thessalonicherbrief und die frühe paulinische Evangeliumsverkündigung. Zur Frage einer Entwicklung der paulinischen Theologie," *BZ* 35 (1991): 180-203 (with a copious reappraisal of previous research).

92. See, e.g., F. Hahn, "Gibt es eine Entwicklung in den Aussagen über die Rechtfertigung bei Paulus?" *EvTh* 53 (1993): 342-64, 354-55; H. Hübner, *Biblische Theologie des Neuen Testaments: Die Theologie des Paulus* (Göttingen: Vandenhoeck & Ruprecht, 1993), 2.41-56 (insofar as he touches on the question); partly from other perspectives and premises, R. Riesner, *Die Frühzeit des Apostels Paulus: Studien zur Chronologie, Missionsstrategie und Theologie* (WUNT 71; Tübingen: Mohr, 1994), 297-369, especially 339-49, 357-58.

The Function of 1 Thessalonians 2:1-12
and the Use of Rhetorical Criticism:
A Response to Otto Merk

Jeffrey A. D. Weima

Two specific problems arise from a study of 1 Thess 2:1-12. The first issue is very specific and narrowly focused: What is the function of Paul's autobiographical statements in 1 Thess 2:1-12? The second issue is more broad in scope and hence somewhat more complex: What are the validity and interpretive value of applying the methods of rhetorical criticism and epistolary analysis to 1 Thess 2:1-12 and, more generally, to the Pauline letters as a whole?

1. The Function of 1 Thessalonians 2:1-12:
Autobiographical Paraenesis or Apology?

Until relatively recent times there had been widespread agreement that Paul in 1 Thess 2:1-12 was in some real sense defending himself. Although scholars debated the exact identity of his opponents in Thessalonica, they did agree that the charges implied in 2:1-12 were actual accusations brought against Paul. Thus in the late 1960s Walter Schmithals could say with justification, "On this point the exegetes from the time of the Fathers down to the last century have never been in doubt."[1]

---

1. Walter Schmithals, "The Historical Situation of the Thessalonian Epistles," in *Paul and the Gnostics* (Nashville: Abingdon, 1972), 123-218, especially 151.

The situation changed dramatically, however, with the publication of Abraham Malherbe's 1970 article on the possible Cynic background of 1 Thess 2:1-12.[2] On the basis of striking parallels between Paul's language in this passage and a speech of Dio Chrysostom, Malherbe argued that the apostle in 2:1-12 is not defending himself against actual accusations but that his statements here are part of the traditional *topos* and vocabulary of a philosopher depicting himself. Malherbe concluded, therefore, that the function of 2:1-12 is not apologetic but paraenetic: Paul is presenting his conduct and that of his fellow missionaries as a model for the Thessalonian believers to follow.

Subsequent studies, especially those making use of insights from rhetorical criticism, have similarly concluded that Paul in this passage is not defending himself from attack but presenting himself as a model to be imitated. The sweeping popularity of this new interpretation is evident in the fact that, with a couple of notable exceptions,[3] virtually all recent commentators have rejected the traditional, apologetic interpretation of 2:1-12 and opted instead for its exclusively paraenetic or exemplary function.[4]

---

2. Abraham Malherbe, "'Gentle as a Nurse': The Cynic Background to I Thess ii," *NovT* 12 (1970): 203-17. Republished in his *Paul and the Popular Philosophers* (Minneapolis: Fortress, 1989), 35-48.

3. Perhaps the most vigorous defender of the traditional view among contemporary exegetes has been Traugott Holtz: in addition to his chapter in this volume, see his article "Der Apostel des Christus: Die paulinische 'Apologie' 1. Thess. 2,1-12," in *Als Boten des gekreuzigten Herrn* (Festschrift W. Krusche; eds. Heino Falcke, Martin Omnasch, and Harald Schultze; Berlin: Evangelische Verlagsanstalt, 1982), 101-16, and his commentary, *Der erste Brief an die Thessalonicher* (Neukirchen: Neukirchener Verlag, 1986).

4. To cite a few examples, see, e.g., George Lyons, *Pauline Autobiography: Toward a New Understanding* (SBLDS 73; Atlanta: Scholars Press, 1985), 185; Wolfgang Stegemann, "Anlaß und Hintergrund der Abfassung von 1 Th 2,1-12," in *Theologische Brosamen für Lothar Steiger* (ed. Gerhard Freund and Ekkehard Stegemann; Heidelberg: Esprint, 1985), 397-416; Robert Jewett, *The Thessalonian Correspondence: Pauline Rhetoric and Millenarian Piety* (Philadelphia: Fortress, 1986), 73; Charles A. Wanamaker, *Commentary on 1 and 2 Thessalonians* (NIGTC; Grand Rapids: Eerdmans, 1990), 91; Frank W. Hughes, "The Rhetoric of 1 Thessalonians," in *The Thessalonian Correspondence* (ed. Raymond F. Collins; BETL 87; Leuven: Leuven University Press–Peeters, 1990), 101; Johannes Schoon-Janßen, *Umstrittene 'Apologien' in den Paulusbriefen. Studien zur rhetorischen Situation des 1. Thessalonicherbriefes, des Galaterbriefes und des Philipperbriefes* (GTA 45; Göttingen: Vandenhoeck & Ruprecht, 1991), 39-65; Abraham Smith, *Comfort One Another: Reconstructing the Rhetoric and Audience of 1 Thessalonians* (Literary Currents in Biblical Interpretation; Louisville: Westminster/John Knox, 1995), 78-79; Earl J. Richard, *First and Second Thessalonians* (SP

The widespread acceptance of this new view is illustrated in the essay by Otto Merk.[5] After making a number of helpful comments about the close relationship of 2:1-12 to the following section (2:17–3:13), as well the passage's external boundaries and internal structure, Merk cites in an approving manner the conclusion of Johannes Schoon-Janßen, namely, that Paul in 1 Thess 2:1-12 by no means defends himself but instead here presents himself to the supportive congregation in Thessalonica as "a model to be emulated."[6] Although this position is not forcefully argued in the remainder of the essay, similar statements are found scattered throughout the third and lengthiest section of this work.[7] The reader is thus well prepared for the conclusion that Paul presents himself in 1 Thess 2:1-12 as "a model and imitation for the congregation."[8] Thus Merk joins the widespread consensus among contemporary interpreters that this passage has an exclusively paraenetic focus.

I am not convinced, however, that the shift in scholarly opinion regarding the function of 1 Thess 2:1-12 is justified. Admittedly, many exegetes in the past have overinterpreted the antithetical statements in this passage and made unwarranted conclusions about the specific charges to which Paul was supposedly responding and the specific opponents who brought these charges. Nevertheless, a number of factors suggest that Paul is not merely presenting himself to the Thessalonian believers as a model to be imitated but that he is, in fact, defending the actions and motives of his original ministry among them.

First, the thanksgiving section of the letter (1:2-10) contains a lengthy reference to the mission-founding activity of Paul and his coworkers: "our gospel was not among you in word alone but also in power and in the Holy Spirit and in much conviction, as you know what kind of men we were among you because of you" (1:5). A comparison of this thanksgiving section with the thanksgiving sections of Paul's other letters highlights the unique character of this passage. Whereas in all other thanksgivings Paul focuses *on*

11; Collegeville, Minn.: Liturgical Press, 1995), 88-89; Beverly R. Gaventa, *First and Second Thessalonians* (IBC; Louisville: John Knox, 1998).

5. Otto Merk, "1 Thessalonians 2:1-12: An Exegetical-Theological Study," 89-113 in this volume.

6. Merk, "1 Thessalonians 2:1-12," 112.

7. Merk, "1 Thessalonians 2:1-12." See, e.g., his comments about v 2 on pp. 100-103 and his comments about vv 5-6 on pp. 104-5.

8. Merk, "1 Thessalonians 2:1-12," 112.

his readers and his thanksgiving to God for *them,* here Paul focuses on *himself* and the righteous character of *his* activity among them. One is struck, however, not just by the mere presence of this unparalleled statement in a thanksgiving section but also by the prominent location, the length, and the apparent defensive tone of this statement. For in addition to using an antithetical construction, Paul here deviates from his typical manner of referring to the gospel and employs the personal pronoun "our" (τὸ εὐαγγέλιον ἡμῶν), thereby stressing the key role that he and his fellow missionaries played in the Thessalonians' acceptance of the gospel message.[9] Paul also feels the need to use not one but three noun phrases to describe the true nature of his preaching activity among them ("in power," "in the Holy Spirit," and "in much conviction"). But even this is not enough, apparently, to make his point. Thus he adds a simple form of the disclosure formula ("you know . . ."),[10] by which he appeals to their firsthand knowledge of his and his fellow missionaries' ethical conduct among them.

When these unique features of the thanksgiving section are combined with the fact that this epistolary unit typically functions to foreshadow the central concerns of the letter as a whole,[11] it would seem natural to conclude that Paul in 1 Thessalonians is very much concerned about defending his character and already here in the thanksgiving anticipates the lengthy defense that he will present at the beginning of the letter-body. It is difficult to believe that Paul would deviate so significantly from his standard epistolary practice of referring in the thanksgiving section only to his readers if, in fact, he was simply interested in presenting himself as an example for others to follow.

Second, the recognition of 2:17–3:10 as an "apostolic *parousia*"[12] also

9. The term εὐαγγέλιον occurs some 60 times in the Pauline corpus, very often accompanied by the phrase "of God" or "of Christ." The personal pronoun "our" or "my" with "gospel" is found only six times (Rom 2:16; 16:25; 2 Cor 4:3; 1 Thess 1:5; 2 Thess 2:14; 2 Tim 2:8).

10. Terrence Y. Mullins, "Disclosure as a Literary Form in the New Testament," *NovT* 7 (1964): 44-50.

11. Paul Schubert, *Form and Function of the Pauline Thanksgivings* (Berlin: Töpelmann, 1939), 77: "Each thanksgiving not only announces clearly the subject matter of the letter, but also foreshadows unmistakably its stylistic qualities, the degrees of intimacy and other important characteristics." Peter T. O'Brien, *Introductory Thanksgivings in the Letters of Paul* (NovTSup 49; Leiden: Brill, 1977), 15: "We note in these periods an epistolary function, i.e., to introduce and indicate the main theme(s) of the letters."

12. R. Funk, "The Apostolic *Parousia:* Form and Significance," in *Christian History and Interpretation* (Festschrift J. Knox; ed. W. R. Farmer, C. F. D. Moule, and R. R. Niebuhr;

suggests that Paul is indeed concerned in this letter with defending himself. The other apostolic *parousias* found in Paul's writings (Rom 15:14-33; Philem 22; 1 Cor 4:14-21; Gal 4:12-20; Phil 2:19-24) never use the apostle's presence in an exemplary manner but typically function to exert his authority over his readers. As Robert Funk notes: "All of these [i.e., references to either the writing of the letter, the sending of his emissary, or his own impending visit] are media by which Paul makes his apostolic authority effective in the churches. The underlying theme is therefore the apostolic parousia — the presence of apostolic authority and power."[13]

The function of the apostolic *parousia* of 1 Thessalonians, however, is slightly different than elsewhere in Paul's letters. For in 2:17–3:10 Paul makes his *parousia* or "presence" more powerfully felt among the Thessalonians not so much to exert his apostolic authority as to reassure them of his continued love and care for them.[14] The need for Paul to reassure the Thessalonians of this fact was due to his sudden separation from them (2:17-20) and the subsequent persecution (3:1-5) they had to endure — events that apparently left Paul feeling vulnerable to criticism for his failure thus far to return to them. The apostolic *parousia* thus serves as an effective literary device by which Paul emphasizes his "presence" among the believers in Thessalonica in such a way that his readers are reassured of his ongoing love for them and any lingering uncertainty over his inability to return is removed.

There appears to exist, therefore, a parallel between the function of the apostolic *parousia* of 2:17–3:10 and the function of the autobiographical section of 2:1-12 — a parallel that strengthens the claimed apologetic function of this latter passage. Just as 2:17–3:10 is a defense of Paul's *present* absence from the Thessalonians *(apologia pro absentia sua)*, so 2:1-12 (or 2:1-16) is a defense of Paul's *past* ministry among them *(apologia pro vita sua [et labore sua])*.[15]

Cambridge: Cambridge University Press, 1967), 249-68. See especially his summary statements on 249 and 266. See also the work on apostolic *parousia* by L. Ann Jervis, *The Purpose of Romans: A Comparative Letter Structure Investigation* (JSNTSup 55; Sheffield: JSOT Press, 1991), 110-31.

13. Funk, "Apostolic *Parousia*," 249.

14. Jervis, *Purpose of Romans:* "Thus the dominant function of the apostolic *parousia* of 1 Thessalonians is to express Paul's love for his Thessalonian converts and to encourage them in their faith" (116).

15. These Latin phrases for the function of 2:1-16 and 2:17–3:10 are found in a num-

Third, a variety of unique features about the antithetical statements in 2:1-12 provide further compelling evidence that Paul is concerned with defending the integrity of his character and actions during his mission-founding work among them. It is here, of course, with these antithetical statements, that some of the strongest criticisms against the traditional view are typically made. George Lyons, in his influential study of Pauline autobiography, has been especially critical of those who find a polemical context in the apostle's antithetical statements:

> Antithetical constructions require a literary and rhetorical rather than historical explanation. They were far too common in the normal synagogue preaching of Hellenistic Judaism and the moral discourses of itinerant Cynic and Stoic philosophers in clearly non-polemical settings to assume, as the consensus of New Testament scholarship has done, that Paul's antithetical constructions uniformly respond to opposing charges.[16]

More recently, Steve Walton states of our passage: "The antithetical style used in 2:1-12 does not necessarily mean that the views on the 'not' side actually exist: opponents are an unnecessary hypothesis."[17]

Despite these objections, however, the antithetical statements of 2:1-12 contain a number of unique and striking features that support the traditional apologetic view:

(a) Paul appeals two times in the passage to God as a "witness" (2:5: "God is a witness"; 2:10: "You and God are witnesses"). The apostle rarely invokes God as a witness in his letters,[18] and our passage is the only place where he does it twice.

(b) Paul claims twice in verse 4 that God has "examined" him and his coworkers ("examined [δεδοκιμάσμεθα] by God to be entrusted with the

---

ber of the older commentators, including James Moffatt, *The First and Second Epistles to the Thessalonians* (London: Hodder & Stoughton, 1910), 4, 26, 29; J. E. Frame, *Epistles of St. Paul to the Thessalonians* (ICC; Edinburgh: T. & T. Clark, 1912), 14, 17, 140; W. Hendriksen, *Thessalonians, Timothy and Titus* (Grand Rapids: Baker, 1955), 74. It is difficult to ascertain who first coined this language.

16. Lyons, *Pauline Autobiography,* 184.

17. Steve Walton, "What Has Aristotle to Do with Paul? Rhetorical Criticism and 1 Thessalonians," *TynB* 46.2 (1995), 244.

18. In addition to the two occurrences in 1 Thess 2:1-12, Paul calls upon God as a "witness" only three other times: Rom 1:9; 2 Cor 1:23; Phil 1:8.

gospel . . . God who examines [δοκιμάζοντι] our hearts"). This language of "examination" adds weight to the legal-like language of verses 5 and 10, where the apostle appeals to both God and the Thessalonians as witnesses and so further supports a polemical context.[19]

(c) Our passage contains a very heavy concentration of antithetical statements. Elsewhere in 1 Thessalonians nine such statements can be found (1:5, 8; 2:13, 17; 4:7, 8; 5:6, 9, 15). These antithetical statements, however, are scattered throughout the letter, whereas five occurrences can be found in just the first eight verses of 2:1-12 (vv 1-2, 3-4, 4b, 5-7a, 8b). Furthermore, in contrast to other antithetical statements in the letter, all of the five instances in 2:1-8 are autobiographical: they refer to Paul and his coworkers. Finally, some of these five autobiographical antithetical statements are clearly being emphasized with the repeated use of the negative: there is a threefold occurrence of the negative in the antithetical statement of verses 3-4 and a fivefold occurrence of the negative in the antithetical statement of verses 5-7a.

The unique features in the antithetical statements of 2:1-12 noted above lead me to paraphrase the words of Shakespeare: "Methinks that Paul doth protest too much" and, one could justly add, in a too personal and emotionally charged manner to view this passage as having only an exemplary function. Bruce Johanson has similarly observed "the perceptible agitation and what appears to be a concerned insistence visible in the repetitive οὐ . . . ἀλλά antitheses in 2:1-8."[20] Therefore, although the mere presence of antithetical statements does not necessarily prove the existence of a polemical context, the several unique features of the antithetical statements in 2:1-12 strongly suggest that Paul here is not merely presenting himself as a model to be imitated but rather is countering accusations of

19. In considering possible criticisms raised against Paul in 1 Thess 2:1-12, Michael Goulder observes that "the denials, especially in the first verses, seem to cover more than this [i.e., more than an exhortation to the community to imitate Paul's conduct], and the appeals to God (v. 4, 'who tests our hearts'; v. 10) reinforce the impression that Paul is countering accusations" ("Silas in Thessalonica," *JSNT* 48 [1992]: 94). Goulder further argues for the creative but improbable position that the false teachings in the Thessalonian church were due to the work of Silas, who represented the Jerusalem church, so that the Thessalonian letters are the first evidence of the profound cleft that existed between the Pauline and the Jerusalem missions.

20. B. Johanson, *To All The Brethren: A Text-Linguistic Approach to 1 Thessalonians* (Uppsala: Almqvist & Wiksell, 1987), 54.

some kind. When it is further recognized that Paul explicitly identifies opponents who are persecuting the church (2:14, συμφυλεταί), this creates an even greater presumption that the antithetical statements of 2:1-12, even if they have a rhetorical flair, correspond to a historical reality.[21]

Fourth, another remarkable feature of 1 Thess 2:1-12 is Paul's repeated appeals to the firsthand knowledge that the Thessalonians have about him and, more specifically, about his conduct during his original ministry among them. The disclosure formula in the simple form οἴδατε occurs eight times in the letter as a whole, with four of these occurrences within the boundaries of this relatively brief passage (2:1, 2, 5, 11; see also 1:5; 3:3[4]; 4:2; 5:2). Yet another appeal in this passage to the personal knowledge the Thessalonians have about Paul is found in verse 9 with the use of the introductory expression "For you remember, brothers" (μνημονεύετε γάρ, ἀδελφοί). Finally, the second appeal to God as a witness in verse 10 (ὑμεῖς μάρτυρες καὶ ὁ θεός) also includes the Thessalonian believers themselves (note the emphatic position of ὑμεῖς) as those who have observed with their own eyes the "holy, righteous, and blameless" conduct of the missionaries.

Thus there are no less than six explicit appeals in 2:1-12 to the firsthand knowledge that the readers have of Paul and his original ministry among them. As Traugott Holtz observes in his essay in this volume: "The intensity of the appeal to the church's own experience with their apostle is singular. It lends to this section a special urgency that goes beyond purely grateful recollections."[22] It is important to recognize that these repeated appeals to the firsthand knowledge of the Thessalonians are not, as elsewhere in the letter, directed to the teaching and commands that the apostles had previously shared with them[23] but to the moral conduct and behavior of the apostles during their original ministry among them.

Paul's preoccupation in 2:1-12 with reminding the Thessalonians of what they actually know about his past conduct among them is, admit-

21. See Moisés Silva, *Explorations in Exegetical Method: Galatians as a Test Case* (Grand Rapids: Baker, 1996), 106, who makes this point with respect to the Galatians letter.
22. Holtz, "Zum Hintergrund von 1 Thess 2,1-12": "The intensity of the appeal to the church's own experience with their apostle is singular. It lends to this section a special urgency which goes beyond purely grateful recollections."
23. So 3:3; 4:2; 5:2. The one exception in 1:5 is readily explained as Paul's attempt in the thanksgiving section to foreshadow the lengthy discussion of the missionaries' conduct in 2:1-12.

tedly, not clear proof of the passage's apologetic function. Nevertheless, when seen in the light of the other major points noted earlier in this response, such a fixation is more readily understandable in an actual polemical context than as an indirect appeal to imitation.

What, then, should be concluded about the view of Merk and the vast majority of other contemporary exegetes concerning the paraenetic function of 1 Thessalonians 2:1-12? Evidence in support of this conclusion might be seen in the two verses surrounding our passage that refer to the topic of imitation: 1:6 and 2:14. The first reference, however, is not a command to imitate Paul and his coworkers but is simply a declaration: "You became imitators of us and of the Lord." The second reference is also a declarative statement and, more importantly for our purposes, does not even involve the apostles: "For you became imitators of the churches of God in Christ Jesus in Judea." Since the letter thus contains not even one explicit exhortation to imitate Paul and his coworkers, the widespread claim that 2:1-12 is exclusively paraenetic and completely devoid of any apologetic function would appear to be an exaggeration.[24] If such a hortatory purpose is, in fact, at work in 2:1-12, it can only be a secondary function.[25] For the evidence surveyed above — some based on epistolary considerations, others based on more traditional exegetical observations — confirms my contention that the traditional view of this passage has been too quickly abandoned and that the primary function of 2:1-12 is an apologetic one.[26]

---

24. John Gillman, "Paul's Εἴσοδος: The Proclaimed and the Proclaimer (1 Thess 2,8)," in Collins, *The Thessalonian Correspondence*, 68: "It is undoubtedly an exaggeration to call 2:1-12 exclusively paraenetic. . . . Another, perhaps more pressing function of the autobiographical section, is its apologetic concern."

25. A secondary paraenetic function is recognized by I. Howard Marshall, *1 and 2 Thessalonians* (NCBC; Grand Rapids: Eerdmans, 1983), 61; Gillman, "Paul's Εἴσοδος," 68; Eduard Verhoef, *Tessalonicenzen* (Kampen: Kok, 1995), 28-30. After arguing that 2:1-12 has an "anticipative apologetic function," Johanson goes on to state: "At the same time, the foregoing rhetorical interpretation does not allow the apologetic character of 2:1-12 to disappear behind implicit paraenetic and philophronetic functions that are obviously also present" (*To All the Brethren*, 165).

26. This conclusion is still valid regardless of whether Paul is responding to actual accusations raised against him or to potential charges that he feared might be made (see the comments of Johann S. Vos in this volume [81-88], who makes a distinction between an "apology" that is directed toward concrete accusations against Paul in the past and a "self-recommendation" that is directed toward potential objections in the future). For in either situation the function of 2:1-12 remains the same: Paul in this passage is attempting to de-

Although not all the factors discussed are equally significant, they have the cumulative effect of legitimizing the claim that Paul in 2:1-12 is, in fact, defending himself. This apologetic function plays an important role in reestablishing the trust and confidence of Paul's readers such that they will obey the instructions that he will yet give them in this letter.[27]

2. Rhetorical Criticism:
Evaluation of a Contemporary Interpretive Method

The second important issue arising from a study of 1 Thess 2:1-12 concerns the broader and more complex question of method: What are the validity and relative value of applying the methods of rhetorical criticism and epistolary analysis to 1 Thess 2:1-12 and, more generally, to the Pauline letters as a whole?

This is a matter that Merk does not really address in any substantive way in his paper. Although he makes a few general comments in support of using insights from rhetorical criticism and cites approvingly from several scholars who engage in a rhetorical analysis of 1 Thess 2:1-12, his essay largely engages in a traditional, exegetical-theological analysis of the passage. I say this not at all as a criticism of his work, but only as an observation. Whereas the essays of Karl Donfried and Traugott Holtz were intended to make use of the methods of rhetorical criticism and epistolary analysis respectively, the assignment of Merk was to examine 2:1-12 from an exegetical-theological perspective, and this he has done quite well. His essay, therefore, illustrates the fact that, as helpful as the newer methods of rhetorical criticism and epistolary analysis may be, these contemporary

---

fend himself and so reestablish the trust and confidence of his readers. As Aristotle observed: "One way of removing prejudice is to make use of the arguments by which one may clear oneself from disagreeable suspicion; *for it makes no difference whether this suspicion has been openly expressed or not*" (*Ars rhetorica* 3.15.1). Johanson thus comments: "While concrete accusations could be quite naturally expected from the addressees' persecuting fellow-countrymen as well as unbelieving Jews (2:14-16), even this presupposition is not necessary to explain 2:1-12, although such accusations are quite likely to have occurred" (*To All the Brethren*, 165).

27. For a fuller defense of the apologetic function of 1 Thess 2:1-12, as well as a reconstruction of the historical context of this passage in which this apologetic function is readily understood and so also further validated, see Jeffrey A. D. Weima, "An Apology for the Apologetic Function of 1 Thessalonians 2:1-12," *JSNT* 68 (1997): 73-99.

approaches only *supplement* and do not *supplant* the need to engage in a traditional exegetical analysis of the text.[28]

I question, however, an assumption found not only in Merk's essay but in many of the other papers presented in this Seminar as well, namely, the conviction that it is legitimate to engage in a rhetorical analysis of the Pauline letters. If rhetorical criticism is defined very broadly as the "art of persuasion," then I readily grant that Paul uses rhetoric in his letters. It is also clear that Paul employs a variety of literary or so-called "rhetorical" devices that are universally practiced in the everyday use of language and that do not necessarily provide evidence for the training in and conscious use of the ancient rhetorical rules (e.g., Paul's use in 1 Thess 4:9 and 5:1 of *paralipsis,* a rhetorical device that allows speakers or writers to address a subject that they outwardly claim does not need to be addressed). Nevertheless, I have a number of objections to the now common practice of taking the ancient Graeco-Roman rules for speech and applying them in a direct and wholesale manner to the interpretation of Paul's letters.[29]

First, there is the problem of mixing the genre of a speech (oral discourse) with that of a letter (written discourse). If one takes seriously the fact that Paul wrote letters, then the most important source for understanding Paul's letters must naturally be the letter-writing practices of his day, not the rules for oral discourse. The two relevant ancient epistolary handbooks, *Epistolary Types,* falsely attributed to Demetrius of Phaleron (ca. first century B.C.E.), and *Epistolary Styles,* falsely attributed to Libanius (ca. 400-600 C.E.), contain no justification for the application of rhetorical rules to letters. After surveying these two documents, Dennis Stamps concludes:

28. Jan Lambrecht, "A Structural Analysis of 1 Thessalonians 4–5" (163-78 in this volume): "In all structural analyses form and content cannot be separated" (p. 175).

29. Three types of rhetorical criticism are practiced in NT studies. The first is a historically based rhetorical criticism (often called "ancient rhetoric") in which the biblical text is analyzed according to rhetorical categories gleaned from the ancient rhetorical handbooks and ancient rhetorical compositions. The second is a modern-based rhetorical criticism (often called "new rhetoric") in which the biblical text is analyzed according to contemporary rhetorical categories that focus on the persuasive effect of the text without necessary recourse to the ancient rhetorical conventions. This second type is more of a philosophically based approach that concentrates on argumentation: its structure, premises, and techniques. The third type is a hybrid that tries to combine the insights of "ancient rhetoric" with that of "new rhetoric." My objections to the use of rhetoric are directed primarily to the first and third types.

So while both handbooks are concerned with developing a theory of letter writing and as a consequence with the rhetorical matter of selecting the proper response to a situation, in particular selecting the type of letter appropriate to the sender's relationship with the addressee and the particular occasion, *neither specifically relates letter writing to the five traditional aspects of rhetorical practice: invention, arrangement, style, memory and delivery, or to the three traditional species of rhetoric: judicial, deliberative and epideictic.*[30]

When one turns to the ancient rhetorical handbooks, the same picture emerges. The rhetorical handbooks contain very few references to letters, commenting only on the subject of style and saying virtually nothing about the key rhetorical topics of invention and arrangement. Yet it is precisely in these two areas of invention and arrangement that many New Testament scholars have spent most of their energies in applying the rules of ancient rhetoric to Paul's letters. Such exegetes, for example, are typically very concerned with determining the kind of proofs that Paul uses (either "inartificial" proofs, which involve appeals to various laws, witnesses, documents, and historical events, and/or "artificial" proofs, which involve appeals to *pathos, ethos,* or *logos*), classifying Paul's letters according to one of the three types of argument (judicial, deliberative, or epideictic), and outlining Paul's letters under the classical headings of *exordium, narratio, probatio,* and *peroratio.*[31] Stanley Porter, however, after examining the rhetorical handbooks with respect to their treatment of letters, comes to following conclusion:

> One can be certain from the evidence of the ancient rhetorical handbooks themselves of only one thing: with regard to epistles only matters

---

30. Dennis L. Stamps, "Rhetorical Criticism of the New Testament: Ancient and Modern Evaluations of Argumentation," in *Approaches to New Testament Study* (ed. Stanley E. Porter and David Tombs; JSNTSup 120; Sheffield: Sheffield Academic Press, 1995), 144-45 (emphasis mine).

31. The only two Greek rhetorical handbooks dating prior to the time of Paul (Aristotle's *Ars rhetorica* and Anaximenes' *Rhetorica ad Alexandrum*) claim that a speech consists of *four* major parts. Yet many modern exegetes who engage in a rhetorical analysis of Paul's letters divide his correspondence into *five* or *six* parts on the basis of the Latin rhetorical handbooks, despite the fact that these handbooks are written in Latin and are all dated well after the life of the apostle. For further comments on this problem, see Edgar Krentz, "1 Thessalonians: Rhetorical Flourishes and Formal Constraints" (287-318 in this volume).

of style were discussed in any significant way, virtually always with epistles mentioned in contrast to oratory. There is, therefore, little if any theoretical justification in the ancient handbooks for application of the formal categories of the species and organization of rhetoric to analysis of the Pauline epistles.[32]

Therefore, the evidence of both the epistolary handbooks and the rhetorical handbooks seriously calls into question the common practice of using the ancient Graeco-Roman rules of rhetoric as a key to interpret Paul's letters. As Traugott Holtz observes: "The application of rhetorical theory to letters stands, methodologically, on shaky ground."[33]

Second, there is no concrete evidence that Paul knew or was ever trained in ancient rhetoric. This is never proven but simply assumed by many advocates of the rhetorical method. Some believe that the use of rhetoric was so pervasive in the ancient world that Paul must have inductively appropriated these rules for speech. Thomas Olbricht, for example, claims that rhetoric "so permeated Hellenistic culture that it seems inconceivable for Paul to have escaped altogether rhetorical insight or, at minimum, a familiarity with Greek literature so affected."[34] Richard Longenecker similarly states: "The forms of classical rhetoric were 'in the air', and Paul seems to have used them almost unconsciously for his own purposes."[35] Others infer from the argumentation of Paul's letters that he must have known rhetoric or been trained in this discipline. Thus Frank Hughes, commenting about the apostle's literary skills in 1 Thessalonians, concludes:

> Such a persuasive response, coupled with the skillfully crafted triad of virtues in 1:3, the listing of the *propositiones* in the *partitio* (3:11-13), including their careful and subtle recapitulation in the *peroratio* (5:4-11), all *suggest* that Paul either learned rhetoric in school or had developed an extraordinary gift for the subject in which he grasped the

---

32. Stanley E. Porter, "The Theoretical Justification for Application of Rhetorical Categories to Pauline Epistolary Literature," in *Rhetoric and the New Testament: Essays from the 1992 Heidelberg Conference* (ed. Stanley E. Porter and Thomas H. Olbricht; JSNTSup 90; Sheffield: JSOT Press, 1993), 115-16.

33. Holtz, "On the Background of 1 Thessalonians 2:1-12" (70 in this volume).

34. Thomas H. Olbricht, "An Aristotelian Rhetorical Analysis of 1 Thessalonians," in *Greeks, Romans, and Christians: Essays in Honor of Abraham J. Malherbe* (eds. D. L. Balch, E. Ferguson, and W. A. Meeks; Minneapolis: Fortress, 1990), 221.

35. Richard N. Longenecker, *Galatians* (WBC; Dallas: Word, 1990), cxii-cxiii.

appropriateness of various rhetorical precepts for his letter without ever having formally learned them.[36]

At odds with this conclusion, however, is the high improbability that Paul would have received such Hellenistic training as part of his pharisaical instruction,[37] especially since he most likely belonged to the more conservative school of Shammai. With respect to Paul's earlier childhood training, very little, of course, can be known with certainty. Martin Hengel concludes that Paul likely received his elementary education in a Greek-speaking *Jewish* school where, among other things, he received basic training in speech in order to facilitate public speaking in the synagogue. This training in speech, however, "did not correspond to the Attic-style school rhetoric of the time" and was "not orientated on classical literary models."[38] It seems unlikely, then, that Paul received, either early or late in life, any formal training in rhetorical theory[39] (see also Paul's self-characterization of his speaking ability in 2 Cor 11:6, which is discussed below).

Third, even if Paul did know or had been trained in ancient rhetoric, there is evidence that he deliberately chose not to engage in such oratorical practices. It seems clear from his extant letters to the Corinthians — the very location from which he wrote to the Thessalonians — that the believers there did not like the unprofessional manner of Paul's speech and his unsophisticated public presentation (2 Cor 10:10: "his bodily presence is weak and his speech of no account"). They went so far in their criticism of Paul's abilities as to charge him with being "unskilled" [ἰδιώτης] in public speaking — a charge that the apostle apparently acknowledges (2 Cor 11:6: "even if I am unskilled in speaking"). Yet it seems clear from a number of statements in 1 Corinthians 1–2 where

36. Frank W. Hughes, "The Social Situations Implied by Rhetoric" (251-52 in this volume; emphasis mine). Hughes here is also quoted approvingly by Karl Donfried, "The Epistolary and Rhetorical Context of 1 Thessalonians 2:1-12" (40 in this volume).

37. Gerald M. Philipps has argued that there is no specific mention nor general awareness of Hellenistic rhetoric in the Talmud and that the rabbis seem to have been unfamiliar with this discipline. See his "The Place of Rhetoric in the Babylonian Talmud," *Quarterly Journal of Speech* 43 (1957): 390-93 and "The Practice of Rhetoric at the Talmudic Academies," *Speech Monographs* 26 (1959): 37-46.

38. Martin Hengel, *The Pre-Christian Paul* (London: SCM, 1991), 58. See also his comments on p. 38.

39. So also R. Dean Anderson Jr., *Ancient Rhetorical Theory and Paul* (Kampen: Kok Pharos, 1996), 249.

Paul speaks about his own preaching that he deliberately chose not to present the gospel in the kind of professional, rhetorical manner that the Corinthians wanted:[40]

> "For Christ did not send me to baptize but to preach the gospel, not with eloquent wisdom (ἐν σοφίᾳ λόγου) in order that the cross of Christ might not be emptied of its power" (1:17).
>
> "When I came to you, brothers, I did not come proclaiming to you the mystery of God in lofty words or wisdom (ὑπεροχὴν λόγου ἢ σοφίας)" (2:1).
>
> "My speech and my message were not in persuasive words of wisdom (ἐν πειθοῖς σοφίας λόγοις) but in demonstration of the Spirit and of power, in order that your faith might not rest in the wisdom of men but in the power of God" (2:4-5).
>
> "And we speak this [i.e., the gospel message] not in words taught by human wisdom (ἐν διδακτοῖς ἀνθρωπίνης σοφίας λόγοις) but in words taught by the Spirit" (2:13).

A consideration of these statements within the larger context of Paul's relationship with the Corinthians leads Bruce Winter to the following conclusion: "Paul, as a matter of principle, did not 'display his speeches rhetorically or according to the received form of the sophists' (*On Rhetoric* 2.139, XI). He renounced the use of oratory in preaching as inappropriate, for it was designed to draw attention to the messenger and his rhetorical abilities, and not the content of his message."[41] In another article dealing specifically with 1 Thess 2:1-12, Winter similarly concludes: "Paul as preacher had reflected . . . on the use of classical rhetoric for the presenta-

---

40. Although there continues to be debate over the exact evaluation of rhetoric by Paul in these opening chapters of 1 Corinthians, there is an increasing recognition that the apostle's statements here ought to be viewed against the context of Greco-Roman rhetoric and that this subject matter played a crucial role in the problems he faced in Corinth. See, e.g., Steven M. Pogoloff, *Logos and Sophia: The Rhetorical Situation of 1 Corinthians* (SBLDS 134; Atlanta: Scholars Press, 1992); Duane Litfin, *St. Paul's Theology of Proclamation: 1 Corinthians 1–4 and Greco-Roman Rhetoric* (SNTSMS 79; Cambridge: Cambridge University Press, 1994); Michael A. Bullmore, *St. Paul's Theology of Rhetorical Style: An Examination of 1 Corinthians 2:1-5 in the Light of First-Century Graeco-Roman Culture* (San Francisco: International Scholars Publications, 1995).

41. Bruce Winter, "Is Paul among the Sophists?" *RTR* 53 (1994): 35.

tion of his message and rejected it."[42] Some years earlier Edwin Judge reached the same conclusion:

> The technical term ἰδιώτης which they [the Corinthians] applied to him [2 Cor 11:6] . . . means that he was not qualified for the career which he might have been thought to have assumed, that of a public lecturer. This would have required university-level training under a recognized sophist (or 'professor'), and would have been instantly recognizable in his mastery of the complex arts of platform rhetoric. Whether Paul might have had such training at Jerusalem is not clear. *But it is certain that he refused absolutely to practice it if he did.*[43]

In fact, if Paul had made use of rhetorical devices in his first letter to the Thessalonians, he would have invited the very charge that he sought to avoid in 2:1-12, namely, that he was just a typical wandering philosopher who used impressive speech and sophisticated arguments for financial gain and personal glory.

Some final considerations may be briefly raised. First, there is the evidence of the early church. It is striking that the church fathers, despite the rhetorical training that many of them received, never interpreted Paul's letters or any other part of Scripture from the perspective of rhetorical theory. The one possible exception is Augustine, who, in the fourth and final volume of his *On Christian Doctrine,* was seeking to defend Paul against certain unidentified Christians who had criticized the eloquence of the Bible.[44] Yet even in this apologetic context where it is in Augustine's interest to highlight any possible connection between Paul's letters and the categories of Graeco-Roman rhetoric, this church father (and former professor of rhetoric!) comments only generally on Paul's style and makes no mention of the topics of invention and arrangement. And the other church fathers not only failed to interpret the Bible using rhetorical categories, but they generally considered Paul's word choice and syntax (i.e., the rhetorical topic of style) to be rather unsophisticated and his argumentation to be at times obscure.[45]

---

42. Bruce Winter, "The Entries and Ethics of Orators and Paul (1 Thessalonians 2:1-12)," *TynB* 44 (1993): 74.

43. Edwin A. Judge, "Cultural Conformity and Innovation in Paul: Some Clues from Contemporary Documents," *TynB* 35 (1984): 12-13 (emphasis mine).

44. Augustine, *De doctrina Christiana* 4.6.10; 4.7.14.

45. See especially the interesting summary of comments from the church fathers on

Second, I wonder whether the nature of the relationship between Paul and his audience made the conscious use of ancient rhetoric inappropriate. Rhetorical speeches were typically given before an unknown or nonfriendly audience of equal (public assembly: deliberative or demonstrative speech) or greater (courtroom: judicial speech) status. Paul, by contrast, is writing to those with whom he has a close personal relationship (note, e.g., the heavy use of the vocative "brothers") and from an authoritative position as an apostle of Jesus Christ (note, e.g., his self-descriptions in the letter openings).

Finally, the purpose of rhetorical theory was to aid the *creation* of speeches, not the interpretation of these oral discourses. Due caution ought to be exercised, therefore, in applying the rules of ancient rhetoric retrogressively to Paul's letters for the purpose of interpretation.[46]

3. Conclusion

Although the essay of Merk contains many helpful insights into a variety of exegetical issues found in 1 Thess 2:1-12, I disagree with his conclusion that the central concern of Paul in this passage is to present himself as a model to the Thessalonian church. Although such a concern may well be part of the apostle's aim, the evidence strongly suggests that his primary purpose here is apologetic. In a context where the "fellow citizens" of the Thessalonian believers were not only oppressing the church but also questioning the motives of their leader, Paul begins the letter-body with an autobiographical reminder of his original ministry among them that in a pointed fashion defends his integrity, and so reestablishes the trust and confidence of his readers. This renewed trust in the apostle (and thus also in his message) would not only encourage the Thessalonians believers to stand firm in the midst of their suffering but also ensure that they would obey the instructions which he would yet give them in this letter.

With regard to the larger question of method, significant objections can be raised to the current widespread practice of taking the ancient

Paul's style provided by Eduard Norden, *Die antike Kunstprosa: Vom vi. Jahrhundert v. Chr. bis in die Zeit der Renaissance* (3rd ed.; Darmstadt: Wissenschaftliche Buchgesellschaft [1898], 1958), 501-6.

46. This concern is raised by both Porter, "Rhetorical Categories in Pauline Literature," 105 and Anderson, *Ancient Rhetorical Theory and Paul,* 256.

Graeco-Roman rules for speech and applying them in a direct and indiscriminate manner to the interpretation of Paul's letters. Although Paul is very much involved with the general "art of persuasion" and employs in his letters a variety of literary or so-called "rhetorical" devices, there is no compelling evidence that he employed the classical rules of Graeco-Roman rhetoric in the writing of his letters. This conclusion does not necessarily mean that there is nothing to be gained by comparing Paul's letters with the rhetorical practices that were so much a part of the Graeco-Roman culture in which he preached and wrote.[47] It does, however, seriously undermine the conviction held by many interpreters today that Paul's letters ought to be interpreted through the grid of the ancient rhetorical rules and also calls into question the accompanying belief that this method better than any other holds the hermeneutical key that will unlock the true meaning of the apostle's writings.

---

47. See the brief but helpful comments of Anderson, *Ancient Rhetorical Theory and Paul*, 255.

PART 2

1 THESSALONIANS:
THE METHODOLOGICAL DEBATE

Thanksgivings in 1 Thessalonians 1–3

Jan Lambrecht

In his 1983 article "Saint Paul and the Apostolic Letter Tradition," John Lee White states that "Paul was the first to popularize the letter as an authoritative form of communication within Christianity."[1] He calls Paul the "founder of the apostolic letter" and stresses "the religious nature of the epistolary setting."[2] This last point follows from the fact that Paul's letters were meant to be read in public Christian gatherings. Besides considering the liturgical influences on the style, it is a rather common approach today to reckon with the rhetorical character of Paul's letters.[3] Therefore, possi-

---

1. J. L. White, "Saint Paul and the Apostolic Letter Tradition," *CBQ* 45 (1983): 433-44, here 436. See H. Koester, "I Thessalonians — Experiment in Christian Writing," in *Continuity and Discontinuity in Church History* (Festschrift G. H. Williams; SHCT 19; Leiden: Brill, 1979), 33-44: ". . . this carefully composed writing is actually an experiment in the composition of literature which signals the momentous entry of Christianity into the literary world of antiquity. The consequences of this experiment cannot be underestimated. . . . I Thessalonians testifies to the creative moment, it is 'the Christian letter in the making'" (33).

2. White, "Saint Paul," 437.

3. We may here refer to our recent study, "Rhetorical Criticism and the New Testament," *BPTF* 50 (1989): 239-53. See J. L. White, "New Testament Epistolary Literature in the Framework of Ancient Epistolography," in *ANRW* 25.2, 1733: "To be sure, the apostle Paul, who is the primary model for all NT epistles, is influenced by rhetorical traditions, like the *diatribe*, by the Jewish/Christian homily and by other forms of persuasion, common to a more literary style." More specifically for 1 Thessalonians, see R. Jewett, *The Thessalonian Correspondence: Pauline Rhetoric and Millenarian Piety* (FFNT; Philadelphia: Fortress, 1986), and B. C. Johanson, *To All the Brethren: A Text-Linguistic and Rhetorical Approach to I Thessalonians* (ConBNT 16; Stockholm: Almqvist & Wiksell, 1987).

ble liturgical as well as rhetorical impacts must be duly taken into consideration in the analysis of 1 Thessalonians 1–3.

One can assume that during his second missionary journey Paul's stay in Thessalonica was rather brief, even if probably somewhat longer than the four weeks that Acts 17:1-10 seems to suggest.[4] After his departure Paul was in Athens, and from there he sent Timothy to Thessalonica. Timothy has returned and is now with Paul in Corinth. He has brought with him good news about the young Christian congregation. Paul very much desires to visit the Thessalonians again, but this is impossible for the time being (see 1 Thess 2:17–3:8). Therefore, he writes a letter, "to be read to all the brethren" (5:27), in which he thanks God extensively for all the blessings and good tidings. Yet the content of this letter manifests other reasons for writing. The Christians suffer persecutions; they grieve because of those who have died: Do deceased fellow Christians have a future? The Thessalonians need exhortation. Moreover, Paul must defend himself.

As far as we know, 1 Thessalonians is Paul's first letter; it is the oldest New Testament written document that has been preserved. "Wie kaum ein anderer Brief steht das kleine Schreiben an die Thessalonicher den Anfängen der Gemeinde noch unmittelbar nahe. . . . Sein Anliegen ist, die noch junge, bedrohte Gemeinde beim dem ersten Anfang zu erhalten."[5]

The letter can easily be divided into two major parts, the first with thanksgiving and apology (1 Thessalonians 1–3), the second with exhortations and instructions (1 Thessalonians 4–5). In this presentation we are concerned only with the first part. A cursory reading of 1 Thessalonians 1–3 at once reveals a repeated movement from the Thessalonians *(a)* to the writer *(b)* and back again: in the *a* sections the addressees are to the fore, whereas in the *b* sections Paul clearly deals with himself. We may use this movement for the following tentative structuring. After the initial salutation (1:1) we have:

> *a:* Thanksgiving for the Thessalonians' faith and example (1:2-10)
> *b:* Apology with regard to stay in Thessalonica (2:1-12)
> *a:* Thanksgiving for the acceptance of the word (2:13-16)

---

4. See, e.g., the critical remarks of E. Best, *A Commentary on the First and Second Epistles to the Thessalonians* (BNTC; London: Black, 1972), 5-7: "Luke's limitation of the stay to four weeks is incorrect" (7).

5. G. Bornkamm, *Paulus* (UB 119D; Stuttgart: Kohlhammer, 1969), 81.

b: Intentions and actions after departure (2:17–3:8)
a: Thanksgiving for all the joy (3:9-10).

The first half of the letter then ends with a solemn prayer for Paul himself as well as for the Thessalonians (3:11-13).

The question arises whether this provisionally structured overview is correct and, if so, whether it could be more specified and better justified. Furthermore, does structure help us to get a reliable insight into Paul's line of thought? And does it reveal particular aspects of his theology? Let us start with the thanksgiving sections in 1 Thessalonians 1–3.

1. A Threefold Thanksgiving

As is well known, in 1 Thessalonians Paul thanks God three times by means of the following sentences, each of which forms a distinct grammatical unit: 1:2-5, 2:13, and 3:9-10.

a. A First Grammatical Analysis

In the first and second thanksgivings Paul uses three identical features: (1) the principal verb εὐχαριστοῦμεν; (2) the dative object: τῷ θεῷ; and (3) a temporal adverb: πάντοτε or ἀδιαλείπτως. In both thanksgivings a fourth feature provides the reason for gratitude, respectively περὶ πάντων ὑμῶν and a ὅτι clause. The first thanksgiving is further expanded by means of three participial clauses (1:2b-5) introduced by μνείαν ποιούμενοι (v 2), μνημονεύοντες (v 3) and εἰδότες (v 4, explained at the end by the motivating ὅτι clause of v 5). The participles modify the principal verb. In the much shorter second thanksgiving the ὅτι clause (2:13) also elaborates the motivation.

The third thanksgiving is somewhat special. Grammatically it is a rhetorical question. The main verb is replaced by the expression τίνα . . . εὐχαριστίαν δυνάμεθα . . . ἀνταποδοῦναι (3:9). The second feature, the dative τῷ θεῷ, is present, but the third, the adverb of time, had to be omitted since Paul speaks here of one specific motive: all the joy he feels for the Thessalonians at Timothy's return.[6] This concrete situation con-

---

6. See P. T. O'Brien, *Introductory Thanksgivings in the Letters of Paul* (NovTSup 49;

stitutes precisely the fourth feature. The reason for giving thanks is provided, as in the other thanksgivings, by what the Thessalonians have
done. Regarding this third thanksgiving we must also mention the subordinate participial clause introduced by δεόμενοι; it points forward to
the future: "night and day earnestly praying that we may see you face to
face . . ." (3:10). It strikes the reader that Paul, notwithstanding his concrete, once-only thanking in verse 9, again mentions constant prayer in
verse 10: "night and day."

b. Paul Schubert

In his 1939 monograph *Form and Function of the Pauline Thanksgivings*,
Paul Schubert states that "Paul's epistolary thanksgivings must be considered genuine examples of a definite and widely used Hellenistic
epistographical pattern, which had a precise function on the specific level
of epistolary writing."[7] The thanksgiving is a formal section of most of
Paul's letters; it concludes the letter opening, indicates the purpose of the
letter, and sometimes outlines its basic topics.

Schubert distinguishes two types of thanksgiving in Paul. Four
items are identical in both types: the principal verb of the entire period,
the personal object τῷ θεῷ, a temporal phrase or temporal adverb, and a
pronominal object phrase περὶ (or ὑπὲρ) ὑμῶν.[8] The first type, if complete, possesses three more syntactical units. The fifth unit contains a
temporal participial clause with a temporal adverbial phrase; the sixth a
causal participial clause and/or adverbial phrase; the seventh a subordinate final clause introduced by ἵνα, ὅπως, or εἰς with the infinitive.[9] The
second type, a variant of the first, does not possess participial clauses; its
"final" clause is introduced by the causal ὅτι.[10] According to Schubert

---

Leiden: Brill, 1977), 156: εὐχαριστοῦμεν, "together with the temporal adverbs πάντοτε or
ἀδιαλείπτως, signifies regular thanksgiving. The phrase in question (3:9) is *punctiliar and
particular*, denoting Paul's immediate reaction to Timothy's good news." See also p. 266.

7. P. Schubert, *Form and Function of the Pauline Thanksgivings* (BZNW 20; Berlin:
Töpelmann, 1939), 173.

8. Schubert, *Form and Function*, 63.

9. Schubert, *Form and Function*, especially 53-62.

10. Schubert, *Form and Function*, especially 51-53. "Final" clause here means the last
member, the terminal clause, whereas in the first type it is at the same time a real purpose

1 Thess 1:2-5 belongs to the first type (but the final clause is missing), as does 3:9-10. 1 Thess 2:13 follows the second type (but περὶ ὑμῶν is missing).[11] Schubert, however, refuses to speak of "really three separate thanksgivings" and of the material in between them as "two real digressions."[12] "Indeed, we are forced to view 2,13ff. and 3,9ff. as . . . repetitions, serving to unify formally the entire section from 1,2–3,13."[13] The so-called digressions are "by no means digressions but, from the point of view of form, function and content, are on the contrary fully legitimate and indeed constitutive elements of the general Pauline thanksgiving pattern."[14] For Schubert, "the thanksgiving itself constitutes the main body of 1 Thessalonians. It contains all the primary information that Paul wished to convey."[15] Since, just as in the other letters, the paraenetical section (chaps. 4 and 5) forms but the conclusion, "the thanksgiving *is* the letter."[16] Although such bold affirmations have often been accepted and repeated recently,[17] three critical questions may be asked.

(final) clause. Table II on pp. 54-55 presents an overview of the syntactical units of all the thanksgivings of the *corpus Paulinum* (thus also of Col 1:3-8 and 9-10; 2 Thess 1:2-10, 11-12; 2:13-14; and Eph 1:15-19) and even of passages such as 2 Cor 1:10-11 and Eph 1:15-19, where no strict thanksgivings are present. The discussion of the two types is already to be found on pages 34-39 and continues on pp. 62-67.

11. Schubert, *Form and Function*, 16-27.

12. Schubert, *Form and Function*, 18.

13. Schubert, *Form and Function*, 18. See, e.g., also O'Brien, *Thanksgivings*, 141: "What appeared to be three separate thanksgivings . . . were in fact one introductory thanksgiving in which the basic εὐχαριστῶ-formula was repeated twice, thus unifying the whole section, chapters 1:2 to 3:13." We may compare these passages with the autonomous thanksgiving of 2 Cor 2:14-17 (τῷ δὲ θεῷ χάρις . . .), which interrupts the narrative and is not resumptive at all. See J. Lambrecht, "Structure and Line of Thought in 2 Cor 2:14–4:6," *Bib* 64 (1983): 344-80, 347-53; M. E. Thrall, "A Second Thanksgiving Period in II Corinthians," *JSNT* 16 (1982): 101-24, 113-19. F. O. Francis, "The Form and Function of the Opening and Closing Paragraphs of James and I John," *ZNW* 61 (1970): 110-26, 111-17, investigates the cultivation of a twofold opening form (e.g., a double thanksgiving or blessing) in the Hellenistic letter.

14. Schubert, *Form and Function*, 18.

15. Schubert, *Form and Function*, 26.

16. Schubert, *Form and Function*, 26.

17. See especially O'Brien, *Thanksgivings*. On pp. 4-15 this author presents the previous research (for Schubert see pp. 6-8 and the assessment and outlook on pp. 10-15). He discusses 1 Thessalonians 1–3 on pp. 141-66. See also C. J. Roetzel, *The Letters of Paul: Conversations in Context* (Atlanta: Knox, 1975), 21-22; S. K. Stowers, *Letter Writing in Greco-Roman Antiquity* (LEC 5; Philadelphia: Westminster, 1986), 21-22.

Do chapters 4–5 function as a mere conclusion? Must we postulate two types of thanksgiving in Paul and, therefore, in 1 Thessalonians 1–3? In what sense do the digressions of 1 Thessalonians 1–3 belong to the thanksgivings? The answer to the first question can be brief. Since 1 Thessalonians lacks a so-called dogmatic part and, moreover, since chapters 4–5 contain not only paraenesis but also "dogmatic" information (see 4:13-18; 5:1-11), it would seem advisable not to exclude the long chapters 4 and 5 from the body of the letter, especially if "body" is understood in a nontechnical sense.[18]

c. One Pauline Thanksgiving Pattern?

A careful reconsideration of those genuine Pauline writings that contain one or more thanksgivings[19] may both simplify and nuance Schubert's structural proposals. No more than three basic constituents are present:

1. the stable "kernel" of the main clause (present);
2. the reason for gratitude, that is, the "memory" (past); and
3. a "petition" (future).

1. The first constituent, the "kernel," contains three elements: the principal verb, God, and a temporal adverb.

(a) The initial item varies between εὐχαριστῶ (Rom 1:8; 1 Cor 1:4; Phil 1:3; Philem 4), εὐχαριστοῦμεν (1 Thess 1:2; 2:13), and εὐχαριστίαν δυνάμεθα . . . ἀνταποδοῦναι (1 Thess 3:9).[20] This principal verb (or verbal expression) is in the present: a "continuous" present ("always, without interruption").

---

18. See C. J. Bjerkelund, *Parakalô. Form, Funktion und Sinn der parakalô-Sätze in den paulinischen Briefen* (BTN 1; Oslo: Universitetsforlaget, 1967), 134: "Will man an der traditionellen Dreiteilung der paulinischen Briefe, Introduktion, Corpus, Abschluss, festhalten, dann besteht unserer Auffassung nach das Corpus aus 4,1–5,11." See now also Johanson, *To All the Brethren,* pp. 61-67, who defends a broad concept of the letter-body (1:2–5:24).

19. Rom 1:8-10; 1 Cor 1:4-9; Phil 1:3-11; 1 Thess 1:2-5; 2:13; 3:9-10; Philem 4-7.

20. See Ps 115:3 (LXX): τί ἀποδώσω τῷ κυρίῳ περὶ πάντων. . . . In this presentation we refer to Paul, although the first person plural may (sometimes) include Paul's fellow workers.

(b) The second item has a simple τῷ θεῷ (1 Cor 1:4; 1 Thess 1:2; 2:13; 3:9) or τῷ θεῷ μου (Rom 1:8 — "through Jesus Christ" is added; 1 Cor 1:4 — variant reading; Phil 1:3; Philem 4).

(c) The temporal adverb is πάντοτε (1 Cor 1:4; 1 Thess 1:2; Philem 4; Phil 1:3-4 reads: ἐπὶ πάσῃ τῇ μνείᾳ ὑμῶν πάντοτε ἐν πάσῃ δεήσει μου) or ἀδιαλείπτως (1 Thess 2:13), but it is absent in Romans and 1 Thessalonians 3.

2. The second constituent, the "memory," is rather composite, yet its different elements are better taken together.

(a) Almost every thanksgiving starts by indicating the addressees as the reason for gratitude: περί or ὑπὲρ (πάντων) ὑμῶν (Phil 1:3-4 states: "I thank my God," ἐπὶ πάσῃ τῇ μνείᾳ ὑμῶν). That expression is absent in the repeated thanksgiving of 1 Thess 2:13 (but see the second person plural in the ὅτι clause) and in Philem 4 (but see μνείαν σου ποιούμενος).

(b) Some thanksgivings continue then with a temporal participial clause and/or the mention of prayer. 1 Thess 1:2 reads: μνείαν ποιούμενοι ἐπὶ τῶν προσευχῶν ἡμῶν[21] (see almost the same wording in Philem 4). Romans 1 starts a new sentence in verse 9: "For God is my witness, whom I serve with my spirit in the gospel of his Son, ὡς ἀδιαλείπτως μνείαν ὑμῶν ποιοῦμαι πάντοτε ἐπὶ τῶν προσευχῶν μου." Phil 1:4 has μετὰ χαρᾶς τὴν δέησιν ποιούμενος. Such a syntactical unit is absent from 1 Cor 1:4 as well as from 1 Thess 2:13 and 3:9. Remembering (or praying) qualifies the act of thanking. Paul thanks God while and because he actually remembers the past (and present) of his addressees;[22] he does it during his prayers.[23]

(c) The specific grounds or reasons for Paul's gratitude can be introduced in different ways: by causal participles (μνημονεύοντες and εἰδότες in 1 Thess 1:3-4; ἀκούων in Philem 5) or by ἐπί and dative indicating mo-

---

21. Here and in Rom 1:9 ἀδιαλείπτως has a temporal sense. It remains uncertain whether ἀδιαλείπτως (end of 1 Thess 1:2) qualifies ποιούμενοι or μνημονεύοντες.

22. M. H. Bolkestein, *De brieven aan de Tessalonicenzen* (De prediking van het NT; Nijkerk: Callenbach, 1974), 22-23, appropriately mentions that "remembering" possesses an OT background. He adds: "Paulus 'gedenkt' de gemeente in de verwachting dat God haar 'gedenkt'" (23).

23. It is not impossible that within this second constituent, which gratefully recalls the past, the motif of "prayer" already points forward to the future and thus announces the third constituent. It would seem that J. H. Roberts, "Transitional Techniques to the Letter Body in the 'corpus Paulinum,'" in *A South African Perspective on the New Testament* (Festschrift B. M. Metzger; ed. J. H. Petzer and P. J. Hartin; Leiden: Brill, 1986), 187-201, separates thanksgiving and prayer too much (see, e.g., pp. 188, 191, and 192).

tives (1 Cor 1:4; Phil 1:5; 1 Thess 3:9). The reasons can also be contained in a ὅτι clause (Rom 1:8; 1 Cor 1:5-7; 1 Thess 1:5; 2:13).[24]

3. Most thanksgivings also possess the third constituent, a "petition" for the future (or its equivalent). In Rom 1:10 εἴ πως follows a δεόμενος; verses 11-12 further explain Paul's desires concerning the future. In Phil 1:6-7 Paul states: "πεποιθὼς αὐτὸ τοῦτο, ὅτι he who began a good work in you will bring it to completion at the day of Jesus Christ; as it is right for me . . ."; verses 8-11 then elaborate Paul's intention. In 1 Thess 3:10 we read: νυκτὸς καὶ μέρας ὑπερεκπερισσοῦ δεόμενοι εἰς τὸ ἰδεῖν . . . καὶ καταρτίσαι; the grammatically independent verses 11-13 become a prayer in wish-form. In Philem 6 the petition is introduced by a simple ὅπως.[25] Such a petition, however, is missing in 1 Cor 1:4-6 (but see the eschatological outlook in vv 7-9), and also, but understandably, in 1 Thess 1:2-5 and 2:13 (see 3:11-13!).[26]

24. In Rom 1:8 and 1 Cor 1:5 the ὅτι appears to be causal. Even if this is not the case in 1 Thess 1:5 and 2:13, ὅτι perhaps indicating the content of "knowing" and "giving thanks," the clauses certainly present the reasons for gratitude. J. E. Frame, *Epistles of St. Paul to the Thessalonians* (ICC; Edinburgh: T. & T. Clark, 1912), e.g., prefers the causal sense both in 2:13 (107) and in 1:5: "We infer your (pretemporal) election from the fact that (ὅτι = 'because' . . .) the Spirit was in us who preached . . ." (78-79).

25. Schubert, *Form and Function,* writes: "Philem 4-7 is the briefest of all the full (= first type) thanksgivings" (12). "The 'normal' word order is more effectively exemplified by the thanksgiving of Phm, which for this reason was chosen as the 'standard'" (63).

26. We may add a few remarks on the thanksgivings of 2 Thess 1:3-12 and 2:13-14 and on Col 1:3-8:

	2 Thess 1	2 Thess 2	Col 1
1a	3	13	3
b	3	13	3
c	3	13	(3?)
2a	3	13	(3?)
b	—	—	3
c	3-10	13-14	4-8
3	11-12	—	(9ff.)

In the two thanksgivings of 2 Thess 1 a, b, c and 2a are almost identical. There is no verb of remembering nor reference to prayer (2b). In both cases the reason is introduced by ὅτι. In the first thanksgiving the "petition" (3) is a new sentence with προσευχόμεθα . . . ἵνα. In both thanksgivings the eschatological dimension is very prominent; see 1:11-12 and 2:13-14.

With regard to Col 1:3-8 one must notice that the expression πάντοτε περὶ ὑμῶν προσευχόμενοι most probably forms 2b (then there is no 1c with πάντοτε nor 2a with περὶ ὑμῶν). From v 9 onward we have a new sentence: the author prays for the future well-being of the Colossians.

We may schematically present our findings in the following tables:

Table 1 — Structure of Pauline Thanksgivings

1 "Kernel" (present): a I thank;
                                b God;
                                c always.

2 "Memory" (past): a for you;
                                b remembering (you) in my prayers;
                                c specific reasons.

3 "Petition" (future).

	Rom 1	1 Cor 1	Phil 1	1 Thess 1	1 Thess 2	1 Thess 3	Philem
1a	8	4	3	2	13	9	4
b	8	4	3	2	13	9	4
c	—	4	3-4	2	13	—	4
2a	8	4	4	2	—	9	—
b	9-10	—	4	2	—	—	4
c	8-9	4-6	5	3-5	13	9	5
3	10	(7-9)	6-7	—	—	10	6

Table 2 — Pauline Thanksgivings Structured

Rom 1:8, 9-10

1a   8 Πρῶτον μὲν εὐχαριστῶ

b   τῷ θεῷ μου διὰ Ἰησοῦ Χριστοῦ

c

2a   περὶ πάντων ὑμῶν

c   ὅτι ἡ πίστις ὑμῶν καταγγέλλεται ἐν ὅλῳ τῷ κόσμῳ. 9 μάρτυς γάρ
      μού ἐστιν ὁ θεός, ᾧ λατρεύω ἐν τῷ
      πνεύματί μου ἐν τῷ εὐαγγελίῳ τοῦ υἱοῦ αὐτοῦ,

b   ὡς ἀδιαλείπτως μνείαν ποιοῦμαι 10 πάντοτε ἐπὶ τῶν προσευχῶν
      μου

3   δεόμενος εἴ πως ἤδη ποτὲ εὐοδωθήσομαι ἐν τῷ θελήματι τοῦ θεοῦ
      ἐλθεῖν πρὸς ὑμᾶς.

1 Cor 1:4-6

1a 4 Εὐχαριστῶ
b τῷ θεῷ μου
c πάντοτε
2a περὶ ὑπῶν
b
c ἐπὶ τῇ χάριτι τοῦ θεοῦ τῇ δοθείσῃ ὑμῖν ἐν Χριστῷ Ἰησοῦ, 5 ὅτι ἐν
παντὶ ἐπλουτίσθητε ἐν αὐτῷ, ἐν παντὶ λόγῳ καὶ πάσει γνώσει,
6 καθὼς τὸ μαρτύριον τοῦ Χριστοῦ ἐβεβαιώθη ἐν ὑμῖν,
(?3 7 ὥστε ὑμᾶς μὴ ὑστερεῖσθαι ἐν μηδενὶ χαρίσματι ἀπεκδεχομένους
τὴν ἀποκάλυψιν τοῦ κυρίου ἡμῶν Ἰησοῦ Χριστοῦ: 8 ὅς ... 9 ...
τοῦ κυρίου ἡμῶν.)

Phil 1:3-7

1a 3 Εὐχαριστῶ
b τῷ θεῷ μου
c ἐπὶ πάσῃ τῇ μνείᾳ ὑμῶν 4 πάντοτε ἐν πάσῃ δεήσει μου
2a ὑπὲρ πάντων ὑμῶν,
b μετὰ χαρᾶς τὴν δέησιν ποιούμενος
c 5 ἐπὶ τῇ κοινωνίᾳ ὑμῶν εἰς τὸ εὐαγγέλιον ἀπὸ τῆς πρώτης ἡμέρας
ἄχρι τοῦ νῦν,
3 6 πεποιθὼς αὐτὸ τοῦτο, ὅτι ὁ ἐναρξάμενος ἐν ὑμῖν ἔργον ἀγαθὸν
ἐπιτελέσει ἄχρι ἡμέρας Χριστοῦ Ἰησοῦ· 7 καθώς ἐστιν δίκαιον ἐμοὶ
τοῦτο φρονεῖν ὑπὲρ πάντων ὑμῶν, διὰ τὸ ἔχειν με ἐν τῇ καρδίᾳ
ὑμᾶς, ἔν τε τοῖς δεσμοῖς μου καὶ ἐν τῇ ἀπολογίᾳ καὶ βεβαιώσει τοῦ
εὐαγγελίου συγκοινωνούς μου τῆς χάριτος πάντας ὑμᾶς ὄντας.

1 Thess 1:2-5

1a 2 Εὐχαριστοῦμεν
b τῷ θεῷ
c πάντοτε
2a περὶ πάντων ὑμῶν
b μνείαν ποιούμενοι ἐπὶ τῶν προσευχῶν ἡμῶν, ἀδιαλείπτως
c 3 μνημονεύοντες ὑμῶν τοῦ ἔργου τῆς πίστεως καὶ τοῦ κόπου τῆς
ἀγάπης καὶ τῆς ὑπομονῆς τῆς ἐλπίδος τοῦ κυρίου ἡμῶν Ἰησοῦ
Χριστοῦ ἔμποσθεν τοῦ θεοῦ καὶ πατρὸς ὑμῶν, 4 εἰδότες, ἀδελφοὶ
ἠγαπημένοι ὑπὸ [τοῦ] θεοῦ, τὴν ἐκλογὴν ὑμῶν, 5 ὅτι τὸ εὐαγγέλιον
ἡμῶν οὐκ ἐγενήθη εἰς ὑμᾶς ἐν λόγῳ μόνον ἀλλὰ καὶ ἐν δυνάμει καὶ
ἐν πνεύματι ἁγίῳ καὶ [ἐν] πληροφορίᾳ πολλῇ, καθὼς οἴδατε οἷοι
ἐγενήθημεν [ἐν] ὑμῖν δι᾽ ὑμᾶς.

3

1 Thess 2:13

1a 13 Καὶ διὰ τοῦτο καὶ ἡμεῖς εὐχαριστοῦμεν
 b τῷ θεῷ
 c ἀδιαλείπτως,
2a
 b
 c ὅτι παραλαβόντες λόγον ἀκοῆς παρ' ἡμῶν τοῦ θεοῦ ἐδέξασθε οὐ
    λόγον ἀνθρώπων ἀλλὰ καθώς ἐστιν ἀληθῶς λόγον θεοῦ, ὃς καὶ
    ἐνεργεῖται ἐν ὑμῖν τοῖς πιστεύουσιν.
3

1 Thess 3:9-10

1a 9 Τίνα γὰρ εὐχαριστίαν δυνάμεθα
 b τῷ θεῷ ἀνταποδοῦναι
 c
2a περὶ ὑμῶν
 b
 c ἐπὶ πάσῃ τῇ χαρᾷ ᾗ χαίρομεν δι' ὑμᾶς ἔμπροσθεν τοῦ θεοῦ ἡμῶν,
3   10 νυκτὸς καὶ ἡμέρας ὑπερεκπερισσοῦ δεόμενοι εἰς τὸ ἰδεῖν ὑμῶν
    τὸ πρόσωπον καὶ καταρτίσαι τὰ ὑστερήματα τῆς πίστεως ὑμῶν;

Philem 4-6

1a 4 Εὐχαριστῶ
 b τῷ θεῷ μου
 c πάντοτε
2a
 b μνείαν σου ποιούμενος ἐπὶ τῶν προσευχῶν μου,
 c 5 ἀκούων σου τὴν ἀγάπην καὶ τὴν πίστιν, ἣν ἔχεις πρὸς τὸν κύριον
    Ἰησοῦν καὶ εἰς πάντας τοὺς ἁγίους,
3   6 ὅπως ἡ κοινωνία τῆς πίστεώς σου ἐνεργὴς γένηται ἐν ἐπιγνώσει
    παντὸς ἀγαθοῦ τοῦ ἐν ἡμῖν εἰς Χριστόν.

d. Conclusions

From our analysis several conclusions can be drawn. First, "the thanksgiving structure is characterized by a basic bipolarity, a double focus around which all thoughts center: the addressant and the addressee."[27] Paul tells the Thessalonians that his thanking, directed to God, occurs in his prayers: to give thanks is to pray. Second, Paul provides us with an actual thanksgiving report. Thanksgiving essentially means remembering the past. Moreover, at the end it almost spontaneously becomes asking for the future. Whether Paul intentionally applied this simple but impressive three-dimensional time structure is hard to say. This may have been the result of a subconscious compulsion. Third, there can be no doubt that Paul uses typical vocabulary with more or less fixed expressions in a fairly stereotyped order. Paul is, however, anything but a slave of a schematic pattern. He freely varies words as well as constructions. He can omit elements; he breaks off, interrupts, and repeats; he sometimes changes the order. There is no need at all to distinguish with Schubert two major types of Pauline thanksgiving.[28]

The first three conclusions concern all Pauline thanksgivings. A fourth conclusion brings us back to 1 Thessalonians 1–3. In the light of the presence of the third constituent, the "petition," in 3:9-10 we easily understand its absence in the first two thanksgivings. So also the presence of elements in the first thanksgiving of 1:2-5 explains those missing from 2:13. As already stated, 3:9 is strictly speaking not a repetition of the first two thanksgivings. A fifth conclusion must not be omitted. That Paul freely spreads out his thanksgiving over the three chapters in no way pleads against the integrity of 1 Thessalonians. One remains somewhat baffled at the ease with which certain scholars use the three thanksgivings as an argument for their hypothetical conflation of two letters or a so-called interpolation of 2:13-16.[29]

27. Schubert, *Form and Function,* 37. This author very much stresses the epistolary situation over and against a so-called liturgical form (e.g., "I thank you, God . . ."). He formulates "the most important thesis" of his study as follows: "The Pauline thanksgivings are characteristically and basically epistolary in form and function" (38).

28. Schubert, *Form and Function,* 181, states that "both Pauline types . . . have their parallels in the papyrus documents." This is a rather misleading conclusion since a fair number of Schubert's items are rarely present in those papyrus letters.

29. See R. F. Collins, "Apropos the Integrity of I Thess," *ETL* 65 (1979): 67-106; now also in *The Thessalonian Correspondence* (ed. R. F. Collins; BETL 87; Leuven: Leuven University Press–Peeters, 1990), 96-135, especially 114-24 (The Compilation Theories) and 97-114 (The Interpolation Theories). For more recent references see in the same volume pp. 73-74 and 14-15. See also Jewett, *Thessalonian Correspondence,* 31-36. Koester, *"Experiment,"* 38, n. 12, writes: "Any attempt to assign part of I Thess 1:2–3:13 to two different letters . . . disregards the careful composition. . . ." Does such a statement not plead against his own acceptance of 2:13-16 as an interpolation?

A proof of redactional freedom can be found in the three different ways in which Paul introduces the specific reasons (2c) in 1 Thessalonians: two participles (1:3-4), ὅτι (2:13), and ἐπί (3:9). One must realize that 1 Thessalonians is Paul's first letter and that Paul is here probably in the process of "creating" his structured thanksgiving. It would seem methodologically wrong to start, as Schubert does, with the later letters that provide the standard types and then to state that 1 Thessalonians contains a "highly complex though formally orthodox thanksgiving."[30] When Paul composed 1 Thessalonians, that "formal orthodoxy" did most probably not yet exist.

A further proof of Paul's epistolary liberty is provided by his digressions. Since Paul, in 1:6-10 as well as in 2:14-16, elaborates in independent sentences on the Thessalonians' faith and their exemplary Christian life, it seems preferable to consider these passages as still pertaining, admittedly in a loose way, to the thanksgivings. As will be shown in greater detail in the next paragraph, this also applies, but in a still much looser way, to the passages 2:1-12 and 2:17–3:8.

We must not forget 3:11-13.[31] It has already been said that within the threefold thanksgiving only 3:10, "a petitionary prayer report," belongs to the third constituent and clearly looks forward to the future. Therefore, "the movement from verse 9 to verse 10 marks a major turning-point in the whole letter."[32] The sentence comes to an end in verse 10. Between verse 10 and verse 11 there is a shift. From verse 11 onward Paul no longer

---

30. *Form and Function,* 23. See our n. 25 for Schubert's comment on the standard form of Philem 4-7. Koester, *"Experiment,"* 38-39, very much stresses Paul's creativity. He calls 1 Thess 1:2–3:13 a proem in which the general form of a traditional genre is still visible: (1) remembrance of past relationships (1:2-10); (2) explanation of the writer's behavior (2:1-12); and (3) discussion of the present situation (2:17–3:13). But he notes: "However, in each instance Paul forces the traditional topos to convey a message which cannot be contained in the conventional frame" (36). See also H. Koester, "Apostel und Gemeinde in den Briefen an die Thessalonicher," in *Kirche* (Festschrift G. Bornkamm; ed. D. Lührmann and G. Strecker; Tübingen: Mohr, 1980), 287-98, especially 289-92.

31. See R. Jewett, "The Form and Function of the Homiletic Benediction," *ATR* 51 (1969): 18-34; G. P. Wiles, *Paul's Intercessory Prayers: The Significance of the Intercessory Prayer Passages in the Letters of St Paul* (SNTSMS 24; Cambridge: Cambridge University Press, 1974), 52-63; R. F. Collins, "Paul at Prayer," *Emmanuel* 88 (1982): 412-19; now also in Collins, *Studies on the First Letter to the Thessalonians* (BETL 66; Leuven: Leuven University Press–Peeters, 1984), 356-64, 360-62.

32. O'Brien, *Thanksgivings,* 157 (with references to other exegetes).

reports on prayer but actually prays. "It is characteristic of Paul's letters that he frequently slips into some short prayer."[33] Verses 11-13 constitute a wish-prayer: Αὐτὸς δὲ ὁ θεὸς καὶ πατὴρ ἡμῶν καὶ ὁ κύριος ἡμῶν Ἰησοῦς κατευθύναι τὴν ὁδὸν ἡμῶν πρὸς ὑμᾶς. . . . Since in verses 11 and 12 Paul expands the intentions already mentioned in verse 10, it is most appropriate to consider this wish-prayer as pertaining to the "petition" constituent, if not grammatically, certainly from the point of view of content. Moreover, one should duly measure the solemnity and all-encompassing character of this eschatological prayer climax: God the Father and the Lord Jesus, Paul and the Thessalonians, growth and abundance in love to one another and to all, purity and holiness before God "at the coming of our Lord Jesus with all his saints" (v 13).[34]

Recent studies warn us to see the Pauline thanksgiving only as the equivalent of the rather rare examples in the Greek letter.[35] There may have been Old Testament and Jewish influences as well.[36] James M. Robinson mentions "Schuberts wohl gelungene Beweisführung für den brieflichen und hellenistischen Charakter" of the Pauline thanksgivings but detects also "eine formale Verbindung" of them "mit jüdischen . . . und früh-christlichen Gebeten."[37] Already in the OT and Judaism a blessing of

---

33. L. Morris, *The First and Second Epistles to the Thessalonians* (NICNT; Grand Rapids: Eerdmans, 1959), 110.

34. See at the end of the letter: "May αὐτὸς δὲ ὁ θεὸς τῆς εἰρήνης sanctify you wholly; and may your spirit and soul and body be kept sound and blameless at the coming of our Lord Jesus Christ. He who calls you is faithful, and he will do it" (5:23-24).

35. See the state of the question in W. G. Doty, *Letters in Primitive Christianity* (GBS; Philadelphia: Fortress: 1973), 31-33. Best, *Thessalonians,* 65, rightly notes: "The 'thanksgiving', though occurring sometimes, was not a regular part of contemporary letters and Paul would therefore appear to have largely evolved a new form for himself." White, "Saint Paul," 438, underlines a major difference: ". . . a similar thanks-offering phrase to the deity is sometimes found in the letter opening of Hellenistic correspondence but, ordinarily, the thanks is given because the writer himself has been rescued from danger. . . . In the case of Paul, however, thanks is offered because of the activity of his recipients. . . ." See White, "Epistolary Literature," 1741.

36. See references and discussion in O'Brien, *Thanksgivings,* 10-13. B. Rigaux, *Saint Paul et ses lettres. État de la question* (SN.S 2; Paris-Bruges: Desclée de Brouwer, 1962), 169-70, concludes his brief consideration as follows: ". . . il ne semble pas que l'usage épistolaire paulinien de l'action de grâces doive son origine à une influence externe. Mieux vaut penser que Paul, selon une habitude juive, commençait ses discours par une action de grâces et que cet usage de la prédication a passé dans sa correspondence" (170).

37. J. M. Robinson, "Die hodajot-Formel in Gebet und Hymnus des Frühchristen-

God's mighty works often becomes a petition for further graces and mercy. Klaus Berger, too, maintains that the form, content, and function of the thanksgiving in the early Christian letter cannot be deduced completely from the Hellenistic letters. In his opinion, a Christian thanksgiving often functions there as the rhetorical *captatio benevolentiae* in a spoken discourse.[38]

2. Apology and Report

In 2:1 as well as in 2:17 there is a change of perspective, a shift of focus: from addressees to author. In 2:1-12 Paul depicts in great detail his personal way of acting, his attitude during his first stay in Thessalonica; in 2:17–3:8 he further deals with his own desires and decisions in the time period from his departure until the writing of the letter.

a. John L. White

In his doctoral dissertation published in 1972, John Lee White studied the body of the Greek letter.[39] With regard to 1 Thessalonians he first refers to Schubert: "I endorse, heartily, both Schubert's suggestion that the thanksgiving has a singularly important epistolary function and that I Thessalonians does not have a 'body' of doctrinal or practical information like Paul's letters customarily have. I propose, nevertheless, that the

---

tums," in *Apophoreta* (Festschrift E. Haenchen; ed. W. Eltester and F. H. Kettler; BZNW 30; Berlin: Töpelmann, 1964), 194-235, quotation on 202. See, e.g., White, "Epistolary Literature," 1741-42; Johanson, *To All the Brethren*, 68-69; and Roetzel, *Letters*, 22: ". . . the apostle has grafted onto this traditional epistolary form materials from liturgical tradition."

38. K. Berger, "Apostelbrief und apostolische Rede/Zum Formular frühchristlicher Briefe," *ZNW* 65 (1974): 190-231, especially 219-24. We may quote his conclusion: "Die These über die Herkunft der Danksagung aus dem hellenistischen Brief wäre daher erheblich abzuschwächen, Präformiert ist höchstens die Stelle einer Danksagung im Brief . . . , Form, Inhalt und Funktion sind von anderer Art, aber, wo es um captatio geht: gleichwohl aus der antiken Rhetorik verständlich" (224).

39. J. L. White, *The Form and Function of the Body of the Greek Letter: A Study of the Letter-Body in the Non-Literary Papyri and in Paul the Apostle* (SBLDS 2; Missoula, Mont.: Scholars Press, 1972). See also J. L. White, "Greek Documentary Letter Tradition Third Century B.C.E. to Third Century C.E.," *Semeia* 22 (1982): 89-106; and "Epistolary Literature."

body *is* a structural element — though, to be sure, taken up into, shaped by, and logically dependent on, the thanksgiving.[40]

White also agrees with Jack T. Sanders that the disclosure formula of 2:1-2 opens the body of the letter.[41] For White, 2:1–3:13 constitute the whole body and can be divided into four sections: body-opening (2:14), body-middle (2:5-16), body-closing (2:17–3:10), and eschatological climax (3:11-13).[42] Hendrikus W. Boers calls the passage 2:1-12 Paul's "apostolic apology."[43] But such a terminology clearly points to the heading "apostolic *parousia*," which Robert W. Funk proposed for 2:17–3:8.

b. Robert W. Funk

In an article that appeared in the 1967 Festschrift for John Knox, Robert W. Funk detects in Paul's letters the literary genre that he refers to as the "apostolic *parousia*" because in it the apostle's authority is made effective as though he were actually present (see 1 Cor 5:3-5).[44] The results of this study are often referred to. Funk opines that Paul regards his apostolic

---

40. White, *Body,* 116-17.

41. J. T. Sanders, "The Transition from Opening Epistolary Thanksgiving to Body in the Letters of the Pauline Corpus," *JBL* 81 (1962): 348-62, 355-56. In this article Sanders wants "to show that the transition from the εὐχαριστῶ period at the opening of a Pauline letter to the body of the letter is more formally structured than Schubert realized" (348). See also T. Y. Mullins, "Disclosure: A Literary Form in the New Testament," *NovT* 7 (1964): 44-50. J. L. White, "Introductory Formulae in the Body of the Pauline Letter," *JBL* 90 (1971): 91-97, distinguishes six formulae that may introduce the body of the Pauline letter: Disclosure Formula, Request Formula, Joy Expression, Expression of Astonishment, Statement of Compliance, and Formulaic Use of Verb of Hearing or Learning. Both Sanders and White see in 1 Thess 2:1-2 a type of disclosure formula. See White, "Epistolary Literature," 1743-44, and the new proposals in the thorough study of Roberts, "Transitional Techniques," especially 191-96.

42. White, *Body,* 125-27. The "body" proper imparts information; the "body-closing" is rather designed to further personal contact. See also R. W. Funk, *Language, Hermeneutic, and Word of God: The Problem of Language in the New Testament and Contemporary Theology* (New York: Harper, 1966), 270.

43. H. Boers, "The Form Critical Study of Paul's Letters: I Thessalonians as a Case Study," *NTS* 22 (1975-76): 140-58, 152-53, and 158. See also his discussion of Sanders on pp. 143-45 and White on p. 150.

44. R. W. Funk, "The Apostolic 'Parousia': Form and Significance," in *Christian History and Interpretation* (Festschrift J. Knox; ed. F. D. Moule and R. R. Niebuhr; Cambridge: Cambridge University Press, 1967), 249-68.

presence in a threefold way: the letter, the emissary, and his personal presence. These aspects "are media by which Paul makes his apostolic authority effective in the churches."[45] "These items tend to converge in one more or less discrete section of the letter."[46] That section, mostly at the end of the letter-body, possesses a formal structure. Funk analyzes twelve Pauline passages, seven of which represent the apostolic *parousia* proper.[47]

From the example Rom 15:14-33 five elements can be distinguished:[48]

(1) a γράφω ὑμῖν . . . , stating Paul's disposition or purpose in writing (vv 14-15a);
(2) the basis of Paul's apostolic relation to the recipients (vv 15b-21);
(3) implementation of the apostolic *parousia* (vv 22-28);
(4) invocation of divine approval and support for the apostolic *parousia* (vv 30-32a); and
(5) benefit from the apostolic *parousia* (v 32b).

These elements, however, are not present in all texts, nor are they always present in exactly the same sequence. So in 1 Thess 2:17–3:13 only the last

45. See Funk, "Parousia," 249. See also, e.g., White, "Saint Paul": "The implementation of Paul's apostolicity (or of his apostolic *parousia*, as Funk calls it) is, in ascending order of importance, the letter, the dispatch of an emissary, and Paul's own presence" (440). On pp. 441-42 White discusses what for him constitutes a "fourth medium of Paul's authority": ". . . the rehearsal of his past conduct with the recipients and/or his reminder of previous instruction (= the *parenesis*). . . . Regarding this fourth dimension of Paul's apostolicity . . . it is noteworthy that whereas the three preceding aspects of his apostolicity are situational, being directed to the occasion of the letter, the parenetic appeal to the Christian tradition is general in intent . . ." (441). See also White, "Epistolary Literature," 1746-48. It would seem that Koester, "Apostel," 292, underestimates the aspect of apostolic letter presence. On pp. 287-92 of this study he overemphasizes the identity of eschatological faith experience in apostle and congregation.

46. Funk, "Parousia," 249. He writes on p. 226: "Owing to Paul's understanding of the significance of his apostolic presence to his congregations, Paul gathers the items which may be scattered about in the common letter or appended as additional information into one more or less discrete section. . . ."

47. Funk, "Parousia," 258. See the schematic presentation of the twelve examples on pp. 253-54. The seven real passages are: Rom 15:14-33; 1 Cor 4:14-21; 2 Cor 12:14–13:13; Gal 4:12-20; Phil 2:19-24; 1 Thess 2:17–3:13; Philem 21-22.

48. Funk, "Parousia," 252-53. See the discussion in Boers, "Case Study," 146-53, especially 146-49, and White, "Epistolary Literature," 1744-50.

three appear: (3) implementation (2:17–3:5), (4) invocation (3:10a, 11-13), and (5) benefit (3:6-9, 10b).[49]

The implementation of the apostolic *parousia* is the major theme of the genre. It can be further divided into:

- Paul's desire to see the Thessalonians (2:17b);
- his wish to come to them (2:18a);
- the hindrance (2:18b);
- the dispatch of an emissary (3:2-5);
- his prayer for a personal visit (3:10a).

So the complete movement is present: "Paul is eager to come, hopes to come, but he has suffered delay, encountered some obstacle, which forces him to send an envoy in the meantime. However, his hopes will eventually be realized, God willing. . . ."[50]

c. Franz Schnider and Werner Stenger

In 1987 Franz Schnider and Werner Stenger published their well-documented *Studien zum neutestamentlichen Briefformular.*[51] For Schnider and Stenger,

---

49. 1 Thess 2:17–3:8 was called a "travelogue" in R. W. Funk, *Language, Hermeneutic, and Word of God*, 269.

50. Funk, "Parousia," 260. See, e.g., T. Holtz, *Der erste Brief an die Thessalonicher* (EKKNT; Zürich: Benziger Verlag; Neukirchen: Neukirchener Verlag, 1986), 114: "Auch wenn man in der Annahme eines festen Schemas vorsichtig urteilen wird: sprechen die angeführten Gründe doch für einen einheitlichen Entwurf des ganzen Abschnitts."

51. F. Schnider and W. Stenger, *Studien zum neutestamentlichen Briefformular* (NTTS 11; Leiden: Brill, 1987). We may refer here first to the section "Die briefliche Danksagung" (pp. 42-49). (a) Along with Sanders and White, these authors see 1 Thess 2:1-2 as a disclosure formula. This type of formula enables us in all genuine Pauline letters "die brieflichen Danksagungen gegenüber dem folgenden Kontext abzugrenzen" (43). The formula is introduced by two constitutive elements: "Brethren" and "a reference to the addressees' knowing." One should keep in mind that "die Formel in allen Fällen auch einen *Perspektivenwechsel* markiert. In der brieflichen Danksagang stehen nämlich immer die *Adressaten* im Mittelpunkt der Betrachtung, in dem der Formel folgenden Kontext wird der Blick auf den *Briefschreiber* gelenkt" (44). (b) Like Schubert and O'Brien, they underline "dass die Danksagungen als ganze nicht an Gott gerichtet sind, sondern eher Berichte an die Adressaten über ein die Gemeinde betreffendes Dank- und machmal Bittgebet des Briefschreibers gegenüber Gott darstellen" (47). (c) Like Berger (see n. 38) and many others,

1 Thess 2:1-12 and 2:17–3:8 form a double epistolary recommendation, a twofold "briefliche Selbstempfehlung."[52] They contend that Sanders and White one-sidedly compare Paul's "Briefformular" with that of the ancient private letter. But according to Schnider and Stenger Paul in his letters combines the genres of the written letter and those of the spoken discourse. "Sicher folgt Paulus bei der Abfassung seiner Briefe keinem klassischen Handbuch der Rhetorik, doch nötigt ihn die Adresse seiner Briefe, nicht nur briefstilgemäss sondern auch rhetorisch zu verfahren."[53]

The two authors refer to Wilhelm Wuellner's analysis of Rom 1:13-15. In this passage Paul establishes his ethical quality ("Ethosbeschaffung"!). The passage is an epistolary recommendation.[54] Schnider and Stenger find such recommendations, well delineated, in all Paul's letters.[55] In 1 Thessalonians the "Selbstempfehlung" occurs in Paul's long reference to his "Erstpräsenz" (2:1-12) and further to his plans and decisions after his departure (2:17–3:8).[56]

Whereas by means of the thanksgiving Paul makes the addressees present to himself, in the epistolary recommendation he himself becomes present to the addressees.[57] This kind of recommendation has no epistolary origin;[58] it is occasioned precisely by the discourse function of Paul's letters. The recommendation "dient dazu, dem brieflichen Redner rednerischen Glaubwürdigkeit gegenüber den Adressaten zu verschaffen."[59] Different topics are at home in such a recommendation: the desire to be

---

they emphasize evident rhetorical influences: "Die besondere Form der Rede als Brief führt zur Kombination epistolarer wie rhetorischer Gesichtspunkte. Rhetorisch besehen hat die briefliche Danksagung die Funktion einer captatio benevolentiae des Redners vor seinem Publikum" (51).

52. Schnider-Stenger, *Briefformular,* 50-59: "Die briefliche Selbstempfehlung."

53. Schnider-Stenger, *Briefformular,* 50-52; cited text on 51.

54. Schnider-Stenger, *Briefformular,* 51-52. See W. Wuellner, "Paul's Rhetoric of Argumentation in Romans: An Alternative to the Donfried-Karris Debate over Romans," *CBQ* 38 (1976): 332-51.

55. Besides Rom 1:13-15, Schnider-Stenger, *Briefformular,* 54, indicate 1 Cor 1:10–4:21, 2 Cor 1:8–2:17, Gal 1:8-10, Phil 1:12-30, and Philem 7-9.

56. Schnider-Stenger, *Briefformular,* 53, especially n. 12.

57. Schnider-Stenger, *Briefformular,* 51-52: "Dass die Rede ein Brief ist, hat zur Folge, dass in der *captatio benevolentiae* die Gegenwart der Adressaten beim Briefschreiber, und im Ethos-Abschnitt die Gegenwart des Briefschreibers bei den Adressaten laut wird" (52).

58. Schnider-Stenger, *Briefformular,* 59.

59. Schnider-Stenger, *Briefformular,* 58.

present (by letter, by envoy, in person); prayer for the congregation; appeal to the believers' feelings; references to the first and foundational visit; the writer's exemplary behavior. . . .[60]

d. Evaluation

Nobody should despise these and other analyses of Paul's so-called digressions in 1 Thessalonians 1–3. The indication of obvious breaks at 2:1 (αὐτοὶ γὰρ . . . , ἀδελφοί) and 2:17 (ἡμεῖς δέ, ἀδελφοί), which in the opinion of some authors enables us to delineate the thanksgivings and detect the beginning of new sections, the gathering of striking parallels in Pauline and non-Pauline letters, the careful study of topics with regard to apology and travelogue, the search for stereotyped formulae as well as the determination of their function, the discussion of different aspects of apostolic presence, and even the naming of newly found literary genres: all these efforts, and many more, may be helpful in our understanding of Paul.[61]

The danger, however, lies in exaggeration, in increasingly inventive speciousness, in too much, often farfetched and strained, genre hunting. One might wonder whether Paul consciously starts the body of his letter in 2:1, deliberately composes in an apostolic *parousia* 2:17–3:13, or really intends a twofold epistolary recommendation in 2:1-12 and 2:17–3:8. Even to attribute to Paul a more or less spontaneous, subconscious following of preexisting patterns may constitute here an unwarranted postulate.[62]

---

60. Schnider-Stenger, *Briefformular*, 54-59.

61. F. F. Bruce, *1 and 2 Thessalonians* (WBC 45; Waco: Word, 1982), 54, referring to "apostolic *parousia*, travelogue, body," notes somewhat depressingly: "Such matters of definition and classification vary from one student to the next."

62. We may mention what I. H. Marshall, *1 and 2 Thessalonians* (NCBC; Grand Rapids: Eerdmans, 1983), says on p. 8 with regard to "apostolic apology" and "apostolic *parousia*": "This characterisation of both sections of the letter is justified in terms of their content and the parallels detected with similar material in other letters. However, a closer analysis of the parallels suggests that it is over-precise and perhaps misleading to think of these as two specific 'formal' parts of Pauline epistles which constitute structural elements in them. It would appear rather to be the case that here we have two themes which recur — for good contextual reasons — in various of Paul's letters and in which he naturally expresses himself in similar ways." See Johanson, *To All the Brethren*, 6; Holtz, *Thessalonicher*, 29: "So deutlich sich . . . aber bestimmte formale Strukturen als verhältnismässig feste Bestandteile der paulinischen Briefe aufweisen lassen, so deutlich ist Paulus doch nicht an sie gebunden;

Before appealing to a compulsory obedience to given genres one should always first try a more natural procedure. What in this emotional letter is more self-explanatory than our two autobiographical reports? The Thessalonian addressees would hardly be amazed that Paul after his expanded praise of them refers to his own intentions, his personal behavior, and his mood. The division into two sections, one dealing with his first stay in Thessalonica (2:1-12) and the other narrating what happened after he left (2:17–3:8), is logical, and hardly accidental. Moreover, the contents of these sections are most probably not just conventional literary topics. Paul's sufferings in Philippi and the opposition in Thessalonica (2:2), as well as the Thessalonians' persecutions (2:14) and afflictions (3:3-4), were clearly historical realities. Not only is Paul's telling of his desire to visit the Thessalonians again, his sending of Timothy from Athens, and Timothy's return a true historical report, but there also appears no reason why Paul's description of his visible apostolic endeavors as well as his internal attitude should be merely language sanctioned by style and tradition. Finally, especially in 2:1-12, the highly sensitive tone leads us to see this apology as true to life, to personal attacks.[63]

e. The Structure of 1 Thessalonians 1–3

Granted the foregoing somewhat commonsense reflections, the initial questions return: Is there a definite structure in 1 Thessalonians 1–3? To what degree does the threefold thanksgiving dominate these chapters? What is Paul's train of thought?

---

er gestaltet die Form seiner Briefe entsprechend der jeweiligen Briefsituation"; Roetzel, *Letters*, 22: ". . . Paul does not slavishly follow precut patterns: but creates his own. Moreover, we should not assume that this was a conscious exercise on Paul's part . . ."; Best, *Thessalonians*, 35, with regard to the thanksgiving: "Paul was both too profound a thinker and too excitable a personality to be held within the categories of a fixed pattern of letter writing." Roberts, "Transitional Techniques," 190-91, rightly warns against a too easy use of the term "formula": ". . . I would suggest that we speak rather of techniques than of formulae . . ." (190).

63. See H. Schlier, "Auslegung des 1. Thessalonicherbriefes," *BiLe* 3 (1962): 89-97: "Es scheint uns seltsam, dass der Apostel so scheinbar Selbstverständliches hervorhebt. Aber so selbstverständlich ist es nicht. Und wahrscheinlich nötigen ihn Verdächtigungen in Thessalonich dazu. Vielleicht hatten die Thessalonicher schlimme Erfahrungen mit anderen religiösen Wanderpredigern gemacht. Wahrscheinlich gehören die Anklagen zum Verleumdungsfeldzug seiner Gegner" (91).

It would seem that in 1 Thessalonians 1–3 Paul's thanksgiving is to a certain degree indeed the controlling factor.[64] Yet, there are undeniably expansions, digressions, and interruptions. One must notice how the indication of reasons for gratitude develops both grammatically and ideally into a more independent narrative. This occurs already at 1:6 (καὶ ὑμεῖς μιμηταὶ ἐγενήθητε καὶ τοῦ κυρίου): Paul depicts in 1:6-10 the Thessalonians' conversion faith as an example to others. It occurs again at 2:14 (ὑμεῖς γὰρ μιμηταὶ ἐγενήθητε, ἀδελφοί, "of the churches . . . in Judea"): Paul points in 2:14-16 to the persecutions on the part of the Gentiles and compares them with the Jewish hostility. From the point of view of content these developments certainly still belong to the thanksgivings.

One must further recognize how easily these expansions brought Paul to his personal apologetical narrative (2:1-12: *apologia pro vita sua*) and the subsequent report (2:17–3:8: *apologia pro absentia sua*). At 2:1 and 2:17 there is twice undoubtedly a *Perspektivenwechsel,* from addressees to writer. But even these passages are connected to the thanksgivings. By means of the expression διὰ τοῦτο in 2:13 Paul subsumes what precedes into his gratitude,[65] and the χαρά of 3:9, which is caused by the good news brought by Timothy, provides the concrete ground for a renewed thanksgiving. So, we see: within the broad range of giving thanks Paul moves from the Thessalonians to himself and back again to the Thessalonians, to repeat later the same movement.

64. So the whole of 1 Thessalonians is thanksgiving. Schubert, *Form and Function,* points to its "excessive length." "It comprises, as we have seen, 43 verses, if its maximum possible length be taken into account; and it constitutes almost exactly three-fifths of the entire letter" (17). See O'Brien, *Thanksgivings,* 164. Some commentators hesitate, e.g., Bruce, *Thessalonians,* 43: "It is better to recognize 2:13 as introducing a further thanksgiving: the opening words διὰ τοῦτο καὶ ἡμεῖς εὐχαριστοῦμεν are too emphatic to be merely resumptive of εὐχαριστοῦμεν in 1:2, and the apologia of 2:1-12 is an integral part of the letter and no mere digression."

65. Boers, "Case Study," incorrectly, or at least one-sidedly, translates καὶ διὰ τοῦτο . . . in 2:13: "And for the following (reason) . . ." (151). The expression, however, refers back to what is said in the previous verses, perhaps especially to the end of v 12. See, e.g., Johanson, *To All the Brethren,* 95-96. But see also B. Rigaux, *Saint Paul. Les Épîtres aux Thessaloniciens* (EtB; Paris: Gabalda; Gembloux: Duculot, 1956): "διὰ τοῦτο a toujours une relation à ce qui précède: relation subordinative et consécutive; cependant très souvent la locution introduit un motif spécial et l'ajoute au général déjà mentionné. Ici l'objet spécial est introduit par ὅτι." The καὶ after τοῦτο can be taken either with ἡμεῖς (word order!) or along with εὐχαριστοῦμεν even with διὰ τοῦτο "so that the point is that Paul has a fresh or further reason for thanksgiving: or simply that he wants to emphasise the reason" (437); see, e.g., Marshall, *Thessalonians,* 76-77, quotation on 77.

In the thanksgiving the three time dimensions make themselves felt. Paul informs his Thessalonians how he thanks and prays. Actual thanking, thanking in the present (and always!), automatically contains remembrance of the past. Paul lavishly elaborates on it. The future, however, is not absent either. Paul speaks of future growth in virtue, more abundant love. Above all, there is the eschatological outlook, already at 1:10 (the wrath to come, see 2:16) and 2:12 (God's kingdom), but especially in 3:13 (Jesus' *parousia;* see 1:10 and 2:19).

Present, past, and future, as well as the double focus of addressees and writer in their relation to God and Jesus Christ, appear to have been the structuring factors of Paul's thought in 1 Thessalonians 1–3. Of course, over and against the first thanksgiving in 1:2-5, the thanksgiving of 2:13 is repetitive and, just as the first, rather static ("always, constantly"). The third of 3:9-10 refers to a more advanced point in history, a recent, peculiar event and Paul's joy at the return of Timothy. So also, a progressive trend in time is secured by the report of 2:17–3:8 after that of 2:1-12.

Robert Jewett distinguishes three types of outlines: thematic (topical), epistolary (e.g., opening, body, and closing), and rhetorical (e.g., *exordium, narratio, probatio,* and *peroratio*).[66] Must our outline remain "adequate" in the strict sense, so much so that we cannot use thematic divisions within an epistolary frame? The answer to this question is hardly positive, for two reasons. First, the body of each Pauline letter possesses its own specific content. Second, Paul himself does not appear to follow given structures. On the condition that one does not completely separate nor unduly isolate the individual passages, the division given at the beginning of this presentation holds:

1:1: salutation
    a 1:2-10: thanksgiving
        b 2:1-12: apological report
    a 2:13-16: thanksgiving
        b 2:17–3:8: report on the intervening period
    a 3:9-10: thanksgiving
3:11-13: eschatological wish-prayer.

66. In Jewett's book, *Thessalonian Correspondence,* there is no reference to Funk's "apostolic *parousia*" nor to White's studies of the letter-body. I must confess difficulty in seeing how a radical rhetorical division of 1 Thessalonians such as, e.g., Jewett, pp. 72-76 and 221, proposes (*exordium,* 1:1-5; *narratio,* 1:6–3:13; *probatio,* 4:1–5:22; *peroratio,* 5:23-28) is plausible.

Along with matters of content, this division takes into account the thanksgiving constituents starting at 1:2, 2:13, and 3:9, the shift of focus from addressees to author at 2:1 and 2:17, and the relatively independent character of 3:11-13 both grammatically and formally (wish-prayer).

3. God, Paul, and the Thessalonians

The concrete occasion for writing 1 Thessalonians was Timothy's return. As is obvious from chapters 4 and 5, Paul wanted to provide his addressees with an exhortation and complementary instruction. He also wanted to express his joy and to report how he thanks God for the authentic Christian life active in Thessalonica. Having now reached an insight into the rather unpretentious structure of chapters 1–3 and, through it, into Paul's engaging train of thought, in our third and final section we would like to offer a brief consideration of the Thessalonians' faithful life, Paul's apostolic existence, and God's irresistible gospel.[67]

a. The Christians in Thessalonica

Paul's prayerful thanksgiving oscillates between God's election of the Thessalonian Christians and their final destiny. His thanksgiving starts with the impressive remembrance of their work of faith, labor of love, and steadfastness of hope (1:3).[68] These past and present qualities found their origin in God's election, which was historically concretized in the arrival of the gospel and the conversion of the Thessalonians. Those Christians

67. Because of this choice special questions such as, e.g., Paul's use of pre-Pauline traditions in 1:9-10 and 2:14-16, as well as a detailed verse-by-verse exegesis or the consideration of the letter's integrity, have to be omitted.

68. See B. Rigaux, "Vocabulaire chrétien antérieur à la première épître aux Thessaloniciens," in *Sacra Pagina* (ed. J. Coppens et al.; BETL 13; Gembloux: Duculot, 1959), 2.387-88; and, among others, O'Brien, *Thanksgivings:* "This is the first use of the Christian triad faith-love-hope; and although it was probably not created by Paul, in its present form it may well have been his coinage. . . . In its present context the order is the most natural ('Faith rests on the past; love works in the present; hope looks to the future'); while hope has the prominent place one would expect in a letter devoted so largely to eschatological teaching" (148). But see also Best, *Thessalonians*, 67: "Since all the non-Pauline references to the triad are clearly later than Paul it is possible that Paul himself is its creator."

thus became imitators of the apostles and the Lord and, in their turn, an example to other believers (1:6-7). One can reconstruct the line coming from God and the Lord Jesus Christ and going through the apostles to the Thessalonians, and through them further to others. In his thanksgiving Paul does not fail to point out that, with the acceptance of God's word and in the midst of the ensuing Christian life, there is bound to be much affliction and persecution (3:3-4).[69]

Thanksgiving becomes prayer for the future. There is no Pauline thanksgiving without concern and care regarding the future. Paul humbly prays that he may visit his addressees again (3:11). However, the explicit intention of that visit and of all his prayer is that Paul may comfort his fellow Christians and supply what is still lacking in their faith. They should grow in love; but the final aim is that they remain steadfast and that God establish them unblamable in holiness at the coming of Christ (see 3:12-13).[70]

b. Paul's Apostolic Existence

It may seem strange that Paul interrupts his thanksgiving twice to speak with great passion of his apostolic existence. Has Timothy brought besides the good news also a report of accusations, of doubts regarding Paul's in-

---

69. The first person plural of κείμεθα (v 3) and μέλλομεν is most probably inclusive: Paul and the Thessalonians. Koester, "Experiment," 38, points to the new Christian view of a traditional theme, i.e., to Paul's reinterpretation of the sorrows and tribulations: "They are no longer caused by temporary physical separation, but are seen as the fundamental condition of Christian existence. . . ." A. J. Malherbe, *Paul and the Thessalonians: The Philosophic Tradition of Pastoral Care* (Philadelphia: Fortress Press, 1987), 30, reconstructs the outline of a typical Pauline sermon preached to the Gentiles. But he adds, "Such Christian preaching to Gentiles, which spoke to the emotion as well as the reason of the hearers, was taken over from Hellenistic-Jewish propaganda which had already appropriated popular philosophic thought."

70. White, "Epistolary Literature," 1745, refers to an unpublished essay on Galatians by N. A. Dahl, who "suggests that Paul conceived of his apostolic commission not only in terms of being a herald to the nations but also in connection with the necessity of preparing pure and blameless Gentile congregations for the day of Christ. Whereas the idea of apostolicity is announced already in the opening address, the sense of responsibility regarding the end time surfaces, initially, in the eschatological conclusions with which Paul rounds off the opening prayers of thanksgiving."

tegrity? Recently Abraham Malherbe presented an overview of data with which reliable Cynic philosophers defended their position. He more specifically refers to Dio Chrysostom. "Paul's description of his Thessalonian ministry in 1 Thess. ii is strikingly similar to the picture sketched by Dio, both in what is said and in the way in which it is formulated."[71] By means of his defense Dio intends to get the sympathy and confidence of his listeners. In reality Dio was not accused. Malherbe's conclusion with regard to Paul is hardly correct: "We cannot determine from his description that he is making a personal apology."[72] Paul's purpose, according to Malherbe, is mainly exhortation; the description is meant as a pattern for the Thessalonians. However, not only the very nature of this letter but also the frequent appeal to veracity[73] decisively plead against Malherbe's hesitation.[74]

Three main characteristics in the "mirror" of 2:1-12 deserve our attention. Paul first underlines his παρρησία, his courage, his free, open, and bold preaching of the gospel in the face of great opposition (vv 1-2).[75] Paul then emphasizes repeatedly his pure intention. His appeal does

71. A. J. Malherbe, "'Gentle as a Nurse': The Cynic Background to I Thess. II," *NTS* 12 (1970): 203-17, 216.

72. Malherbe, "'Gentle as a Nurse,'" 217; Boers, "Case Study," 150; and Stowers, *Letter Writing*, 25-26, agree. See Malherbe, *Paul:* "There is no evidence in the letter to suggest that Paul's rehearsal of his dealing with the Thessalonians is a defense against charges that had been brought against him or that he suspected might be leveled at him. . . . His self-description is therefore not apologetic, but parenetic" (74).

73. See the use of οἴδατε in 2:1, 2, 5, μνημονεύετε in 2:9, and especially ὑμεῖς μάρτυρες καὶ ὁ θεός in 2:10 and θεὸς μάρτυς in 2:5.

74. For a presentation and refutation of the thesis of Malherbe (or his predecessors like M. Dibelius), see Marshall, *Thessalonians,* 61; Koester, "Experiment," 41-42; Holtz, *Thessalonicher,* 92-95; Jewett, *Correspondence,* 92 and 102-3; and Johanson, *To All the Brethren,* 164-65. But for others see R. F. Collins, "Paul as Seen through His Own Eyes: A Reflection on the First Letter to the Thessalonians," *LS* 8 (1980-81): 348-82; now also in Collins, *Studies,* 175-208. In the section, "A Frame of Reference: Philosophers, Statesmen, and Prophets" (*Studies,* 183-91), he argues that 1 Thess 2:1-12 is not a real apology, and prefers the heading "autobiographical confession." See also H.-D. Betz, "The Problem of Rhetoric and Theology according to the Apostle Paul," in *L'apôtre Paul: Personnalité, style et conception du ministère* (ed. A. Vanhoye; BETL 73; Leuven: Leuven University Press, 1986), 16-48, especially 21-23.

75. See Phil 1:20: ". . . it is my eager expectation and hope that I shall not be at all ashamed, but that with full courage (πάσῃ παρρησίᾳ) now as always Christ will be honored in my body, whether by life or by death."

not spring from error or uncleanness; it is not made with guile. Paul does not speak to please human beings: he does not use words of flattery or a cloak for greed. God is his witness (vv 3-6). Thirdly, Paul's whole behavior is commanded by his missionary ardor. Although, as an apostle of Christ, he might have made demands, Paul worked night and day not to burden his Christians; he was affectionately gentle as a nurse; he was as a father with his children; he exhorted and encouraged them out of genuine love (vv 7-12).[76]

From the report in 2:17–3:8 we also grasp somewhat Paul's true-to-life feelings, his sincere, deep alliance with his Thessalonian Christians. Paul's concern is their spiritual well-being, their perseverance, and their eschatological salvation.

c. God's Irresistible Gospel

Paul writes his letter to "the church of the Thessalonians in God the Father and the Lord Jesus Christ" (1:1). In 1 Thessalonians 1–3 God is very prominent.[77] Not only does Paul state that he is thanking God always and constantly, he also emphasizes that God is the beginning (1:4) and the end (3:13) of Christian life. The same God is also the origin and permanent witness of Paul's own ministry (2:4 and 5). Moreover, God is active in his apostles and their gospel. Therefore, the gospel arrives "in power and the Holy Spirit and with full conviction" (1:5).[78] And from Thessalonica, where it is accepted,[79] the word of God sounds forth in Macedonia and Achaia, yes, everywhere (1:7-8).

Of course, human response and acceptance are needed. Yet, God's initiative possesses, as it were, an irresistible dynamic. Paul thanks God because the Thessalonians received "the word of God not as the word of men but as what is really is, λόγον θεοῦ, ὃς καὶ ἐνεργεῖται ἐν ὑμῖν τοῖς

76. See Malherbe, *Paul*, 58-60, where he distinguishes the "pastoral care" of Paul from that of the moral philosophers whose methods Paul uses.

77. See, e.g., Koester, "Experiment," 36, with regard to 1:1-10: "Repeatedly Paul introduces 'God'... in an almost importunate fashion..." (with references to 1:3, 4, 8, and 9).

78. According to Best, *Thessalonians*, 143, Paul "does not offer his thanksgiving to the Thessalonians but to God, for what the Thessalonians are, they are by the grace of God."

79. Koester, "Apostel," 269, pointedly remarks: "Es ist . . . der Glaube der neu Bekehrten: der 'als Wort des Herrn' wirkt. . . ."

πιστεύουσιν" (2:13).[80] The powerful, effective word of God or, as Paul calls it in this same letter, τὸ εὐαγγέλιον τοῦ θεοῦ (2:2, 8, 9), τὸ εὐαγγέλιον τοῦ Χριστοῦ (3:2), τὸ εὐαγγέλιον ἡμῶν (1:5),[81] is at work and remains compellingly active in the believers and, through them, in the world.

80. See Heb 4:12: ". . . the word of God is living and active (ἐνεργής), sharper than a two-edged sword. . . ."

81. In 1:5 "gospel" may be personalized. See Rigaux: *Thessaloniciens*, "L'évangile est une force pour le salut (*Rom* 1:16) et c'est déjà cette pensée qui est sous-jacente ici. Il est une force de vie" (373).

A Structural Analysis of 1 Thessalonians 4–5

Jan Lambrecht

1. Introduction

In my previous essay, "Thanksgivings in 1 Thessalonians 1–3,"[1] I devoted much attention to the epistolary thanksgiving in 1 Thessalonians 1–3 and

---

1. J. Lambrecht, "Thanksgivings in 1 Thessalonians 1–3," in *TD*, 135-62. Originally in *The Thessalonian Correspondence* (ed. R. F. Collins; BETL 87; Leuven: Leuven University Press–Peeters, 1990), 183-205; also in Lambrecht, *Pauline Studies* (BETL 115; Leuven: Leuven University Press–Peeters, 1994), 319-41.

Five studies in *The Thessalonian Correspondence* are of particular interest to our topic: J. Chapa, "Consolatory Patterns? 1 Thess 4,13.18; 5,11," 220-28; F. W. Hughes, "The Rhetoric of 1 Thessalonians," 94-116; R. Kieffer, "L'eschatologie en 1 Thessaloniciens dans une perspective rhétorique," 206-18; A. Vanhoye, "La composition de 1 Thessaloniciens," 73-86; W. Wuellner, "The Argumentative Structure of 1 Thessalonians as Paradoxical Encomium," 117-36.

On 1 Thessalonians 1–3, see now also J. Schoon-Janßen, *Umstrittene 'Apologien' in den Paulusbriefen. Studien zur rhetorischen Situation des 1. Thessalonicherbriefes, des Galaterbriefes und des Philipperbriefes* (GTA 45; Göttingen: Vandenhoeck & Ruprecht, 1991); P. Arzt, "The 'Epistolary Introductory Thanksgiving' in the Papyri and in Paul," *NTS* 36 (1994): 29-46: "The combination of a report of a prayer and/or the μνεία-motif with a thankgiving to God for the addressees derives from Paul's personal intention and not from a common epistolary convention" (45). Compare this with my conclusions in "Thanksgivings," in *TD*, 145-49: "One must realize that 1 Thessalonians is Paul's first letter and that Paul is here probably in the process of 'creating' his structured thanksgiving" (in *TD*, 147). See J. Murphy-O'Connor, *Paul the Letter-Writer: His World, His Options, His Skills* (GNS 41; Collegeville, Minn.: The Liturgical Press, 1995), 55-64.

offered a brief discussion of items such as the "body" of the letter, the "apostolic *parousia*," and the "epistolary recommendation." There I stated that the delineation of the thanksgivings and the detection of the beginning of new sections, "the gathering of striking parallels in Pauline and non-Pauline letters, the careful study of topics with regard to apology and travelogue, the search for stereotyped formulae as well as the determination of their function, the discussion of different aspects of apostolic presence, and even the naming of newly found literary genres: all these efforts, and many more, may be helpful in our understanding of Paul."[2]

In addition I stated: "The danger, however, lies in exaggeration, in increasingly inventive speciousness, in too much, often far-fetched and strained, genre hunting. One might wonder whether Paul consciously starts the body of his letter in 2:1, deliberately composes an apostolic *parousia* in 2:17–3:13, or really intends a twofold epistolary recommendation in 2:1-12 and 2:17–3:8. Even to attribute to Paul a more or less spontaneous, subconscious following of preexisting patterns may constitute here an unwarranted postulate."[3]

The proposal I made there concerning the structure of 1 Thessalonians 1–3 is based on a combination of epistolary and thematic criteria.[4] The same combination will now apply to the examination of the second part of the letter, chapters 4 and 5, where the "surface" structure is examined, utilizing Paul's development of thought, often revealed by formal elements and by the use of different literary genres.

2. Analysis of 1 Thessalonians 4–5

There is an almost general consensus that distinguishes the paraenetic sections 4:1-12 and 5:12-22 from the eschatological middle section 4:13–5:11.[5] B. C. Johanson is convinced that in 1 Thessalonians "the main 'point' of the

2. Lambrecht, "Thanksgivings," in *TD*, 154.
3. Lambrecht, "Thanksgivings," in *TD*, 154.
4. Lambrecht, "Thanksgivings," in *TD*, 157-58.
5. See, e.g., I. H. Marshall, *1 and 2 Thessalonians* (NCBC; Grand Rapids: Eerdmans, 1983), 10-11, distinguishes three areas: general morality (sexual morality and idleness); teaching about the *parousia;* and life together. His division is: 4:1-12 (Exhortation to Ethical Progress), 4:13–5:11 (Instruction and Exhortation about the Parousia), and 5:12-24 (Instruction for Life in the Church).

communication lies in the . . . major text-sequence of 4:1–5:24."[6] He puts forward the ring-composition "A = 4:1-12, B = 4:13–5:11 and A' = 5:12-24."[7] He also compares 4:13-18 with 5:1-11, but at the same time stresses the differences of these passages vis-à-vis the framing ones (4:1-12 and 5:12-22): "Both subsequences formally close with an admonition beginning with the lexical recurrence of παρακαλεῖτε ἀλλήλους. Abundant use of apocalyptic motifs is made in both sections in contrast to what precedes and follows and both make use of creedal material, namely, ὅτι Ἰησοῦς ἀπέθανεν καὶ ἀνέστη (4:14); Ἰησοῦ Χριστοῦ τοῦ ἀποθανόντος ὑπὲρ ἡμῶν (5:9-10). There is also the general conceptual recurrence of σὺν κυρίῳ ἐσόμεθα (4:17) in ἅμα σὺν αὐτῷ ζήσωμεν (5:10) with the references to the οἱ κοιμώμενοι, οἱ νεκροὶ/οἱ ζῶντες, οἱ περιλειπόμενοι of the former sequence echoed in the word-play in εἴτε γρηγορῶμεν εἴτε καθεύδωμεν ἅμα σὺν αὐτῷ ζήσωμεν in 5:10."[8]

The end of the letter consists of a last prayer (5:23-24) and final recommendations (5:25-28). Because of the parallelism in both content and wording of this prayer with the one at the end of the first part, 3:11-13, it seems better also to consider 5:23-24, this second eschatological wish-prayer — almost a benediction — as a kind of conclusion of what precedes, not yet the beginning of the formal ending.[9] Regarding 5:23, verse

---

6. B. C. Johanson, *To All the Brethren: A Text-Linguistic and Rhetorical Approach to I Thessalonians* (ConBNT 16; Stockholm: Almqvist & Wiksell, 1987), 160. For an evaluation of this important monograph, see, e.g., Kieffer, "Eschatologie," 208-9 and Vanhoye, "Composition." This last author fully recognizes the merits of Johanson's text-centered analyses. Yet he remains severe in his overall judgment: "Devenue plus technique, l'étude de la composition s'exprime en un langage esotérique, hérissé de néologismes et d'abréviations, ce qui, assurément, ne rend pas facile le processus de communication entre le lecteur et le commentateur. Un effort démesuré est nécessaire pour comprendre le 'métalangage' utilisé par ce dernier et pour vérifier si l'analyse exprimée dans le métalangage correspond réellement à des données du texte. Le métalangage donne à toute affirmation une apparence d'infaillibilité scientifique. Il rend plus difficile la tâche de démasquer les erreurs possibles" (74). Moreover, among other points, Vanhoye thoroughly criticizes Johanson's qualification of the function of chapters 1–3 as (only) a preparatory *captatio benevolentiae:* "Il me semble qu'il faut reconnaître, au contraire, que 1 Thessaloniciens est avant tout une lettre, où 'la fonction épistolaire de contact' est prédominante" (86). The first part of 1 Thessalonians is much more than a preparation for the second (82-86).

7. Johanson, *To All the Brethren,* 143.

8. Johanson, *To All the Brethren,* 118-19 (quotation on 118). He mentions also the "common emphasis on not being like οἱ λοιποί who grieve without hope (4:13) and who are spiritually asleep (5:6)" (118-19).

9. In both prayers we have the introductory expression αὐτὸς δὲ ὁ θεός and the term

24 functions as a motivating clause: such a prayer can be formulated since we are sure that the God who calls us will also do what we pray for.[10] This verse is thus connected with the prayer; verses 23-24 belong together.

In 5:25 we have the beginning of 5:25-28 with ἀδελφοί. Just as Paul has been praying for the Thessalonians, so also the Thessalonians must pray for him: "pray for us." To a certain extent, therefore, verse 25 is also still linked with verses 23-24.[11] A letter appropriately ends with final requests and greetings. In verses 26-28 there are three sentences: Greet the brothers with a holy kiss; I adjure you by the Lord that this letter be read to all the brothers; and the grace of our Lord Jesus Christ be with you — an admonition (v 26), an adjuration (v 27),[12] and a final greeting (v 28).

a. Paraenesis

The two sections that I called paraenetic, 4:1-12 and 5:12-22, correspond to each other through the genre itself: accumulations of exhortation.

ἀμέμπτους or ἀμέμπτως. The Thessalonians should be blameless at the day of Jesus' *parousia* (in each prayer: ἡ παρουσία τοῦ κυρίου ἡμῶν Ἰησοῦ (Χριστοῦ). The two prayers are manifestly eschatological. See P.-E. Langevin, "L'intervention de Dieu selon I Thes 5,23-24," in *Thessalonian Correspondence*, 236-56; J. A. D. Weima, "The Pauline Letter Closings: Analysis and Hermeneutical Significance," *BulBR* 5 (1995): 177-97.

10. See, e.g., Langevin, "L'intervention," 246.

11. Johanson, *To All the Brethren*, 65-66: ". . . not only is there a thematic shift at 5:25 . . . , but also a shift from a predominantly persuasive-exhortational . . . to a predominantly phatic communicative function. The transition is, however, not abrupt, but has soft features in that the request for prayer follows naturally upon Paul's immediately preceding wish-prayer for the addressees."

12. E. R. Richards, *The Secretary in the Letters of Paul* (WUNT II/42; Tübingen: Mohr, 1991), 179-81, points to the first person singular in v 27: "Throughout the letter, the stereotyped formulae are always in the plural. After the final greetings, however, in verse 26, there is a request in the singular (v. 27). . . . Moreover, the previous requests have been rather abstract and 'spiritual', but this request is very pragmatic and stands in contrast to the rest of the epistle. Perhaps it is an indication of Paul taking the pen to affix a closing greeting (v. 28) and adding a personal request as well" (179-80). This may then reveal secretarial assistance in the writing of 1 Thessalonians. See also H. Binder, "Paulus und die Thessalonicherbriefe," in *The Thessalonian Correspondence*, 87-93, who defends a co-authorship in the two letters to the Thessalonians (Paul and especially Silvanus, "der 'zweite Mann'," who represented "den Autoritätsanspruch Jerusalems," 88) and speaks of "a häufiger Autorenwechsel" (91); Murphy-O'Connor, *Paul the Letter-Writer*, especially 16-20.

Moreover, it is hardly accidental that a number of terms are the same, especially at each beginning. In 4:1 as well as in 5:12 there is a petition formula and, within it, the verb ἐρωτῶμεν, the personal pronoun ὑμᾶς, the vocative ἀδελφοί, and the expression ἐν κυρίῳ ('Ιησοῦ). In 4:1 and 5:14 one may add the presence of παρακαλοῦμεν, and in 4:3 and 5:18 the remarkable repetition of τοῦτο γὰρ . . . θέλημα θεοῦ.[13] To be sure, the sections also differ. In the second section the sentences are mostly shorter and, as it were, more nervous. While 4:1-12 give general moral admonitions, 5:12-22 focus on community life.

Περὶ δέ in 4:9 indicates a new start, but the division within 4:1-12 is almost completely topical. After the very emphatic opening of verses 1-2, which introduce the second part in its entirety,[14] the letter gives three warnings: warnings against unchastity (vv 3-8: dangers will come from the pagan past of the converts), to obey the love commandment (vv 9-10: the flower of Christianity), and concerning quiet and honest work (vv 11-12: apocalyptic complacency, a danger that may have its origin in Christians' expectation of the imminent return of their Lord and could scandalize τοὺς ἔξω).[15] Lexical elements in verses 1-2 and verses 10-12 reveal an inclusion:

13. We may also point to the presence of ἀπέχομαι in 4:3 and 5:22 and of πνεῦμα in 4:8 and 5:19. Johanson, *To All the Brethren*, 143, moreover, mentions ἁγιασμός, ἁγιασμῷ, ἁγιάσαι (4:3, 7; 5:23), ἐκάλεσεν ἡμᾶς/καλῶν ὑμᾶς (4:7; 5:24)."

14. The phrase λοιπὸν οὖν, ἀδελφοί ("finally, therefore, brothers") in 4:1 might seem to announce the end. See 2 Cor 13:11, λοιπόν, ἀδελφοί, and Phil 4:8, τὸ λοιπόν, ἀδελφοί. Yet by itself it is not. See Johanson, *To All the Brethren*, 112: "Here in I Thess 4:1 the evidence is seen to support taking λοιπὸν οὖν as generally inferential ('then' or 'and so') in relation to 1:2–3:13 in view of its exordial-like character [?]. Thus it seems to mark a major text-sequential transition to the text-sequence containing the main message of the letter." U. Schnelle, "Die Ethik des 1. Thessalonicherbriefes," in *The Thessalonian Correspondence*, 295-305, especially 302, stresses that the transition is linked (οὖν) with the eschatological content of 3:13, which just precedes.

15. As is well known, not all exegetes would agree that in vv 3-8 Paul deals only with unchastity; some claim that v 6 speaks of honesty in business (τὸ μὴ ὑπερβαίνειν καὶ πλεονεκτεῖν ἐν τῷ πράγματι τὸν ἀδελφὸν αὐτοῦ). Yet v 7 with (a) ἐκάλεσεν . . . ὁ θεός, (b) ἐν ἁγιασμῷ, and (c) ἀκαθαρσία constitutes an inclusion with (a) θέλημα τοῦ θεοῦ, (b) ὁ ἁγιασμός, and (c) πορνεία in v 3. Is it, therefore, not better to explain v 6 according to the overall theme of vv 3-8?

Another point of discussion is the question to what extent Paul's exhortations refer to a concretely existing situation in Thessalonica (see the distinction between "aktuell" and "usuell"). See J. Lambrecht, "A Call to Witness by All: Evangelisation in 1 Thessalonians," in

ἀδελφοί, ὑμεῖς, παρακαλέω, and περισσεύω μᾶλλον in 4:1 and 4:10; περιπατέω in 4:1 and 4:12; παραγγελία in 4:2 and παραγγέλλω in 4:11.[16]

Thus, I see three small subdivisions in 5:12-22: verses 12-13, verses 14-15, and verses 16-22. Verse 12 begins with ἐρωτῶμεν δὲ ὑμᾶς, ἀδελφοί, and verse 14 with the parallel παρακαλοῦμεν δὲ ὑμᾶς, ἀδελφοί; the brief clauses in verses 16-18a, after the long sentence of verse 15, in their own manner indicate a new beginning.[17] While in verse 12 the address "brothers" refers to all fellow Christians in Thessalonica, the terms "you, brothers" in verse 14 presumably point to those who may become or are the first local church leaders; it envisions their specific duties toward Christians and non-Christians (εἰς πάντας, v 15). It would seem that from verse 16 onward the second person plural is again directed to all Thessalonians. If this way of interpreting is valid, one would have an a-b-a′ composition: all Christians–leaders–all Christians. The unit a′ begins with three imperatives (brief clauses); then follows the emphatic motivation: "for this is the will of God in Christ Jesus for you" (see 4:3); finally, there are five imperatives (a "pentad," five brief clauses that treat in a delicate manner the way in which the working of the Spirit has to be judged).[18] One may perhaps consider εἰρηνεύετε (end of v 13) and (ὁ θεὸς) τῆς εἰρήνης (v 23) as an inclusion.

b. Eschatology

The central eschatological section, 4:13–5:11, requires careful consideration. We will do so in four steps.

Pauline Studies, 343-59, especially 352-55 (bibliography on 360-61); U. Schnelle, "Ethik," 295-305 ("usuell"); Johanson, *To All the Brethren*, e.g., 113-18.

On 4:9-12, see the recent study of J. S. Kloppenborg, "ΦΙΛΑΔΕΛΦΙΑ, ΘΕΟΔΙΔΑΚΤΟΣ and the Dioscuri: Rhetorical Engagement in 1 Thessalonians 4.9-12," *NTS* 39 (1993): 265-89 (περὶ δέ is epistolary shorthand introducing a matter of common concern; φιλαδελφία is known in Thessalonica as the near proverbial virtue of the divine twins Castor and Polyceudes; θεοδίδακτος is a term probably coined by Paul himself to convey the idea of divine instruction).

16. See Johanson, *To All the Brethren*, 113.
17. See Johanson, *To All the Brethren*, 136-39.
18. See Lambrecht, "A Call to Witness," 356-57.

1. Because of the threefold presence of the preposition περί in 4:9, 4:13, and 5:1, one could be tempted to underestimate the structural qualities of the text. Does περί not indicate a loose sequence of themes and topics? Such a question is strengthened by the strikingly similar outlook of 4:9 and 5:1-2:

> 4:9: περὶ δὲ τῆς φιλαδελφίας
> 5:1-2: περὶ δὲ τῶν χρόνων καὶ τῶν καιρῶν
> 4:9: οὐ χρείαν ἔχετε γράφειν ὑμῖν
> 5:1: οὐ χρείαν ἔχετε ὑμῖν γράφεσθαι
> 4:9: αὐτοὶ γὰρ ὑμεῖς θεοδίδακτοί ἐστε
> 5:2: αὐτοὶ γὰρ ἀκριβῶς οἴδατε.

In both passages the δέ is progressive and announces a new theme ("now concerning . . ."). In both passages Paul stresses that the Thessalonians do not need to have anything written to them; they already know.

Yet in 4:13 the caesura is much greater and the situation appears to be different. The preposition περί does not stand at the beginning of the sentence; the tone is more personal: Paul no longer deals with "virtues" but with information about the future of deceased Christians. That is a matter that the Thessalonians do not yet seem to know.[19]

2. The beginning and the end of the section correspond to each other as far as content and vocabulary are concerned. One may compare the following elements from 5:9-11 and 4:13-18:

5:9: ὁ θεός	4:14: ὁ θεός
The Lord Jesus Christ	4:14, 15, 16, 17
5:10: ἀποθανόντος	4:14: ἀπέθανεν
wake, sleep	4:13, 15-17: alive, asleep
ἅμα	4:17: ἅμα
σὺν αὐτῷ	4:17: σὺν αὐτῷ
"we"	4:17: ἐσόμεθα
5:11: διὸ παρακαλεῖτε	4:18: ὥστε παρακαλεῖτε
ἀλλήλους	ἀλλήλους

---

19. For the disclosure formula "we would not have you ignorant" in 4:13, see also Rom 1:13; 11:25; 1 Cor 10:1; 12:1; 2 Cor 1:8. See Johanson, *To All the Brethren*, 120: The formula "not only serves to signal a transition to a different topic but also the introduction of new information, as indicated by θέλομεν together with the noetic verb."

Just as in 4:13-18, Paul deals in 5:9-11 with the final destination of all Christians, dead and living alike. Both passages provide information that must make possible mutual consolation. It would seem that one can understand the particle ὅτι of 5:9 in a pregnant way: for (this we should know, namely, that) God has destined us. . . . If the two passages thus correspond to one another, then (1) from 5:10 (τοῦ ἀποθανόντος ὑπὲρ ἡμῶν ἵνα . . . σὺν αὐτῷ ζήσωμεν) one may conclude that in 4:14 the same strict causal connection between Christ's death and our resurrection is implicitly present, and (2) from 4:16-18 it is evident that ζήσωμεν in 5:10 (= σωτηρία, 5:9) implies both resurrection (4:16) and "being always with the Lord" (4:17).

The paraenetic character of both passages is the same: because Christians are aware of their eschatological future — no destination for wrath but vocation to obtain salvation through the Lord Jesus Christ, that is, lasting life with him — they must not grieve (4:13); rather, they must comfort and encourage one another (4:18 and 5:11).

Moreover, the passages 4:13-18[20] and 5:9-11 constitute an inclusion. This confirms the correctness of the general assumption that 4:13–5:11 is a coherent section, a large thematic unity.

3. The remaining verses, 5:1-8, are different. There is another type of information and exhortation. Paul here stresses something that the Thessalonians are supposed to know already: the sudden, unexpected, and imminent coming of the Lord, "as a thief in the night" (v 2). Paul also emphasizes that Christians are not in darkness (they know and, morally speaking, they are children of light and day); therefore, the coming day should not surprise them. Paul here distinguishes, not between dead and living (i.e., between two kinds of Christians) as in the two framing passages, but between Christians and other people who say "there is peace and security"; sudden destruction will come upon those people, and there will

---

20. See J. Delobel, "The Fate of the Dead according to 1 Thessalonians 4 and 1 Corinthians 15," in *The Thessalonian Correspondence,* 340-47. According to J. Aletti, "Paul et la rhétorique. Etat de la question et propositions," in *Paul de Tarse* (ed. J. Schlosser; LD 165; Paris: Cerf, 1996), 27-50: "Paul combine très souvent les parallélismes et le cadre conceptuel de la rhétorique argumentative" (33). For the "micro-unité" 4:13-18, he indicates the "parallèles lexicaux," as well as the "composition discursive": A = *introduction* (v 13: annonce du thème); B = *propositio* (l'apodose, v 14b); C = *preuves* (vv 15-17); D = *conclusion* (v 18: exhortation) (33-34).

170

be no escape. This demarcation is signaled by "you yourselves" (v 2) and "when they say" (v 3; see οἱ λοιποί, v 6).[21]

The exhortation is no longer to console one another but to "keep awake and be sober" (v 6). Verses 7-8 give the motivation and repeat that admonition: "For those who sleep sleep at night, and those who are drunk get drunk at night. But, since we belong to the day, let us be sober, and put on the breastplate of faith and love, and for a helmet the hope of salvation." Moreover, the exhortation is "given a particularly gentle pastoral tone due to the hortatory subjunctives used in the whole letter."[22]

One more difference between 5:1-8 and the framing units. In verses 6-8 the verbs καθεύδω and γρηγορέω are employed metaphorically,[23] just as "night" and "darkness, and "day" and "light" in verses 4-8. A rather strange shift occurs in 5:9-10: here the equally metaphorical sense of καθεύδω is "to be dead" (see κοιμωμάω in 4:13-15), and that of γρηγορέω "to be (still) alive" (see ζάω in 4:15, 17).

4. We can now draw some conclusions to this structural analysis. It appears that 4:13–5:11 consists of three units, of which the third corresponds to the first; this section thus has a concentric feature:

a: 4:13-18: because of the future resurrection comfort one another;
b: 5:1-8: because of the near but uncertain date be sober and awake;
a': 5:9-11: because of the final salvation encourage one another.

Of course, contentwise the three units are not so different; they are linked together. Moreover, verses 9-10 of chapter 5 function as motivation for the exhortation to keep awake and to be sober (see ὅτι at the beginning of v 9).[24] Finally, the very last verse, 5:11, is probably more than the exhor-

---

21. However, this distinction, together with the expression οἱ λοιποί (5:6), occurs already in 4:13: οἱ λοιποὶ οἱ μὴ ἔχοντες ἐλπίδα.

22. Johanson, *To All the Brethren*, 133. The concentric structure proposed by C. Focant, "Les fils du Jour (1 Thes 5,5)," in *The Thessalonian Correspondence*, 348-55, especially 350-53, is hardly convincing.

23. See μεθύω ("to get drunk," 5:7) and νήφω ("to be sober," 5:6 and 8). In v 7a the sense of καθεύδω is most probably literal ("to sleep").

24. See T. Söding, "Der Erste Thessalonicherbrief und die frühe paulinische Evangeliumsverkündigung. Zur Frage einer Entwicklung der paulinischen Theologie," in *BZ* 35 (1991): 180-203: "Dass Glaube, Liebe und Hoffnung zur eschatologischen Rettung führen, folgt nach dem 1Thess aus dem Heilshandeln Gottes in Jesus Christus" (197). See n. 49 on ὅτι "als Verbindung zwischen 5,8 und 5,9." Johanson, *To All the Brethren*, 134, however, nu-

tation that follows from 5:9-10. In some way it functions as the conclusion of the whole section 4:13–5:11 (see the introductory διό in 5:11). It is also quite possible that παρακαλεῖτε in verse 11 differs in meaning from the same imperative in 4:18: no longer consolation of those who grieve because of their deceased fellow Christians, but encouragement and "upbuilding" or, more concretely, exhortation to vigilance as in 5:6-8. The addition of both καὶ οἰκοδομεῖτε εἰς τὸν ἕνα and καθὼν καὶ ποιεῖτε in 5:11 confirms this suggestion for a shift of meaning. One might even compare this last expression with καθὼς καὶ περιπατεῖτε at the beginning of the second half of the letter, 4:1.

c. Structure

One can hardly put forward that Paul wanted to give to the second part of his letter to the Thessalonians a structure similar to that of the first part. Yet, if this analysis has any value, there is a striking similarity; like chapters 1–3, chapters 4–5 mainly consist of five internally related units and a wish-prayer:[25]

> 4:1-2: introductory paraenesis
>   a 4:3-12: paraenesis
>   b 4:13-18: final destiny of Christians
>   a 5:1-8: paraenesis
>   b 5:9-11: final destiny of Christians
>   a 5:12-22: paraenesis
> 5:23-24: eschatological wish-prayer

The paraenesis in the a-units contains moral exhortation and admonishments. The exhortation present at the end of the b-units asks for mutual consolation and encouragement. Of course the movement from paraenesis (a) to information (b) should not eclipse the distinct eschatological character of the three middle units, 4:13–5:11. Moreover, all paraenesis in

---

ances: Verses 9-10b "should not be seen so much as giving the motivation for the exhortations to sober vigilance as giving the theological-christological basis of their status."

25. Compare the differing chiastic and alternating patterns in Johanson, *To All the Brethren*, 151.

1 Thessalonians serves an eschatological purpose.[26] Finally, the surprising similarity in structure between 1 Thessalonians 1–3 and 1 Thessalonians 4–5 should not cover up the great differences of content: thanksgiving is not paraenesis, and autobiographical apology is not eschatological information.

3. Methodological Reflections

It will now be useful to return to a reflection on the method.[27] Three items require a brief comment. What is the relevancy of content in each proposal of structure? What type of letter is 1 Thessalonians? What are the main characteristics of this particular letter, the first written by Paul?

a. The Relevancy of Content

In his discussion of the rhetoric of the Thessalonian letters, Jewett writes: "Prior to the appearance of the rhetorical studies . . . , the research that has been done on the structure . . . fell in two general categories: analyses of the logical or thematic development, and analyses of the epistolary form."[28] One gets the impression that there are three types of structure: thematic, epistolary, and rhetorical.

Yet one has only to look further than the main divisions of both the epistolary form (e.g., salutation, thanksgiving, body, and greetings) and

26. For the connection between paraenesis and eschatology, see, e.g., Söding, "Der Erste Thessalonicherbrief," 188: "Die Paraklese zielt auf die Vorbereitung der Glaubenden für den 'Tag des Herrn' (5,2), an dem sie heilig und untadelig dastehen sollen (3,12f; 4,3-8; 5,23)"; and 193: "Die gesamte Paraklese des 1Thess steht im Zeichen der Vorbereitung auf die Parusie des Kyrios. . . ."

27. See Lambrecht, "Thanksgivings," 192-94 and 198-202. For broad and balanced methodological reflections, see Johanson, *To All the Brethren,* with regard to rhetorics, especially 157-72; Aletti, "Paul et la rhétorique"; Murphy-O'Connor, *Paul the Letter-Writer,* especially 65-98; and my more general study "Rhetorical Criticism and the New Testament," *BPTF* 50 (1989): 239-53.

28. R. Jewett, *The Thessalonian Correspondence: Pauline Rhetoric and Millenarian Piety* (FFNT; Philadelphia: Fortress, 1986), 63-78 and charts on 216-21; cited text on 68. See, e.g., the rhetorical approach by C. A. Wanamaker, *The Epistles to the Thessalonians* (NIGTC; Grand Rapids: Eerdmans, 1990), 45-50 (for a critical discussion, see Aletti, "Paul et la rhétorique," 35-36).

the rhetorical pattern (e.g., *exordium, narratio, probatio,* and *peroratio*) in order to see immediately the entrance of the content considerations.[29] This is a first remark. The second concerns the possible identification of sections of the letter. So one would be willing to qualify the report of 2:1-12 and 2:17–3:8 as a *narratio* and the thanksgiving of 2:1-10 as an *exordium,* but one can hardly call 4:1–5:22 a *probatio.* There is the danger of forcing a text into the straitjacket of a so-called common pattern.[30] This calls for a third remark. Although an author can sometimes follow a given form, a literary genre, almost unconsciously, a more sophisticated pattern supposes an intended effort. In order to conclude that such a pattern is present, formal and topical indications are needed. It would seem that they are lacking in 1 Thessalonians as far as the proposed rhetorical structure is concerned. A fourth remark: with regard to the "body" of the letter and its arrangement two factors are of much more importance than a given pattern. First, attention must be given to the situation in Thessalonica with, on the one hand, the praiseworthy conduct of Christians and, on the other, their specific difficulties regarding moral life and doctrine. Second, the

29. We may refer to the divisions within the "body" of the letter and quote Jewett, *Thessalonian Correspondence,* 70: "There is usually a proper identification of the epistolary prescript and postscript as well as a portion of the thanksgiving. But such categories are interspersed with topical titles. . . ." Is this, however, not equally true of what Jewett himself does on, e.g., p. 75, regarding 4:9-12? These verses are part of the *"probatio"* and constitute "the second proof concerning the communal ethic." The division is as follows: 1. Reiteration of previous grounding and accomplishment of the love ethic (4:9-10a); 2. The admonitions (4:10b-12): a. Continue in the ethic (v. 10b), b. Live quietly (v. 11a), c. Be self-supporting (v. 11b), d. Gain public respect (v. 12a), e. Be independent (v. 12b). The same applies to Hughes, *Rhetoric,* 109-16 (= "A Rhetorical Summary of 1 Thessalonians," extremely detailed).

30. See Vanhoye, "Composition," 82 and 78-79: The rhetorical patterns "s'efforcent de faire entrer le texte de l'épître dans le lit de Procuste que la rhétorique classique a défini pour les discours et non pour les lettres." See also the careful remarks of Johanson, *To All the Brethren,* 141-42, regarding 5:12-24 as *peroratio.* His conclusion: "While these observations do not qualify 5:12-24 as a *peroratio* characteristic of orations as such, there are nevertheless sufficient peroration-like characteristics to justify taking 5:12-24 as a whole to function as the conclusion not merely of the text-sequence 4:1–5:24, but of the whole letter-body (1:2–5:24)" (142). For the whole of 4:1–5:24, see 72-74, 78, and 161-63. See Johanson's reflection at the beginning of his monograph: a "text-centered analysis is necessary in order to be able to judge the extent to which conventional influence has controlled individual expression or to which the individual author has bent and shaped the conventional into something new and appropriate to the situation in hand" (6).

free and creative talent of Paul as a writer should not be underestimated. Finally, one should bear in mind that a so-called thematic structure must not neglect the formal criteria. In all structural analyses form and content cannot be separated.

b. What Kind of Letter?

I will try to answer two questions. The first is: Should one consider 1 Thessalonians as a letter of consolation? In two recent studies Juan Chapa took up this question in reaction to Karl Donfried and A. Smith, who attempted to interpret 1 Thessalonians as such a letter.[31] Chapa first examines what is meant by consolation in antiquity and highlights the three elements in a letter of consolation: sympathy, consolation proper, and explicit exhortation.[32] He recognizes that in the church of Thessalonica there seem to have been two sources of affliction: hostility (up to persecution) and the death of some Thessalonians.[33]

31. J. Chapa, "Is First Thessalonians a Letter of Consolation?" *NTS* 40 (1994): 150-60, and "Consolatory Patterns"; A. Smith, *The Social and Ethical Implications of the Pauline Rhetoric in 1 Thessalonians* (Unpub. Ph.D diss.; Vanderbilt University, 1989), 170; K. Donfried, "The Theology of 1 Thessalonians as a Reflection of Its Purpose," in *To Touch the Text* (Festschrift J. A. Fitzmyer; ed. M. P. Horgan and P. J. Kobelski; New York: Crossroad, 1989), 243-60, especially 243-44 and 259-60: ". . . we understand 1 Thessalonians not primarily as a 'paraenetic' letter but as a 'paracletic' letter, as a *consolatio*" (243-44); "1 Thessalonians is a λόγος παραμυθητικός to a Christian church suffering the effects of persecution . . . an encouragement to the discouraged" (260). See also Donfried, "1 Thessalonians, Acts and Early Paul," in *The Thessalonian Correspondence*, 3-26. For an introduction in ancient letter-writing see, e.g., A. J. Malherbe, *Ancient Epistolary Theorists* (SBLSBS 19; Atlanta: Scholars Press, 1988), 1-14; Richards, *Secretary*, 129-53, as well as the appendix on 211-16; Murphy-O'Connor, *Paul the Letter-Writer*.

32. On the presence of exhortation in a letter of consolation, see Chapa, "Letter of Consolation," 151-53: "Explicit exhortation was . . . the natural connotation of consolation" (152); ". . . the exhortation to accept bravely the misfortune which is connatural to the human condition, not to be overcome excessively by grief and, in consequence, to neglect one's duties" (151).

33. Chapa, "Letter of Consolation," 150-56. See, e.g., Söding, "Der Erste Thessalonicherbrief," 182-83. For Donfried, "Theology," 254-56, it is probable that persecution in Thessalonica has led to occasional deaths. He suggests that "the dead who are referred to in 1 Thess 4:13-18 are those who may have died in some mob-action type of persecution in Thessalonica" (254). The two sources of affliction are thus linked. Rightly? Donfried refers

Chapa then gives a survey of the passages in 1 Thessalonians that could function in a letter of consolation.[34] In 2:17-18 Paul's mention of his inability to visit Thessalonica may have a consolatory purpose. In 2:2 Paul refers to his own suffering and so expresses his sympathy. In 3:3-4 Paul perhaps aims "to lessen the sorrow of those who were suffering, through the consideration of the universality and inescapability of sorrow and pain."[35] Moreover, he stresses that suffering was to be expected. In 1:6-10 Paul praises the noble Christian conduct of the Thessalonians; such praise can easily be regarded as a source of consolation. In 2:14-15 he refers to the sufferings of Christ and the churches of Judaea; as is well known, examples of people with similar experiences of grief may have a consolatory intention. Chapa mentions that "Paul's continuous exhortation, especially in chapters 4 and 5, might be seen as a response to circumstances of sorrow and affliction, which could have put at risk the fulfillment of Christian obligations";[36] such exhortations may possess a consolatory purpose.

For Chapa "it is clear that 1 Thessalonians contains some rhetorical strategies current in literature of consolation which seem to fit a situation of some sort of crisis caused by sorrow or affliction in the Christian community at Thessalonica, like the death of some of its members or the consequences which persecution has left among them."[37] However, because an overall linking scheme is missing, he hesitates. "Is then 1 Thess a letter of consolation? I do not think one can give a definite and precise answer to this question."[38] His final word is: "If we should not formally classify 1 Thessalonians as a 'letter of consolation,' we may, nevertheless, be justified in calling it a consoling letter without intending to exclude other valid purposes."[39] Is not the consoling character of 1 Thessalonians thus not overly stressed by Chapa?

---

to his earlier study, "The Cults of Thessalonica and the Thessalonian Correspondence," *NTS* 31 (1985): 336-56, especially 349-50, and to the same conclusion by J. S. Pobee, *Persecution and Martyrdom in the Theology of Paul* (JSNTSup 6; Sheffield: JSOT Press, 1985), 113-14.

34. Chapa, "Letter of Consolation," 156-59.

35. Chapa, "Letter of Consolation," 158.

36. Chapa, "Letter of Consolation," 158-59.

37. Chapa, "Letter of Consolation," 159.

38. Chapa, "Letter of Consolation," 160.

39. Chapa, "Letter of Consolation," 160. See also the critical approach by Murphy-O'Connor, 95-98: ". . . the value of epistolary classification of whole letters must be considered extremely dubious" (98).

The second question is a rhetorical one. Does 1 Thessalonians belong to demonstrative (epideictic) or to deliberative speech? The first type of speech wants to praise a present situation and to confirm the addressees in their conduct,[40] while the second looks to the future and exhorts to new and better action.[41] To what extent can this rhetorical distinction be applied to 1 Thessalonians? It would appear that, because of the situation in Thessalonica, a choice between the two kinds of languages is unnecessary and should be avoided. The needs of Christians may have differed from person to person and from family to family. In his letter Paul speaks of both present and future; he wants to reaffirm good conduct as well as bring people back to the right behavior.

c. The Peculiar Structure of 1 Thessalonians

In an ancient letter, including a Pauline letter, one normally expects a salutation at the beginning and greetings at the end. 1 Thessalonians respects this rule. After the salutation most Pauline letters begin with a thanksgiving, and then the "body" follows. Already here the first letter to the Thessalonians goes its own way. The thanksgiving of 1 Thessalonians is scattered over the first half of the letter and certainly belongs to the "body" of this particular letter.

One may expect some requests or recommendations after the "body" of a letter and before its "closing." Sometimes a distinction can be made

---

40. See Chapa, "Letter of Consolation," 153-54. Chapa thinks that 1 Thessalonians is "epideictic"; equally, e.g., Jewett, *The Thessalonian Correspondence*, 71-72; Wanamaker, *Thessalonians*, 47-48; Hughes, "Rhetoric," 97 and 106-7; Kieffer, "Eschatologie," 211-12; S. Walton, "What Has Aristotle To Do with Paul? Rhetorical Criticism and 1 Thessalonians," *TynB* 46 (1995), 229-50. Wuellner, "Argumentative Structure," calls the genre of 1 Thessalonians more specifically a "Paradoxical Encomium" (encomiastic = epideictic). Yet see Murphy-O'Connor, 70: "However justified this [rhetorical] classification may be in theoretical terms, it is manifest that a huge abyss separates 1 Thessalonians from the classic display discourses . . ." (display rhetoric = epideictic rhetoric).

41. See Johanson, *To All the Brethren*, 166: ". . . there is the future-oriented focus in the response-changing function of dissuasion from grief and incipient doubt, besides in the response-reinforcing, more general admonitions to advance in leading a life pleasing to God." Since the response-changing function is the most important of the letter, Johanson concludes: "As for the rhetorical genre, the one to which I Thess would have the closest resemblance is the deliberative one" (189).

between a doctrinal (dogmatic) part and an exhortative (paraenetic) part (see Romans 1–11 and 12–15). Again, 1 Thessalonians is different. Chapters 4 and 5 are more than paraenesis; they contain doctrine as well; these chapters, too, belong to the "body" of the letter. However, this special outlook of Paul's first letter should not hinder one's view of its peculiar and even artistic structure.[42]

42. For Wuellner, however, this is, I think, still the "literary" structure. He sees "Paul's rhetoric of argumentation and . . . the rhetorical structure of 1 Thessalonians as distinct from both the traditionally more familiar concern for discrete rhetorical features *in* 1 Thessalonians, and for *literary* structures" ("Argumentative Structure," 127-28). By rhetorical criticism he means, above all, "the rhetoric, the type of persuasion, of 1 Thessalonians" (135). "Better than any other modern critical approach it brings to comprehension (which is more than explanation) what all exegetical methods *want* to 'explain' — the text's 'power' (G. Kennedy)" (135-36).

On the Use of Elements of Ancient Epistolography in 1 Thessalonians

Johannes Schoon-Janßen

In recent years I have repeatedly concerned myself with the connection between ancient letter theory, Graeco-Roman rhetoric, and the Pauline letters. This was not due to an interest in researching the apostle's exact level of education or in elucidating the Jewish-Christian educational system of the first century C.E.; instead, it grew solely out of a desire to determine more exactly the historical background of a given Pauline letter and, as a result, to understand better his statements and to translate them more effectively for the contemporary reader. In classical terms this means that I am not interested in the form of these letters for form's sake, but rather in discovering the *Sitz im Leben* of the respective writing by approaching it from the perspective of *Formgeschichte*, that is, the attempt to understand better the background of the writing.

For this reason, in my 1991 dissertation *Umstrittene "Apologien" in den Paulusbriefen*, I examined several Pauline letters from both an epistolographical and rhetorical perspective and thereby repeatedly sought to ascertain the *Sitz im Leben* of the elements thus identified.[1] Whoever looks for elements of ancient epistolography in Paul's letters in this way is thereby situated in an astonishingly long line of historical research.

---

1. Johannes Schoon-Janßen, *Umstrittene "Apologien" in den Paulusbriefen. Studien zur rhetorischen Situation des 1. Thessalonicherbriefes, des Galaterbriefes und des Philipperbriefes* (GTA 45; Göttingen: Vandenhoeck & Ruprecht, 1991).

1. A Brief Overview of Epistolographical Research
in New Testament Studies since
Von Wilamowitz-Moellendorff and Deißmann

Already U. von Wilamowitz-Moellendorff, in his 1907 work *Die Grie-chische Literatur des Altertums*, considered Paul one of the great letter-writers of antiquity.[2] In the period following, important studies of Paul's letter-style were published by Adolph Deißmann, in his book *Licht vom Osten*;[3] F. Exler, in his work *The Form of the Ancient Letter — A Study in Greek Epistolography*;[4] and O. Roller, in his study *Das Formular der paulinischen Briefe*.[5] In 1939 Paul Schubert published *Form and Function of the Pauline Thanksgivings*,[6] and the thesis of this book has recently been taken up anew, primarily by Jan Lambrecht[7] and Peter Arzt.[8] The aspect of Schubert's work that has certainly contributed to ongoing research and is undoubtedly of lasting value is the approach that infers *situation* from the *form* of the letter. Likewise very important is H. Koskenniemi's book, *Studien zur Idee und Phraseologie des griechischen Briefes bis 400 n. Chr.*,[9] published in 1956, in which the author discussed, among other things, the relationship of ancient rhetoric to epistolography. Especially valuable for the relation between ancient epistolography and the Pauline letters is Klaus Thraede's 1970 work, *Grundzüge griechisch-römischer Brieftopik*,[10] in which he examines primarily the elements of ancient friendship letters and

2. U. von Wilamowitz-Moellendorff, *Die Griechische Literatur des Altertums* (2nd ed.; Berlin/Leipzig: Teubner, 1907).

3. A. Deißmann, *Licht von Osten* (Tübingen: Mohr, 1923) (English translation: A. Deißmann, *Light from the Ancient East* [Grand Rapids: Baker, 1978]).

4. F. X. J. Exler, *The Form of the Ancient Letter: A Study in Greek Epistolography* (Washington: Catholic University of America, 1923).

5. O. Roller, *Das Formular der paulinischen Briefe: Ein Beitrag zur Lehre vom antiken Briefe* (BWANT 4.6; Stuttgart: Kohlhammer, 1933).

6. P. Schubert, *Form and Function of the Pauline Thanksgivings* (BZNW 20; Berlin: Alfred Töpelmann, 1939).

7. J. Lambrecht, "Thanksgiving in 1 Thessalonians 1–3," in *The Thessalonian Correspondence* (ed. R. F. Collins; BETL 87; Leuven: Leuven University Press–Peeters, 1990), 183-205, and now in *TD*, 135-62.

8. P. Arzt, "The 'Epistolary Introductory Thanksgiving' in the Papyri and in Paul," *NovT* 36 (1994): 29-46.

9. H. Koskenniemi, *Studien zur Idee und Phraseologie des griechischen Briefes bis 400 n. Chr.* (Helsinki: Akateeminen Kirjakauppa, 1956).

10. K. Thraede, *Grundzüge griechisch-römischer Brieftopik* (Munich: Beck, 1970).

finds them again, among other places, in a number of passages from Paul's letters.

In 1972, in *Der Apostel Paulus und die sokratische Tradition,* Hans-Dieter Betz interpreted 2 Corinthians 10–13 epistolographically as a "Verteidigungsbrief" (defense letter).[11] Other works that take up and develop Thraede's approach come from Abraham J. Malherbe,[12] Karl P. Donfried,[13] Hans-Dieter Betz,[14] Robert Jewett,[15] Michael Bünker,[16] John L. White,[17] Stanley K. Stowers,[18] Franz Schnider and Werner Stenger,[19] Juan Chapa,[20] and others.[21] The application of elements of ancient epistolography is useful for this essay primarily because, from the application of certain epistolary themes, one can make assertions about the *situation* of the letter, that is, the relationship that Paul has with a given church at the time of the letter's formulation (on this, see especially the above-mentioned works of Schubert, Koskenniemi, Thraede, Donfried, Jewett, and Bünker).

11. H.-D. Betz, *Der Apostel Paulus und die sokratische Tradition* (BHT 45; Tübingen: Mohr/Siebeck, 1972).

12. A. J. Malherbe, "Ancient Epistolary Theorists," *OJRS* 5 (1977): 3-77; "Exhortation in First Thessalonians," *NovT* 25 (1983): 238-56.

13. K. P. Donfried, "False Presuppositions in the Study of Romans," in *The Romans Debate* (ed. K. P. Donfried; rev. ed.; Minneapolis: Augsburg, 1991), 102-27.

14. H.-D. Betz, *Galatians* (Hermeneia; Philadelphia: Fortress, 1979); *2 Corinthians 8 and 9* (Hermeneia; Philadelphia: Fortress, 1985).

15. R. Jewett, "Romans as an Ambassadorial Letter," *Int* 36 (1982): 5-20.

16. M. Bünker, *Briefformular und rhetorische Disposition im 1. Korintherbrief* (GTA 28; Göttingen: Vandenhoeck & Ruprecht, 1984).

17. J. L. White, "New Testament Epistolary Literature in the Framework of Ancient Epistolography," *ANRW* II.25.2 (Berlin and New York: Walter de Gruyter, 1984), 1730-56.

18. Stanley K. Stowers, *Letter Writing in Graeco-Roman Antiquity* (Philadelphia: Fortress, 1986).

19. F. Schnider and W. Stenger, *Studien zum neutestamentlichen Briefformular* (NTTS 11; Leiden: E. J. Brill, 1987).

20. J. Chapa, "Consolatory Patterns? 1 Thes 4,13.18; 5,11," in *The Thessalonian Correspondence,* 220-28; "Is First Thessalonians a Letter of Consolation?" *NTS* 40 (1994): 150-60.

21. See the additional literature cited in Schoon-Janßen, *Umstrittene "Apologien,"* 168-82, and Arzt, *Thanksgiving,* 29-30.

2. Elements of Ancient Epistolography in 1 Thessalonians

The elements of epistolary theory of classical antiquity, which are in fact found quite often in 1 Thessalonians, belong to that aspect of theory related to friendship letters. This is not accidental, since the oldest work on Greek letter style that has come down to us — a writing that draws on sources of the first century B.C.E. and compiles them by means of redaction during the first, second, or third century C.E.[22] — defines the letter per se as a friendship letter.

The writing in question is an excursus in the study attributed to Demetrius of Phaleron, Περὶ ἑρμενείας,[23] where, in the course of §§223-35, the author characterizes the letter, with some qualifications, in the following way. He speaks of the simplicity of the letter (§223), which should, however, be somewhat more developed than a conversation (τοῦ διαλόγου) and which is sent as a kind of gift (δῶρον) (§224). With regard to its style, the letter should not correspond to a festive speech, but rather to the way one speaks with a friend (πρὸς φίλον) (§225). Asyndeta are not suitable for a letter (§226). Nevertheless, it should contain much personal information (τὸ ἠθικόν), since every person writes a letter more or less as an image of his or her own soul and since one can know the inner thoughts (τὸ ἦθος) of the writer nowhere better than from a letter (§227). Letters should not be treatises headed by a greeting — like many of Plato's letters (§228) — and they should not be written in a formal style, as if one were writing not a letter but rather a defense speech (δίκην), which would be not only ridiculous, but also unfriendly (οὐδὲ φιλικόν) (§229). Some items are unsuitable for a letter (e.g., treatises on the dialectical arts or on scientific questions [§230]), since a brief letter is intended as a friendly gesture (φιλοφρόνησις), with the presentation of uncomplicated circumstances (περὶ ἁπλοῦ πράγματος ἔκθεσις) in simple words (§231). Also, proofs can (as an exception) be presented in a letter (§233). When it concerns missives to cities and kings, the person of the addressee is to be respected and a more formal style (ἐξηρμένη) employed, although not the style of a treatise (§234). Thus, the letter should be a mixture of charming and simple styles (§235). One also learns, especially from §§225, 229, and 231, that

---

22. Regarding the dating, see Thraede, *Grundzüge*, 19-21.
23. Demetrius, Περὶ ἑρμενείας, §§223-35, in *Demetrius Phalereus de Elocutione* (ed. L. Radermacher; Stuttgart: Teubner, 1967), 47-49.

Demetrius understands a letter, as a rule, to be a written communication *between friends*, whereas letters to cities and kings were treated as a special case.

Friendship letters play a prominent role in the oldest Greek letter-writer that has been preserved for us, which is also incorrectly attributed to Demetrius[24] and was written in Egypt sometime after Περὶ ἑρμενείας.[25] Here the φιλικός-type is treated most thoroughly[26] as the first of twenty-one categories of letters. That the various letter types overlap at many points is clear from a comparison of the letter of friendship (φιλικός)[27] with the letter of sympathy (παραμυθητικός),[28] letter of praise (ἐπαινετικός),[29] the letter of advice (συμβουλετικός),[30] and the letter of congratulations (συνχαρητός).[31] In his description of the friendship letter, Pseudo-Demetrius[32] emphasizes that separation from the letter's recipient can only be limited to a *merely physical* one[33] and that through the means of the letter a conversation, albeit indirect, is enabled.

As the starting point of their studies on the ancient letter, both Koskenniemi[34] and Thraede[35] analyze the very writings we have mentioned. Whereas Koskenniemi also examines several different kinds of letters and bases his work essentially on Greek-language papyrus letters from Egypt,[36] Thraede deals consistently with the friendship letter of classical antiquity.[37]

---

24. See Thraede, *Grundzüge*, 26.

25. Thraede, *Grundzüge*, 54-55.

26. It consists of twenty lines in the edition by Weichert: *Demetrii et Libanii qui feruntur Typoi Epistolikoi et Epistolimaioi Charaktēres* (ed. V. Weichert; Leipzig: Teubner, 1910), 1-12.

27. Weichert, *Typoi epistolikoi*, 2-3.

28. Weichert, *Typoi epistolikoi*, 4-5.

29. Weichert, *Typoi epistolikoi*, 6-7.

30. Weichert, *Typoi epistolikoi*, 7.

31. Weichert, *Typoi epistolikoi*, 10-11.

32. Weichert, *Typoi epistolikoi*, 2-3; this text can also be found in Thraede, *Grundzüge*, 25-26.

33. Extract from the exemplary letter: τῷ σώματι μόνον πάσχω, Weichert, *Typoi epistolikoi*, 3, lines 6-7.

34. Koskenniemi, *Studien*, 21-27, 54-56.

35. Thraede, *Grundzüge*, 17-27.

36. Koskenniemi, *Studien*, 64-87.

37. In fact, due to the age and significance of the friendship letter precisely at the time the New Testament writings came into being, I consider this procedure justified and even imperative.

I now turn to some of Thraede's insights.[38] He recognizes already in pre-Christian writers such as Cicero,[39] Ovid, Seneca, and Pliny certain motifs unique to friendship letters that were in part taken up in the New Testament and then immediately developed into a friendship letter system, primarily by a series of Christian letter-writers of late antiquity. These motifs include primarily the following:

a) the letter as a conversation *(per litteras colloqui)*;[40]
b) the ἄπων/πάρων or the παρουσία or the μνεία motif, which[41] could first of all develop into the motif "unity in the spirit";[42] second, by way of the notion "unity in friendship,"[43] these motifs could also evolve into[44] the motif of "being bound together in love";[45] and, third, in Thraede's listing of letter motifs of late antiquity, these motifs appear again, along with the εἰκών ψυχῆς motif,[46] under the collective concept of "making the person present";[47]
c) the "present in the spirit" motif,[48] which is closely tied to the παρουσία motif (the παρουσία motif[49] is taken up also in the New

38. For Demetrius, the friendship letter is the basic form of the letter per se, which is the reason why I concentrate, in the following discussion, on Thraede's reflections, which are rooted in this notion.

39. A standard work on the rhetoric of Cicero is C. J. Classen's *Recht-Rhetorik-Politik. Untersuchungen zu Ciceros rhetorischer Strategie* (Darmstadt: Wissenschaftliche Buchgesellschaft, 1985), 41; see also the literature listed on 371ff.

40. See Ovid evidence in Thraede, *Grundzüge*, 49; similarly, already in Cicero; references for this are found in Thraede, *Grundzüge*, 27-38.

41. See Ovid evidence in Thraede, *Grundzüge*, 52-55; similarly, already in Cicero; references are found in Thraede, *Grundzüge*, 39-47.

42. Thraede, *Grundzüge*, 109.

43. Thraede, *Grundzüge*, 126.

44. Regarding the notion "unity in friendship," the recollection of Demetrius, Περὶ ἑρμενείας, particularly §224 (the letter as δῶρον) and §231 (the letter as φιλοφρόνησις), could, in my opinion, have played a role.

45. Thraede, *Grundzüge*, 126.

46. See also already Περὶ ἑρμενείας §227!

47. Thraede, *Grundzüge*, 146-61.

48. Thraede, *Grundzüge*, 55-61.

49. This motif is also considered by Koskenniemi, *Studien* — quite apart from his other usual procedure — as one of three that are decisive for general academic letter theory. In addition to the notion of the *parousia* (38-42), he mentions that of *philophronesis* (35-37) and that of *homilia* in the sense of being together (42-47).

Testament; see 1 Thess 2:17, 1 Cor 5:3, and Col 2:5);[50] and

d) the thematization of consolation and longing,[51] which in late antiquity is taken up again as the πόθος motif.[52]

In the following discussion I would like to demonstrate that, of the motifs found in 1 Thessalonians, παρουσία is not the only one, and, further, that it is found in several times. In 1 Thessalonians the "letter as conversation" motif does not appear explicitly; however, of the concepts mentioned, the ἄπων/πάρων or the παρουσία or the μνεία motif appears twice at the very beginning, namely, in 1:2 and 1:3 (Εὐχαριστοῦμεν τῷ θεῷ πάντοτε περὶ πάντων ὑμῶν μνείαν ποιούμενοι ἐπὶ τῶν προσευχῶν ἡμῶν, ἀδιαλείπτως μνημονεύοντες ὑμῶν τοῦ ἔργου τῆς πίστεως καὶ τοῦ κόπου τῆς ἀγάπης καὶ τῆς ὑπομονῆς τῆς ἐλπιδος τοῦ κυρίου ἡμῶν Ἰησοῦ Χριστοῦ ἔμπροσθεν τοῦ θεοῦ καὶ πατρὸς ἡμῶν). Both in verse 2 (ὑμῶν μνείαν ποιούμενοι) and verse 3 (μνημονεύοντες ὑμῶν . . .) the μνεία motif is given as a friendship letter *topos*. This anchoring of one's presence in remembering is in both cases extended by Christians: both are concerned with remembering in prayer before God (εὐχαριστοῦμεν τῷ θεῷ πάντοτε περὶ πάντων ὑμῶν). Additionally, in verse 3 the concepts ἔργον, κόπος, and ὑπομονή are consciously supplied; they are later taken up, to some degree, in 2:9 (μνημονεύετε γάρ, ἀδελφοί, τὸν κόπον ἡμῶν καὶ τὸν μόχθον· νυκτὸς καὶ ἡμέρας ἐργαζόμενοι) and then (this time functioning paraenetically) in 4:11 (καὶ ἐργάζεσθαι ταῖς [ἰδίαις] χερσὶν ὑμῶν, καθὼς ὑμῖν παρηγγείλαμεν). Similarly, the triad πίστις, ἀγάπη, and ἐλπίς is consciously introduced in verse 3, so that it may likewise be used paraenetically in 5:7-8 (οἱ γὰρ καθεύδοντες νυκτὸς καθεύδουσιν καὶ οἱ μεθυσκόμενοι νυκτὸς μεθύουσιν· ἡμεῖς δὲ ἡμέρας ὄντες νήφωμεν ἐνδυσάμενοι θώρακα πίστεως καὶ ἀγάπης καὶ περικεφαλαίαν ἐλπίδα σωτηρίας). The μνεία-motif in 1 Thess 1:2-3 is expanded both times; in the second it is additionally supplemented by a double triad,[53] so that simultaneously the basis for part of the later paraenesis is established.

The analysis of friendship letter motifs found in 2:17 is not entirely simple. If Thraede used 2:17a as an example for the παρουσία *topos*,[54] then

---

50. Thraede, *Grundzüge*, 95-106.

51. Ovid evidence in Thraede, *Grundzüge*, 61-64.

52. Thraede, *Grundzüge*, 165-68.

53. In this regard, see also W. Marxsen, *Der erste Brief an die Thessalonicher* (Zürich: Theologischer Verlag, 1979), 35.

54. Thraede, *Grundzüge*, 95-97.

one must, at this point, differentiate, go beyond Thraede, and classify 2:17b as including a letter *topos:* ἡμεῖς δέ, ἀδελφοί, ἀπορφανισθέντες ἀφ' ὑμῶν πρὸς καιρὸν ὥρας, προσώπῳ οὐ καρδίᾳ (2:17a). Being separated "in person, not in heart" naturally expresses a form of presence, though it fits better into the category of "present in spirit": περισσοτέρως ἐσπουδάσαμεν τὸ πρόσωπον ὑμῶν ἰδεῖν ἐν πολλῇ ἐπιθυμίᾳ (2:17b). The emphasis on the fervent attempts to see the addressees face to face, further strengthened by the expression ἐν πολλῇ ἐπιθυμίᾳ, is a very clear written example of the pre-Pauline friendship letter motif of yearning, which in post-Pauline letter theory is designated as the πόθος motif.

A mixture of the μνεία and πόθος motifs is found in 3:6: . . . ἐλθόντος Τιμοθέου . . . καὶ εὐαγγελισαμένου ἡμῖν . . . ὅτι ἔχετε μνείαν ἡμῶν ἀγαθὴν πάντοτε, ἐπιποθοῦντες ἡμᾶς ἰδεῖν καθάπερ καὶ ἡμεῖς ὑμᾶς. We have here an enhancement of the μνεία and πόθος motifs by the Thessalonians, even if reported indirectly, to the level of a Pauline πόθος confession. Connected to this is the consolation motif in 3:7: διὰ τοῦτο παρεκλήθημεν, ἀδελφοί, ἐφ' ὑμῖν . . . διὰ τῆς ὑμῶν πίστεως. The consolation that Paul had been given by the Thessalonians is certainly rooted primarily in their faith. From the context, however, it is evident that this faith is closely related to the fact that they remember Paul with fondness and yearn to be with him (v 6). In 3:10 the πόθος motif appears again: νυκτὸς καὶ ἡμέρας ὑπερεκπερισσοῦ δεόμενοι εἰς τὸ ἰδεῖν ὑμῶν τὸ πρόσωπον. Here also, Paul again expresses a tender bond with the Thessalonians by using this motif of the friendship letter.

1 Thess 4:13-18 is permeated with the consolation motif, although this motif becomes clear primarily in the framing verses of the passage (13 and 18): Οὐ θέλομεν δὲ ὑμᾶς ἀγνοεῖν, ἀδελφοί, περὶ τῶν κοιμωμένων, ἵνα μὴ λυπῆσθε καθὼς καὶ οἱ λοιποὶ οἱ μὴ ἔχοντες ἐλπίδα (4:13). The function of this passage is clear: the addressees should not be sad that, prior to the *parousia* of the Lord, members of their church have died whose fate now appears uncertain to them. Thus Paul can urge: Ὥστε παρακαλεῖτε ἀλλήλους ἐν τοῖς λόγοις τούτοις (4:18). The closing of 4:13-18, with its παρακαλεῖτε ἀλλήλους in verse 18, supports what was said in verse 13. Also in 5:11 a similar challenge appears: Διὸ παρακαλεῖτε ἀλλήλους καὶ οἰκοδομεῖτε εἰς τὸν ἕνα, καθὼς καὶ ποιεῖτε. The παρακαλεῖτε in verse 11, at the end of the section 5:1-11, points, in my opinion, in two different directions. Both "consoling" and mutual "admonishing" are involved here: the passage emphasizes both the consoling indicative of salvation (especially

186

5:4-5 and 5:8a, 9-10) and the admonishing imperative (5:6, 8b),[55] which is derived from the former.

An additional friendship letter motif found in 1 Thessalonians is the "joined in love" motif, which, although not recorded prior to Paul, developed from the pre-Pauline motif "present in spirit." It is found in 1 Thessalonians for the first time in 2:8: οὕτως ὁμειρόμενοι ὑμῶν εὐδοκοῦμεν μεταδοῦναι ὑμῖν οὐ μόνον τὸ εὐαγγέλιον τοῦ θεοῦ ἀλλὰ καὶ τὰς ἑαυτῶν ψυχάς, διότι ἀγαπητοὶ ἡμῖν ἐγενήθητε. Within the context of this verse, Paul reports the good relationship he developed with the Thessalonians while visiting them, though the ἀγαπητοὶ ἡμῖν ἐγενήθητε, at least in Paul's view, was still valid even at the time 1 Thessalonians was composed. This is confirmed by the second occurrence of the "joined in love" motif in 1 Thessalonians: ὑμᾶς δὲ ὁ κύριος πλεονάσαι καὶ περισσεύσαι τῇ ἀγάπῃ εἰς ἀλλήλους καὶ εἰς πάντας καθάπερ καὶ ἡμεῖς εἰς ὑμᾶς (3:12). Decisive in this regard is the abbreviated afterthought (καθάπερ καὶ ἡμεῖς εἰς ὑμᾶς), which states that Paul himself is also bound in love to the Thessalonians.

Apart from the explicit friendship letter motifs already discussed, a few other formal indications from the general structure of the letter indicate that Paul's relationship to his church was, at a minimum, not bad. First of all, it is striking that in the praescript Paul refrains from mentioning the term "apostle" when referring to the name of the sender. Obviously, he could have done this: the plural ἀπόστολοι is mentioned in 2:7, and he uses the term in most of his letters (Galatians, 1 and 2 Corinthians, and Romans). Evidently, an emphasis on his authority in relationship to the Thessalonians was unnecessary at the time the letter was written; or, indeed, the practice may not yet have been established, since controversies that could have provoked such a stress had not yet flared up in any of the Pauline churches. Additionally, it is striking that in 1:2 a detailed *prooemium* begins that, for good reason, is absent in Galatians, since the relationship to the churches there is very strained. As a result, the "we-you" structure in 1:2-6 becomes quite obvious. The "we-you" relationship that stands behind this usage is characterized quite positively by Paul in 1:6 by the use of μιμητής. This is also expressed by the address ἀδελφοὶ ἠγαπημένοι ὑπὸ θεοῦ.

In 2:1-12 Paul reminds the Thessalonians of his first, joyful visit with them and thereby establishes in their memory a genuine basis for the con-

---

55. See what has been said about 5:7-8 within the context of the discussion of 1:3 above.

tinued positive development of the church. The expositions remind one of the friendship letter *topos* "unity in friendship." The thesis of the emphasis on friendship between sender and receiver in 1 Thess 2:1-12 can be further substantiated if one compares it[56] with §§88b-100a of Cicero's work *Laelius de Amicitia*.[57] Written in the year 44 B.C.E. in the context of a pre-Ciceronian teaching about friendship,[58] this essay is concerned with the relation between friendship *(amicitia)*, honesty *(fides*[59] or *veritas*[60]), and flattery *(adulatio*[61] or *adsentatio*[62]). As the fundamental source, Steinmetz identified the Greek concepts of φιλία, παρρησία, and κολακεία,[63] whereby the relation is such that παρρησία always belongs to true friendship and can, under certain circumstances, also disclose itself in exhortation (νουθεσία) and reproach (ἐγκλήματα),[64] while κολακεία (flattery) is a sure sign for a falsely understood friendship.[65]

Indeed, both ἐπαρρησιασάμεθα in 1 Thess 2:2 and οὔτε γάρ ποτε ἐν λόγῳ κολακείας ἐγενήθημεν in 2:5 fit well into this scheme. Also relevant is Paul's emphasis on the fact that he never gained financially from the Thessalonians, to whom he was bound in friendship (2:5; οὔτε ἐν προφάσει πλεονεξίας), and that he had never used their friendship for other personal advantages (2:6; οὔτε ζητοῦντες ἐξ ἀνθρώπων δόξαν οὔτε ἀφ' ὑμῶν οὔτε ἀπ' ἄλλων). These themes are similar to Cicero's detailed teaching on friendship,[66] which claims that genuine friendship and the seeking of personal advantage are mutually exclusive.

---

56. On the use of elements of ancient friendship instruction by Paul and on the following, see Betz, *Galatians*, 220-37.

57. On the dating, see M. Schanz and C. Hosius, *Geschichte der Römischen Literatur bis zum Gesetzgebungswerk des Kaisers Justinian, 1. Teil: Die Römische Literatur in der Zeit der Republik* (4th ed.; Munich: Beck, 1927), 518-19.

58. See in this regard F.-A. Steinmetz, *Die Freundschaftslehre des Panaitios* (Wiesbaden: Steiner, 1967), 193, who has shown that, with regard to sources, Cicero's treatise was based largely on a Greek source written by Panaitios of Rhodes, a second-century-B.C.E. Stoic!

59. Cicero, *Amicitia* (ed. Robert Combes; Paris: Les Belles Lettres, 1971), §88b.

60. Cicero, *Amicitia*, §§89ff.

61. Cicero, *Amicitia*, §§91-92.

62. Cicero, *Amicitia*, §§89.91b and 93ff.

63. Steinmetz, *Freundschaftslehre*, 151-54.

64. Steinmetz, *Freundschaftslehre*, 151.

65. Steinmetz, *Freundschaftslehre*, 154.

66. Cicero, *Amicitia*, §§26-32.

With respect to epistolography, the final verses of 1 Thessalonians are also of interest. In 5:23 a kind of blessing is imparted, and in 5:26 cordial, though not very specific, greetings are given (ἐν φιλήματι ἁγίῳ), both of which point to a friendly relationship between Paul and the church. This impression is somewhat relativized by verse 27, where Paul adjures (ἐνορκίζω) the addressees before God to read the letter to *all* the brothers (πᾶσιν τοῖς ἀδελφοῖς), whereby he utilizes not only his own authority but even the Lord's.

This suggests that the reading of the letter to everyone in the congregation was important for Paul precisely because the letter contained important nonphilophronetic sections that were not self-evident, such as exhortation (e.g., in relation to the work ethic) and "instruction" (hope of resurrection). This is probably linked to Paul's inexperience in writing letters to churches, and in no way causes a rupture in the friendship with the Thessalonians. Beyond this, we also observe a writing that moves beyond a purely friendship letter toward instruction and exhortation.[67] In fact, the various paraenetic uses of the extended friendship letter motif, especially in 1:2-3, have already hinted at this.

The use of epistolographic elements in 1 Thessalonians, therefore, can be summarized as follows: 1 Thessalonians contains a number of similarities to the *topics* found in ancient friendship letters. On the one hand, one should not give too much weight to the use of these *topics*, since many are used *conventionally*. On the other hand, it must nevertheless be remembered that these *topics* are conventional precisely for *a friendship letter* and not for an instructional or a business letter. Indeed, Paul *consciously* approaches the Thessalonians as *a friend*.

Concerning the probable *Sitz im Leben* of 1 Thessalonians, it can be asserted that 1 Thessalonians is essentially a letter of friendship from Paul to

---

67. In 1983 Abraham Malherbe identified a clear exhortative function for 1 Thessalonians ("Exhortation in First Thessalonians," *NovT* 25 [1983]: 238-56, especially 238), and in 1986 he even calls the entire epistle a pure example of the "paraenetic letter" genre (*Moral Exhortation: A Graeco-Roman Sourcebook;* Philadelphia: Fortress, 1986), 80. In the same year, the same is done by W. A. Meeks, *The Moral World of the First Christians* (Philadelphia: Fortress, 1986), 126; see also Stowers, *Letter Writing,* 96. I am indeed of the opinion that 1 Thessalonians also exhibits paraenetic characteristics. This cannot, however, mean that abuses are rampant in the church, nor that the relationship of the apostle to the church is troubled. Paul approaches the Thessalonians rather in the manner of a parent (see 2:7, 11), as an intimate and trusted friend who, at the same time, as role model, consoles and admonishes.

his church in Thessalonica. It is a letter in which the apostle praises the church greatly, yet simultaneously admonishes it to pursue honorable work and, with pastoral concern, also provides consoling new information[68] regarding the fate of the dead at the time of the *parousia*. In this way, Paul presents himself not as an exceptional teacher, but rather as a pastoral friend.

3. 1 Thessalonians and Graeco-Roman Rhetoric: A Brief Overview

Although the question regarding the link between Paul's letters and Graeco-Roman rhetoric has increasingly come to the fore in recent years, it is by no means a new issue.[69] Already at the turn of this century, F. G. Heinrici[70] and J. Weiss[71] argued for the significance of ancient rhetoric in the interpretation of Paul's letters over against the objections of E. Norden[72] and P. Wendland.[73] The topic was raised again in the 1920s by M. Dibelius, who adopted a rhetoric-friendly position.[74]

---

68. Along with Chapa ("Is First Thessalonians a Letter of Consolation?" 159-60), I see much consolation in 1 Thessalonans, but not necessarily that it is a genuine "letter of consolation."

69. At a minimum one should mention: B. C. Johanson, *To All the Brethren: A Text-Linguistic and Rhetorical Approach to I Thessalonians* (Stockholm: Almqvist & Wiksell, 1987); A Vanhoye, "La Composition de 1 Thessaloniciens," *The Thessalonian Correspondence,* 73-86; F. W. Hughes, "The Rhetoric of 1 Thessalonians," *The Thessalonian Correspondence,* 94-116; W. Wuellner, "The Argumentative Structure of 1 Thessalonians as Paradoxical Encomium," *The Thessalonian Correspondence,* 117-36; and J. S. Kloppenborg, "ΦΙΛΑΔΕΛΦΙΑ, ΘΕΟΔΙΔΑΚΤΟΣ and the Dioscuri: Rhetorical Engagement in 1 Thessalonians 4.9-12," *NTS* 39 (1993): 265-89. See also Schoon-Janßen, *Umstrittene "Apologien,"* 19-25.

70. G. Heinrici, *Der zweite Brief an die Korinther* (8th ed.; KEK 5; Göttingen: Vandenhoeck & Ruprecht, 1900).

71. J. Weiss, *Beiträge zur Paulinischen Rhetorik* (Festschrift B. Weiss; Göttingen: Vandenhoeck & Ruprecht, 1897), 165-247, especially 169-70.

72. E. Norden, *Die antike Kunstprosa* (2 vols.; appeared first in 1898; cited according to the unaltered 3rd ed.; Darmstadt: Wissenschaftliche Buchgesellschaft, 1958), especially 502-7.

73. P. Wendland, *Die Hellenistisch-römische Kultur in ihren Beziehungen zu Judentum und Christentum* (HNT I.2; Tübingen: Mohr, 1908), especially 20; *Die urchristlichen Literaturformen* (Tübingen: Mohr, 1912), especially 349.

74. M. Dibelius, *Geschichte der urchristlichen Literatur II, Apostolisches und Nach-apostolisches* (Leipzig: Teubner, 1926), especially 11.

In 1972 Hans-Dieter Betz utilized a rhetorical approach in his previously mentioned book on 2 Corinthians 10–13, and, again in 1975, in his article "The Literary Composition and Function of Paul's Letter to the Galatians."[75] This latter study served as the foundation for his commentary on Galatians, which was published four years later.[76] In this important work Betz interpreted Galatians as a defense speech by Paul, influenced by classical antiquity and embedded in an epistolary framework.

In subsequent years a number of distinguished studies on Pauline rhetoric were written. Wilhelm Wuellner[77] needs to be included in this list because of his emphasis on the significance of the "rhetorical situation" for the interpretation of Paul's letters.[78] George A. Kennedy[79] has published a number of important studies on ancient rhetoric, including his 1984 book *New Testament Interpretation through Rhetorical Criticism*, which is of particular value for theologians. The aim of rhetorical analysis, in Kennedy's view, is to uncover the *intention* of the author and the *manner in which* the author transmits this intention to the audience through a text.[80]

---

75. Hans-Dieter Betz, "The Literary Composition and Function of Paul's Letter to the Galatians," *NTS* 21 (1975): 353-79.

76. Hans-Dieter Betz, *Galatians: A Commentary on Paul's Letter to the Churches in Galatia* (Hermeneia; Philadelphia: Fortress, 1979).

77. W. Wuellner, "Greek Rhetoric and Pauline Argumentation," in *Early Christian Literature and the Classical Intellectual Tradition* (Festschrift R. M. Grant; ed. W. R. Schoedel and R. L. Wilken; ThH 53; Paris: Beauchesne, 1979), 177-88; W. Wuellner, "Paul's Rhetoric of Argumentation in Romans," *CBQ* 38 (1976): 330-51 (reprinted in *The Romans Debate* [ed. Karl P. Donfried; Minneapolis: Augsburg, 1991], 128-46); W. Wuellner, "Toposforschung und Torahinterpretation bei Paulus und Jesus," *NTS* 24 (1978): 463-86; W. Wuellner, "The Argumentative Structure."

78. W. Wuellner, "Toposforschung," 468; this emphasis goes back to Lloyd F. Bitzer, "The Rhetorical Situation," *Philosophy and Rhetoric* (1968): 1.1-14; it was later carried forward by E. Schüssler Fiorenza, "Rhetorical Situation and Historical Reconstruction in 1 Corinthians," *NTS* 33 (1987): 386-403.

79. G. A. Kennedy, *The Art of Persuasion in Greece* (Princeton: Princeton University Press, 1963); *The Art of Rhetoric in the Roman World* (Princeton: Princeton University Press, 1972); *Classical Rhetoric and Its Christian and Secular Tradition from Ancient to Modern Times* (Chapel Hill: University of North Carolina Press, 1980); *Greek Rhetoric under Christian Emperors* (Princeton: Princeton University Press, 1983); *New Testament Interpretation through Rhetorical Criticism* (Chapel Hill: University of North Carolina Press, 1984).

80. Kennedy, *Rhetorical Criticism*, 12: "The ultimate goal of rhetorical analysis, briefly put, is the discovery of the author's intent and of how that is transmitted through a text to an audience."

In his 1984 book *Formgeschichte des Neuen Testaments,* Klaus Berger[81] also deals with the genre of larger textual units. For a systematic study of chapters, Berger uses the ancient "divisions into deliberative *(symbouleutikon),* epideictic *(epideiktikon),* and judicial *(dikanikon)* texts, that is, texts which aim to activate or admonish the reader (symbouleutic); texts which aim to impress him (epideictic); and texts which aim to clarify decisions for him (dikanic)."[82] The question regarding the "genre" of a biblical text certainly seems to me to have some bearing on the interpretation of the respective text. As far as 1 Thessalonians is concerned, Frank Witt Hughes classifies the oldest Pauline epistle as belonging to the epideictic genre,[83] in distinction from G. A. Kennedy,[84] who, for example, considers 1 Thessalonians a deliberative/symbouleutic letter. 1 Thessalonians, in my judgment, belongs more nearly to the epideictic genre,[85] although it does contain elements of admonition that are anticipated in the opening section and then clearly articulated in 1 Thess 4:11-12. Nevertheless, in my judgment 1 Thessalonians is not determined by these admonitions. The tone of the letter is set by the very good relationship between the apostle and the church, as is evident from the frequent usage of components from the friendship letter.

The primary intention of the letter is not paraenetic[86] (epistolary theory!) or symbouleutic (rhetorical theory!), but *more likely* friendly/pastoral (epistolary theory!) and epideictic (rhetorical theory!). In stating this, however, I wish to emphasize firmly the words *"more likely"* and thus not to absolutize this thesis.

In light of these tentative results the thesis that 1 Thess 2:1-12 is an apology in which Paul reacted to criticisms made against him can be eliminated. This conclusion is valid whether one considers 2:1-12 as a passage

---

81. K. Berger, *Formgeschichte des Neuen Testaments* (Heidelberg: Quelle & Meyer, 1984), 17.

82. "Einteilung in symbuleutische, epideiktische und dikanische Texte, d.h. Texte, die den Leser aktivieren oder mahnen wollen (symbuleutische); Texte, die ihn beeindrucken wollen (epideiktische), und Texte, die ihm eine Entscheidung verdeutlichen wollen (dikanische)." Berger, *Formgeschichte,* 17.

83. Hughes, "Rhetoric," 94-116.

84. Kennedy, *Rhetorical Criticism,* 102.

85. On the reasons, see Schoon-Janßen, *Umstrittene "Apologien,"* 47-50, especially nn. 58, 61, and 62.

86. Contra Malherbe, "Exhortation in First Thessalonians," 238.

belonging to the *topos* "unity in friendship" (which seems to me the most appropriate solution), the letter of friendship as previously described, or whether one considers 2:1-12 within the framework of rhetorical theory, either as an example of apostolic *imitatio* having paraenetic character (thus classifying it with the symbouleutic/deliberative genre) or as an approbatory description of the past (thus classifying it with the epideictic/ demonstrative genre).

4. Results

1 Thessalonians contains many features reminiscent of the *topic* of ancient friendship letters, including the important fact that Paul consciously approaches the Thessalonians as a friend. The speech genre of 1 Thessalonians comes closest to the genus epideictic. Reasons for such a classification include the *topoi* of praise and blame (although less frequent) as well as the dominant feeling of love.[87] Such love is rooted in a profound sympathy for the church, a factor that again reveals Paul's positive relationship to these Christians in Thessalonica. Such a reading, however, would suggest that the paraenetic section 4:10b-12 clearly falls outside the framework of pure praise.

As far as a possible *Sitz im Leben* for 1 Thessalonians, it is essentially a letter of friendship from Paul to the church that he founded in Thessalonica in which the apostle highly commends the community but also specifically admonishes it to pursue honorable work. In addition, Paul, as a result of his pastoral concern, shares consoling new information about the fate of the dead at the time of the *parousia*. As a result of this approach it is evident that the apostle does not present himself as a superior teacher, but, rather, as an empathetic friend. Alleged previous criticisms against Paul by the church are highly unlikely and should, therefore, be excluded thoroughly in the interpretation of 1 Thessalonians.

---

87. See Schoon-Janßen, *Umstrittene "Apologien,"* 48-49, nn. 58 and 62.

The Rhetoric of Letters

Frank W. Hughes

One of the questions raised by the SNTS Thessalonian Correspondence Seminar is how the methods and results of both form criticism and rhetorical criticism can be integrated to produce the most adequate analysis of 1 Thessalonians. In this context it will be useful to raise some methodological issues related specifically to a rhetorical analysis of 1 Thessalonians as a way of introducing my previous analysis of the subject, "The Rhetoric of Letters."[1]

1. Methodological Notes on Rhetorical Criticism

Can rhetorical criticism and form criticism be successfully integrated? The answer lies in how one does rhetorical criticism. This, in turn, depends on what system of rhetoric undergirds one's practice of rhetorical criticism.[2]

---

1. Frank W. Hughes, *Early Christian Rhetoric and 2 Thessalonians* (JSNTSup 30; Sheffield: JSOT Press, 1989), especially chap. 2, "The Rhetoric of Letters," 19-50. By the kind permission of JSOT Press, this chapter is reprinted as part of this essay. Also relevant to this discussion is my detailed rhetorical analysis of 1 Thessalonians: Frank W. Hughes, "The Rhetoric of 1 Thessalonians," in *The Thessalonian Correspondence* (ed. Raymond F. Collins; BETL 87; Leuven: Leuven University Press–Peeters, 1990), 94-116.

2. Frank W. Hughes, "Rhetorical Criticism," in the *Mercer Dictionary of the Bible* (ed. Watson E. Mills; Macon: Mercer University Press, 1990), 763-64; see also Duane F. Watson and Alan J. Houser, *Rhetorical Criticism of the Bible: A Comprehensive Bibliography with*

For some rhetorical critics, the use of categories of Graeco-Roman rhetoric is not of great interest, and so integration with the form criticism of letters is probably neither desirable nor possible. Other rhetorical critics of letters have come to rhetorical criticism through form criticism (either of the Gospels or of the letters), and so the integration of the insights of form criticism with those of rhetorical criticism is presupposed. Some early rhetorical critics seem not to have been aware that they were doing rhetorical criticism, but thought they were doing a more adequate kind of form criticism, using models explicitly drawn from Graeco-Roman rhetoric.

Yet before we even deal with the integration of rhetorical criticism with form criticism at all, some scholars will object to doing rhetorical criticism of letters as it is now being done. Duane F. Watson states very crisply: "A vigorous debate transpires concerning the extent that Greco-Roman rhetorical theory influenced the epistolary genre in antiquity. One facet of this debate concerns the relationship between rhetoric and the epistles of the New Testament, particularly those of Paul."[3] One extreme side of this "vigorous debate" asserts that since rhetorical theory was developed for use in speeches, it is not legitimate to use rhetorical theory to deal with letters, especially the phenomenon of the arrangement or *dispositio* of letters.[4] The other side of the debate, represented by a variety of rhetorical critics, myself included, counters with a number of arguments in favor of using rhetorical theory to help interpret letters. Since it is well known that epistolary theory was developed somewhat separately from rhetorical theory, the same sources do not tell us anything about *both* the rhetoric of speeches *and* of letters. Hence, if we are looking for material on the arrangement of speeches we can turn to the rhetorical handbooks of Aristotle (looking back at pre-Aristotelian rhetoric as well), Cicero, the pseudo-Ciceronian *Rhetorica ad Herennium,* and Quintilian; we can also turn to actual speeches of Cicero, Demosthenes, and quite a few other Greek and Roman orators to see how the precepts of rhetoric were worked out in practice. In so doing we observe how a long tradition of teaching on

---

Notes on History and Method (Biblical Interpretation Series, 4; Leiden: E. J. Brill, 1994), 109-15.

3. Duane F. Watson in Watson and Houser, *Rhetorical Criticism of the Bible,* 120.

4. See especially C. Joachim Classen, "Paul's Epistles and Ancient Greek and Roman Rhetoric," in *Rhetoric and the New Testament: Essays from the 1992 Heidelberg Conference* (ed. Stanley E. Porter and Thomas H. Olbricht; JSNTSup 90; Sheffield: JSOT Press, 1993), 265-91.

arrangement is continually made more and more complex as one proceeds from Aristotle, through Cicero, to Quintilian. In addition, historians of Christianity can gain knowledge about the development of tradition from the way older rhetorical tradition is dealt with by Quintilian in the context of reflection on his own successful career of rhetorical instruction. In looking for instruction about the writing of letters, the scholar will find little surviving material in the epistolary handbooks.[5] In comparison with the New Testament, most of what survives is significantly later. Much of this extant material in the epistolary handbooks, as well as other scattered information concerning the writing of letters, has primarily to do with the *inventio* (invention, or, better, the use of topics) and *elocutio* (style) of letters (and this material is strongly related to rhetoric), with almost no references to the *dispositio* of letters. What little there is focuses mostly on the opening and closing of letters, with little instruction about the bodies of letters. A statement by one of the newer participants in the "vigorous debate," Jeffrey T. Reed, is worth quoting at some length:

> Certain functional parallels, nevertheless, do exist between the epistolary theorists and letter writers and the customary rhetorical arrangement. In the same way that epistolary openings function to expose the general nature of the relationship between the sender and the recipient (be it positive or negative), so also the *exordium* serves to generate a positive relationship of trust and compliance between the speaker and listener, that is, to build ἦθος. The same may be said of the epistolary closing and the *conclusio*. One type of letter particularly lended itself to creating ἦθος, the friendly type. . . . The epistolary body, which communicated the message(s) of the sender, least parallels the rhetorical categories of, for example, *narratio, propositio, probatio* and *confirmatio*. However, because the epistolary body was open to various mediums of communication, one must at least concede the possibility of finding a rhetorical arrangement here.
>
> In summary, the three standard epistolary components (opening, body, closing) share some similarity with the four principal patterns of rhetorical arrangement *(exordium, narratio, confirmatio, conclusio)*. But the similarity is functional, not formal. In other words, there is no necessary connection between the basic theory of epistolary structure and the

5. Abraham J. Malherbe, *Ancient Epistolary Theorists* (SBLSBS 19; Atlanta: Scholars Press, 1988).

technical teachings about rhetorical arrangement. The similarities may be explained in light of the modern linguistic realization that language is often pragmatically used in different genres to do similar things. More importantly, the epistolary theorists and letter writers say nothing explicit about structuring letters according to a rhetorical arrangement.[6]

The silence of the rhetorical handbooks concerning letters parallels the silence of the epistolary handbooks concerning rhetorical *dispositio,* since it was considered highly undesirable to try to do persuasion by letters. The reasons for this are not difficult to imagine for those who know rhetorical theory. Since before the time of Aristotle, rhetorical theory had five parts: invention, arrangement, style, memory, and delivery. A letter would lack the last two of these elements: memory and delivery. To say positive things about doing rhetoric by letters would put rhetorical teachers in the position of telling their students that two of the subjects they taught were not absolutely important; and their nonimportance would make declamation, one of the most important avenues of rhetorical instruction, absurd. Hence, rhetorical handbooks are definitely the wrong places to look for much that is positive concerning the persuasive power of letters! This ambiguity of rhetoricians doing rhetoric by letters is still the best explanation of the silence of the rhetorical handbooks concerning letters.

Yet just because rhetorical theory was silent concerning letters does not mean that rhetoricians did not actually write letters in attempts to persuade the readers (and/or hearers) of the letters to change attitudes or actions. And how best to arrange the material in the letters? In *De oratore* 2.49 Cicero portrays an imaginary dialogue between Antonius and Catulus, two well-known Roman orators. In this passage Antonius asks, "And what if, as often happens to the most excellent men, messages *(mandata)* have to be communicated from a general at a meeting of the Senate, or conveyed from the Senate to a general or to any prince or nation? Because, on occasions of this sort, a *genus* of rhetoric more elaborate *(accuratiore)* than the ordinary has to be employed, does it therefore seem to follow that this sort of speaking *(pars etiam haec causarum)* should be accounted a distinct department of oratorical activity, or should be fitted out with its own peculiar rules?" "Definitely not," Catulus replied, "since

---

6. Jeffrey T. Reed, "Using Ancient Rhetorical Categories to Interpret Paul's Letters: A Question of Genre," in Porter and Olbricht, *Rhetoric and the New Testament,* 292-304; the quotation is from 307-8.

the ability acquired by a ready speaker, from the treatment of his other subjects and topics, will not fail him in situations of that description."[7] In other words, no further *genus* of rhetoric other than the conventional three *genera* (epideictic, deliberative, and judicial) is needed: a "ready speaker" will be able to take the precepts from the three *genera* as they stand and make modifications from them to fit the situation. Clearly this does not mean that letters are the same as speeches; but Cicero portrays Catulus as saying that letters (or other forms of *mandata*, which are clearly written missives rather than oral speeches) could use various rhetorical features drawn from the conventional precepts about speeches.

What Jeffrey Reed concluded above is that the similarities between letters and speeches are functional and not formal. This fact is not problematic since rhetoric in the practical sense is functional. What is important is that the section of a letter designated as an *exordium* be at the beginning of the letter and attempt to acquire the goodwill of the readers/hearers and state the subjects that will be dealt with in the rest of the letter. If 1 Thess 1:1-10 functions in this way, then it is plausible to call it the *exordium*. No form critic, as far as I know, doubts that rhetorical style could affect letters, and few form critics doubt that conventional topics drawn from rhetorical discourse could also be used in letters. If there is little or no objection against rhetorical style and invention being used in letters, it is hard to see why it is unlikely that some rhetorical elements of arrangement could also be found in letters. This is why the rhetorical analyses Demosthenes' *Epistle 1* by Jonathan A. Goldstein and me are significant.[8] My conclusion then and now is

---

7. Cicero, *De oratore* 2.49; the English translation is modified from that of the Loeb Classical Library. The Loeb translation misleadingly translates *num quia genere orationis in eiusmodo causis accuratiore est utendum* as "because, on occasions of this sort, a style of diction more elaborate than the ordinary has to be employed." This imprecise translation of *genere orationis* by "style of diction" is highly misleading. For a critique of this interpretation of Cicero on this point, see Stanley E. Porter, "The Theoretical Justification for Application of Rhetorical Categories to Pauline Epistolary Literature," in Porter and Olbricht, *Rhetoric and the New Testament*, 100-122; his critique of my interpretation of this passage is found on pp. 115-16, n. 40. I argue that *genere orationis* means what it most commonly means in Latin rhetoric, i.e., a *genus* of rhetoric, meaning one of the three *genera* such as the *genus iudiciale*, the *genus deliberativum*, or the *genus demonstrativum*. This construal of *genere orationis* allows me to conclude that Cicero portrays Catulus as saying that letters could have features of one or more of the *genera orationis* and that no fourth *genus* was necessary.

8. Hughes, *Early Christian Rhetoric*, 47-50; Jonathan A. Goldstein, *The Letters of Demosthenes* (New York and London: Columbia University Press, 1968), 176-81.

that if Demosthenes wrote a letter using rhetoric, it confirms that such a letter could be written, despite the silence of the handbooks from antiquity on this subject. As is well known, Demosthenes was the most famous Greek orator and the most famous deliberative orator. What Demosthenes actually did (as well as what he was reputed to do) could be as much a part of subsequent rhetorical instruction as was any handbook of rhetoric.

Thus the relationship between rhetoric and letters is in a very important sense an open question. A significant way of bringing further clarity to this situation is through the scholarly investigation of the rhetorical features of letters, looking for some of the features one finds in rhetorical speeches, yet always being aware of the differences between speeches and letters. The pragmatic nature of Pauline letters, viewed within the larger context of his apostolic mission, suggests that Paul would use virtually any linguistic means at his disposal (short of what is described in 1 Thess 2:3, 5) to make his letters as persuasive as possible. The task of the rhetorical critic of letters is to discover all elements that make the letter persuasive, whatever they may be and whatever their source. There is no reason why a methodological synthesis of form criticism of letters and rhetorical criticism of letters cannot be forged.

2. Epistolary Rhetoric and the Pauline Corpus

The "quest of the rhetorical Paul" is not a new search. Even during the lifetime of Paul, his adversaries recognized that the letters of Paul had a powerful persuasive effect. In 2 Cor 10:10, Paul preserved a negative comment of his enemies about himself: "For they say, 'His letters are weighty and strong, but his bodily presence is weak, and his speech is despicable.'" Thus the enemies of Paul were contrasting the power of Paul's letters with the apparent weakness of his oratory. This evaluation by Paul's enemies, however, ran counter to the usual evaluation of the rhetorical effectiveness of letters as compared with the physical presence and polished delivery of an orator. The greatest Greek orator, Demosthenes, wrote in a letter, "It is a difficult thing, I know, for advice conveyed by letter to hold its ground, because you Athenians have a way of opposing many suggestions without waiting to understand them."[9] Isocrates, the famous Greek teacher of rhetoric, wrote at

---

9. Demosthenes, *Epistle* 1.3; the English translation is in Demosthenes, *Funeral*

length in two of his extant letters about why he preferred not to write letters, relating this in one instance mainly to the nonunderstanding by the audience of the letter,[10] and in another instance mainly to the letter's not having the prestige of the speaker and devices of oral delivery.[11] Thus, if this negative attitude toward letters was the general attitude of rhetors, Paul's enemies' contention that Paul's letters were "weighty and strong," though his physical presence and oral delivery were weak, indicates that Paul's letters were understood as powerful documents of rhetoric by Paul's enemies.[12]

Since the first century, other writers have commented on Paul's use of rhetoric, among whom the most prominent was Augustine of Hippo, a well-educated teacher of rhetoric and later a Christian bishop and theologian. In his work *De doctrina Christiana,* book 4 of which is a Christian rhetorical handbook that uses rhetorical works by Cicero such as *De inventione* and *Orator* to describe early Christian rhetoric, Augustine analyzed biblical literature and its rhetorical styles. He found, for example, that Paul used the device called *klimax* in Greek and *gradatio* in Latin in Rom 5:3-5, as well as another ornament "which our [Latin] writers call *membra* and *caesa,* and the Greeks call *kola* and *kommata.*" 2 Corinthians was offered by Augustine as an example of *refutatio:* "Writing to the Corinthians in the second epistle he refutes certain persons, pseudo-apostles from among the Jews, who had attacked him."[13] Going on, Augustine

---

Speech, Erotic Essay, Exordia, Letters (trans. N. W. and N. J. DeWitt; LCL; Cambridge: Harvard University Press, 1949).

10. Isocrates, *Epistle 1.2,* to Dionysius.

11. Isocrates, *To Philip* 25-26.

12. On the relation of literary to oral rhetoric, see especially G. A. Kennedy, *Classical Rhetoric and Its Christian and Secular Tradition from Ancient to Modern Times* (Chapel Hill: University of North Carolina Press, 1980), 108-19. For a listing of patristic interpretations of this passage, see V. P. Furnish, *II Corinthians* (AB 32A; Garden City, N.Y.: Doubleday, 1984), 468. A more recent view of this passage and of the success of Paul's literary rhetoric is found in W. A. Meeks, *The First Urban Christians: The Social World of the Apostle Paul* (New Haven: Yale University Press, 1983), 72, where Meeks comments: "some Corinthians have complained that, while Paul's letters are 'weighty and strong,' his 'bodily presence is weak and [his] speech despicable' (2 Cor 10:10). The claims which Paul makes just before this (10:14) are themselves claims about rhetorical ability, the ability 'to take every thought captive.' In 11:6 he admits to nonprofessional status *(idiotēs)* as an orator, but claims to possess *gnōsis.* That is an argument of the same order: Paul rhetorically boasts that he is no mere sophist."

13. Augustine, *De doctrina Christiana* 4.12; English translation: *On Christian Doctrine: St. Augustine* (trans. D. W. Robertson, Jr.; Library of Liberal Arts; Indianapolis: Bobbs-Merrill, 1958).

showed that he understood very well the "foolish discourse" of Paul in 2 Cor 11:16-30, commenting, "And since he was forced to praise himself, attributing this praise to a kind of folly of his own, how wisely and how eloquently he speaks!" He then quoted 2 Cor 11:16-30, and concluded, "Those who are awake will see how much wisdom lies in these words. With what a river of eloquence they flow even he who snores must notice."[14] These are references to what was already a commonplace about an ideal rhetoric: an ideal rhetoric included a marriage of wisdom *(sapientia)* and eloquence *(eloquentia)*.[15] Hence Augustine cited Paul's letters as examples of Christian eloquence par excellence: "surely, if we offer anything of his as an example of eloquence, we shall offer it from those Epistles which even his critics who wished to have his word seem contemptible confessed to be 'weighty and strong.'"[16]

Augustine by no means stands alone as a rhetorical critic of the New Testament. In the early nineteenth century, the German lexicographer Christian Gottlob Wilke as a rhetorical critic was primarily concerned with the investigation of the smaller rhetorical forms, particles, and sentence structure. His pedantic *Die neutestamentliche Rhetorik* concerned itself with the aesthetic form of New Testament discourses, attempting to investigate each "rhetorisches Moment" ("rhetorical element").[17] Wilke did decide that Paul was "as a writer more difficult to characterize than the remaining New Testament writers,"[18] though Paul's rhetoric was described as "clever."[19] Interestingly enough, Wilke distinguished a rhetorical style in the "accepted genuine" letters that was different from that of the epistles to the Ephesians and Colossians, which was also different from that of the Epistle to the Hebrews.[20] He did, however, accept both Thessalonian epistles as genuine.

The discussion of Pauline rhetoric was advanced by the article of Johannes Weiss published in 1897. Weiss began his 82-page essay, "Beitrage zur Paulinischen Rhetorik," by stating

14. Augustine, *De doctrina Christiana* 4.12.

15. Cicero, *De inventione* 1.1-5; *De oratore* 3.142-43; see 2.33 and 3.125.

16. Augustine, *De doctrina Christiana* 4.15.

17. C. G. Wilke, *Die neutestamentliche Rhetorik: Ein Seitenstück zur Grammatik des neutestamentlichen Sprachidioms* (Dresden & Leipzig: Arnold, 1843), IX.

18. Wilke, *Die neutestamentliche Rhetorik,* 469.

19. Wilke, *Die neutestamentliche Rhetorik,* 471.

20. Wilke, *Die neutestamentliche Rhetorik,* 475.

That Paul in his letters, which it is generally recognized he dictated and which are so expressed for public reading, laid down prominent oratorical features of the day, is not something new. The question is only how this rhetorical element should be explained and evaluated.[21]

Though Weiss rightly characterized the work in his article as "fragmentary" and as "suggestions," he did give an essentially positive assessment of Paul's rhetoric.

But what Paul lacks in *Kunstprosa* [art prose], he makes up for somewhat in his carefully written letters through a sure rhetorical movement, which works not without a gripping artistry, often through symmetry, rhythm, flourish, and sonority.[22]

For Weiss, an extraordinary element that made Paul's discourses oratorical was Paul's use of parallelism, which Weiss believed to be modeled on the Hebrew *parallelismus membrorum*.[23] Even though parallelism was for Paul "only a model,"[24] Weiss used it to identify patterns in a number of passages, including 1 Corinthians 13.[25] Later on in the same article he attempted to determine the rhetorical structure of Romans using similar criteria.[26] At the end of the article, Weiss concluded that further work by specialists on Paul who understood Graeco-Roman rhetoric was needed.[27]

In 1898, Eduard Norden's *Die antike Kunstprosa* surveyed classical literature from the standpoint of the practical equation of rhetoric with artistic prose style.[28] This erudite scholar found Paul's rhetoric sadly lacking:

Paul is an author which I barely, with great difficulty, understand. This is clear to me for two reasons: First, his method of argumentation has a

---

21. J. Weiss, "Beiträge zur Paulinischen Rhetorik," in *Theologische Studien* (Festschrift B. Weiss; Göttingen: Vandenhoeck & Ruprecht, 1897), 165-274; the quotation is from p. 165.

22. Weiss, "Beiträge," 167.

23. Weiss, "Beiträge," 168.

24. Weiss, "Beiträge," 184.

25. Weiss, "Beiträge," 184-98; the quotation is from p. 198.

26. Weiss, "Beiträge," 211-47.

27. Weiss, "Beiträge," 247.

28. E. Norden, *Die antike Kunstprosa vom VI. Jahrhunderts vor Christus in die Zeit der Renaissance* (Leipzig: B. G. Teubner, 1898, 1913; repr. Darmstadt: Wissenschaftliche Buchgesellschaft, 1958).

strange style; and second, his style, all things considered, is indeed unhellenic.[29]

Although Norden held that Paul's writing was not without power, especially because of his use of rhetorical devices such as repetition and antithesis,[30] his attitude toward Paul's rhetoric was basically quite negative. Two years later, Carl Friedrich Georg Heinrici countered Norden's negative judgment about Paul as a rhetorical writer with a more positive assessment in an appendix, "Zum Hellenismus des Paulus" ("On the Hellenism of Paul"), to his commentary on 2 Corinthians.[31] Heinrici concluded that

> Paul's style is individual and gripping. Despite its various limitations, it has a unified character. No classicist, no Hellenist has written thus, and also no church father. The Hellenistic Jew overwhelmed by his Lord stands for himself. His mode of expression was not conditioned by imitation (μίμησις), but through the original, vivid power of his intellectual formation.[32]

Johannes Weiss's student Rudolf Bultmann wrote his doctoral dissertation comparing Pauline literature to the Cynic-Stoic diatribe, and he demonstrated several rhetorical figures in popular philosophical literature, with parallels in Pauline letters.[33] Significant advances in the rhetorical understanding of Pauline literature were to wait some sixty years.[34] In 1968, Edwin A. Judge published a very interesting article in which he examined the question of whether Paul was indeed a "layman in rhetoric" (ἰδιώτης τῷ λόγῳ), as he said he was in 2 Cor 11:6.[35] In 1961, Judge had

---

29. Norden, *Die antike Kunstprosa*, 499.

30. Norden, *Die antike Kunstprosa*, 498-510.

31. C. F. G. Heinrici, *Der zweite Brief an die Korinther, mit einem Anhang: Zum Hellenismus des Paulus* (MeyerK 6; 8th ed.; Göttingen: Vandenhoeck & Ruprecht, 1900), 436-58. On Heinrici and Norden, see H.-D. Betz, *2 Corinthians 8 and 9: A Commentary on Two Administrative Letters of the Apostle Paul* (Hermeneia; Philadelphia: Fortress, 1985), 129, n. 2.

32. Heinrici, *Der zweite Brief an die Korinther*, 453.

33. R. Bultmann, *Der Stil der paulinischen Predigt und die kynisch-stoische Diatribe* (FRLANT 13; Göttingen: Vandenhoeck & Ruprecht, 1910; repr. 1984).

34. In favor of understanding Paul's letters as rhetorical, with a review of patristic attitudes to Pauline rhetoric, is a short statement by W. A. Jennrich, "Classical Rhetoric in the New Testament," *CJ* 44 (1948-49): 30-32.

35. E. A. Judge, "Paul's Boasting in Relation to Contemporary Professional Practice," *AusBR* 16 (1968): 37-50.

suggested that the early Christians understood themselves as a kind of "scholastic community,"[36] and that "Paul found himself a reluctant and unwelcomed competitor in the field of professional 'sophistry' and that he promoted a deliberate collision with its standards of value."[37] Judge argued that "the verdict of the Fathers would be that Paul used no asteistic irony in admitting he was a layman in speech, but accepted the charge that he was in order to confound it."[38] Like Weiss before him, Judge concluded that ". . . we must urgently look for the scholars who will be able to give us control of the New Testament art of speech."[39]

Those who survey what critics up to and including Judge have said about Paul's use of rhetoric will note that most of the discussion has been centered around examinations of style; and even for many contemporary classicists and New Testament scholars, there is an explicit or implicit equation of rhetoric with style and the smaller rhetorical figures. The kind of rhetorical criticism of Pauline literature that has appeared in the 1970s and since is of a markedly different sort, a rhetorical criticism no longer *primarily* concerned with the elucidation of style or the identification of smaller rhetorical figures or of a particular sentence structure. The works of Hans-Dieter Betz, Wilhelm Wuellner, George A. Kennedy, Robert Jewett, and others have focused on the understanding of whole documents as rhetorical discourses. Consequently their rhetorical criticism has stemmed from the identification of traditional parts of a rhetorical discourse (as taught in various ancient rhetorical handbooks) with parts of actual Pauline letters. In 1975, Hans-Dieter Betz published a seminal article, "The Literary Composition and Function of Paul's Letter to the Galatians," in which he argued that Paul wrote Galatians having in mind the standard parts of a rhetorical speech, and that rhetorical criteria should be used to interpret that letter.[40] In 1976, Wilhelm Wuellner wrote an article in which he argued that the structure of Romans followed the pattern of a rhetorical speech, followed in 1979 by another article explor-

36. E. A. Judge, "The Early Christians as a Scholastic Community," *JRH* 1 (1960-61): 4-15 and 125-37.

37. Judge, "Paul's Boasting," 47, referring to his earlier article, "The Early Christians as a Scholastic Community."

38. Judge, "Paul's Boasting," 42.

39. Judge, "Paul's Boasting," 46.

40. H.-D. Betz, "The Literary Composition and Function of Paul's Letter to the Galatians," *NTS* 21 (1975): 353-79.

ing the rhetorical structure of 1 Corinthians 13.[41] Late in 1979 appeared Hans-Dieter Betz's large commentary on Galatians, which was structured around his rhetorical analysis of that epistle as an "apologetic letter."[42] In 1982, Robert Jewett published an article, "Romans as an Ambassadorial Letter," in which he argued that Romans is a rhetorical letter in which Paul attempted to unify the Roman house-churches so that they could support his projected mission to Spain.[43] In 1984 George A. Kennedy published *New Testament Interpretation through Rhetorical Criticism,* which was the first work to teach rhetorical criticism as a method of New Testament interpretation of both epistles and Gospels. The following year Betz brought out another commentary, *2 Corinthians 8 and 9,* which used rhetorical criteria to explain many of the literary features of these letter fragments, comparing them with administrative correspondence in the Hellenistic period and other letters such as Cicero's.[44]

Michael Bünker's study of the rhetoric of 1 Corinthians integrates studies of rhetorical *dispositio* (arrangement) with epistolographic studies of Hellenistic letters.[45] He identifies various sections of the canonical 1 Corinthians with traditional parts of rhetorical speeches. The lengthy study of the argumentation of Romans 9–11 by Folker Siegert uses rhetorical precepts as found in Chaim Perelman's *New Rhetoric* to guide the analysis of that most

41. W. Wuellner, "Paul's Rhetoric of Argumentation in Romans," *CBQ* 38 (1976): 330-51, repr. in *The Romans Debate* (ed. Karl P. Donfried; rev. ed.; Peabody, Mass.: Hendrickson, 1991), 152-74; Wuellner, "Greek Rhetoric and Pauline Argumentation," in *Early Christian Literature and the Classical Intellectual Tradition* (Festschrift Robert M. Grant; ed. William R. Schoedel and Robert L. Wilken; ThH 54; Paris: Beauchesne, 1979), 177-88.

42. H.-D. Betz, *Galatians: A Commentary on Paul's Letter to the Churches in Galatia* (Hermeneia; Philadelphia: Fortress, 1979); for criticism of this work, see the penetrating review by W. A. Meeks in *JBL* 100 (1981): 304-7, as well as W. D. Davies in *RSRev* 7 (1981): 310-18, repr. in Davies, *Jewish and Pauline Studies* (Philadelphia: Fortress Press, 1984), 172-88; see especially G. A. Kennedy, *New Testament Interpretation through Rhetorical Criticism* (Studies in Religion; Chapel Hill: University of North Carolina Press, 1984), 144-52.

43. R. Jewett, "Romans as an Ambassadorial Letter," *Int* 36 (1982): 520. This article was written in preparation for Jewett's forthcoming two-volume commentary on Romans in the Hermeneia series, which will utilize rhetorical criticism as well as other types of criticism.

44. Betz, *2 Corinthians 8 and 9,* especially 129-44. See the significant review of this book by Stanley K. Stowers in *JBL* 106 (1987): 727-30.

45. M. Bünker, *Briefformular und rhetorische Disposition im I. Korintherbrief* (GTA 28; Göttingen: Vandenhoeck & Ruprecht, 1984).

difficult section of Romans, relating Paul's argumentation to theories of semiotics as well as rhetoric.[46] In 1984 Klaus Berger's *Formgeschichte des Neuen Testaments* also appeared; it gathers New Testament literary forms under the three *genera* of rhetoric.[47] Every year sees more and more papers presented at the Annual Meeting of the Society of Biblical Literature in both the Rhetorical Criticism section and the Pauline Epistles section that use and develop rhetorical criticism of New Testament epistles. Rhetorical criticism is becoming more and more widely recognized as a method of interpretation of Pauline literature, as well as other biblical literature.[48]

The discussion of the rhetorical function of letters was also advanced by Abraham J. Malherbe's useful article, "Ancient Epistolary Theorists," which was published in 1977.[49] In this work Malherbe collected and translated several of the ancient epistolary (letter-writing) handbooks that date from approximately the first century B.C.E. to the sixth century C.E. Malherbe stated that

> Epistolary theory in antiquity belonged to the domain of the rhetoricians, but it was not originally part of their theoretical systems. It is ab-

46. F. Siegert, *Argumentation bei Paulus gezeigt an Röm 9–11* (WUNT 34; Tübingen: J. C. B. Mohr, 1985); see also C. Perelman and L. Olbrechts-Tyteca, *The New Rhetoric: A Treatise on Argumentation* (Notre Dame: University of Notre Dame Press, 1969).

47. K. Berger, *Formgeschichte des Neuen Testaments* (Heidelberg: Quelle & Meyer, 1984); see also Berger, "Hellenistische Gattungen im Neuen Testament," in *ANRW* II.25.2 (ed. W. Haase; Berlin & New York: Walter de Gruyter, 1984), 1031-32 and 1831-85; as well as Berger, "Apostelbrief und apostolische Rede: Zum Formular frühchristlicher Briefe," *ZNW* 65 (1974): 190-231.

48. For a recent collection of essays that were first presented in the Rhetorical Criticism section of the Society of Biblical Literature, most of which deal with the Hebrew Bible, see *Art and Meaning: Rhetoric in Biblical Literature* (ed. D. J. A. Clines, D. M. Gunn, and A. J. Hauser; JSOTS 19; Sheffield: JSOT Press, 1982). For recent methodological surveys, see V. K. Robbins and J. H. Patton, "Rhetoric and Biblical Criticism," *Quarterly Journal of Speech* 66 (1980): 327-50; R. Jewett, *The Thessalonian Correspondence: Pauline Rhetoric and Millenarian Piety* (FFNT; Philadelphia: Fortress Press, 1986), 63-68; F. W. Hughes, "New Testament Rhetorical Criticism and Its Methodology," paper presented in the Rhetorical Criticism section of the Society of Biblical Literature Annual Meeting, November 1986 in Atlanta; D. E. Knorr, "The Rhetorical Consensus: A Proposed Methodology for the Study of Paul's Use of the Old Testament," paper presented at the Midwest regional meeting of the Society of Biblical Literature, February 20, 1986, at Andrews University; W. Wuellner, "Where Is Rhetorical Criticism Taking Us?" *CBQ* 49 (1987): 448-63.

49. A. J. Malherbe, "Ancient Epistolary Theorists," *OJRS* 5 (1977): 3-77.

sent from the earliest extant rhetorical handbooks, and it only gradually made its way into the genre.[50]

Malherbe did point out, however, that "Demetrius's" handbook *De elocutione* ("On Style"), which has been dated from the third century B.C.E. to the first century C.E., included a discussion of letters and their styles.[51] "Demetrius" taught that, of the four conventional styles of rhetoric, the elevated style, the graceful style, the plain style, and the forcible style, letters should be written in a combination of the plain style and the graceful style. "Demetrius" also compared letters to dialogues: a letter was in the same style as a dialogue and constituted one part of a dialogue (*De elocutione* 223). Although Malherbe never defined a clear relationship between rhetoric and letters (nor did Heikki Koskenniemi in his classic study of Greek letters),[52] nevertheless he showed that letter-writing instruction was indeed part of the conventional curriculum of grammar schools in the early empire.[53] He also pointed out that "Cicero did know rhetorical prescriptions on letters and was probably familiar with handbooks on letter writ-

---

50. Malherbe, "Ancient Epistolary Theorists," 4.

51. "Demetrius," *De elocutione* 223-35; see Malherbe, "Ancient Epistolary Theorists," 4-5, including nn. 11-13. A convenient edition of *De elocutione* is that of W. R. Roberts, *Demetrius: On Style* ([bound together with Aristotle's *Poetics* and "Longinus," *On the Sublime*]; LCL; Cambridge: Harvard University Press, 1927). See also the text of *De elocutione* 223-35 with comments in K. Thraede, *Grundzüge griechisch-römischer Brieftopik* (*Zet* 48; Munich: C. H. Beck, 1970), 17-25.

52. H. Koskenniemi, *Studien zur Idee und Phraseologie des griechischen Briefes bis 400 n. Chr.* (AASF, B102/2; Helsinki: Suomalaien Tiedakatemie, & Wiesbaden: Otto Harrassowitz, 1956); on rhetoric and letters see especially pp. 19-34. Koskenniemi demonstrated on the basis of the epistolary handbooks that letters act to provide a means of furthering *philophronēsis* (goodwill between the writer and the readers, 35-37), *parousia* (the presence of the writer with the readers even though the writer is physically absent, 38-42), and *homilia* (conversation between writer and readers, 42-47). While it is certainly true that letters did and do provide a means of communication and commonality between writer and readers, this tells us more about the relation between the form and the intention of letters, but less about the relation between the content and the intention. In particular, epistolary theories such as this tell us little about how the argumentative structure of a particular letter works. For material that directly impacts the relation between the content of discourses and their intention, one must turn to rhetoric. That there was an overlap between rhetorical theory and letters is hardly surprising, primarily because acquiring goodwill and furthering relationships were important concerns of rhetoricians. On the acquiring of goodwill, see below my discussion of the *exordium* in the rhetorical handbooks.

53. Malherbe, "Ancient Epistolary Theorists," 12-15.

ing."[54] Yet Cicero's comments on letter types were, according to Malherbe, ". . . not the basis for an epistolographic system, nor are they part of such a system. They are rather practical, conventional means of finding an appropriate form for important situations to which letters are addressed."[55] On the other hand, systems of rhetoric, as we know several of them from the extant rhetorical handbooks, are sometimes not much more than "practical, conventional means of finding an appropriate form" to meet situations of contingency in which a persuasive response is needed. In fact, Malherbe's phrase is not far distant from Aristotle's classic definition of rhetoric, "the faculty for finding the available means of persuasion in any subject whatsoever."[56]

Two studies of different aspects of Graeco-Roman epistolography that appeared in 1986 also inform the discussion about epistolary rhetoric. John L. White's collection, *Light from Ancient Letters,* is limited to documentary letters written on papyri, excluding Hellenistic royal correspondence and "literary" letters.[57] On "literary" letters, White comments, "The use of rhetorical techniques, especially in the theological body of Paul's letters, indicates that a knowledge of these traditions is quite relevant to the study of early Christian letters."[58] White mentions the "Christian letter tradition . . . in which a Christian leader wrote a letter of instruction to a Christian community under his leadership."[59] White sees Paul as the creator of this tradition, when he wrote to churches he had previously founded. At the end of his collection, White gives an overview of Greek letter-writing, where he considers various school traditions of letter-writing and modern theories of letter-writing, to some degree based on the epistolary handbook Τύποι Ἐπιστολικοί ("Epistolary Types," dated from the third century B.C.E. to the third century C.E.) falsely attributed to Demetrius of Phalerum, as well as the epistolary handbook Ἐπιστολικοὶ Χαρακτῆρες ("Epistolary Characters," dated from the fourth to the sixth centu-

54. Malherbe, "Ancient Epistolary Theorists," 7.

55. Malherbe, "Ancient Epistolary Theorists," 7; see H. Koskenniemi, "Cicero über die Briefanen (genera epistularum)," *Arctos* 1 (1954): 97-102.

56. Aristotle, *Ars rhetorica* 1.2.1.

57. J. L. White, *Light from Ancient Letters* (FFNT; Philadelphia: Fortress, 1986).

58. White, *Light,* 3.

59. White, *Light,* 19; see White, "Saint Paul and the Apostolic Letter Tradition," *CBQ* 45 (1983): 433-44, and White, "New Testament Epistolary Literature in the Framework of Ancient Epistolography," in *ANRW* II.25.2, 1730-56.

ries C.E.) falsely attributed to Libanius.[60] To a certain extent, following the epistolary types (and within the limits of "nonliterary" or documentary letters), White is able to categorize various letters as "letters of instruction and recommendation," "letters of petition," and "family letters."

Especially useful are White's well-documented lists of standard epistolary formulae, including formulae in the opening and closing of the letters and formulae in the letter-body. These latter formulae include disclosure formulae, such as "Therefore I wrote you in order that you may know ... ," similar to Paul's formula, "We do not want you to be ignorant, brothers, concerning. . . ."[61] Other formulae include "statements of reassurance, concern, and other conventions," as well as various requests and instructions.[62] White's characterization of "statements used to persuade, coerce, or threaten"[63] could be seen to impinge rather directly on theories of rhetoric, the "art of persuasion."

Stanley K. Stowers' book, *Letter Writing in Greco-Roman Antiquity*, seeks to understand the New Testament letters by means of theories and letter types found primarily in the epistolary handbooks of Pseudo-Demetrius and Pseudo-Libanius. Stowers' work also interacts in important ways with rhetorical traditions. Essentially accepting the Aristotelian division of rhetoric into three *genera*, Stowers finds that most Graeco-Roman letter types were associated with epideictic rhetoric, whose standard topics were praise and blame.[64] He also finds that

60. White, *Light*, 187-220. The Greek text of these handbooks is found in *Demetrii et Libanii qui feruntur Typoi Epistolikoi et Epistolimaioi Charaktēres* (ed. V. Weichert; Leipzig: B. G. Teubner, 1910); the English translation of these texts is found in Malherbe, "Ancient Epistolary Theorists."

61. White, *Light*, 204-5; see 1 Thess 4:13.

62. White, *Light*, 206-8.

63. White, *Light*, 205-6.

64. S. K. Stowers, *Letter Writing in Greco-Roman Antiquity* (LEC 5; Philadelphia: Westminster, 1986). On letters and epideictic rhetoric see pp. 27-28; see Stowers' discussion of letter types and the *genera* of rhetoric on pp. 51-57. Elsewhere, Stowers emphasizes the need "to compare Christian letters to the whole range of letters and to approach them with a knowledge of ancient epistolary and rhetorical theory" (23). On the following page, evidently concerning rhetorical criticism, Stowers writes, "Recently there has been a revival of interest in the study of Greek and Roman rhetoric on the part of some New Testament scholars. A few classical scholars have also taken an interest in the New Testament and ancient rhetoric. Important beginnings have been made, beginnings that often take up the leads of scholars from the beginning of this century who were steeped in classical literature. It is too early, however, to speak of definitive results or widespread agreement among researchers."

Two types of letters, the accusing and the apologetic, clearly fall under judicial rhetoric. The letter of advice would also clearly seem to belong to deliberative rhetoric. Most other kinds of letters could be conceived of as belonging to epideictic, which had two departments, praise and blame.[65]

Stowers argues, however, that epistolary classification "according to the three species of rhetoric only partially works. This is because the letter-writing tradition was essentially independent of rhetoric."[66]

A monograph on letters by Hermann Peter, *Der Brief in der rö-mischen Literatur,* published in 1901, understood Graeco-Roman letter-writing as part of rhetorical tradition.[67] Peter argued that official letters were seen in Greek tradition as substitutes for or representations of public speeches ("letter and speech were looked upon as belonging together");[68] thus teaching about letters was a natural part of Graeco-Roman education, particularly within rhetorical schools. Peter argued that the systematic rules taught in rhetorical schools had a powerful influence on all kinds of speeches and letters.[69]

There is no doubt that Paul (and, for that matter, other authors whose writings are preserved in the Pauline corpus) intended his letters to be persuasive, and that what is being persuaded varies greatly from letter to letter. It is true that rhetorical rules and precepts were developed for oral discourses, but it is also not unreasonable to believe that rhetorical principles were used either directly or indirectly in the composition of letters, for several reasons. Graeco-Roman rhetoric had often affected the composition of written discourses, since Aristotle mentions a style proper to written discourses in his discussion of rhetorical styles,[70] and since Isocrates, the Athenian statesman and the most influential teacher

---

65. Stowers, *Letter Writing,* 52.

66. Stowers, *Letter Writing,* 52.

67. H. Peter, *Der Brief in der römischen Literatur: Literargeschichtliche Untersu-chungen und Zusammenfassungen* (ASGW.PH 20/3; Leipzig: B. G. Teubner, 1901; repr., Hildesheim: Georg Olms, 1965).

68. Peter, *Brief,* 14.

69. Peter, *Brief,* 19.

70. Aristotle, *Ars rhetorica* 3.12.2. On the effect of rhetoric on Latin prose style, see A. D. Leeman, *Orationis Ratio: The Stylistic Theories and Practice of the Roman Orators, His-torians, and Philosophers* (2 vols.; Amsterdam: Adolf M. Hakkert, 1963), as well as the review of this work by G. A. Kennedy in *AJP* 87 (1963): 237-41.

of rhetoric in his day, was well known for the elegant literary style of his orations.[71] In the midst of discussions of rhetorical styles, Quintilian and Apollonius of Tyana mention a style appropriate to letters.[72] Most notably, Cicero in his mature work, *De oratore,* has one of his rhetorical heroes argue that when official messages, presumably in the form of letters, must be sent to or from the Senate and must be written in an elaborate style, no other genus of rhetoric (beyond the traditional three *genera*) is needed, "since the ability acquired by a ready speaker, from the treatment of his other subjects and topics, will not fail him in situations of that description."[73] Thus Cicero argued that (1) it is quite natural for letters written for official purposes to use rhetoric, and (2) letters could be understood as belonging to (or at least being strongly affected by) the three traditional *genera* of rhetoric. Similarly, it seems clear that Pauline letters were official and relatively public communications from Paul to various churches he had founded, since in the earliest of his extant letters, Paul ordered, "I adjure you by the Lord to read the letter to all the brethren" (1 Thess 5:27; see Col 4:16).

Another set of connections between rhetoric and letters includes the treatment of letters in the two Hellenistic epistolary handbooks cited above. The handbook of Pseudo-Demetrius advised its readers that twenty-one epistolary types were in existence. Examination of the names of these types shows that several of the types are named with technical terminology from Graeco-Roman rhetoric, as witnessed in the rhetorical handbooks. For example, the "blaming" (μεμπτικός) type and the "praising" (ἐπαινετικός) type seem to be clearly related to epideictic rhetoric because the standard topics of this genus of rhetoric are praise and blame. In Aristotle's *Ars rhetorica,* epideictic rhetoric is described as a *genos* of rhetoric in 1.2.3, and then in 1.3.5 and 1.3.7 the phrase "those who praise or blame" (τοῖς ἐπαινοῦσι καὶ ψέγουσι; οἱ ἐπαινοῦντες καὶ οἱ ψέγοντες)[74] is employed as a synonym for those who do epideictic rhetoric. The

---

71. On Isocrates, see Kennedy, *Art of Persuasion in Greece,* 174-203; J. F. Dobson, *The Greek Orators* (London: Methuen, 1918; repr. Chicago: Area, 1974), 126-59; on the literary style of Isocrates, see Dionysius of Halicarnassus, *Isocrates* 2-3, 11-20.

72. Quintilian, *Institutio oratoria* 9.4.19; Apollonius of Tyana, *Epistle* 19.

73. Cicero, *De oratore* 2.49; the English translation is by E. W. Sutton and H. Rackham, *Cicero: De oratore,* two vols. (LCL; Cambridge: Harvard University Press, 1942).

74. Aristotle uses ψέγειν for "blame" rather than μέμφεσθαι.

συμβουλευτικός ("advising") type of letter would seem to be related to the genus of rhetoric called συμβουλευτικόν (deliberative).[75] Similarly, the ἀπολογητικός ("defensive") type of letter shares its title with one of the parts of judicial rhetoric, ἀπολογία or "defense."[76] The ψεκτικός ("vituperative") letter seems to have a name similar to the ψεκτικόν ("vituperative") kind of rhetoric, which along with "enkomiastic" (ἐγκωμιαστικόν) rhetoric seems to constitute the genus of epideictic rhetoric in *Rhetorica ad Alexandrum*.[77] It appears, therefore, that some of the technical terminology of rhetorical style, topics, and *genera* became part of the terminology of the relatively little we know of systematic teaching about letters.

The relation between rhetoric and letters may also be viewed from the perspective of mediaeval rhetoric. In the Middle Ages, rhetoric developed greatly in the direction of literary (as opposed to oral) discourses, although the art of preaching *(ars praedicandi)* was by no means neglected. The two most important literary *artes* were the art of verse-writing *(ars poetriae)* and the art of letter-writing *(ars dictaminis)*. One of the most important contributions to the mediaeval art of letter-writing was the *Dictaminum radii* (or *Flores rhetorici*) of Alberic of Monte Cassino, a "teacher in the oldest continuously operating Benedictine monastery in Europe," who "inherited the ancient traditions of learning which went back to Benedict himself."[78] In the *Dictaminum radii*, written about 1087, there is an unmistakable correlation between the use of rhetoric and written works. This work concentrated on material at the beginning of written rhetorical discourses, the *exordium* and the *captatio benevolentiae* (the acquisition of goodwill), and Alberic devoted the longest treatment in this treatise to the relationship between the *salutatio* (salutation of letters) and the *exordium* (3.5-6), clearly showing that he had letters in mind, as does "his statement that the first thing to consider is 'the person to whom and the person from whom it is sent.'"[79] Alberic showed that he had the *partes orationis* in mind when he wrote, "After the salutation [belongs] the *exor-*

---

75. Aristotle, *Ars rhetorica* 1.3.3 et passim. For a list of Pseudo-Demetrius's twenty-one letter types, see White, *Light*, 203.

76. Aristotle, *Ars rhetorica* 1.10.1.

77. *Rhetorica ad Alexandrum* 1421b9.

78. J. J. Murphy, *Rhetoric in the Middle Ages: A History of Rhetorical Theory from Saint Augustine to the Renaissance* (Berkeley: University of California Press, 1974) 203, including nn. 19 and 20.

79. Murphy, *Rhetoric in the Middle Ages*, 206.

dium," and "after the *exordium* the narration. . . ."[80] In his other work *Breviarium de dictamine,* Alberic frequently referred to letters, and it is hard to dispute James J. Murphy's conclusion "that Alberic's school at Monte Cassino was actively engaged in discussing the nature of letters."[81]

In an anonymous work written around 1135 and called *Rationes dictandi,* which reflects "the basic doctrines of the *ars dictaminis*" that "were crystallized in the region of Bologna,"[82] the fourth of its thirteen sections taught that letters have five parts, namely, *salutatio, benevolentiae captatio, narratio, petitio,* and *conclusio.* Thus it is clear that the *partes orationis* had been adapted into standard letter parts in the region of Bologna no later than the early twelfth century.[83] A wider provenance for the understanding of letters in rhetorical categories is suggested by other mediaeval and Byzantine works,[84] as well as by Erasmus's *De conscribendis epistolis,* which treated letters according to the three traditional *genera* of rhetoric and according to the *partes orationis.*[85]

The fact that letter-writing is so firmly established in the mediaeval appropriation of Graeco-Roman rhetoric suggests that the composition of letters may have been more than a peripheral concern in the actual practice of rhetors, particularly in the Hellenistic period. A more adequate explanation of the paucity of instruction about letters in the earliest rhetorical handbooks would center around the fact that rhetorical tradition in the Hellenistic period gave primary emphasis to judicial rhetoric, as opposed to deliberative and epideictic rhetoric. By the time of Cicero, the *Rhetorica ad Herennium,* and Quintilian, instruction in rhetorical schools concentrated on judicial rhetoric,[86] and these handbooks themselves tended to define the other *genera* of rhetoric in terms of judicial rhetoric. The fact that it was rhe-

---

80. *Dictaminum radii* 3.6, quoted from Murphy, *Rhetoric in the Middle Ages,* 206.

81. Murphy, *Rhetoric in the Middle Ages,* 207.

82. Murphy, *Rhetoric in the Middle Ages,* 220.

83. Murphy, *Rhetoric in the Middle Ages,* 224-25.

84. L. Rockinger, *Über Briefsteller und Formelbücher in Deutschland während des Mittelalters* (Munich: J. G. Weiss, 1861); H. Rabe, "Aus Rhetoren-Handschriften: 9. Griechische Briefsteller," *RMP* 64 (1909): 284-309, with the literature referred to there.

85. Erasmus, *De conscribendis epistolis,* in *Omnia opera Desiderii Erasmi Roterodami recognita et adnotatione critica instructa notisque illustrata* (Amsterdam: North Holland Publishing Co., 1971), with introduction and notes by J.-C. Margolin, I/2.153-579.

86. E. P. Parks, *The Roman Rhetorical Schools as a Preparation for the Courts under the Early Empire* (Johns Hopkins University Studies in Historical and Political Science 63/2; Baltimore: Johns Hopkins University Press, 1945).

torically undesirable to write letters, as stated earlier in this chapter, as well as the fact that the teaching in handbooks tended to teach about and presuppose ideal situations, as Cicero complained,[87] made it unlikely that the rhetorical handbooks would give much attention to letters. Yet rhetoric, particularly deliberative rhetoric, had traditionally been centered around the need for men to speak up for their own interests, and that of their city, in front of political bodies that had the power to make decisions that would affect their future. A letter, lacking the ἦθος and delivery of the rhetor, was considered a very poor substitute for the rhetor's own presence, a substitution that would be made only in the direst of straits, such as that exemplified by Demosthenes' *Epistle 1*, which we shall analyze later in this chapter. Demosthenes, Paul, and others wrote the letters they did because, being far away from the people they had to persuade, they had no other option. Since the doing of crucial kinds of persuasion by letters was so undesirable, it is unlikely that rhetorical teachers would want to make letters a part of rhetorical theory. On the other hand, given the fact that instruction in rhetoric was given by grammar teachers as well as by rhetorical teachers,[88] and given the fact that letters of famous persons appear to have been a part of rhetorical instruction,[89] one can be skeptical about an absolute separation between rhetorical instruction and grammatical instruction, so that instruction about letters could very well have taken place within the context of learning specific strategies of persuasion. Although the major domain of rhetoric, in the Hellenistic period and before it, was the spoken persuasive word, the fact that Paul's letters could be considered "weighty and strong" by his most professionally competent rhetorical enemies (2 Cor 10:10) suggests that Paul was able to make letter-writing into a fine art. The notion that Paul might use rhetorical principles and patterns in doing persuasion by letter does not speak against the quality of his rhetoric; rather, it speaks strongly in favor of his rhetorical creativity.

The publication of White's *Light from Ancient Letters*, of course, raises the issue of the multiplicity of kinds of letters to which early Christian letters can be compared. The papyrus letters we have exhibit a remarkable diversity in function, if not in form. The parallels between documentary (or "nonliterary") letters and New Testament letters, especially in the

---

87. *De oratore* 1.86-87; 1.105.
88. Suetonius, *De grammaticis et rhetoribus* 4; Quintilian, *Institutio oratoria* 2.1.1-6.
89. Rabe, "Aus Rhetoren-Handschriften," 289.

more formulaic parts of letters at their beginnings and ends, can be quite precise. John White's interesting form-critical analysis of the body of the Greek letter tells us much about certain components of Hellenistic documentary letter tradition, in terms of both form and function.[90] However, epistolographic studies generally do not make it clear just how form is related to the *content* of particular letters. Form-critical studies can indeed explain how parts of letters are constructed (at least some of the parts), but they seem less helpful when it comes to explaining *why* certain letter formulae were used rather than others.

The question that rhetorical analysis of letters can answer, that epistolographic analysis alone does not appear to answer very well, is this: Just how are the structure and function of a letter related to its content and the intention of its writer? If this question can be answered, then scholars will be well on their way toward answering one of the most traditional questions asked by form critics, that is, What was the *Sitz im Leben* ("situation in life" in which the literature was composed) of the document being examined? I propose that rhetorical criticism can help scholars to identify the lived situation of letters in the Pauline corpus,[91] primarily because the use of certain rhetorical *genera* and topics seems to presuppose certain situations. If this is indeed the case, then rhetorical criticism can help us learn more not only about the language of letters, but about the intention of authors in writing them.

3. The *Genera* of Rhetoric

One of the major features of Aristotle's famous handbook "The Art of Rhetoric" (here referred to as *Ars rhetorica*) is its logical division of rhetoric into three "kinds" (εἴδη or γένη), or, in Latin, *genera* (plural of *genus*). The three *genera* of rhetoric are deliberative (συμβουλευτικόν), judicial

---

90. J. L. White, *The Form and Function of the Body of the Greek Letter: A Study of the Letter-Body in the Non-Literary Papyri and in Paul the Apostle* (2nd ed. corrected; SBLDS 2; Missoula: Scholars Press, 1972).

91. On the widening of a definition of the *Sitz im Leben* to include "all typical situations of contact between text and social reality," see especially K. Berger, *Einführung in die Formgeschichte* (Tübingen: Francke Verlag, 1987), especially 156-61 (quotation from 161). For a cogent critique of the limitations of form criticsm, see J. Muilenburg, "Form Criticism and Beyond," *JBL* 88 (1969): 148, especially 4-5.

(δικανικόν), and epideictic (ἐπιδεικτικόν).[92] In Aristotle's rhetorical system, they were linked and differentiated through the phenomenon of time.

> Further, to each of these a special time is appropriate: to the deliberative the future, for the speaker, whether he exhorts or dissuades, always advises about things to come; to the forensic the past, for it is always in reference to things done that one party accuses and the other defends; to the epideictic most appropriately the present, for it is the existing condition of things that all those who praise or blame have in view. It is not uncommon, however, for epideictic speakers to avail themselves of other times, of the past by way of recalling it, or of the future by way of anticipating it.[93]

Thus, Aristotle taught here that epideictic rhetoric had to do with the past and future, as well as the present, although the proper time for deliberative rhetoric was the future and the proper time for judicial rhetoric was the past. Since Aristotle noted elsewhere that the present was also an appropriate time for deliberative rhetoric,[94] it would not be too much to say that the overlapping of subjects and topics in time became an illustration of, if not a justification for, the overlapping of the *genera* of rhetoric in Aristotle's understanding.

Judicial (or "forensic") rhetoric dealt with defense and accusation, and its normative locus was the law courts. When a rhetor was either defending his client or acting as a prosecutor, the arguments in the case had to do with past actions that the accused did or did not do, as well as the overall character of the accused. One of the greatest examples of judicial rhetoric was Demosthenes' speech *De corona* ("On the Crown"), in which the orator defended himself, his deeds and words, against the attack of his enemy Aeschines.[95] Epideictic rhetoric included praise and blame of things in the present; praise was much more common than blame. Funeral speeches, such as the famous funeral speech of Pericles found in Thucydides' *History of the*

---

92. Aristotle, *Ars rhetorica* 1.3.3.

93. *Ars rhetorica* 1.3.4.

94. *Ars rhetorica* 1.6.1 and 1.8.7.

95. On *De corona* in particular and on Demosthenes in general, see J. F. Dobson, *Greek Orators*, 199-267, especially 223-24; see also G. A. Kennedy, *Art of Persuasion in Greece*, 206-36, especially 232-36; L. Pearson, *The Art of Demosthenes* (American Philological Association Special Publications, 4; Chico, Calif.: Scholars Press, 1981), 178-99, with bibliography on 1-3.

Peloponnesian War 2.35, are some of the most important examples of epideictic rhetoric.[96] Deliberative rhetoric, as its Greek name συμβουλευτικόν suggests, was rhetoric given before the council (βουλή) and which argued for or against specific actions by the body politic that would affect the future for good or ill. Thus in Aristotle's view, the successful deliberative rhetor argued his case on the basis of what was expedient and/or harmful to the hearers of the speech. The related topics of honor and justice, therefore, were to be introduced in the context of what is expedient and/or harmful to the audience to whom the rhetor is speaking.

Aristotle's rhetorical system became practically canonical within the realm of rhetoric, for a variety of reasons. First, though the Aristotelian system of rhetoric was taken up and modified by Cicero in *De inventione* and Quintilian in *Institutio oratoria,* the Aristotelian system had become quite influential before Cicero,[97] partially because Aristotle's system had much in common with the earlier systematization of Isocrates.[98] Second, Aristotle's understanding of the relations among the three *genera* of rhetoric is intrinsically brilliant and logical. Judicial rhetoric really did deal with defense and accusation on the basis of deeds done in the past. Epideictic rhetoric really did deal with the praise and blame of people and things, mostly for aspects of their existence in the present, though overlapping with the past and future as well. And when a rhetor spoke before a deliberative body, the goal of the speech was generally to advise that body on making decisions that would affect that body's existence and well-being in the future. Thus, since the best guides for the future have always been the past and present, even though the genus of deliberative rhetoric really did deal mostly with the future, there is a necessary overlap with the past and present in this genus as well. Hence, Aristotle's categorization of rhetoric into the three *genera,* relating them and yet differentiating them on the basis of time, can be considered one of the most important developments in the history of rhetoric. In addition, the relating of the three *genera* by Aristotle through time is quite consistent with the universal character of rhetoric itself, as defined by Aristotle.[99]

Although it is clear that rhetoric had been practiced in each of the

96. See Kennedy, *Art of Persuasion in Greece,* 154-203.

97. R. Volkmann, *Die Rhetorik der Griechen und Römer in systematischer Obersicht* (2nd ed.; Leipzig: B. G. Teubner, 1885), 19-22.

98. See especially F. Solmsen, "The Aristotelian Tradition in Ancient Rhetoric," *AJP* 62 (1941): 35-50 and 169-90.

99. *Ars rhetorica* 12.1.

three *genera* of rhetoric well before Aristotle,[100] it is nonetheless true that the first "creator of a systematic and scientific 'Art' of Rhetoric is Aristotle."[101] Moreover, the organization of rhetoric into the three *genera* of judicial, epideictic, and deliberative rhetoric became and remained an important foundation for the understanding and teaching of rhetoric well into the Middle Ages and Renaissance.

4. The Parts of Rhetorical Discourses *(partes orationis)*

The rhetorical handbooks from Graeco-Roman antiquity, beginning with Aristotle's *Ars rhetorica*, exhibit a remarkable amount of consensus concerning the standard parts of the rhetorical discourse *(partes orationis)*. Aristotle wrote in *Ars rhetorica* 3.13.4, "These divisions are appropriate to every speech, and at most the parts are four in number, *exordium* (προοίμιον), statement (πρόθεσις), proof (πίστις), and epilogue (ἐπίλογος)." The statement of the case may at times include a narrative (διήγησις), though Aristotle taught that this was not necessary for every speech, since a narration truly belonged to judicial rhetoric.[102] Cicero's *De inventione* taught that the parts of a discourse were six in number: *exordium, narratio, partitio, confirmatio, reprehensio,* and *conclusio*.[103] Cicero's *De partitione oratoria* taught that there were four parts of a discourse: *exordium, narratio, confirmatio* and *reprehensio* (together), and *peroratio*.[104] Quintilian listed different parts of speeches according to the different *genera* of rhetoric; according to him, ju-

---

100. A. Hellwig, *Untersuchungen zur Theorie der Rhetorik bei Platon und Aristoteles* (Hyp 38; Göttingen: Vandenhoeck & Ruprecht, 1973); D. A. G. Hinks, "Tria genera causarum," *CQ* 30 (1936): 170-76; F. Solmsen, "Aristotelian Tradition in Ancient Rhetoric"; Volkmann, *Rhetorik der Griechen und Römer;* Kennedy, *Art of Persuasion in Greece,* 26-82; on deliberative rhetoric see especially I. Beck, "Untersuchungen zur Theorie des Genos Symbuleutikon" (Unpubl. Dr. Phil. diss.; University of Hamburg, 1970). For a collection of texts and fragments of rhetorical handbooks before Aristotle, see *Artium Scriptores. Reste der voraristotelischen Rhetorik* (ed. L. Radermacher; Sitzungsberichte der österreichischen Akademie der Wissenschaften, philosophisch-historische Klasse, 227/3; Wien: Rudolf M. Rohrer, 1951), as well as the older collection, *Rhetores Graeci* (ed. L. Spengel; Leipzig: B. G. Teubner, 1894).

101. J. H. Freese, "Introduction" to *Aristotle. The "Art" of Rhetoric* (LCL; Cambridge: Harvard University Press, 1926), xxii.

102. *Ars rhetorica* 3.13.3.

103. Cicero, *De inventione* 1.19.

104. Cicero, *De partitione oratoria* 27.

dicial rhetorical discourses have these parts: *prooemium, narratio, probatio, refutatio,* and *peroratio.*[105] In deliberative rhetoric an *exordium* was not always required, though the beginning of a speech "must have some resemblance to an *exordium.*"[106] However, appeals to the emotions were required in deliberative rhetoric, probably referring to the content of the *peroratio.*[107] We may assume that a proof was required, since it is absurd to have a rhetorical discourse without a proof, either confirmatory or refutational. A *narratio* was not required in deliberative rhetoric, but one might frequently be introduced.[108] In 4.Preface.6, Quintilian set forth his program for books 4-6, namely the explication of the *prooemium,* the *narratio,* the *probatio* (either confirmatory or refutational), and the *peroratio,* although his actual discussion included the *exordium* (4.1), the *narratio* (4.2), the *propositio* (4.4), the *partitio* (4.5), proofs (5), and the *peroratio* (6.1).

The *Rhetorica ad Herennium,* which seems to come from the early first century B.C.E., also taught about various parts of the rhetorical discourse: *exordium, narratio, divisio, confirmatio, confutatio,* and *conclusio.*[109] As late as the sixth century C.E., Boethius wrote: "This rhetorical discourse has six parts, the *prooemium,* which is the *exordium,* the narrative, the partition, the confirmation, the refutation, the peroration; and these are the parts of the instrument of the rhetorical discipline."[110]

Thus in the above rhetorical handbooks, which date from the fourth century B.C.E. to the sixth century C.E., one can see a large amount of consensus, as represented in the following table:[111]

105. Quintilian, *Institutio oratoria* 3.9.1.

106. *Institutio oratoria* 3.8.6.

107. *Institutio oratoria* 3.8.12.

108. *Institutio oratoria* 3.8.11.

109. See the introduction to the Loeb edition of (Cicero) *Ad C. Herennium: De ratione dicendi (Rhetorica ad Herennium)* (LCL; Cambridge: Harvard University Press, 1954), translated and with an introduction by H. Caplan on vii-xliv; for authorship, see pp. vii-xiv. The *partes orationis* quoted are found at *Rhetorica ad Herennium* 1.4.

110. Translation by E. Stump in *Boethius' De topicis differentiis* 1208C (Ithaca: Cornell University Press, 1978).

111. In *Handbuch der literarischen Rhetorik,* H. Lausberg gives a similar but much more detailed chart that takes the rhetorical tradition even further forward and shows that the consensus concerning the *partes orationis* does continue well into the fifth century C.E. (Munich: Max Hueber Verlag, 1960; 2. Aufl., 1973); see the chart on 1.148. However, on the dangers of using Lausberg's learned *Handbuch* uncritically, see the review by A. E. Douglas, *CLR* 12 (1962): 246-47.

Greek	Latin
προοίμιον	*exordium*
διήγησις	*narratio*
πρόθεσις, et al.	*partitio, propositio*
πίστις	*probatio,* often divided into *confirmatio* and *reprehensio*
ἐπίλογος	*peroratio.*

The best explanation of the similarities and differences among the various rhetorical handbooks is the living tradition of rhetoric itself, which included a variety of understandings of what rhetoric was; whether it was a good thing, a bad thing, or something quite neutral that could be used in different ways; what the purposes of rhetoric were; how one went about learning and teaching rhetoric; whether rhetoric was primarily an oral or a literary phenomenon; and whether or not it was an honorable thing to persuade people by aiming at their emotions. In the light of the complexity of this intellectual and practical tradition which predates Socrates and stretches into the Middle Ages and Renaissance, the consensus as to what the *partes orationis* are and do is quite stiking.[112]

Assuming that this consensus reflects an ongoing tradition of teaching about how speeches should be put together *(dispositio)*, it should be possible to analyze rhetorical discourses according to precisely these categories, if the parts of the discourses do really seem to do what the handbooks say they should do. In other words, since there is wide agreement in the extant handbooks (several of which are based on older handbooks no longer extant), it should be possible to do rhetorical criticism on discourses based on the precepts of these handbooks. Hence this study will proceed by summarizing the consensus in the extant handbooks as to the nature and functions of the *partes.*

The Exordium

The rhetorical handbooks agree that the rhetorical discourse has an introduction, which is called *prooimion* in Greek or *prooemium* or *exordium* in Latin. Aristotle wrote:

112. D. E. Knorr, "Rhetorical Consensus."

The exordium [*prooimion*] is the beginning of a speech, as the prologue [πρόλογος] in poetry and the prelude in flute-playing: for all these are beginnings, and as it were a paving the way for what follows.[113]

The *exordium* of discourses did exactly that: it introduced the rhetor and his subject to the audience. In epideictic rhetoric, Aristotle says, the *exordia* derive from the topics of blame and praise.[114] Judicial rhetoric's *exordia*, according to Aristotle,

> provide a sample of the subject, in order that the hearers may know beforehand what it is about . . . so then he who puts the beginning, so to say, into the hearer's hand enables him, if he holds fast to it, to follow the story. . . . So then the most essential and special function of the exordium is to make clear what is the end or purpose of the speech.[115]

However, Aristotle recognized that other reasons for *exordia* included the weaknesses of the audience.[116] These other forms of *exordia* are "remedies" for such weaknesses of the audience.[117] The most important type of "remedy"-*exordium* is the appeal to the audience. For this, then,

> The reason is obvious. The defendant, when about to introduce himself, must remove all obstacles, so that he must first clear away all prejudices; the accuser must create prejudice in the epilogue, that his hearers may have a livelier recollection of it. The object of an appeal to the hearer is to make him well disposed or to arouse his indignation, and sometimes to engage his attention or the opposite. . . .[118]

Aristotle quoted Homer to end his discussion of *exordia* in judicial rhetoric:

> And since it is rightly said, "Grant that on reaching the Phaeacians I may find friendship or compassion," the orator should aim at exciting these two feelings.[119]

In Aristotle's system, deliberative rhetoric "borrows its exordia from

---

113. *Ars rhetorica* 3.14.1.
114. *Ars rhetorica* 3.14.2.
115. *Ars rhetorica* 3.14.6.
116. Freese in *Aristotle: The "Art" of Rhetoric*, 431, n. g.
117. *Ars rhetorica* 3.14.7.
118. Aristotle, *Ars rhetorica* 3.14.7.
119. *Ars rhetorica* 3.14.11, quoting Homer, *Odyssey* 7.327.

judicial," though Aristotle said *exordia* are "uncommon" in deliberative rhetoric, since in this *genus* of rhetoric the hearers should be familiar with its subject. Thus, the task of deliberative rhetoric is to "excite or remove prejudice, and to magnify or minimize the importance of the subject."[120] According to Aristotle, the task of the epideictic orator is to "make the hearer believe that he shares the praise, either himself, or his family, or his pursuits, or at any rate in some way or other."[121]

Cicero's *De inventione* 1.20 gives rules for *exordia:*

> An *exordium* is a passage which brings the mind of the auditor into a proper condition to receive the rest of the speech. This will be accomplished if he [the auditor] becomes well-disposed, attentive, and receptive.[122]

Further instruction by Cicero on the *exordium* takes the form of audience psychology, that is, how to make the audience well disposed toward the orator, given the mood the audience is in and the nature of the case.[123] Conversely, of an *exordium* that does not perform these functions, Cicero says, "nothing surely can be worse than that."[124]

Quintilian deals with the *exordium* in 4.1 of his *Institutio oratoria*. Its optimal definition included the notion that this section of a discourse "is designed as an introduction to the subject on which the orator has to speak."[125] The "sole purpose" of the *exordium* for Quintilian, as for the young Cicero, "is to prepare our audience in such a way that they will be disposed to lend a ready ear to the rest of the speech."[126] Much of the rest of Quintilian's treatment of the *exordium* agrees with the treatment by the young Cicero in *De inventione,* especially the notion that the orator goes about making his audience "well-disposed, attentive, and ready to receive instruction" *(si benevolum, attentum, docilem fecerimus).*[127]

---

120. *Ars rhetorica* 3.14.12.

121. *Ars rhetorica* 3.14.11.

122. *De inventione* 1.20.

123. *De inventione* 1.20-21.

124. *De inventione* 1.26. On the securing of goodwill in Cicero's own practice, see P. Prill, "Cicero in Theory and Practice: The Securing of Goodwill in the *Exordia* of Five Forensic Speeches," *Rhetorica* 4 (1986): 93-109.

125. *Institutio oratoria* 4.1.1.

126. *Institutio oratoria* 4.1.5.

127. *Institutio oratoria* 4.1.5; see *De inventione* 1.20: "si eum benivolum, attentum,

The Narratio

Aristotle gave guidance concerning the διήγησις (*narratio* in Latin) in *Ars rhetorica* 3.16, based on the needs of each of the three *genera* of rhetoric. "In the epideictic style the narrative should not be consecutive, but disjointed."[128] In defense (a part of judicial rhetoric), "the narrative need not be so long, for the points at issue are either that the fact has not happened or that it was neither injurious nor wrong nor so important as asserted. . . ."[129] The narrative "should be of a moral character" if the subject admits of a moral end.[130] The narrative might also "draw upon what is emotional by the introduction of such of its accompaniments as are well known, and of what is specially characteristic of either yourself or of the adversary."[131] In the narrative, the rhetor may also introduce himself and his adversary as being "of a certain moral character."[132] However, in deliberative rhetoric, "narrative is very rare, because no one can narrate things to come."[133] This clearly relates to Aristotle's understanding of the proper times of each of the *genera* of rhetoric. Deliberative rhetoric deals properly with the future, since the rhetor, "whether he exhorts or dissuades, always advises about things to come."[134] Judicial rhetoric was proper to the discussion of the past, "for it is always in reference to things done that one party accuses and the other defends." Epideictic rhetoric appertains "most appropriately to the present, for it is the existing condition of things that all those who praise or blame have in view. It is not uncommon, however, for epideictic speakers to avail themselves of other times, of the past by way of recalling it, or of the future by way of anticipating it."[135] Thus, according to Aristotle's system, a deliberative discourse is unlikely to have a *narratio*.

In *De inventione* 1.27 Cicero gave rules for the *narratio:* "The narra-

---

docilem confecerit." See also the statement in *Rhetorica ad Herennium* 1.6: "ut adtentos ut dociles, ut benivolos auditores habere possimus," and 1.7: "Quoniam igitur docilum, benivolum, adtentum auditorem habere volumus. . . ."

128. *Ars rhetorica* 3.16.1.
129. *Ars rhetorica* 3.16.6.
130. *Ars rhetorica* 3.16.8.
131. *Ars rhetorica* 3.16.10.
132. *Ars rhetorica* 3.16.10.
133. *Ars rhetorica* 3.16.16.
134. *Ars rhetorica* 1.3.4.
135. *Ars rhetorica* 1.3.4.

tive is an exposition of events that have occurred or are supposed to have occurred." Cicero distinguished three kinds of *narrationes*:

> one which contains just the case and the whole reason for the dispute; a second in which a digression is made beyond the strict limits of the case for the purpose of attacking somebody, or of making a comparison, or of amusing the audience in a way not incongruous with the business at hand, or for amplification. The third kind is wholly unconnected with public issues, which is recited or written solely for amusement but at the same time provides valuable training.[136]

The three important characteristics of the *narratio* of whatever type are that it should be "brief, clear, and plausible" *(ut brevis, ut aperta, ut probabilis sit).*[137] With regard to brevity, Cicero advised orators to begin with what needs to be said but not to burden the reader or listener with useless details.[138] Clarity is to be achieved in a *narratio* "if the events are presented one after another as they occurred, and the order of events in time is preserved so that the story is told as it will prove to have happened or will seem possible to have happened."[139] Plausibility will be achieved in the *narratio* "if it seems to embody characteristics which are accustomed to appear in real life."[140] In addition to this, Cicero advises, "one must also be on guard not to insert a narrative when it will be a hindrance or of no advantage."[141] Thus, a *narratio* "is also useless when the audience has grasped the facts so thoroughly that it is of no advantage to us to instruct them in a different fashion. In such a case one must dispense with narrative altogether."[142]

Quintilian dealt with the *narratio* in *Institutio oratoria* 4.2. He taught that the *narratio* is not indispensable, since some *causae* were so brief as to require "only a brief summary rather than a full statement of the facts."[143] Also, some *causae* did not require a *narratio* as they are "well known to the judge or have been correctly set forth by a previous speaker."[144] Quintilian

---

136. *De inventione* 1.27.
137. *De inventione* 1.28.
138. *De inventione* 1.28.
139. *De inventione* 1.29.
140. *De inventione* 1.29.
141. *De inventione* 1.30.
142. *De inventione* 1.30.
143. *Institutio oratoria* 4.2.4.
144. *Institutio oratoria* 4.2.5.

did advise that the *narratio,* when there was one, should follow immediately upon the *exordium,* unless there was some special reason for not doing so.[145] Quintilian defined the *narratio* in 4.2.31: "The statement of facts [*narratio*] consists in the persuasive exposition of that which either has been done, or is supposed to have been done. . . ." On the nature of the *narratio,* Quintilian referred to earlier traditions: "Most writers, more especially those of the Isocratean school, hold that it should be lucid, brief, and plausible [*lucidam, brevem, verisimilem*] (for it is of no importance if we substitute clear [*perspicuam*] for lucid, or credible or plausible [*probabilem credibilemve*]). I agree with this classification of its qualities. . . ."[146] Hence, Quintilian was in essential agreement here with Cicero's *De inventione,* especially in the ways that one causes the *narratio* to have these qualities,[147] although Quintilian's treatment is much more fulsome than Cicero's. In dealing with *narratio, Rhetorica ad Herennium* 1.12 had a categorization into three types of *narrationes* similar to that in *De inventione* 1.27, quoted above. Also, a *narratio* should have three properties: brevity, clarity, and plausibility *(ut brevis, ut dilucida, ut veri similis sit),*[148] as *De inventione* and Quintilian also advised. The discussion of *narratio* here is also based on the exposition of how to get these three qualities in the *narratio,* in 1.14-16. Hence, the *Rhetorica ad Herennium* correctly concluded: "In what I have thus far said I believe that I agree with the other writers on the art of rhetoric. . . ."[149]

The Partitio

There is no single equivalent to *partitio* in Greek rhetoric, but several terms such as πρόθεσις, προκατασκευή, περιβολή, προέκθεσις, and ὑπόσχεσις seem to be the Greek equivalents of the *partitio,* which is also known as the *propositio.*[150] In *De inventione* 1.31-34, Cicero discusses the *partitio.* In his understanding the *partitio* takes two forms *(partes).*[151] In

145. *Institutio oratoria* 4.2.25-28.
146. *Institutio oratoria* 4.2.31-32.
147. *Institutio oratoria* 4.2.36-60.
148. *Rhetorica ad Herennium* 1.14.
149. *Rhetorica ad Herennium* 1.16.
150. Volkmann, *Rhetorik der Griechen und Römer,* 167-69.
151. *De inventione* 1.31.

both forms the goal is to make the *causa* clear and to help determine the nature of the controversy. The first form is a statement of agreements and disagreements with the opponents; "as a result of this some definite problem is set for the auditor on which he ought to have his attention fixed." In the second form of *partitio,*

> the matters which we intend to discuss are briefly set forth in a methodical way. This leads the auditor to hold definite points in his mind, and to understand that when these have been discussed the oration will be over.[152]

The first form of *partitio,* namely the statement of agreement and disagreement with opponents, "should," in Cicero's words, "turn the subject of agreement to the advantage of the speaker's case."[153] The second form of *partitio,* that which contains an *expositio* of topics to be discussed, ought to have three qualities: "brevity, completeness, and conciseness [*brevitas, absolutio, paucitas*]."[154] These qualities then became the subject of discussion in 1.32-33. Brevity was defined as the use of no unnecessary word. Completeness in the *partitio* meant that everything that is argued in the discourse was mentioned in the *partitio.*[155] Conciseness in the *partitio* meant not confusing *genus* with *species,* as well as only mentioning *genera.*[156]

Quintilian discussed the *partitio* in *Institutio oratoria* 4.5, in which he defined it as the enumeration in order of *propositiones.*[157] The *propositio* as discussed in 4.4 seems to constitute the beginning of each proof. Its goal was to state what the question to be decided was. This might include a statement of agreements and disagreements with opponents. Thus the *partitio,* as discussed in 4.5, "will, if judiciously employed, greatly add to the lucidity and grace of the speech [*lucis et gratiae confert*]."[158] It did this by "isolating the points from the crowd in which they would otherwise be lost and placing them before the eyes of the judge" and by setting limits on

---

152. *De inventione* 1.31.
153. *De inventione* 1.31.
154. *De inventione* 1.32.
155. *De inventione* 1.32.
156. *De inventione* 1.33.
157. *Institutio oratoria* 4.5.1.
158. *Institutio oratoria* 4.5.22.

the arguments so that the listener or reader could be aware of what part of the argument had been completed.[159] Thus *propositiones,* whether they are single or multiple, must first be "clear and lucid [*aperta atque lucida*]." Second, "it must be brief [*brevis*] and contain no unnecessary word."[160] Redundancy was to be avoided by not confusing *genus* and *species* and thus not enumerating *species* that are part of a *genus* mentioned.[161] Quintilian's treatment is very much in agreement with that in Cicero's *De inventione* 1.32, as discussed above.

The *Rhetorica ad Herennium,* also like Cicero, understood that the *partitio* (which it calls the *divisio*) had two *partes.*[162] The first *pars* included a statement of agreements and disagreements with opponents, and the second *pars* (called *distributio*) included enumeration and exposition of the points that would be discussed in the *probatio.* Cicero in *De inventione* had understood these two *partes* as different forms of the *partitio;* the *Rhetorica ad Herennium* seems to understand that each *divisio* included both *partes.*[163] Nevertheless, the *divisio* in the *Rhetorica ad Herennium* seems to be based on the *partitio* found elsewhere in Latin rhetoric. Indeed, the *Rhetorica ad Herennium* taught that the exposition "consists in setting forth briefly and completely [*breviter et absolute*], the points we intend to discuss";[164] as compared with "brevity, completeness, conciseness [*brevitas, absolutio, paucitas*]" in *De inventione* 1.32.

The Probatio

The proof (Greek πίστις; Latin *probatio* or *confirmatio/reprehensio* [or *refutatio*]) is considered the most important part of the rhetorical discourse, truly its *sine qua non.* The proof is the core of the discourse; everything that goes before it leads up to it, and the *peroratio* serves to underscore it.

Without a proof there simply is no rhetorical discourse, since nothing has been persuaded. Aristotle's *Ars rhetorica* 3.13.4 says, "so then the

159. *Institutio oratoria* 4.5.22-23.
160. *Institutio oratoria* 4.5.26.
161. *Institutio oratoria* 4.5.27.
162. *Rhetorica ad Herennium* 1.17.
163. *Rhetorica ad Herennium* 1.17.
164. *Rhetorica ad Herennium* 1.17.

necessary parts of a speech are the statement of the case and the proof. These divisions are appropriate to every speech, and at most the parts are four in number — exordium, statement, proof, epilogue." Aristotle includes refutation and comparison as part of the proof, since both refutation and comparison prove something.[165] Methods that may be employed in the proofs are discussed in 3.17.3–18.7. Amplification is especially appropriate for epideictic speeches, "as a rule, to prove that things are honorable or useful."[166] Deliberative rhetoric may be characterized by arguments "that certain consequences will not happen, or that what the adversary recommends will happen, but that it will be unjust, inexpedient, or not so important as supposed."[167] Examples (παραδεί-γματα), according to 3.17.5, were "best suited to deliberative oratory and enthymemes to judicial. The first [deliberative] is concerned with the future, so that its examples must be derived from the past; the second [judicial] with the question of the existence or non-existence of facts, in which demonstrative and necessary proofs are more in place; for the past involves a kind of necessity."[168]

In *De inventione* Cicero divided the proof into two parts, the *confirmatio* and the *reprehensio*. *Confirmatio* was defined as the "part of the oration which by marshalling arguments lends credit, authority, and support to our case."[169] The *reprehensio* was

> that part of an oration in which arguments are used to impair, disprove, or weaken the confirmation or proof in our opponents' speech. It utilizes the same sources of invention that confirmation does, because any proposition can be attacked by the same methods of reasoning by which it can be supported. . . . Therefore the rules for the invention and embellishment of arguments may properly be transferred from what has been said before to this part of the oration.[170]

In *Institutio oratoria* Quintilian devoted essentially all of book 5 to proofs. For Quintilian, the proof was the most important part of the dis-

---

165. *Ars rhetorica* 3.13.4.
166. *Ars rhetorica* 3.17.3.
167. *Ars rhetorica* 3.17.4.
168. *Ars rhetorica* 3.17.5.
169. *De inventione* 1.34.
170. *De inventione* 1.78.

course, since "there can be no suit in which the proof is not absolutely necessary."[171] Hence, Cicero and Quintilian agree on the existence of this part and its place within the structure of the speech.

The same is true of the *Rhetorica ad Herennium,* which reads, "The entire hope of victory and the entire method of persuasion rest on proof and refutation, for when we have submitted our arguments and destroyed those of the opposition, we have, of course, completely fulfilled the speaker's function."[172] Differing kinds of proofs and refutations were advised for the different *genera* of rhetoric, based on the topics that were to be discussed. For example, the proofs in deliberative rhetoric were discussed in 3.8; since the end of deliberative rhetoric, according to *Rhetorica ad Herennium,* is advantage (which had the two subdivisions of the consideration of security and the consideration of honor), the proofs in deliberative rhetoric were properly based on these two topics, which can be further subdivided. Thus in deliberative rhetoric the proof and refutation "establish in our favour the topics explained above, and refute the contrary topics."[173] Consequently the proof and refutation according to the *Rhetorica ad Herennium* served the same basic purposes as the proof and refutation according to other rhetorical handbooks.

The Peroratio

The *peroratio* (Greek ἐπιλόγος) forms the end of rhetorical discourses, hence the term for it in the *Rhetorica ad Herennium,* the *conclusio.*[174] Aristotle said that the ἐπιλόγος is the last of the four parts of the discourse,[175] and that it has four functions: "to dispose the hearer favourably towards oneself and unfavourably towards the adversary; to amplify and to deprecate; to excite the emotions of the hearer; to recapitulate."[176] Aristotle goes on to give the general reason for the ἐπιλόγος and its placement at the end of the discourse: "For after you have proved that you are truthful and that the adversary is false, the natural order of things is to praise ourselves,

171. *Institutio oratoria* 5.Preface.5
172. *Rhetorica ad Herennium* 1.18.
173. *Rhetorica ad Herennium* 3.8.
174. *Rhetorica ad Herennium* 1.4.
175. *Ars rhetorica* 3.13.4.
176. *Ars rhetorica* 3.19.

blame him and put the finishing touches."[177] In disposing the audience favorably to one's case (and unfavorably toward that of one's adversary, if there is one), Aristotle advised, "One or two things should be aimed at, to show that you are either relatively or absolutely good and the adversary either relatively or absolutely bad."[178] The excitement of the emotions of the audience was fairly self-explanatory. By way of recapitulation, the ἐπίλογος should give a summary statement of the proofs.[179]

Cicero defined the *peroratio* as the "end and conclusion of the whole speech."[180] The *peroratio* had three parts: the "summing-up" *(enumeratio)*, the "exciting of indignation [against the enemy]" *(indignatio)*, and the "arousal of pity and sympathy" *(conquestio)*. The *enumeratio*, according to Cicero, "is a passage in which matters which have been discussed in different places here and there throughout the speech are brought together in one place and arranged so as to be seen at a glance in order to refresh the memory of the audience."[181] The *indignatio* "is a passage which results in arousing great hatred against some person, or violent offense at some action."[182] The skilled rhetor had numerous means at his disposal for *indignatio*, including "all the attributes of persons or things . . . or any method of arousing enmity."[183] The opposite of the arousal of sympathy against the adversary was the arousal of sympathy in favor of one's own argument or person, the *conquestio*. This was done, according to *De inventione*, by the use of sixteen *loci* (in Greek, τόποι) or "commonplaces" that relate to the worthiness of one's case and the person of the defendant and that seek to arouse feelings of mercy from the audience.[184]

Quintilian's treatment of the *peroratio* is found in book 6. Clearly drawing on earlier rhetorical traditions, Quintilian divided the *peroratio* ("which some call the completion [*cumulum*] and others the conclusion [*conclusio*]")[185] into two types, "for it may deal either with facts or with the

---

177. *Ars rhetorica* 3.19.1.
178. *Ars rhetorica* 3.19.1.
179. *Ars rhetorica* 3.19.4.
180. *De inventione* 1.98.
181. *De inventione* 1.98.
182. *De inventione* 1.100.
183. *De inventione* 1.100.
184. *De inventione* 1.107-9.
185. *Institutio oratoria* 6.1.1.

emotional aspects of the case."[186] *Enumeratio* was defined as the "repetition and grouping of the facts, which the Greeks call ἀνακεφαλαίωσις [i.e., recapitulation]."[187] The appeal to the emotions may be employed by either defendant or plaintiff, though these would naturally appeal to different emotions.[188] Quintilian summed up his long treatment of *peroratio* as follows:

> It is therefore the duty of both parties to seek to win the judge's goodwill and to divert it from their opponent, as also to excite or assuage his emotions. And the following brief rule may be laid down for the observation of both parties, that the orator should display the full strength of his case before the eyes of his judge, and, when he has made up his mind what points in his case actually deserve or may seem to deserve to excite envy, goodwill, dislike or pity, should dwell on those points by which he himself would be most moved were he trying the case.[189]

The *Rhetorica ad Herennium* referred to the *peroratio* as the *conclusio*. It was equated by this author to the Greek ἐπίλογος, and it consisted of three parts, "the summing up, amplification, and appeal to pity [*enumeratione, amplificatione, et commiseratione*]."[190] The *enumeratio* here was equivalent to the *enumeratio* according to Quintilian.[191] *Amplificatio* was "the principle of using Commonplaces to stir the hearers."[192] The *Rhetorica ad Herennium* lists ten commonplaces that could be used for this. *Commiseratio* was the stirring up of pity in the audience.[193] Like Cicero,[194] the author of *Rhetorica ad Herennium* advised that the appeal to pity must be brief, "for nothing dries more quickly than a tear."[195]

In summary, there is clearly a wide consensus between Aristotle and extant Latin handbooks as to what the *partes orationis* were and what they did in and for the discourse. The *exordium* introduced the rhetor to the au-

186. *Institutio oratoria* 6.1.1.
187. *Institutio oratoria* 6.1.1.
188. *Institutio oratoria* 6.1.9.
189. *Institutio oratoria* 6.1.11.
190. *Rhetorica ad Herennium* 2.47.
191. *Rhetorica ad Herennium* 2.47.
192. *Rhetorica ad Herennium* 2.47
193. *Rhetorica ad Herennium* 2.50.
194. *De inventione* 1.109.
195. *Rhetorica ad Herennium* 2.50.

dience and might state the *causa*. The *narratio*, if there was one, stated the facts in the case. The *partitio*, if there was one, could either state the agreements and disagreements with the adversary or could list (or allude to) the arguments to be made in the proof. The *probatio* proved the case and might refute the adversary, if there was one. The *peroratio* summed up the arguments and amplified them, and it frequently excited the emotions of the audience either for one's case, against one's adversary's case, or both.

5. Traditions of Deliberative Rhetoric

Aristotle's *Ars rhetorica* seems most classically Aristotelian in that it defined the *genera* of rhetoric in terms of three τέλοι, as Grimaldi has pointed out,[196] but in fact Aristotle's τέλοι of each *genus* of rhetoric were actually equivalent to the topics that were traditionally associated with them. Hence the τέλοι of deliberative rhetoric included "the expedient or harmful," which were positive and negative forms of the topic of advantage, that is, the advantageous and the disadvantageous. With regard to other traditional topics of deliberative rhetoric, such as the topics of honor and justice, Aristotle advised that they were "included as accessory" to the topics of the expedient and the harmful.[197] Thus Aristotle's system of rhetoric included a ranking of topics, with honor and justice understood as subsidiary topics of the topic of advantage, which implied that the rhetor introduced the topic of honor not separately from the topic of advantage, but *in terms of* the topic of advantage. In other words, the rhetor advised the βουλή that he addressed that they should do the honorable thing because it is advantageous to be honorable. For all practical purposes, then, honor was identified with one's reputation, in Aristotle's system of rhetoric.[198]

Aristotle's interaction with rhetoric, however, was not confined to the rather late treatise *Ars rhetorica*. Early in his life he had written a collection of opinions about rhetoric by rhetoricians, entitled Συναγωγή τέχνων,

---

196. W. M. A. Grimaldi, *Aristotle, Rhetoric I: A Commentary* (New York: Fordham University Press, 1980), 80.

197. Aristotle, *Ars rhetorica* 1.3.5.

198. It is interesting that this ordering of the topics of rhetoric, in which advantage precedes and includes honor, is exactly opposite the ordering of the young Cicero in *De inventione* 2.12; 2.156.

a "gathering together of 'arts' [of rhetoric]."[199] Tradition has it that one of the rhetorical works included by Aristotle in his now-lost Συναγωγή τέχνων was the τέχνη of Isocrates. George Kennedy has argued that the fragments of Isocrates' τέχνη we now have do not conform to the well-developed style of Isocrates, but that they may be genuinely Isocratean by virtue of having come from the summary of Isocrates' teaching in Συναγωγή τέχνων, and that information about Isocrates' teaching could have come through oral tradition or through an internal document in his school.[200] Interestingly enough, Plutarch tells us that Demosthenes learned Isocrates' τέχνη secretly,[201] and one must agree with Kennedy that this "puzzling story can perhaps best be explained if knowledge of this handbook was not supposed to exist outside of the school."[202] Cicero in *De inventione* 2.7 tells us of Isocrates, "there is known to be a text book from his hand, but I have not seen it," and the fifth-century-c.e. rhetorician Syrianus referred to Isocrates' "private" handbook,[203] so the theory of a private handbook of Isocrates has much to commend it. Thus, one must agree with Kennedy that Isocrates' handbook "shows that the contents of rhetorical theory were gradually expanding with the addition of material on style and on kinds of speeches, and it shows something about the state of sophistic rhetoric at the time Aristotle turned his attention to the subject."[204]

Isocrates' *De pace* ("On the Peace"), probably written about 355 b.c.e., is an excellent example of deliberative rhetoric. In it, Isocrates argued for an end to the Second Social War, seeking not a union of all the Hellenes, as he had earlier in his career, but rather, "It is enough for Isocrates now to urge Athens to set her own house in order and to take the lead in a consistent policy of peace, resorting to war only to defend the principle that the states of Hellas have the right to be free."[205] And on what basis did Isocrates argue for peace? Isocrates employed the two topics of advantage and honor, which in this speech constantly flow together.

In *De pace* 18-21 Isocrates argued that the Athenians should make

---

199. On Συναγωγή τέχνων see Kennedy, *Art of Persuasion in Greece,* 13, including n. 9.
200. Kennedy, *Art of Persuasion in Greece,* 70-72, especially n. 40.
201. Demosthenes' use of Isocrates is discussed in Plutarch's *Life of Demosthenes* 5.5.
202. Kennedy, *Art of Persuasion in Greece,* 71-72.
203. Kennedy, *Art of Persuasion in Greece,* 73.
204. Kennedy, *Art of Persuasion in Greece,* 74.
205. G. Norlin, *Isocrates* (LCL; Cambridge: Harvard University Press, 1929), 2.4-5.

peace rather than war because (1) it was to the advantage of the Athenians to end the war, based on considerations of finance and freedom, to pursue peacetime occupations, including farming and maritime trade, and (2) it was to the advantage of the Athenians to end the war because they would enjoy greater security because the Athenians' allies would be more disposed toward true friendship. We can see that the primary topic used is the topic of advantage, and that the topic of honor is subsidiary to the topic of advantage, primarily because to be honorable is to enjoy the blessings of a good reputation. At the end of *De pace,* Isocrates concluded:

> If, then, you will abide by the advice which I have given you, and if, besides, you will prove yourselves warlike by training and preparing for war but peaceful by doing nothing contrary to justice, you will render not only this city but all the Hellenes happy and prosperous. . . . But no matter what course the rest may take, our own position will be honourable and advantageous. . . .

A more telling indication of deliberative rhetoric could hardly be found than the final words of Isocrates just quoted: καλῶς ἕξει καὶ συμφερόντως, a clear use of what were or would become the standard topics of deliberative rhetoric's honor and advantage.

A more famous political speech than the foregoing is Isocrates' *Panegyricus,* which Isocrates delivered in the autumn of 380 B.C.E. Not accidentally, this speech argued in favor of war, along exactly the same lines that *De pace* had argued against war, the topics of advantage and honor.

After Isocrates, the most notable practitioner of deliberative rhetoric was Demosthenes, who was born in Athens in 384 B.C.E. He studied rhetoric with Isaeus, who had studied with Isocrates. The course of Demosthenes' early development as an orator is the subject of many interesting stories, to be found in plenty in Plutarch's *Life of Demosthenes.* His earliest speeches were those of his prosecution of his guardians, *Against Aphobus I* and *II,* which date from 363 B.C.E., Demosthenes' twenty-first year. Although he won his patrimony in court, little of it remained by the time he obtained it, and so Demosthenes became a λογογράφος, a speech-writer. Although Demosthenes' most famous single work is probably *De corona* ("On the Crown"), a brilliant judicial speech in which he defended his life and public career, Demosthenes is best known as the rhetor who mobilized Athens against Philip II of Macedon through his deliberative speeches before the Athenian council, such as his several *Philippic* and *Olynthiac* speeches, as well as lesser-known speeches such as *On the Symmories, For the People of Megalopolis, For the Liberty of the Rhodians, On the Peace,* and *On the Chersonese.* A number of letters bearing Demosthenes' name survive; not all of them have equal claim to authenticity, but Jonathan A. Goldstein has demonstrated the authenticity of and provided a rhetorical analysis of several of them.[206] Whether or not any of them is authentic, it is clear that they demonstrate the use of rhetorical techniques in letters associated with the most famous deliberative rhetor in history.

Demosthenes' *First Philippic* was written around 351 to 340 B.C.E. Kennedy noted that the major focus of the *First Philippic* was the argument on the basis of advantage; honor and justice do not seem to enter into this speech.

> It is assumed that Philip acts in his own interest, and Athens must act in hers. . . . Demosthenes so focuses Athenian interests that the question seems not one of advantage, but of necessity, not the choice of a course of action, but the pursuit of the only possibility. . . . All other rhetorical arguments are only accessory: Athens' failure to act will bring on her the deepest disgrace and will allow Philip to go unpunished, but no honor is promised Athens for action, and disinterested justice is not involved.[207]

The *Third Philippic* was one of Demosthenes' most successful deliberative speeches. Much as in the *First Philippic,* he uses the argument from advantage or expediency almost exclusively. The advantage that was offered to the Athenians was, of course, of no small import: it was nothing less than the salvation of the Athenians from the hands of Philip. In paragraphs 63-69 of this speech Demosthenes used the *exempla* of other cities that Philip had ravaged, a standard feature in deliberative rhetoric, but the reason these negative examples were used is that they were examples of people who acted unwisely toward Philip, to their own disadvantage. Instead of being honored citizens of their own *polis,* they had become slaves, in Demosthenes' view. By the somewhat indirect reference to the social status of the captive subjects of Philip, it is clear that the topic of honor does enter into this argument, although it seems secondary to the topic of ad-

---

206. J. A. Goldstein, *The Letters of Demosthenes* (New York and London: Columbia University Press, 1968).

207. Kennedy, *Art of Persuasion in Greece,* 224.

vantage. Nevertheless, the two arguments work together powerfully in a number of Demosthenes' deliberative speeches, because it was dishonorable to choose not to fight Philip (given the kind of person he was), and, more importantly, it was to the Athenians' great disadvantage not to acknowledge the reality of their conflict with Philip, especially when an early entrance into a war with Philip would have given the Athenians a better chance of protecting Athens from him. Kennedy has shown that the confluence of the arguments from advantage and honor is a standard feature of fourth-century deliberative oratory,[208] and it is easy for us to see why this was the case, after having understood the classification of rhetoric by Aristotle. Aristotle taught, as far as we know for the first time, that the distinctions between the *genera* of rhetoric could be understood on the basis of time. In deliberative rhetoric, a deliberative body (or a deliberative person) is asked to make a decision that will affect the future for good or ill. Hence, the arguments that have always been most effective in deliberative rhetoric are those arguments that showed that the hearers' or readers' own personal advantage (which would be realized in the future) would be affected by the decision that they must make, either by doing something or by not doing anything.

6. A Deliberative Rhetorical Letter: Demosthenes' *Epistle 1*

Perhaps the best proof of the use of rhetoric in ancient letters is not statements about letters in the various rhetorical handbooks, or even epistolary handbooks, but actual letters written by prominent rhetors. Among letters written by Greek rhetors, one should not overlook the letters of Demosthenes, who was known as the greatest Greek orator as well as the greatest deliberative rhetor, and who was clearly one of Cicero's rhetorical heroes.[209] Goldstein showed that Demosthenes' *Epistle 1* was conceived and executed in the style of deliberative rhetoric.[210]

208. G. A. Kennedy, "Focusing of Arguments in Greek Deliberative Oratory," *TAPA* 20 (1959): 131-38.

209. A. Weische, *Ciceros Nachahmung der attischen Redner* (BKAW 2/45; Heidelberg: Winter, 1972); C. W. Wooten, *Cicero's Philippics and Their Demosthenic Model: The Rhetoric of Crisis* (Chapel Hill: University of North Carolina Press, 1983).

210. See the rhetorical analysis of *Epistle 1* in Goldstein, *Letters of Demosthenes,* 176-81; Goldstein's English translation of *Epistle 1* is found on pp. 204-7 of the same work.

In *Epistle 1*, "On Concord," the exiled Demosthenes began with a prayer for divine inspiration for writer and readers, followed by the epistolary prescript. In the *exordium* of this letter, Demosthenes only briefly mentioned the topic of his exile, passing over this topic in order to mention the two topics dealt with in the proof: the advantage of the Athenians, and the importance of making decisions and following them consistently. The two-part proof is then followed by a *peroratio*, which in turn is followed by an exhortation. Although "exhortation" is not a traditional *pars orationis*, according to the handbooks, the presence of exhortations at the end of deliberative orations is consistent with the discussions of deliberative rhetoric in certain rhetorical handbooks, in which the prime task of the deliberative rhetor is exhortation.[211] For facility of study and discussion, we include a brief rhetorical analysis of Demosthenes' *Epistle 1*, showing the *partes orationis* of this letter in outline form.

A Rhetorical Summary of Demosthenes' *Epistle 1*

```
1-4   I.   Exordium
1          A.        Invocation
                     1. Reason for invocation: propriety
                     2. Deities invoked: "all the gods and goddesses"
                     3. Purpose of invocation: "that what is best for
                        the democracy of the Athenians and for
                        those who bear goodwill toward the democ-
                        racy . . . I may be moved to write and the
                        members of the assembly to adopt"
2          B.        Epistolary prescript
                     1. Superscriptio: "Demosthenes"
                     2. Adscriptio: "to the Council and people"
```

211. See especially the discussion of exhortation (and dissuasion) in the pseudo-Aristotelian *Rhetorica ad Alexandrum* in connection with deliberative rhetoric, especially sections 1-2, which are 1421b7 to 1425b35 in the standard editions (see the edition by H. Rackham, *Aristotle: Rhetorica ad Alexandrum,* bound together with Aristotle's *Problems,* books 22-38 [LCL; Cambridge: Harvard University Press, 1957], 275-305). In this system of rhetoric, speeches are divided into three kinds, deliberative, epideictic, and forensic, and these three kinds of rhetoric are divided into seven εἴδη, exhortation, dissuasion, eulogy, vituperation, accusation, defense, and investigation; deliberative rhetoric includes exhortation and dissuasion; see Aristotle, *Ars rhetorica* 1.3.3.

			3. *Salutatio:* "greetings"
2-4	C.		Material concerning the relationship between Demosthenes and the Athenians
			1. First part (not discussed directly): "the question of my return"
3			2. Second part: advantage for the Athenians

                 (a) Aspects of advantage
                    (i) "glory"
                    (ii) "security"
                    (iii) "liberty"
                 (b) Recipients of advantage
                    (i) "not only for you" (= the Athenians)
                    (ii) "but for all the rest of the Greeks"
        3. Third part on the Athenians' making of decisions
                 (a) Stated positively: "provided you adopt the necessary measures"
                 (b) Stated negatively: "if you fail to recognize it or are misled"

3-4	D.		The *causa* (reason) for this letter
			1. Stated in terms of the rhetor: "I felt I had to put before the public my opinion"
			2. Digression on the difficulties of communicating by letters
4			3. Stated in terms of the need of the Athenians
5-7	II.	*Partitio*	
5	A.		Topic of second proof: on establishing concord
	B.		Topic of third proof: on the carrying out of decisions when passed
6	C.		Topic of first proof: on not harboring grudges
7-12	III.	*Probatio*	
7	A.		First proof: on not harboring grudges

        1. Statement of thesis
                 (a) Negatively: the fear of bitterness makes collaborators
                 (b) Positively: those unafraid of bitterness will be tractable

238

2. First argument: public proclamation of not harboring grudges not advantageous

3. Second argument actual practice of not harboring grudges will determine future expectations

8-10   B.   Second proof: on concord

8   1. Statement of thesis

    (a) Negatively: "you must not cast any blame"

    (b) Positively: "you must grant that everyone has done his duty"

9   2. First argument: on the basis of honor

9   3. Second argument: on the basis of advantage

10   4. Third argument: on the basis of Demosthenes' personal experience

11-12   C.   Third proof: on the carrying out of decisions when passed

11   1. Reference to previous communication from Demosthenes on preparatory steps

11-12   2. Statement of thesis: the carrying out of war commands are the tasks of commanding generals

12   3. First argument: those who give advice to you are put in a difficult position

4. Second argument: plans carefully thought out can be spoiled when not implemented correctly

13   III. *Peroratio*

     A.   Transition from previous heading *(e contrario)*: "This time I hope that everything will go well"

     B.   The *exemplum* of Alexander

1. Statement of *exemplum*

2. Consequences of *exemplum*

    (a) First consequence: Alexander succeeding by activity, not by inactivity

    (b) Second consequence: Fortune is now seeking someone to accompany

239

14-16	IV.	Exhortation
14	A.	Concerning commanders
15	B.	Concerning changes of mind (see second proof above)
16	C.	Concerning religious duties
	D.	Final exhortation: "liberate the Greeks!"
16	V.	Epistolary postscript: "Farewell"

7. Conclusions

From the above analysis of Demosthenes' interesting deliberative letter, a letter in which Demosthenes advised the Athenians that they should make a change in public policy that would affect their future, one can see that the *partes orationis* do function in this letter in ways that one would expect from reading about the *partes orationis* in the rhetorical handbooks. There is a clear connection between the *exordium,* the two-part proof, and the *peroratio,* and one could argue that there is also recapitulation of the second proof in the exhortation section, although recapitulation of the first proof seems to be absent. All of the *partes orationis* that are found in Demosthenes' *Epistle 1,* as well as in other letters,[212] are indeed found in the Second Letter to the Thessalonians.

Just as the identification and exposition of the *partes* of Demosthenes' letter are central to the understanding of what and how the writer intended to persuade, so are the identification and exposition of the *partes* of 1 Thessalonians central to the understanding of the rhetoric of this letter.[213]

---

212. Several rhetorical letters that were written in the Hellenistic period, closer to the time of the New Testament, are found in *Royal Correspondence in the Hellenistic Period: A Study in Greek Epigraphy* (ed. C. B. Welles; New Haven: Yale University Press, 1934). In his introduction (xli-l) Welles identifies letters 14, 22, 30, 36, 44, and especially 15 in his collection as rhetorical. These letters, mostly written as honorific communications from kings to subordinates, are generally epideictic in character. See Welles's translation and notes on letter 15, from Antiochus II to Erythrae (78-85). In this letter one can readily identify an *exordium* (including an epistolary prescript and a lengthy *captatio benevolentiae*), a *narratio,* a proof concerning the real reason for the letter (the king's grant of autonomy and tax exemption to the city of Erythrae), an exhortation to the city to act in ways consistent with its previous good record, and an ending greeting.

213. See Hughes, "The Rhetoric of 1 Thessalonians."

The Social Situations Implied by Rhetoric

Frank W. Hughes

1. Definition and Practice of Rhetorical Criticism

Rhetorical criticism of a text, biblical or otherwise, always presupposes a theory of rhetoric that grounds the criticism.[1] Although many theories of rhetoric are in use today, some scholars may think of the choice of a theory to be used as a basis for rhetorical criticism as arbitrary. Since rhetorical criticism is intended to be a supplement to and not a replacement for traditional historical criticism, the rhetorical theory selected ought to be one that has the best potential for historical correlation between itself and the texts being studied.[2] The selection of Graeco-Roman rhetoric will be wise for a number of reasons, among the most important being the pervasiveness of rhetorical schools in the educational system likely to have influenced most of the writers and compilers of the New Testament.[3]

---

1. Frank W. Hughes, "Rhetorical Criticism," in *Mercer Dictionary of the Bible* (ed. Watson E. Mills; Macon: Mercer University Press, 1990), 763-64.

2. David E. Mesner, "The Rhetoric of Citations: Paul's Use of Scripture in Romans 9" (Unpub. Ph.D. diss.; Northwestern University/Garrett-Evangelical Theological Seminary, 1991), a dissertation directed by Robert Jewett. Mesner is now working on a larger project to describe the rhetoric of Romans 9–11.

3. George A. Kennedy, *New Testament Interpretation through Rhetorical Criticism* (Studies in Religion; Chapel Hill and London: University of North Carolina Press, 1984), 8-12; E. Patrick Parks, *The Roman Rhetorical Schools as a Preparation for the Courts under the Early Empire* (Johns Hopkins University Studies in Historical and Political Science 63/2; Bal-

Integral to Graeco-Roman rhetorical theory are the three *genera* of rhetoric that had their roots in social situations.[4] The *genus deliberativum* was the rhetoric that was delivered before deliberative bodies such as the Athenian council, and the *genus iudiciale* was the rhetoric spoken in the context of the law court. The *genus demonstrativum* is more difficult to characterize according to social situation, due to the fact that this *genus* of rhetoric implies a "showing forth" or "display" of flashy speech, which could be done for a wide variety of purposes and in a number of different social settings. In fact, it is evident that various social settings are strongly implied in the consensus of rhetorical theory that extends from Isocrates, through Aristotle and Cicero, on into the time of the New Testament, and reaching its fullest expression in Quintilian. Standard topics were associated with the three *genera* of rhetoric: epideictic rhetoric's standard topics, for example, were praise and blame, and their counterparts in deliberative rhetoric were advantage and honor.

Those wishing to do rhetorical criticism of early Christian literature, especially using Graeco-Roman rhetoric as a model, need to consider the critique of the "neo-Aristotelian" approach to rhetorical criticism made by Edwin Black.[5] Black argued that many aspects of modern and contemporary rhetoric exhibit characteristics that are beyond the scope of the rhetorical categories used by Aristotle. Aristotle's *Art of Rhetoric* presupposed that audiences were basically appropriate to the rhetorical discourses that were presented to them,[6] and that his statements about rhetoric were not descriptive of actual "rhetorical transactions."[7] Black did, however, find the neo-Aristotelian approach quite appropriate and congenial to those who were historians of rhetoric, "[f]or critics to approach the study of movements themselves could not fail to illuminate the history of rhetori-

---

timore: Johns Hopkins University Press, 1945); Stanley F. Bonner, *Education in Ancient Rome: From the Elder Cato to the Younger Pliny* (Berkeley and Los Angeles: University of California Press, 1977), 47-89, 250-333, with bibliography on 388-91. In favor of the likelihood that Paul had undergone a rhetorical education, see Christopher Forbes, "Comparison, Self-Praise, and Irony: Paul's Boasting and the Conventions of Hellenistic Rhetoric," *NTS* 32 (1986): 1-30, especially 22-24.

4. As correctly pointed out by Stanley E. Stowers, *Letter-Writing in Greco-Roman Antiquity* (LEC 5; Philadelphia: Westminster, 1986), 51.

5. Edwin Black, *Rhetorical Criticism: A Study in Method* (New York: Macmillan, 1965; repr. Madison: University of Wisconsin Press, 1978).

6. Black, *Rhetorical Criticism*, 113-14.

7. Black, *Rhetorical Criticism*, 129.

cal practice."[8] Although Black objected to the use of the classical rhetorical perspective in criticism of modern and contemporary discourse, he approved of it to ground a rhetorical criticism that would augment the historical criticism of Greek persuasive documents from the late ancient world. What is less clear, however, is how one would actually employ the traditions of Greek and Roman rhetoric in order to develop a criticism of such ancient Greek and/or Roman texts.

How does one utilize appropriately Graeco-Roman rhetoric for the purpose of doing rhetorical criticism today? The history of rhetoric itself provides several clues. Rhetorical theory was commonly understood to have five parts: invention, arrangement, style, memory, and delivery. Memory and delivery are applicable only to oral discourses, so that leaves primarily the first three to be mined for material relevant to the rhetorical criticism of written correspondence. Greek and Roman rhetoric is complex due to a long history in two languages with regard to both theory and practice. As a result it should not be surprising that New Testament scholars start at different places in the tradition of rhetoric as they attempt to analyze and describe the persuasive character of early Christian texts. New Testament scholars who specialize in Pauline and/or other letters have been rather predictably drawn to arrangement as an obvious and appropriate starting point. Given the highly programmatic character of epistolary thanksgiving prayers, comparison of New Testament documents with Graeco-Roman rhetorical theory lies close at hand. Scholars with a specialty in other parts of the New Testament are more likely to focus their analysis on the "internal argumentation" of persuasive texts. Still others have focused on yet another important aspect of rhetorical practice, *imitatio,* as a way to understand the early Christian utilization of textual sources or patterns found in these texts. Although all three approaches for the analysis of persuasive texts in the New Testament have not at all times been identified as "rhetorical criticism," it can certainly be argued that, depending on one's definition of rhetorical criticism, all three can be understood to be types of rhetorical criticism. In this essay rhetorical criticism will be defined as the identification of the strategies of persuasion used by authors and/or compilers of texts. The goal of such identification is an attempt to gain greater understanding of the author, the audience, and the author's purpose in communicating with that particular audience. Cur-

---

8. Black, *Rhetorical Criticism,* 21.

rently several approaches are used to identify such persuasive strategies in the New Testament and other early Christian texts. The next section will seek briefly to explain two approaches and will then focus in some detail on a third approach.

2. Rhetoric as *Imitatio*

Some of the most interesting and most neglected recent works in New Testament studies have been those of Thomas L. Brodie and Wolfgang Roth, both of whom have argued that several New Testament books have been dominated by *imitatio* of patterns drawn from the Hebrew Bible.[9] *Imitatio* may be defined as the use of texts, persons, and literary patterns from existing literature in the creation of new literature.

For the purposes of this study, we focus on the social setting of Mark as identified by Roth. In *Hebrew Gospel*, Roth collected and presented a considerable amount of evidence to suggest that the Gospel according to Mark was a conscious *imitatio* of the Elijah-Elisha cycle of stories in 1 Kings 17–2 Kings 13. Evidence is provided by a number of important details and features in the Elijah-Elisha narrative that appear to have been recreated and expanded in Mark, including the number of miracles and the performance of various kinds of miracles, as well as the identification of John the Baptizer as Elijah. One can see in this provocative monograph a method of identifying and interpreting the persuasive strategies in Mark by means of the repeated parallels from the Elijah-Elisha cycle. Roth argued that Mark was an attempt at the scriptural legitimization of Jesus by showing that he was a greater religious leader (i.e., prophet and martyr) than were his prototypes in the Hebrew Bible. At the end of his study, the attempt is made to identify Mark's originally intended audience. "If the

---

9. Wolfgang Roth, *Hebrew Gospel: Cracking the Code of Mark* (Oak Park, Ill.: Meyer-Stone, 1988); Roth, "Scriptural Coding in the Fourth Gospel," *BR* 32 (1987): 6-29. On the phenomenon of *imitatio* in general see Thomas L. Brodie, "Greco-Roman Imitation of Texts as a Partial Guide to Luke's Use of Sources," in *Luke-Acts: New Perspectives from the Society of Biblical Literature Seminar* (ed. Charles H. Talbert; New York: Crossroad, 1988), 17-26; as well as Frank W. Hughes, "The Parable of the Rich Man and Lazarus (Luke 16.19-31) and Graeco-Roman Rhetoric," in *Rhetoric and the New Testament: Essays from the 1992 Heidelberg Conference* (ed. Stanley E. Porter and Thomas H. Olbricht; JSNTSup 90; Sheffield: JSOT, 1993), 29-41, with the literature referred to on p. 32, n. 16.

thesis here advanced is granted such a community of readers must have existed — audiences to whom, by the same token, the other gospels also seem to be addressed."[10] It is urged that Mark was a book that included signs that only people who would know the special coding of Mark (its *imitatio* of features of 1 Kings 17–2 Kings 13) would fully comprehend; therefore, the *Sitz im Leben* implied by the text of Mark corresponds in a reciprocal way to the rhetoric of Mark. Roth continues:

> Put more broadly, the gospel's audience constitutes itself to the extent to which its readers, like the disciples and other partners of Jesus that it introduces, succeed or fail in being persuaded that its plot and cast reenact and heighten those of a model found in the Hebrew Bible. To the disciples "the secret of the Kingdom of God" has already been given: they know that 1 K[in]gs 17–2 K[in]gs 13 is the paradigm; they only need to come to the insight that Jesus exceeds Elisha in a manner comparable to the way in which the latter exceeds his forerunner Elijah ([Mk] 8:14-21 . . .).[11]

Roth's literary analysis of Mark has, therefore, a direct relationship to the positing of a plausible social setting for the writer (or compiler or editor) of Mark, as well as the originally intended readers of this Gospel. Using a historical model, the rhetoric of a text implies a situation in response to which the author wrote the text. The identification of authorial intention is based on the content as well as the structuring and enumeration of miracle stories in Mark. Hence Roth's method of rhetorical criticism (or "discourse analysis")[12] can be fully integrated with historical criticism; he never claimed not to be doing historical criticism. Rather, what he did do was to develop and use a different approach to the asking and answering of historical questions about a text and its context.

10. Roth, *Hebrew Gospel,* 123.

11. Roth, *Hebrew Gospel,* 130.

12. Roth, *Hebrew Gospel,* 130 (quotation marks his). Roth did not use the term "rhetorical criticism" to describe his work, but has no objection to this characterization, given a broad definition of rhetorical criticism as the identification of strategies of persuasion in a text.

3. Analysis of Rhetoric as Internal Argumentation

A second method of analysis, this one being explicitly referred to as "rhetorical criticism," has been developed by Burton L. Mack and Vernon K. Robbins in their provocative book, *Patterns of Persuasion in the Gospels*. The major difference between their way of doing rhetorical criticism and the way it is practiced by rhetorical critics such as Betz, Jewett, Watson, Kennedy, Mesner, and others is that Mack and Robbins are more interested in analyzing the internal argumentation than in the identification of the arrangement of an overall document. Mack and Robbins put major emphasis on *inventio* and argumentative figures. Examining carefully what topics the writers or speakers have used *(inventio)* as well as the precise way they set up the matter *(stasis)* and argue it (through enthymeme, contrary, analogy, example, and citation of authority), Mack and Robbins execute a rhetorical analysis that recommends particular social environments. By seeing what early Christian writers have at their disposal and how they argue what they have, one can gain insight into the social location of texts and their authors.

Particularly instructive of the method of rhetorical criticism practiced by Robbins is his treatment of Matt 8:19-22 and Luke 9:57-60.[13] Robbins shows that, on the basis of the schema of the elaboration of the *chreia* as found in Aelius Theon's *Progymnasmata*, the elaboration of the sayings, "Foxes have holes . . ." and ". . . leave the dead to bury their dead," is carried out in markedly different ways in Matthew and Luke. These differences reveal distinct social settings for the sayings in Matthew and Luke. The Matthaean form is more indebted to inductive logic, developing the theme of discipleship through the category of the *ethos* of Jesus and the *exemplum* of "let[ting] the dead bury their own dead." Robbins concludes that, for the Matthaean version of the saying, "[t]he rationale introduces deductive logic into a rhetorical sequence based on inductive logic, grounding the assertions in a well-known situation in domestic life in Mediterranean society."[14] Robbins argues that his analysis has shown that the difference between the presentation of the stories in Matthew and Luke "is significant rhetorically"[15] in that the Lucan version of the same story is

---

13. Burton L. Mack and Vernon K. Robbins, *Patterns of Persuasion in the Gospels* (FFNT: Literary Facets; Sonoma, Calif.: Polebridge, 1989), 69-84.

14. Robbins in Mack and Robbins, *Patterns of Persuasion*, 83.

15. Robbins in Mack and Robbins, *Patterns of Persuasion*, 83.

developed without the introduction of deductive logic, merely using *ethos* and *exemplum*. The social difference in the stories is, after Robbins's expert analysis, easy to identify:

> The issue is whether it is sufficient in the Christian community to ground certain assertions simply in the *ethos* of Jesus, or whether it is advantageous to provide one or more rationales from the arena of common experiences in life. When the reasoning establishes a basis for one or more assertions through a rationale that moves outside the arena of the *ethos* of Jesus, it moves into the realm of elaboration as discussed by Hermogenes.[16]

Hence the rhetorical distance between the ways that the *chreia* is elaborated in the Matthaean and Lucan versions of a Q saying can be a measure of the social distance between the editors/compilers of the two versions of such a saying.

4. Rhetorical Analysis of Letters and Rhetorical *dispositio*

Rhetorical critics have given varying amounts and kinds of attention to the social situations in which the New Testament letters were written. In his pathbreaking commentary on Galatians, Hans-Dieter Betz never referred to his own method as anything but form criticism and/or epistolographic analysis of Galatians.[17] Gerd Lüdemann, who made use of Betz's analysis of Galatians for the purpose of doing Pauline chronology, referred specifically to Betz's work on Galatians as form criticism.[18]

A considerable amount of criticism has been leveled at various rhetorical critics engaged in the analysis of the New Testament, usually to the effect that the identification of *partes orationis* in New Testament letters is often done mechanically and without sufficient consideration of the differences between letters and rhetorical speeches.[19] Yet, on the basis of

---

16. Robbins in Mack and Robbins, *Patterns of Persuasion*, 83-84.

17. Hans-Dieter Betz, *Galatians: A Commentary on Paul's Letter to the Churches in Galatia* (Hermeneia; Philadelphia: Fortress, 1979).

18. Gerd Lüdemann, *Paul, Apostle to the Gentiles: Studies in Chronology* (Philadelphia: Fortress, 1984), 46-59.

19. Many of these objections against rhetorical criticism were answered in my 1989

mentions of letters in rhetorical handbooks (particularly Cicero's statement in *De oratore* 2.49 that another *genus* of rhetoric would not be necessary for a well-trained rhetor in order to write an official letter), as well as
materials illustrative of the appropriation in the Middle Ages and by Erasmus of Graeco-Roman rhetoric in the *ars dictaminis* (art of letter-
writing),[20] it has been argued that letters and speeches should not be
sharply divided from one another. The case for a stronger relationship between rhetoric and letters was made on the basis of the titles of several
epistolary types in the epistolary handbooks.[21] In addition, a fresh rhetorical analysis of Demosthenes' *Epistle 1* is now available, one that had previously been determined as belonging to the genre of deliberative rhetoric by
Jonathan A. Goldstein.[22] This new analysis maintains that, even if rhetorical instruction did not give central attention to letters in rhetorical theory
(probably due to the extreme disadvantage of trying to do persuasion
without *actio*, oral delivery), the practice of rhetoric included letters, especially due to the political necessity for official communications to distant
places.

5. Rhetorical Analyses of the Thessalonian Correspondence

My *Early Christian Rhetoric and 2 Thessalonians* was the first published
rhetorical analysis of 2 Thessalonians.[23] A number of other examinations
of the Thessalonian correspondence have recently been published, the best
known of which are those by Glenn Holland, Bruce Johanson, and Robert
Jewett.[24] Rhetorical analyses of New Testament documents differ markedly

---

monograph: Frank W. Hughes, *Early Christian Rhetoric and 2 Thessalonians* (JSNTSup 30;
Sheffield: JSOT, 1989).

20. Frank W. Hughes, *Early Christian Rhetoric*, 27-28, along with nn. 70-77 on pp.
111-12.

21. Hughes, *Early Christian Rhetoric*, 26-27.

22. Hughes, *Early Christian Rhetoric*, 47-50; Jonathan A. Goldstein, *The Letters of
Demosthenes* (New York and London: Columbia University Press, 1968), 176-81.

23. See n. 19.

24. Glenn S. Holland, *The Traditions That You Received from Us: 2 Thessalonians in
the Pauline Tradition* (HUTh 24; Tübingen: Mohr-Siebeck, 1986); Bruce C. Johanson, *To All
the Brethren: A Text-Linguistic and Rhetorical Approach to 1 Thessalonians* (ConBNT 16;
Stockholm: Almqvist & Wiksell, 1987); and Robert Jewett, *The Thessalonian Correspondence:
Pauline Rhetoric and Millenarian Piety* (FFNT; Philadelphia: Fortress, 1986).

on the basis of three factors: (1) the system of rhetoric being used as the basis for rhetorical criticism; (2) the coherence of the rhetorical criticism with the system of rhetoric that grounds it; and (3) the perceived relationship between rhetorical criticism and form criticism, with its corollary, the perceived relation between rhetoric and epistolography. In order to understand what rhetorical critics have done and are doing, it is vital to realize that different rhetorical critics may be working not only from different presuppositions about how rhetoric worked but also from contrary exegetical presuppositions.

In the case of Johanson's important work on 1 Thessalonians, *To All the Brethren,* two different methods are in significant tension with each other. This is partially due to the acceptance of various theories drawn from modern linguistics as part of his text-linguistic method. Wilhelm Wuellner has identified a methodological difficulty in Johanson's separation of the "ultimate intention" of Paul from the "immediate intention" of the latter's dealing with pastoral issues in the Thessalonian congregation,[25] a distinction that is not reflective of the actual practice of Graeco-Roman rhetoric. What is primary in a rhetorical text is what is argued in that text. All the devices of literary rhetoric, including invention, arrangement, and style, well known as they are in rhetorical theory, are always subservient to the needs of the rhetor in modifying the hearers' attitudes or actions. Whether various motives are immediate or ultimate is an extremely subjective judgment on the part of a rhetorical critic, often based on extraneous presuppositions. What is of primary importance is the identification and recovery of rhetorical strategies; only after the firm identification of such strategies has been made will it be possible to talk about motives. Other criticisms of Johanson's monograph also suggest that the diversity and complexity of the sources that inform us about Graeco-Roman rhetoric are insufficiently acknowledged.

It was precisely this failure to heed the complexity of Graeco-Roman rhetoric that contributed toward Johanson's identification of 1 Thessalonians as belonging to *genus deliberativum.* Such an identification fails to convince.[26] Because it was not shown that the argumentation of 1 Thes-

---

25. Wilhelm Wuellner, "The Argumentative Structure of 1 Thessalonians as a Paradoxical Encomium," in *The Thessalonian Correspondence* (ed. Raymond F. Collins; BETL 87; Leuven: Leuven University Press, 1990), 117-36, here 125-26.

26. F. W. Hughes, "The Rhetoric of 1 Thessalonians," in *The Thessalonian Correspondence,* 94-116.

salonians was on the basis of the advantage of the readers/hearers (since the deliberative topic of honor is rather difficult to isolate from the standard epideictic topics of praise and blame), his classification of 1 Thessalonians as deliberative is not derived from Graeco-Roman rhetoric. Since there is little difference between the *dispositio* of an epideictic and a deliberative discourse (a *narratio* may be had in either one, although it may be omitted or done in a discontinuous fashion in deliberative rhetoric), and since stylistic features exist in all of the three *genera* of rhetoric, Johanson's lack of analysis of the deliberative topic of advantage is quite unanticipated. His failure to demonstrate this topic in 1 Thessalonians makes it impossible to accept his identification of the rhetorical *genus*.[27] In fact, 1 Thessalonians belongs strongly to the *genus* of epideictic rhetoric, as has been shown on the basis of its prolific use of the topics of praise and blame, and on the basis of other features of epideictic rhetoric as noted in Menander Rhetor's handbook.[28] Careful readers of 1 Thessalonians note that the various sections of the letter flow naturally and gradually into each other. Ancient rhetorical theory even allowed for the identification of a special section within the *exordium,* called the *transitus,* precisely because there was such a strong need for a smooth transition between the *exordium* and the *narratio*.[29] The application of Graeco-Roman rhetorical precepts to Hellenistic persuasive letters becomes evident in the mid-to-late first century C.E., when proper allowance is made not only for the special characteristics of letters but also for the diversity and complexity of the rhetorical traditions. The fact that letters have some characteristics (structural and otherwise) that are rather different from oral speeches does not nullify the contention made by rhetorical critics that many persuasive features, identifiable through the rhetorical handbooks and elsewhere, are present in letters.

Moving on from the determination that 1 Thessalonians is an epideictic letter,[30] one may still extrapolate more material that suggests a

27. On the centrality of the topic of advantage in deliberative rhetoric, see George A. Kennedy, "Focusing of Arguments in Greek Deliberative Oratory," *TAPA* 90 (1959): 131-38.

28. See Hughes, "The Rhetoric of 1 Thessalonians," 100, n. 28 and especially p. 107.

29. Quintilian, *Institutio oratoria* 4.1.76-79.

30. The identification of the *genus* of 1 Thessalonians has been confirmed by Robert Jewett, *Thessalonian Correspondence: Pauline Rhetoric;* Wuellner, "The Argumentative Structure of 1 Thessalonians as a Paradoxical Encomium"; and Charles A. Wanamaker, *Commentary on 1 and 2 Thessalonians* (NIGTC; Grand Rapids: William B. Eerdmans, 1990).

social setting for this letter. Since the letter does not concern itself in any depth with charges against Paul (although possibly it addresses suspicions that had been raised against Paul or that he thought might be raised against himself), one can easily conclude that the letter does not fit the judicial *genus* of rhetoric. If it were a judicial letter, one would certainly expect charges made in the *narratio* or elsewhere to be amplified and defended against in the *probatio*. The fact that Paul did not do this suggests that the apostle was not dealing with opponents in Thessalonica at the time he wrote 1 Thessalonians.

In fact, the strong use of epideictic rhetoric, as compared with deliberative and judicial rhetoric, reveals a great deal about the intention of the author in writing the letter. Epideictic rhetoric classically focused on the development of persuasive writing based on values held in common between the rhetor and the audience. Although Paul, like other persuasive writers, was quite capable of using features drawn from all the *genera* of persuasion, the fact that he did not do so in 1 Thessalonians would recommend the centrality of the epideictic topics of praise and blame to what he was trying to accomplish in the letter. Instead of praising the beauty of a mountain or river or of some honorific dead person, the apostle chose to modify this *genus* of rhetoric slightly, so that the recipients of the letter themselves were the object of Paul's praise. Paul's emphasis on praise reinforced the joyful relationship between the Thessalonians and their founder that had existed for some time — though the relationship was troubled by Paul's non-presence in Thessalonica during the congregation's recent difficulties, characterized by the deaths of some in the Thessalonian church. Paul's persuasive response to this bereaved congregation is to praise their faithfulness and love, to explain in an affective manner the reasons for his absence from the city (2:17–3:10), to confirm the teaching that he had given (the first two proofs: 4:1-8 and 4:9-12), and to add instruction that he had not conveyed previously (such as the material in 4:13–5:3). This additional direction is specifically not identified by the apostle as prior teaching but rather as revelation, as a "word of the Lord" (4:15).

Such a persuasive response, coupled with the skillfully crafted triad of virtues in 1:3, the listing of the *propositiones* in the *partitio* (3:11-13), including their careful and subtle recapitulation in the *peroratio* (5:4-11), all suggest that Paul either learned rhetoric in school or had developed an extraordinary gift for the subject in which he grasped the appropriateness of various rhetorical precepts for his letter without ever having formally learned them. What is surprising is not that Paul knew rhetorically effective strategies, but that contemporary scholarship has so hesitatingly acknowledged Paul's rhetorical skill in writing letters. Far more important for the interpretation of 1 Thessalonians than such questions as the location of the transition between *exordium* and *narratio*, or where and how Paul learned rhetoric, is the acknowledgment of Paul's persuasive skill itself.

Whether or not 1 Thessalonians is considered rhetorically successful depends, of course, on one's judgment as to whether or not Paul wrote 2 Thessalonians, and how the audience situation for that rather difficult letter is understood. The enigma is this: if 2 Thessalonians is a pseudonymous letter, how closely does 2 Thessalonians reflect the condition of the Thessalonian congregation or the interest of the author of 2 Thessalonians in doing persuasion through that letter? These latter questions must await further studies of 2 Thessalonians and of the rhetorical character of pseudonymity. The apparently growing consensus that Paul did not write 2 Thessalonians will, hopefully, foster intensified research into the history of Pauline Christianity after the death of Paul.

6. Conclusions

The usefulness and relevance of rhetorical criticism to reconstruct the social situation that caused an author to write a text are dependent on several factors:

(1) Primary among these factors is the nature of the text itself. Some texts are more rhetorically "transparent" than others. 2 Thessalonians has such a transparent rhetorical structure, framed by its *partitio* 2:1-2, which makes it relatively difficult to overlook the fact that it is a rhetorical proof that demonstrates the *propositio* "that the Day of the Lord has not already come." The letter can be called skeletonic because most of its structural elements, with the possible exception of 2 Thessalonians's *exordium* in 1:1-12, are so apparent and so devoid of ornamentation. The major issue for the author of 2 Thessalonians was not his relationship with the congregation in Thessalonica, as was the case in 1 Thessalonians, but the adherence of the intended readers (whoever they were) to what was for him orthodox doctrine. Theological argumentation aside, the skeletonic frame of 2 Thessalonians stands in stark contrast to the complex subtlety of

1 Thessalonians, with its affective *narratio* and its very pastorally oriented third proof "concerning those who have fallen asleep" (4:13–5:3). A compelling rhetorical analysis of both 1 and 2 Thessalonians must recognize the rhetorical particularity of each of these letters. Whereas 2 Thessalonians has a "transparent" and relatively simple rhetoric, 1 Thessalonians has a great deal of intricacy and subtlety.

(2) Though the rhetorical analysis of Pauline and pseudo-Pauline letters has yielded surprisingly vivid insights into the pastoral practices of Paul and his followers,[31] this analytical method has had relatively little to contribute toward understanding the social and cultural situation of the Thessalonians that Paul addressed. Such analyses of 1 and 2 Thessalonians do, however, reveal the intensity and skill with which both these early Christian writers used language in order to modify the attitudes, beliefs, and practices of their readers. Thus, to learn more about the general social and cultural climate of Thessalonica, additional forms of analysis will be needed to accomplish this extremely important task.

(3) Finally, rhetorical analysis can be helpful in reconstructing the historical provenance of letters. The rhetorical situations of these letters are so different from each other (which is quite ironic given the heavy literary dependency of 2 Thessalonians on 1 Thessalonians) that a plausible argument can be made that it is unlikely that the same writer would have written them both, particularly in such close chronological proximity to each other. Further, the most likely historical situation for the rhetorical situation implied in 2 Thessalonians is a crisis in the Pauline church after the death of Paul, a crisis marked by struggles, both theological and political, over the legacy of Paul. If these observations are substantially correct, it should be clear that rhetorical analysis does not proceed directly from the rhetorical text to the historical or social situation of the audience. Rather, the critical "middle term" between these two references is the "rhetorical situation."[32] Therefore it is inappropriate to make an absolute identification between the rhetorical situation and the historical situation to which the text was written. One does not stand here in a one-to-one relation with the other, unless, of course, one can presuppose knowledge

---

31. See Frank W. Hughes, "The Social World of 2 Thessalonians," *Listening: Journal of Religion and Culture* 31 (1996): 105-16.

32. See especially Lloyd F. Bitzer, "The Rhetorical Situation," *Philosophy and Rhetoric* 1 (1968): 1-14.

about who the author was and that the author's view of the situation as presented was a relatively objective and impartial one. Since neither of these factors can be presupposed for the pseudo-Pauline letters, neither can they be presupposed for the authentic letters of Paul! Further investigation needs to be done that acknowledges the difference between *what the text says* about a situation and *the situation itself.* This substantial difference being acknowledged, it stands to reason that the rhetorical situation as dealt with by the writer of a rhetorical discourse and the historical situation observable by others can be understood to be related, but not identical. Particularly where pseudonymity has been identified, one can expect that the rhetorical situation implied by the text might well be different from the historical situation as observed by a disinterested bystander at the actual time and place of the text's composition.

It has been suggested, then, that there are no fewer than three types of rhetorical criticism currently in use. Some are clearly more compatible with historical reconstruction than others. In any event, rhetorical criticism is only *one* of several methods for the analysis of New Testament texts, and its results need to be correlated with the results gained by other methods as well. Rhetorical criticism is surely not "all there is" in the toolbox of biblical scholars. If it is developed carefully, however, with a clear knowledge of what it presupposes in terms of rhetoric and what it requires on the part of critics, then rhetorical criticism has the potential of becoming a valuable key that may help us unlock the meaning of difficult texts and make accessible still concealed authorial intentions.

Epistolary vs. Rhetorical Analysis:
Is a Synthesis Possible?

Charles A. Wanamaker

1. Introduction

Paul's missionary strategy was based on establishing Christian communities and then moving on to new, unevangelized areas (Rom 16:20). This strategy necessitated his using letters, as well as emissaries like Timothy (see 1 Thess 3:1-6), not only for maintaining relations with the communities that he had founded but also for exercising an ongoing pastoral role through nurturing the community.[1] Thus the letters of Paul offer us an invaluable window on the apostle, the communities that he established, and the issues that he and his converts confronted.[2] This led in the past to the letters being read primarily as historical and theological documents, with little attention to their quality as letters.

Around the turn of the twentieth century the work of Adolf Deissmann helped change this by focusing on the letters of early Christianity as part of the letter tradition of the Graeco-Roman world.[3] While

---

1. On this theme see Abraham J. Malherbe, *Paul and the Thessalonians: The Philosophical Tradition of Pastoral Care* (Philadelphia: Fortress, 1987), 61-94.

2. Paul's letters to the Romans and Philemon are somewhat exceptional, Romans because it was addressed to a community that Paul had not established or visited, and Philemon because it is addressed to several individuals, as well as a house-church, and deals with a sensitive personal issue involving a runaway slave and his master.

3. See Adolf Deissmann, *Bible Studies: Contributions Chiefly from Papyri and Inscrip-*

he was wrong to identify the letters of Paul too closely with the papyrus letters, Deissmann, nevertheless, was instrumental in shifting the focus of scholarship away from an exclusively historical and theological perspective to one that took seriously the character of the letters as a particular type of literary production. Subsequent to Deissmann the study of early Christian letters developed in several different directions as scholars devised distinctive strategies for their analysis and interpretation. Two of the most important of these strategies have come to be known as epistolary or form-critical analysis and rhetorical analysis.[4]

In this essay I will explore these two approaches and their contribution to the analysis of 1 Thessalonians with a particular view to assessing whether some form of synthesis is possible between them. As a first step in this paper I will define what I understand by these two types of analyses, and then I will survey various examples of these different forms of analysis in the study of 1 Thessalonians in order to assess critically their contributions to our understanding of 1 Thessalonians. I will conclude by making some suggestions about how these two approaches can be synthesized.

2. Approaches to the Analysis of Early Christian Letters

David Aune has observed that four different techniques, three of which are used in the study of Graeco-Roman letters in general, have been employed for the analysis of early Christian letters by New Testament scholars since the groundbreaking work of Deissmann. These techniques he terms formal literary analysis, thematic analysis, form criticism, and rhetorical analysis.[5] Formal literary analysis, what Stanley Stowers calls "studies of struc-

---

tions to the History of the Language, the Literature and the Religion of Hellenistic Judaism and Primitive Christianity (Edinburgh: T. & T. Clark, 1901) and his later Light from the Ancient East (New York: Doran, 1927).

4. As I will discuss shortly, the terms "epistolary" and "form-critical analysis" need to be defined more carefully and used more circumspectly than has often been the case.

5. David E. Aune, The New Testament in Its Literary Environment (LEC 8; Philadelphia: Westminster, 1987), 183. I have not found any other scholar who states the distinctive types of analysis as clearly as Aune, though they are certainly present in such works as William G. Doty, Letters in Primitive Christianity (Philadelphia: Fortress, 1973), and Stanley K. Stowers, Letter Writing in Greco-Roman Antiquity (LEC 5; Philadelphia: Westminster, 1986), 17-26.

ture and form,"[6] refers to the study of "formulaic features of ancient letters" such as the opening and closing forms of letters and formulae occurring in the beginning and concluding parts of the main body of Graeco-Roman letters, including early Christian letters. Thematic analysis concerns the epistolary *topoi* or commonplace themes such as friendship, consolation, and *paraenesis* or exhortation, and the stock motifs that were used in relation to these themes.[7] Form-critical analysis of early Christian letters, as with its use in the study of the Gospels, concerns the isolation and study of mainly oral forms such as liturgical and paraenetic formulae that have been embedded in the letters as written forms.[8]

Unfortunately, the term "form-critical analysis" is also used in another very different way among those who study Paul's letters. Hendrikus Boers, for example, employs the term "form critical" to refer to what Aune means by formal literary analysis and thematic analysis.[9] This confusion perhaps goes back to the fact that it was the application of form criticism, in the sense of concern for embedded oral forms, which "directed attention to the formal, structural, and stylistic characteristics" of Paul's letters.[10] In any case, from the time of Paul Schubert's groundbreaking study entitled *Form and Function of the Pauline Thanksgivings*,[11] the literary forms found in early Christian letters began to be studied along with similar forms found in other

6. Stanley K. Stowers, "Social Typification and the Classification of Ancient Letters," in *The Social World of Formative Christianity and Judaism* (Festschrift H. Kee; ed. Jacob Neusner, Ernest S. Frerichs, Peder Borgen, and Richard Horsley; Philadelphia: Fortress, 1988), 85.

7. Robert Jewett, *The Thessalonian Correspondence: Pauline Rhetoric and Millenarian Piety* (FFNT; Philadelphia: Fortress, 1986), 68 (see also 216), uses the term "thematic analysis" to refer to the listing of the theological themes and their development by various commentators on 1 Thessalonians. This is very different from what Aune (see also Stowers, "Social Typification," 85) means by thematic analysis.

8. As is well known, this application of form criticism goes back to Martin Dibelius, "Zur Formgeschichte des neuen Testaments (ausserhalb der Evangelien)," *ThR* 3 (1931): 207-42.

9. Hendrikus Boers, "The Form-Critical Study of Paul's Letters. I Thessalonians as a Case Study," *NTS* 22 (1975-76): 140-58. See also Stowers, "Social Typification," 78 (see also 85).

10. Victor Paul Furnish, "Pauline Studies," in *The New Testament and Its Modern Interpreters* (ed. Eldon J. Epp and George W. MacRae; *The Bible and Its Modern Interpreters* 3; Philadelphia and Atlanta: Fortress and Scholars Press, 1989), 322.

11. Paul Schubert, *Form and Function of the Pauline Thanksgivings* (BZNW 20; Berlin: Töpelmann, 1939).

Graeco-Roman letters. The concern with unique letter forms, such as pre-scripts, thanksgivings, and concluding remarks, thus gave rise to the use of the term "form-critical analysis" to refer to this field of inquiry.

Taken together, formal literary analysis and thematic analysis would appear to be what the organizers of the SNTS Seminar on the Thessalonian Correspondence had in mind by the term "form-critical/epistolary analysis." For the sake of terminological clarity I will avoid the use of the term "form-critical" to describe this type of approach.

Aune terms the fourth type of approach to the letters of early Christianity "rhetorical analysis." Rhetorical analysis, when applied to letters, attempts to examine their persuasive character in terms of the forms of argumentation (judicial or forensic, deliberative, and epideictic or demonstrative) and the execution of the argument (invention, arrangement, and style) employed in them. It does so on the grounds that rhetorical theory and practice were pervasive among the educated members of Graeco-Roman society, providing a foundation for all forms of public discourse whether oral or written.[12]

One further crucial dimension in the analysis of early Christian letters involves the importance of the epistolary theorists of antiquity and especially the two extant epistolary handbooks, *Epistolary Types,* incorrectly attributed to Demetrius of Phaleron, and *Epistolary Styles,* attributed to Libanius and on occasion to Proclus.[13] As Abraham Malherbe has observed, both epistolary theory and the epistolary handbooks belonged to the domain of the rhetoricians.[14] Not surprisingly then, ancient epistolary theory, unlike contemporary epistolary analysis, was primarily concerned with the central section of the letter, not the prescript or the letter closing. The handbooks classified letters "through the typification of social interactions" that could be undertaken through the medium of letters.[15] Thus their types were in reality themes for letters written in certain social situations to perform particular social functions.

---

12. See Burton Mack, *Rhetoric and the New Testament* (GBSNT; Minneapolis: Fortress, 1990), 25-31. On Paul's educational background with respect to rhetoric, see Stanley K. Stowers, *A Rereading of Romans: Justice, Jews, and Gentiles* (New Haven: Yale University Press, 1995), 16-21.

13. See Abraham J. Malherbe, *Ancient Epistolary Theorists* (SBLSBS 19; Atlanta: Scholars Press, 1988), for a text and translation of these two handbooks.

14. *Ancient Epistolary Theorists,* 2-3.

15. Stowers, "Social Typification," 78.

In recent years several attempts have been made to classify 1 Thessalonians in terms of the letter types of ancient epistolary theorists. For example, Johannes Schoon-Janßen has classified 1 Thessalonians as a letter of friendship,[16] while Juan Chapa has designated it as a letter of consolation.[17] Unfortunately, I am unable to review this form of analysis in this essay, as my concern is primarily with Aune's categories of formal literary analysis and thematic analysis over against the type of rhetorical analysis that is based directly on rhetorical theory. In what follows I will employ Aune's categories in order both to describe and to assess the contributions of these types of analyses of 1 Thessalonians to understanding the persuasive effects of the letter.

3. Formal Literary Analysis and Thematic Analysis of 1 Thessalonians

Perhaps no issue has proved to be of as much interest to formal literary analysis of Paul's letters in general and 1 Thessalonians in particular as the study of introductory thanksgiving. All of the generally accepted Pauline letters except 2 Corinthians and Galatians have a thanksgiving period following the epistolary prescript. This formal structure in Paul's letters, which is also found in some other Hellenistic letters,[18] was first identified and extensively studied by Schubert in the 1930s.[19]

The analysis of the thanksgiving of 1 Thessalonians has proved particularly complex because formal expressions of thanksgiving occur in three places within the first three chapters of the letter: 1:1-5; 2:13-14; 3:9-13.[20] This led Schubert to argue that the thanksgiving period extended

---

16. See Johannes Schoon-Janßen, *Umstrittene "Apologien" in den Paulusbriefen: Studien zur rhetorischen Situation des 1. Thessalonicherbriefes, des Galaterbriefes und des Philipperbriefes* (Göttingen: Vandenhoeck & Ruprecht, 1991), 39-47, and "On the Use of Elements of Ancient Epistolography in 1 Thessalonians," *TD*, 179-93.

17. Juan Chapa, "Is First Thessalonians a Letter of Consolation?" *NTS* 40 (1994): 150-60.

18. See John L. White, "New Testament Epistolary Literature in the Framework of Ancient Epistolography," in *ANRW* 2.25.2, 1735; and Schubert, *Form and Function*, 35-36.

19. *Form and Function*, 35-36.

20. Walter Schmithals, "Die Thessalonicherbriefe als Briefkompositionen," in *Zeit und Geschichte* (Festschrift R. Bultmann; ed. E. Dinkler; Tübingen: Mohr-Siebeck, 1964),

from 1:2 to 3:13. According to him, 1:6–2:12 and 2:17–3:8, which give the impression of being digressions sandwiched between the expressions of thanksgiving, are in reality formally part of the thanksgiving. For this reason 2:13-14 and 3:9-13 are not separate thanksgivings at all but serve "to unify formally the entire section from 1:2–3:13."[21] This conclusion resulted in Schubert further concluding that 1:2–3:13 constitutes the main body of the letter to the extent that it presents the "primary information" that Paul sought to communicate to his readers.[22] Schubert understood chapters 4 and 5 to be a concluding paraenetic section as in other Pauline letters, and therefore he did not see these chapters as part of the main body of the letter.[23]

Schubert's work has set the terms for much of the subsequent debate regarding the formal literary analysis of 1 Thessalonians as a letter even though many have disagreed with his conclusions regarding the nature and extent of the thanksgiving period in 1 Thessalonians. Jack T. Sanders, for example, argues that the initial thanksgiving period of 1 Thessalonians ends at 1:10 on the basis of the "introductory formula," which he finds in 2:1 ("For you yourselves know, brothers and sisters"). This formula, according to him, introduces the body of the letter. In order to explain the second thanksgiving in 2:13 he maintains that the letter begins again in 2:13, having been initially brought to a conclusion in 2:12, and that the second thanksgiving continues to 3:13.[24] Thus for him 1 Thessalonians has two identifiable thanksgiving periods that are formally distinct from one another.

295-314, uses the existence of three thanksgivings as the bases for arguing that 1 Thessalonians is a composite letter. See also his *Paul and the Gnostics* (Nashville: Abingdon, 1972). For a critical assessment of his compilation theory see my *The Epistles to the Thessalonians: A Commentary on the Greek Text* (NIGTC; Grand Rapids: Eerdmans, 1990), 34-35.

21. Schubert, *Form and Function*, 18.

22. Schubert, *Form and Function*, 26. In coming to this conclusion Schubert was following the lead of Ernst von Dobschütz, *Die Thessalonicher-Briefe* (Nachdruck der Ausgabe von 1909, mit einem Literaturverzeichnis von Otto Merk, Herausgegeben von Ferdinand Hahn; Göttingen: Vandenhoeck & Ruprecht, 1974), 62.

23. Schubert is closely followed by Peter T. O'Brien, *Introductory Thanksgivings in the Letters of Paul* (NovTSup 49; Leiden: E. J. Brill, 1977), 141-61, in seeing 1 Thess 1:2–3:13 as the main letter-body and chapters 4 and 5 as concluding *paraenesis*.

24. Jack T. Sanders, "The Transition from Opening Epistolary Thanksgiving to Body in Letters of the Pauline Corpus," *JBL* 81 (1962): 356.

John L. White agrees with Sanders about the end of the first thanks-giving in 1:10 but refines the explanation of 2:1–3:13 in terms of what he understands to be the formal structure of Paul's letters.[25] Following the salutation and thanksgiving, he sees 2:1–3:13 as the main body of the letter based on "a major transitional construction" in 2:1 in the form of a "disclosure formula."[26] On the basis of what he perceives to be a series of introductory and transitional formulae, he divides the main body into three parts: (1) formal body opening (2:1-4); (2) body-middle (2:5–2:16) with a theoretical segment (2:5-12) and a practical or applicative segment (2:13-16), and (3) body-closing (2:17–3:13), which includes a section on apostolic *parousia*.[27] As with Schubert and Sanders, 1 Thessalonians 4 and 5 contain the standard paraenetic section found in most of Paul's letters along with the formal letter-closing, and, therefore, they are not part of the main body of the letter. Like Sanders, White appears to be struggling with Schubert's claim that the letter-body is exclusively a thanksgiving period. The strength of his own position hinges on his epistolary analysis. This is based on what he has deduced to be the Pauline model of the letter-body, which in turn he sees as having been influenced by the Greek nonliterary letter tradition.

In his discussion of the body-closing White finds several *topoi* that occur in common Greek letters. These are (1) motivation for writing, (2) responsibility phrase, and (3) anticipated visit. In addition, Pauline letters have a confidence formula.[28]

The *topos* "anticipated visit" in the Pauline letters has been subjected to careful analysis by Robert Funk in his often-cited essay on apostolic *parousia*.[29] He argues that the forms giving details of anticipated visits, or travelogues as he terms them, actually concern Paul's three strategies for making his "apostolic authority and power" present. According to Funk,

---

25. John L. White, *The Form and Function of the Body of the Greek Letter: A Study of the Letter-Body in the Non-literary Papyri and in Paul the Apostle* (SBLDS 2; Missoula, Mont.: Scholars Press, 1972), 68-91.

26. White, *Form and Function*, 70.

27. White, *Form and Function*, 70-71, 76-77, 84-86.

28. White, *Form and Function*, 84-86; see also 61-63.

29. Robert W. Funk, "The Apostolic *Parousia*: Form and Significance," in *Christian History and Interpretation* (Festschrift J. Knox; ed. W. R. Farmer, C. F. D. Moule and R. R. Niebuhr; Cambridge: Cambridge University Press, 1967), 249-68. This essay qualified and developed ideas that Funk had originally discussed in his book *Language, Hermeneutic and the Word of God* (New York: Harper and Row, 1966), 264-70.

Paul projects his apostolic authority and power through his letters, through sending apostolic emissaries, and through his own anticipated personal visits. On the basis of an analysis of the apostolic *parousia* segment in Rom 15:14-33, Funk abstracts a fivefold structure for these statements: (1) a statement of "Paul's disposition or purpose in writing," (2) "the basis of Paul's apostolic relation to the recipients," (3) "implementation of the apostolic *parousia*" (with six subfeatures), (4) "invocation of divine approval and support for the apostolic *parousia*," and (5) "benefit from the apostolic *parousia* accruing" (with three subfeatures).[30] Not all of the cases of the form in Paul's undisputed letters contain the complete structure, but a number of the features are present in each letter. In the case of 1 Thessalonians Funk locates the apostolic *parousia* in 2:17–3:13,[31] a point with which White strongly agrees,[32] though Funk does not link it to the body-closing as a formal structure in the way in which White does.

Even a cursory examination of Funk's thirteen examples of apostolic *parousia* segments shows that they lack a clear form and structure. Apart from Rom 15:14-33, only 1 Cor 4:14-21 has all five of the structural features and follows the same order. Among the other eleven examples, none has more than three of the five structural features and they follow no fixed order. Moreover, Funk finds two apostolic *parousia* segments in Romans (Rom 15:14-33 and 1:8-13) and 1 Corinthians (1 Cor 4:14-21 and 16:1-11) and three in 2 Corinthians (2 Cor 8:16-23; 9:1-5; and 12:14–13:13).[33] These examples, along with the others, indicate that there is no fixed location for an apostolic *parousia* segment in Paul's letters. Thus the formal features and the structure of the apostolic *parousia* are abstractions from Paul's letters, although the *topos* would seem to be an important one for Paul.[34]

Boers tackles the problem of the threefold thanksgiving of 1 Thess 1:2–3:13 in yet another way. Following the lead of Birger Pearson,[35] he ar-

---

30. Funk, "Apostolic *Parousia*," 252-53.

31. Funk, "Apostolic *Parousia*," 254.

32. White, *Form and Function*, 91.

33. The case of three in 2 Corinthians is unusual and probably can be explained on the basis of the letter being a composite of at least two independent letters.

34. Funk, "Apostolic *Parousia*," 253, acknowledges that his formal scheme for the apostolic *parousia*, based as it is on Rom 15:14-33, is "a theoretical construct," but then proceeds to ignore the significance of this in the rest of his essay.

35. Birger A. Pearson, "1 Thessalonians 2:13-16: A Deutero-Pauline Interpolation," *HTR* 64 (1971): 79-94.

gues that 2:13-16 is a deutero-Pauline interpolation and that "the elimination of this passage as an interpolation brings about a virtual metamorphosis of I Thessalonians, resolving most of the problems in connection with the form and function of the letter."[36] Once 2:13-16 is excised, 1:2-10 is clearly seen as the opening thanksgiving which "already conveys what is the main purpose of the letter."[37] According to Boers, 2:1-12 is an "apostolic apology" that occurs as "a discreet formal section" in most Pauline letters and therefore cannot function as "the central informative section" of the letter. The following section, 2:17–3:13, serves as the apostolic *parousia* segment. Taken together, 1:2–3:13 with its three distinct segments has a *philophronetic* function.[38]

Unlike the other scholars whom I have discussed, Boers does not view 4:1–5:22 as a traditional paraenetic segment that stands outside the main body of the letter and its principal purpose. Boers is heavily indebted to Carl Bjerkelund's study on *parakalô* periods in Paul's letters, and in particular to his work on 1 Thess 4:1–5:11, for seeing 4:1–5:22 as integral to the main purpose of the letter. Bjerkelund has argued that "wir in 4,1-2 und 4,10 b-12 der Pointe des ganzen Briefes begegnen," and that "will man an der traditionellen Dreiteilung der paulinischen Briefe, Introduktion, Corpus, Abschluss, festhalten, dann besteht unserer Auffassung nach das Corpus aus 4,1–5,11."[39] Boers believes that Bjerkelund has gone too far by claiming that the body of the letter is found in 4:1–5:11, and in fact he maintains that Bjerkelund is ambivalent about this himself.[40] He argues that the purpose of the letter is both *philophronesis,* expressed by Paul's joy and satisfaction with the community at Thessalonica in the three sections forming 1:2–3:13, and *paraenesis,* expressed by Paul's exhortations in 4:1–5:22.[41] The latter is connected to the former through the transitional for-

---

36. Boers, "Form-Critical Study," 152.

37. Boers, "Form-Critical Study," 153.

38. Boers, "Form-Critical Study," 155.

39. Carl J. Bjerkelund, *Parakalô: Form, Funktion und Sinn der parakalô-Sätze in den paulinischen Briefen* (BTN 1; Oslo: Universitetsforlaget, 1967), 134.

40. Boers, "Form-Critical Study," 156.

41. Boers, "Form-Critical Study," 158. In seeing the main purpose of the letter as *philophronēsis* and *paraenesis* Boers acknowledges that he is following the lead of Abraham Malherbe, who presented his views in an unpublished 1972 Society of Biblical Literature seminar paper entitled "1 Thessalonians as a Paraenetic Letter." Malherbe has subsequently incorporated this essay in his "Hellenistic Moralists and the New Testament," *ANRW* 2.26.1, 267-333.

mula of 4:1.[42] Thus he concludes that the letter has a "completely normal form" with a prescript, thanksgiving, apostolic apology, apostolic *parousia*, exhortation, and conclusion.[43]

In recent years, the work of Jan Lambrecht stands out for carrying on the tradition of formal literary analysis of 1 Thessalonians.[44] In the first of his two essays in this volume, he undertakes a critical literary structural analysis of 1 Thessalonians 1–3. Beginning with a detailed study of the thanksgiving periods in Paul's letters, and especially 1 Thessalonians, Lambrecht draws several conclusions worth noting. First, while Paul's thanksgivings employ characteristic vocabulary and relatively established expressions within a fairly fixed order, "He freely varies words as well as constructions," indicating that he was not subject to a predetermined pattern in his thanksgivings.[45] Second, Lambrecht believes that the absence of the regularly occurring "petition" with the first two thanksgiving statements in 1 Thessalonians can be accounted for by its presence with the third one in 3:9-10.[46] Third, he concludes that the "thanksgiving is to a certain degree indeed the controlling factor" in 1 Thessalonians 1–3, though "there are undeniably expansions, digressions, and interruptions" within this structural unit.[47] Employing a combination of what he describes as epistolary and thematic criteria, he proposes the following structure for chapters 1–3:[48]

> 1:1: salutation
>> (a) 1:2-10: thanksgiving
>>> (b) 2:1-12: apologetical report
>> (a) 2:13-16: thanksgiving

---

42. Boers, "Form-Critical Study," 158.

43. Boers, "Form-Critical Study," 158.

44. Jan Lambrecht, "Thanksgivings in 1 Thessalonians 1–3," in *TD*, 135-62 ; originally in *The Thessalonian Correspondence* (ed. Raymond F. Collins; BETL 87; Leuven: Leuven University Press–Peeters, 1990), 183-205. Further now Jan Lambrecht's new essay, "A Structural Analysis of 1 Thessalonians 4–5," in *TD*, 163-78. The important work of Franz Schnider and Werner Stenger, *Studien zum neutestamentlichen Briefformular* (NTTS 11; Leiden: Brill, 1987), has not been available to me.

45. Lambrecht, "Thanksgivings in 1 Thessalonians 1–3," in *TD*, 146.

46. Lambrecht, "Thanksgivings in 1 Thessalonians 1–3," in *TD*, 146.

47. Lambrecht, "Thanksgivings in 1 Thessalonians 1–3," in *TD*, 156.

48. These words are his own for describing the basis of his proposal regarding the structure of 1 Thessalonians 1–3 in his essay "Structural Analysis," in *TD*, 164.

>   (b) 2:17–3:8: report on the intervening period
>   (a) 3:9-10: thanksgiving
>   3:11-13: eschatological wish-prayer[49]

Several features of Lambrecht's analysis merit comment. First, in terms of his own analysis of the thanksgiving form,[50] it is surprising that he includes 1:6-10 in the formal thanksgiving segment since he does not include it in his earlier analysis of 1 Thess 1:2-5. This is undoubtedly because he recognizes that 1:6 begins developing a narrative that is independent of 1:2-5,[51] and, therefore, it should not be included in the opening thanksgiving on structural grounds. Second, his claim that 2:13 links back to 2:12 and the apologetical report on the basis of the transitional phrase διὰ τοῦτο seems questionable to me. The primary reference of διὰ τοῦτο is forward since the expression ὅτι παραλαβόντες λόγον ἀκοῆς in 2:13 clearly provides the reason for the thanksgiving.[52] If this criticism is correct, then it means that the whole of 2:1-12 cannot be "subsumed" into Paul's thanksgiving in 2:13 either structurally or conceptually.[53] This in turn has the serious consequence of calling into question the supposed unified structure of 1 Thessalonians 1–3 since the chapters are no longer controlled by the threefold thanksgiving.

From the perspective of this paper, one further point from Lambrecht's paper on "Thanksgivings in 1 Thessalonians 1–3" requires at-

---

49. Lambrecht, "Thanksgivings in 1 Thessalonians 1–3," in *TD*, 157.

50. See Lambrecht, "Thanksgivings in 1 Thessalonians 1–3," in *TD*, 135-62 but especially 137-49.

51. Lambrecht, "Thanksgivings in 1 Thessalonians 1–3," in *TD*, 147.

52. It must be acknowledged that scholars line up on both sides of the question regarding the reference of the phrase διὰ τοῦτο. I would argue that it is more the preconception that 1:2–3:10 forms a continuous thanksgiving unit than either that the immediate grammar of 2:13 or the immediate content leads to the conclusion that διὰ τοῦτο refers back to 2:12.

53. Given his analysis of the relation between the thanksgiving statement in 2:13-16 and the preceding "apostolic apology," I find it odd that Lambrecht, "Thanksgivings in 1 Thessalonians 1–3," 155 seeks to defend the traditional view that 2:1-12 contains a genuine apology evoked by accusations concerning Paul's integrity. In what way would a defense of his own integrity (2:1-12) lead Paul to give thanks to God without ceasing (2:13a)? Lambrecht, "Thanksgivings in 1 Thessalonians 1–3," 156 seems to forget his own position regarding the back reference of διὰ τοῦτο in 2:13 by relating the thanksgiving to the ὅτι clause of 2:13b.

tention. In a section of his paper in which he evaluates previous discussions on 2:1-12 and 2:17–3:10, he offers a very ambivalent response. After briefly discussing the works of White,[54] Funk,[55] and Franz Schnider and Werner Stenger,[56] Lambrecht first says, "Nobody should despise these and other analyses of Paul's so-called digressions in 1 Thess 1–3."[57] But he then warns against the very type of formal literary analysis and thematic analysis practiced by White, Funk, and Schnider and Stenger:

> The danger, however, lies in exaggeration, in increasingly inventive speciousness, in too much, often farfetched and strained, genre hunting. One might wonder whether Paul consciously starts the body of his letter in 2:1, deliberately composes an apostolic *parousia* in 2:17–3:13, or really intends a twofold epistolary recommendation in 2:1-12 and 2:17–3:8. Even to attribute to Paul a more or less spontaneous, subconscious following of preexisting patterns may constitute here an unwarranted postulate.[58]

This is indeed a serious indictment of the type of formal literary and thematic analysis that has been practiced on 1 Thessalonians as well as other Pauline letters. Coming from Lambrecht, who is committed to this type of approach, this caveat becomes all the more significant. In the section that follows I will offer my own assessment of formal literary and thematic analysis.

4. Assessment of Formal Literary and Thematic Analysis of 1 Thessalonians

The impetus to analyze everything in 1 Thessalonians in terms of one or another epistolary form found elsewhere in Paul has abated over the last decade or so. Scholars have begun to realize that formal literary analysis may have gone too far and thus a reaction has set in. In his 1983 commentary I. Howard Marshall notes that "it is overprecise and perhaps mislead-

---

54. White, *Form and Function.*
55. "Apostolic *Parousia.*"
56. *Briefformular.*
57. Lambrecht, "Thanksgivings," 154.
58. Lambrecht, "Thanksgivings," 154.

ing" to consider the so-called apostolic apology of 1 Thess 2:1-12 and the so-called apostolic *parousia* of 2:17–3:11 "as two specific formal parts of Pauline epistles which constitute structural elements in them."[59] In his view the two proposed forms reflect themes *(topoi)* that regularly recur in Paul's letters and are often expressed in similar fashions but cannot be understood as fixed epistolary forms throughout the Pauline corpus.[60]

Stowers has gone even further, claiming that both the analysis of letters in terms of structure and form (formal literary analysis) and analysis in terms of "characteristic *topoi* and phraseology" (thematic analysis) are overly "reductionistic."[61] These approaches reduce letters to a series of constitutive forms found primarily in their prescripts and conclusions, and to a number of unrelated *topoi* and phrases. The letter-body itself becomes little more than a message to be communicated. From Stowers's point of view this completely misses the real nature of ancient letters as media for social interaction between sender and addressee(s).[62]

To some degree Stowers's criticism does not apply altogether well to the analysis of 1 Thessalonians. Both White and Boers, among others, have attempted to undertake analysis of the letter-body in detail. Where his criticism is trenchant, however, is when it comes to the tendency to reduce letters, in this case 1 Thessalonians, to a series of forms and *topoi* with no real sense of the social function of the letter. As I said in my commentary on 1 and 2 Thessalonians, scholars like White, Boers, Sanders, and others "have not succeeded . . . in explaining the relationships between the individual components or the logic of the letters as integrated literary productions."[63] A good example of this is found in the discussion of 1 Thess 2:1–3:10.

None of the scholars practising formal literary analysis with whom I am familiar, except Lambrecht, has noted that 2:1–3:10 constitutes a narrative of Paul's relations with the Christian community at Thessalonica and his perceptions of the community. The narrative moves from Paul's

---

59. I. Howard Marshall, *1 and 2 Thessalonians* (NCBC; Grand Rapids: Eerdmans, 1983), 8.

60. My analysis of Funk's so-called "apostolic *parousia*" formula above confirms Marshall's point.

61. Stowers, "Social Typification," 85; see Stowers, *Letter Writing*, 22.

62. Stowers, "Social Typification," 85.

63. Wanamaker, *Thessalonians*, 46.

initial missionary activity with the Thessalonians and the nature of his ministry (2:1-12) to his thanksgiving for their reception of the gospel as well as a reflection on their experience of rejection by the dominant society in Thessalonica because of their new convictions (2:13-16). The narrative then takes up Paul's seemingly forced departure and his attempts to return to his converts (2:17-20), followed by his sending of Timothy in his desperation to learn of his converts' situation (3:1-5). The narrative ends with the return of Timothy, who brings the good news that the Thessalonians have remained steadfast and are anxious to see Paul again. This in turn leads to Paul's renewing his thanksgiving and prayer to be allowed to revisit the Thessalonians in order to make good any deficiencies in their faith (3:6-10). To miss so obvious a narrative structure for the sake of analyzing so-called epistolary forms that fragment the narrative into obliteration is one of the fundamental shortcomings of much of the formal literary analysis of 1 Thessalonians.

No less a practitioner of formal literary analysis than White, the scholar who has done most to show us the relation between the nonliterary papyrus letters and the letters of early Christianity, has recognized the limitations of formal analysis. He has recently written,

> My earlier analyses of Paul's letters were overly formalistic and the choice of comparative materials too narrow. I tried to understand the entirety of Paul's letters in terms of conventions found in the nonliterary papyrus letters. It is still feasible to delineate the beginning and end of Paul's letters by such means but, for the large intermediate part of the letter's body, we need to look to the literary letter tradition for our model.[64]

From the point of view of this paper it is noteworthy that White turns to classical rhetoric in his 1993 essay for appropriate tools for the analysis of the letter-body. He does so on the grounds that Paul intended his letters as "an approximation of spoken presence,"[65] and thus the "oral patterns in the body [of Paul's letters] reverberate with the training of the

---

64. John L. White, "Apostolic Mission and Apostolic Message: Congruence in Paul's Epistolary Rhetoric, Structure and Imagery," in *Origins and Method: Towards a New Understanding of Judaism and Christianity* (Festschrift J. C. Hurd; ed. Bradley H. McLean; JSNTSup 86; Sheffield: JSOT, 1993), 148-49.

65. White, "Apostolic Mission and Apostolic Message," 148.

academy" where rhetoric was inculcated for all public-speaking situations.[66]

In the case of 1 Thessalonians the work of Schubert, more than anything else, has bedeviled the analysis of the letter. His conclusion regarding
the threefold thanksgiving of 1 Thessalonians 1–3 as the effective body of
the letter has had extremely serious consequences right up to the present.
It would not be inaccurate to say that nearly every subsequent attempt at
the formal literary analysis of 1 Thessalonians, certainly those I have
looked at for this paper, has been a reaction to Schubert's work. The tendency has been to use the *topos* "thanksgiving" to hold 1 Thess 1:2–3:13 together on the grounds that Paul could only employ a thanksgiving in the
opening section of the letter and therefore 1:2–3:13 must be intercon-
nected. The text is normally subdivided into a series of small formal units
that in some way loosely connect with the dominant theme. A good example of this is the way in which Lambrecht sees 2:1-12 "subsumed" in the
thanksgiving in 2:13 in order to maintain that thanksgiving is the theme
that controls the whole of 1 Thessalonians 1–3.[67]

5. Rhetorical Analysis of 1 Thessalonians

The question of Paul's use of rhetorical skills has been discussed on and off
since the time of the Church Fathers,[68] but the current interest in the formal rhetorical analysis of Paul's letters is little more than two decades old.
The work of Hans-Dieter Betz, especially his work on Galatians,[69] followed
closely by several studies of Wilhelm Wuellner,[70] seem to have revived in-

66. White, "Apostolic Mission and Apostolic Message," 153.

67. See the discussion of Lambrecht above.

68. For a brief history of the discussion of Paul and his use of rhetoric see Hans-
Dieter Betz, "The Problem of Rhetoric and Theology according to the Apostle Paul," in
L'Apôtre Paul: Personnalité, Style et Conception du Ministère (ed. A. Vanhoye; BETL 73;
Leuven: Leuven University Press, 1986), 16-21; and Frank W. Hughes, *Early Christian Rheto-
ric and 2 Thessalonians* (JSNTSup 30; Sheffield: JSOT, 1989), 19-30.

69. See Hans-Dieter Betz, *Der Apostel Paulus und die sokratische Tradition. Eine
exegetische Untersuchung zu seiner "Apologie" 2 Kor 10–13* (BHT 45; Tübingen: Mohr-
Siebeck, 1972); Hans-Dieter Betz, "The Literary Composition and Function of Paul's Letter
to the Galatians," *NTS* 21 (1975): 353-79; Hans-Dieter Betz, *Galatians: A Commentary on
Paul's Letter to the Churches in Galatia* (Hermeneia; Philadelphia: Fortress, 1979).

70. See Wilhelm Wuellner, "Paul's Rhetoric of Argumentation in Romans," *CBQ* 38

terest in the use of Graeco-Roman rhetoric for the analysis of Paul's letters. Since the reemergence of rhetorically oriented investigations much of the emphasis in the study of Paul's letters has been on identifying the genus of the rhetoric in terms of Aristotle's threefold classification system of judicial, deliberative, and demonstrative and the arrangement of the work. But ultimately rhetorical analysis has a much wider purpose, as Kennedy has observed: "The ultimate goal of rhetorical analysis, briefly put, is the discovery of the author's intent and of how that is transmitted through a text to an audience."[71]

The earliest attempt at the rhetorical analysis of 1 Thessalonians known to me is the brief discussion by George Kennedy in his 1984 book.[72] He views 1 Thessalonians as a piece of deliberative rhetoric intended to exhort the recipients to remain firm in their new faith.[73] He offers a limited discussion of the rhetorical arrangement of the letter into an effective structure for invoking a favorable decision from the Thessalonian Christians. He identifies 1:2-10 as the proem, 2:9–3:13 as a narrative, and 4:1–5:22 under the rubric of "headings," a term applied to the relevant topics dealt with in the proof section of a piece of deliberative rhetoric.[74] Oddly he does not designate 2:1-8 in rhetorical terms based on its place in the argumentative structure of the letter. The most obvious thing is to see it as part of the narrative section that runs to 3:13. Instead he asserts that the text is an apology by Paul in the face of imputations regarding his motivations in preaching to the Thessalonians. This Kennedy describes as the "rhetorical problem" Paul seeks to address in the letter.

Kennedy makes several passing references to artistic invention, that part of rhetoric concerned with artistic proof. He notes the presence of *ethos* in Paul's attempts to establish his own credibility and *pathos* in Paul's appeals to the emotions of his readers in both 1:2-10 and 2:9–3:13. He also finds an *enthymeme,* a form of deductive proof based on a logical syllo-

---

(1976): 330-51; Wilhelm Wuellner, "Greek Rhetoric and Pauline Argumentation," in *Early Christian Literature and the Classical Intellectual Tradition* (Festschrift Robert M. Grant; ed. William R. Schoedel and Robert L. Wilken; ThH 54; Paris: Beauchesne, 1979), 177-88.

71. George A. Kennedy, *New Testament Interpretation through Rhetorical Criticism* (Studies in Religion; Chapel Hill: University of North Carolina Press, 1984), 12.

72. Kennedy, *New Testament Interpretation,* 141-44.

73. Kennedy, *New Testament Interpretation,* 142.

74. Kennedy, *New Testament Interpretation,* 142-43. On headings in deliberative rhetoric, see Kennedy, *New Testament Interpretation,* 24.

gism, in 1:5.[75] But he fails to develop this aspect of 1 Thessalonians's rhetoric in any detail.

On the whole Kennedy's observations are undeveloped and far too cursory to be given much weight. For example, it is not clear from Kennedy's presentation what the Thessalonians are being called to "deliberate," that is, what action they are being asked to decide to take in the future. Subsequent analysts of the rhetorical genus of 1 Thessalonians have generally agreed that the letter is epideictic rather than deliberative.[76] This places a certain question mark beside Kennedy's understanding of the arrangement since he himself argues that arrangement is tied to the genus of rhetoric.[77] A somewhat more detailed rhetorical analysis of 1 Thessalonians was offered by Robert Jewett in 1986.[78] His motivation for undertaking a rhetorical study of 1 Thessalonians was not merely literary. He sought to use the rhetoric of the letter to assist him "in the reconstruction of the audience situation and the external circumstances related to the writing."[79] His study is informed not only by classical rhetoric, which he sees as offering a clear insight into how letters were formed in Paul's world, but also by the New Rhetoric and other closely related linguistic theories

75. In Aristotle's formulation of artistic invention *enthymemes,* along with examples, formed the two types of proof used in argumentation.

76. According to Wilhelm Wuellner, "The Argumentative Structure of 1 Thessalonians as Paradoxical Encomium," in Collins, *The Thessalonian Correspondence,* 125. Bruce C. Johanson, *To All the Brethren: A Text-Linguistic and Rhetorical Approach to 1 Thessalonians* (ConBNT 16; Stockholm: Almqvist & Wiksell International, 1987), argues that 1 Thessalonians is deliberative in character. He is to my knowledge the only other scholar, besides Kennedy who argues for this interpretation exclusively. As we will see later Thomas Olbricht, "An Aristotelian Rhetorical Analysis of 1 Thessalonians," in *Greeks, Romans, and Christians* (Festschrift A. Malherbe; ed. David L. Balch, Everett Ferguson, and Wayne A. Meeks; Minneapolis: Fortress, 1990), 225, maintains that 1 Thessalonians has both deliberative and epideictic characteristics, though his discussion seems to indicate that the epideictic predominates. (Unfortunately not only for this point, but for my essay as a whole, Johanson's book has not been available to me.)

77. See Kennedy, *New Testament Interpretation,* 23-25.

78. Jewett, *Thessalonian Correspondence,* 63-78. He points out that the rhetorical analysis of the Thessalonians correspondence is not limited to his discussion of arrangement and *logos,* or logical argumentation, but also includes his analysis of the audience and the circumstances in which the letters were written, the so-called rhetorical situation.

79. Jewett, *Thessalonian Correspondence,* 64. As we will see, Frank Hughes, "The Rhetoric of 1 Thessalonians," in Collins, *The Thessalonian Correspondence,* 94-116, has a similar goal.

that provide a more thorough conception of letters as instruments of communication than is otherwise available.[80]

Like Kennedy, Jewett discusses the rhetorical genus as well as the arrangement of the letter. Unlike Kennedy, he concludes that the letter falls within the genus of epideictic or demonstrative rhetoric rather than deliberative rhetoric. He does so on the grounds that the letter concentrates on the themes of praise and blame, the principal *topoi* of epideictic rhetoric, and has a subsidiary theme of thanksgiving to God that was also associated with epideictic rhetoric.[81] Traditional epistolary analysis appears to still influence Jewett's rhetorical understanding because he sees the main argument present in 1:6–3:13 and claims that it consists of Paul's *narratio* of the grounds for his thanksgiving to God. He then sees the proof section or *probatio* of the letter as addressing concrete areas in the life of the community through enunciating praiseworthy and blameworthy patterns of behavior.[82] This appears to conform to the epistolary analysis of Schubert and others who see the thanksgiving in 1:2–3:13 as the main body of the letter and the paraenetic section of chapters 4 and 5 as a subsidiary theme concluding the letter.

Jewett offers an extremely detailed analysis of the arrangement of the letter. The main structural features of the letter, according to him, are the *exordium* or introduction (1:1-5), the *narratio* or narration (1:6–3:13), the *probatio* or proofs (4:1–5:22), and the *peroratio* or conclusion (5:23-28). With the exception of his description of 3:11-13 as a *transitus*, none of the other subheadings is couched in rhetorical language. Instead they refer to the content of the letter with conventional headings. This is surprising, as is one other matter. Jewett makes no reference to rhetorical invention in the text of 1 Thessalonians. Invention represents one of the five acts in the creation of a persuasive discourse and is that part of rhetoric concerned with planning a discourse and its argumentation. Any attempt at rhetorical analysis without reference to authorial invention is at best only partial and for this reason not altogether satisfying or convincing. The essays by Frank Hughes and Wilhelm Wuellner on the rhetoric of 1 Thessalonians in *The Thessalonians Correspondence*, edited by Raymond F. Collins, constituted a major step forward,[83] but they also show

80. Jewett, *Thessalonian Correspondence*, 64.
81. Jewett, *Thessalonian Correspondence*, 71.
82. Jewett, *Thessalonian Correspondence*, 72.

that rhetorical analysis is anything but an exact science since Hughes and Wuellner come to some very different conclusions in their respective studies.

In introducing his study Hughes makes several important observations about rhetorical analysis and its potential in New Testament studies. First, he observes that the identification of the rhetorical situation of 1 Thessalonians through the comparative use of Graeco-Roman rhetoric can have value for the study of historical issues that are raised by New Testament scholars. Second, rhetorical criticism assumes that whether a particular ancient writer subscribed to the conventions of rhetoric, he or she had as a compositional goal the persuasion of the intended readers regarding beliefs or actions. Third, rhetorical analysis, as Hughes practices it in his study, concerns the "discovery of the writer's rhetorical strategies, in order to understand better the author's persuasive intent."[84]

One final broader point that Hughes makes concerns the place of rhetoric in Graeco-Roman society. Rhetoric was a standard feature of education, giving it wide currency. This means that "rhetorical criticism has the virtue of being a form of analysis whose presuppositions ancient writers are likely to have understood; hence, it is a kind of analysis that has intrinsic historical plausibility."[85] In terms of this essay this is a point to which we will need to return later.

Having determined that 1 Thessalonians should be located in the epideictic genus of rhetoric,[86] Hughes's own rhetorical analysis of 1 Thessalonians focuses primarily on the question of the letter's arrangement. He carefully delineates each rhetorical section of the letter with a description of its function in traditional rhetoric and its content. At several points his analysis differs substantially from that of Jewett. He maintains that the whole of 1 Thess 1:1-10 functions as the *exordium* by serving as a *captatio benevolentiae* to procure the good favor of Paul's readers and as an introduction to the themes to be dealt with later in the letter.[87] The

---

83. Hughes, "Rhetoric," 94-116, and Wuellner, "Argumentative Structure," 117-36.

84. Hughes, "Rhetoric," 94.

85. Hughes, "Rhetoric," 95.

86. Hughes, "Rhetoric," 97. Hughes later (see p. 107) discusses several subgenera of the genus of epideictic rhetoric and seems to imply that 1 Thessalonians may be related to funeral or consolatory speeches.

87. Hughes, "Rhetoric," 97-98.

exordium takes the form of a thanksgiving report with supporting reasons for it.[88]

The *narratio* that follows in 2:1–3:10 develops three themes first enunciated in the *exordium*. The theme of 2:1-20, introduced in 1:5, concerns the type of person Paul proved to be in his ministry to the Thessalonians. Suffering, a subsidiary theme of 2:1-20 found in 2:2, 2:14-16, and again in 2:17, is first announced in 1:6. Finally, according to Hughes, Paul discusses his missionary style in 2:1–3:10 after first mentioning the theme in 1:9.[89]

Hughes describes 3:11-13 as a *partitio*. It functions as a transition from the *narratio* to the *probatio* of the letter. He sees the wish-prayer of 3:12-13 as stating the three *propositiones* to be argued in the *probatio*. The first proof of the *probatio* occurs in 4:1-8 and concerns the correct behavior Paul taught the Thessalonians during his missionary visit. The second proof is found in 4:9-12 and deals with the appropriate behavior to ensure brotherly love. The third and final proof concerns the *parousia* of Christ and the participation of all Christians, whether living or dead, in the resurrection.[90] The proofs of the *probatio* are recapitulated in 5:4-11, according to Hughes, who describes these verses as a *peroratio*.[91] He then describes 5:12-22 as an exhortation that stands outside the formal rhetorical structure of the letter but has analogies with some speeches that end in exhortations to the hearers.[92] He defends his analysis of 5:12-22 as a concluding exhortation by referring to Klaus Berger, who employs epistolary analysis in his discussion of concluding paraenesis in New Testament letters.[93]

On the basis of his rhetorical analysis, Hughes is able to postulate the rhetorical situation of the letter. He sees relative peace and calm in the church at Thessalonica, with Paul attempting to strengthen his already sound relations with the community while addressing his readers' concerns regarding their deceased fellow Christians. The absence of both an

---

88. Hughes, "Rhetoric," 109, mistakenly calls it a prayer.

89. Hughes, "Rhetoric," 98-103.

90. Hughes, "Rhetoric," 103-6. The real issue in 4:13-18 is not the resurrection, as Hughes thinks, but the assumption of Christians to heaven with Christ at the time of his *parousia*. See Wanamaker, *Thessalonians*, 164-75.

91. Hughes, "Rhetoric," 103-5.

92. Hughes, "Rhetoric," 106.

93. See Klaus Berger, "Hellenistische Gattungen im Neuen Testament," in *ANRW* (ed. Hildegard Temporini and Wolfgang Haase; Berlin: W. de Gruyter, 1984), 2.25.2.1348.

apology on Paul's part and an attempt to persuade the readers to accept any clear changes in policy is commensurate with the identification of the letter as epideictic rhetoric.[94]

Several problems emerge in Hughes's treatment. First, while he points to several connections between the *exordium* and the *narratio,* he does not mention any such connections between the *exordium* and the *probatio* section. This is odd since clearly the eschatological theme of 1:9-10 is discussed extensively in 4:13–5:11. Second, by arguing that 5:4-11 constitutes the *peroratio,* or concluding part of the rhetorical arrangement, he is left with defining 5:11-22 as an exhortation that stands outside the formal rhetorical arrangement. This appears to be a questionable analysis since it undermines the carefully structured rhetorical arrangement that he finds in 1:1–5:3. Finally, like Jewett, his treatment is not rhetorical enough in that he fails to discuss rhetorical invention, a crucial factor for understanding the persuasive character of the writing as a whole.[95]

Wuellner offers a substantially different analysis from that of Hughes. He engages in a more holistic rhetorical approach to the letter. In addition, he views 1 Thessalonians as having a far more specific persuasive intention than Hughes.

His analysis begins with a consideration of several preliminary matters. First, he claims that the *exordium,* 1:1-10, is of a special type called *insinuatio.* This type of *exordium* is used "when the credibility of the case under discussion is rated as paradoxical, highly problematic as to its plausibility or cultural/social acceptability, or aptness."[96] The *exordium* evinces its *insinuatio* character through three features: (1) the dissociative argument in 1:3, (2) the first negation in 1:5, and (3) the appearance of "the first *oxymoron* in 1:6" in the words "'much affliction with joy.'"[97] Second, he briefly explores the aims and goals of 1 Thessalonians (the *intellectio/ noesis*) and the decisions that have been made at the level of rhetorical genre, status of the specific aim, the credibility of the status, and the aptness of the choices made for achieving the aim.[98] Wuellner locates the aim

---

94. Berger, "Hellenistische Gattungen im Neuen Testament," 106-7.

95. In fairness Hughes does make one or two passing references to issues that come under the heading "invention," but these remain undeveloped. For example, he does not discuss the crucial interplay between *ethos* and *pathos* in 2:1–3:13.

96. Wuellner, "Rhetorical Structure," 118.

97. Wuellner, "Rhetorical Structure," 118.

98. Wuellner, "Rhetorical Structure," 119.

of the letter as adhering around the "situations of suffering, grief, and perplexity" which Paul seeks to address pastorally in a general way.[99] The issue addressed in the letter, according to Wuellner, involves the "'quality'-status" implied in the *oxymoron* "tribulation with joy." Put somewhat differently, the point at issue in 1 Thessalonians is the paradoxical problem that "the tribulations and griefs experienced and expected are clearly in conflict with, and have a low degree of credibility, and little advocatability, when presented as allegedly compatible with the calling, namely, the life and hope of a religious or cultural community."[100] In attempting to encourage the commitment of the readers who experience the paradoxical situation of the triumph of their faith "in persistently trying and seemingly discrediting circumstances,"[101] Paul's letter conforms to a subgenre of epideictic rhetoric known as *paradoxon enkomion,* according to Wuellner.[102]

The argumentative structure discovered by Wuellner differs substantially from the one proposed by Hughes at most points. As previously noted, he finds the *insinuatio* type of *exordium* in 1:1-10. The actual "thesis" of the argument is found in 1:8-10. During his visit to Thessalonica Paul had functioned as a benefactor to the Christians. This had become typologically significant for them because it had resulted in their turning to the divine benefactor, God in Christ, which in turn led to their living with the duality of serving God in the present while waiting for the *parousia* of God's Son from heaven.[103]

The main argument of 1 Thessalonians is found in 2:1–5:22, according to Wuellner. It confirms the validity of the *oxymoron* "full conviction and joy in full suffering and trial" and the validity of the "'dissociation' of present appearance from future reality; or of faith 'crisis' or 'deficiencies' from faith fullness; or of seeming absence from real presence."[104] The first part of the argument, 2:1–3:13, functions to confirm the paradox of Chris-

---

99. Wuellner, "Rhetorical Structure," 120-21.

100. Wuellner, "Rhetorical Structure," 122-23.

101. The quotation is from Wuellner, "Rhetorical Structure," 133. Apart from the paradox of divine election and suffering, Wuellner, "Rhetorical Structure," 127, notes a second paradox, "the empirical fullness of the spiritual life in the present while 'waiting' for yet fuller completion at the parousia."

102. Wuellner, "Rhetorical Structure," 126.

103. Wuellner, "Rhetorical Structure," 128-29.

104. Wuellner, "Rhetorical Structure," 130.

tian commitment in adversity by using various examples (Paul, the Thessalonians, and the Christians of Judea), who demonstrate the real possibility of commitment in adversity. According to Wuellner, the second part, 4:1–5:22, serves to relate Christian commitment to the requirement of sustained Christian action.[105]

The letter concludes with a *peroratio* in 5:22-28. The *peroratio* functions to recapitulate the main argument (5:23-24) and to give a final emotional appeal (5:25-28).

Wuellner's treatment is far richer than I have been able to portray, but it is not without problems. In the first place, his analysis does not do justice to the totality of the letter. He does not, for example, account for the *narratio* of 2:1–3:10 as a coherent and careful report of Paul's dealings with the community at Thessalonica. It is not enough to say that this material "offers admirable and vituperative models for the case to be argued,"[106] when the material has the more likely rhetorical function of establishing Paul's *ethos* while appealing to the *pathos* of his audience. Secondly, Wuellner does not satisfactorily demonstrate that the coherent argument of the letter revolves around the *oxymoron* of 1:6, "much affliction with joy," and the "constitutive dissociation between the *appearance* of the presence [sic?][107] and the *reality* of the full potential" (his italics)[108] implied in 1:9-10. To do this he would have to look at 1 Thessalonians thought-unit by thought-unit, argument by argument. Unfortunately he does not do so. His treatment of the "main argument" found in 2:1–5:22 is simply too brief to do justice to his claims. In any case, I do not believe that careful analysis will sustain his claims because texts like 2:3-12 do not easily fit into the prescribed argumentative framework.

One further problem is that Wuellner uses two different forms of rhetorical analysis, classical Graeco-Roman and contemporary European and North American.[109] It is not always clear which type of rhetoric he is using in his analysis, nor even whether the two types of rhetoric are compatible with each other. In the end I have the impression that his analysis

105. Wuellner, "Rhetorical Structure," 133.

106. Wuellner, "Rhetorical Structure," 130.

107. I assume that the word "present" is intended. See Wuellner, "Rhetorical Structure," 130.

108. Wuellner, "Rhetorical Structure," 132.

109. See Olbricht, "Aristotelian Rhetorical Analysis," 236, n. 102 for a reservation about this aspect of Wuellner's work.

has more to do with contemporary literary theory than classical rhetoric. He himself says as much: "The rhetorical considerations I will be presenting, therefore, are not part of literary *criticism* (modern or traditional), but part of modern literary *theory*" (his italics).[110] As a result he finds considerable surplus meaning in the text, but not necessarily the meaning of the original rhetoric as a persuasive act by Paul directed at the Christians in Thessalonica.

Appearing in the same year as Hughes's and Wuellner's essays was one by Thomas Olbricht, who sought to apply an authentic Aristotelian rhetorical analysis to 1 Thessalonians. He faults H.-D. Betz for using Latin sources like Cicero and Quintilian, which he maintains Paul would very likely not have known.[111] He argues instead that in the Hellenistic world in which Paul lived the influence of Aristotle on rhetoric was ubiquitous and therefore if Paul was influenced by rhetoric, as seems likely, it would have had Aristotelian roots.[112]

Olbricht begins his analysis by asking what the rhetorical genus or genre of 1 Thessalonians is. He argues that Aristotle would have had to describe a new genre if he had lived in the fourth century C.E. to take account of a context that did not exist in his own day, namely, the church. For this reason and because he sees elements of both deliberative and epideictic rhetoric in 1 Thessalonians itself, Olbricht feels justified in adding a new genre to the traditional three of Aristotle. He calls this new genre "church rhetoric."[113] This rhetoric differs substantially from Aristotle's. It takes account of God's purposes and involvement in human experience and especially in the "acts of God in the community of believers." This in turn has an effect on the proofs, arguments, and style of the rhetoric.[114] In the case of 1 Thessalonians the rhetoric belongs to a subgenre that Olbricht designates as "reconfirmational," though he accepts the classical terms "exhortation" or "paraenesis" as also appropri-

---

110. Wuellner, "Rhetorical Structure," 119. This is also implied in his concluding remarks (Wuellner, "Rhetorical Structure," 135-36).

111. Olbricht, "Aristotelian Rhetorical Analysis," 221. Olbricht would have the same problem with Hughes's work, which I have discussed above.

112. Olbricht, "Aristotelian Rhetorical Analysis," 221. Krentz, "1 Thessalonians," takes a similar approach to Olbricht in restricting his analysis of 1 Thessalonians to Aristotelian rhetorical theory.

113. Olbricht, "Aristotelian Rhetorical Analysis," 225-26.

114. Olbricht, "Aristotelian Rhetorical Analysis," 226.

ate.[115] Thus Olbricht identifies the persuasive intention of 1 Thessalonians as Paul seeking "to reconfirm the young congregation in the matters on which it had been taught, and secondarily to clear up eschatological misconceptions."[116]

In what is probably the best available discussion of the rhetorical proofs used in 1 Thessalonians, Olbricht argues that the dominant form of proof, one of the three aspects of written rhetoric, resides in Paul's implementation of *ethos*. In the main argumentative thrust of 1 Thessalonians, "Paul shows goodwill toward the 'brothers' and avows his own virtue."[117] For example, in 1:2-10 Paul tells his readers of his constant prayers for them and praises them for their Christian virtue demonstrated in their "faith, love, and hope" as well as in their conversion and in their imitation of him and of the Lord. In 1 Thess 2:1–3:6, according to Olbricht, "Paul focused almost exclusively on his own virtue as it related to his relationship with the believers," while from 3:6 onward the *ethos* is directed primarily toward "praise or show of goodwill to the believers."[118] The intention of the proof from *ethos* is to reconfirm the community at Thessalonica. As Olbricht observes, "Confidence in, and the credibility of God, God's messengers, and the members of the community are imperative if Paul's program is to succeed."[119]

Appeals to *pathos* and *logos* are not completely absent in 1 Thessalonians, according to Olbricht's analysis. Paul seeks to arouse the emotions of the readers through "close family and community metaphors" such as those found in 2:7, 11, and 17. He also uses *logos,* or logical proof, which consists of enthymemes and examples, in accord with Aristotle's rhetorical observations. Olbricht makes a strong case for the presence of enthymemes or rhetorical syllogisms in 1:2-10 and especially in the eschatological material of 4:13–5:11, and sees examples, or rhetorical induction, as flowing out of the enthymeme of 1:4-5 regarding the Thessalonians' election.[120]

With respect to style, another of the three aspects of written rhetorical compositions, Olbricht finds 1 Thessalonians to be characterized by

115. Olbricht, "Aristotelian Rhetorical Analysis," 227.
116. Olbricht, "Aristotelian Rhetorical Analysis," 227.
117. Olbricht, "Aristotelian Rhetorical Analysis," 228.
118. Olbricht, "Aristotelian Rhetorical Analysis," 229.
119. Olbricht, "Aristotelian Rhetorical Analysis," 229.
120. Olbricht, "Aristotelian Rhetorical Analysis," 230-32.

stylistic balance. Rhetorical devices, notably parallelisms, are employed but do not predominate. The language is precise and perspicuous, as called for by Aristotle. For example, "Paul's nouns and verbs appear accurate and suited to his purpose," and he uses "vocabulary in a fresh, commanding way."[121] Paul employs a variety of metaphors to give the letter "clarity and liveliness." Of particular interest are the directness of style achieved through the consistent use of first and second person pronouns, and the frequent appeal to the divine to reinforce the argument.[122]

Olbricht bases his understanding of arrangement, the third aspect of written rhetoric, on Aristotle, who expressed a preference for a fourfold division. Thus Olbricht divides the arrangement as follows:

> Prescript, 1:1
> I *Exordium*, 1:2, 3
> II Statement [of the proposition], 1:4-10
> III Proof, 2:1–5:11
> IV Epilogue, 5:12-24
> Postscript, 5:25-28

He admits, however, that the actual statement of the proposition is difficult to determine. Moreover, he makes clear that assessing "the flow of purpose through the argument's divisions" is more important to rhetorical analysis than the actual divisions of the arrangement.[123] In Olbricht's analysis the persuasive intention seems to reside "in declaring the action of God, Christ, and the Holy Spirit — past, present, and future" and sustaining "faith and brotherly love despite affliction."[124]

By his very precise focus on the applicability of an Aristotelian reading of 1 Thessalonians, Olbricht offers a satisfying and generally convincing analysis of the letter. Especially important is his attempt to identify and discuss in a systematic way the three aspects of written rhetoric: proof, style, and arrangement. Whether we should agree to call 1 Thessalonians a piece of "church rhetoric" and identify it as part of a subgenre called "reconfirmational rhetoric" is a moot point, since the themes of friend-

---

121. Olbricht, "Aristotelian Rhetorical Analysis," 233-34.
122. Olbricht, "Aristotelian Rhetorical Analysis," 234-35.
123. Olbricht, "Aristotelian Rhetorical Analysis," 235-36.
124. Olbricht, "Aristotelian Rhetorical Analysis," 236.

ship, *paraenesis*, and even the divine, which predominate in 1 Thessalonians, were part of the discourse of the wider society, and certainly of Paul's own parent community.[125]

6. Assessment of Rhetorical Analysis

The current application of rhetorical analysis to the study of 1 Thessalonians is little more than a decade old, while its reemergence as a tool for the analysis of Paul's letters is little more than two decades old. This makes it early to determine its full potential and its ultimate value in the study of Paul's letters in general and of 1 Thessalonians in particular. Already, however, it has begun to produce noteworthy results, as we have seen above, and thus it is possible to make an initial assessment of its worth for our understanding of 1 Thessalonians as a persuasive discourse.

The possibility of rhetorical analysis results from the recognition that human discourse is purposive in its very essence and involves the attempt to persuade or influence another person to think or believe something, or to do or not do something. Almost as important is the awareness that all human discourse, whether written or spoken, presupposes a situation, similar to the *Sitz im Leben* of form criticism, which has both elicited and shaped the communication. This situation includes the persons involved and their relationship, the issues at stake, the social and cultural setting, and the purposes of the discourse. Rhetorical analysis, as applied to biblical discourse in the form of written texts, seeks to work backward from the text to its rhetorical intention in its rhetorical situation and to the strategies and styles adopted in the text to realize the rhetorical intentions within their rhetorical situation.[126]

One of the major issues that comes out clearly in the studies examined above is that several different types of rhetorical analysis are being practiced. Olbricht engages in a very orthodox Aristotelian form of analysis, though he is able to do so only by claiming that Aristotle would have been forced to develop his theoretical system to take account of the type of

125. On the themes of friendship and *paraenesis* in the letter-writing tradition of antiquity, see Stowers, *Letter Writing*.

126. See Kennedy, *Rhetorical Criticism*, 33-38, for a discussion of the process involved. He points out that the process is not linear but circular in character.

rhetorical situation addressed by Paul. Hughes uses a more eclectic form of classical analysis that draws on Aristotle but also on Latin rhetoricians like Cicero and Quintilian, who were themselves influenced by the Aristotelian tradition. Wuellner, on the other hand, mixes classical and contemporary theory because his goal differs considerable from the others.[127] Hughes and Olbricht want to understand 1 Thessalonians in terms of Paul's intention and possibly as its original recipients would have read it in their sociohistorical context. For this purpose classical rhetoric provides a valuable, if not invaluable, tool for historically oriented analysis. Wuellner, in contrast, recognizes a very different rhetorical situation that includes the time of writing as well as the time of reading. As "cultural conditions and beliefs change," the significance of the text also changes. Thus, in his view, we cannot read 1 Thessalonians as its original readers did, nor would this reading have very much significance if we could. For this reason Wuellner argues that rhetorical analysis

> will emerge as "a dynamic process," not as a system, least of all that of a neo-Aristotelian or neo-Ciceronian system. Rather, it will be imaginative criticism (E. Black), a criticism of the dialogical imaginations (M. Bakhtin) which is cognizant of the Bible as "ideological literature" (M. Sternberg) and of biblical hermeneutics as part of the "politics of interpretation."[128]

Aristotle understood rhetoric as an art in the sense of a skill. It was an art that could be mastered through study, imitation, and practice. It is clear that rhetorical analysis as an approach to 1 Thessalonians, and in fact to the writings of early Christianity in general, is itself an "art" that is only now being developed. Some attempts will inevitably be more successful

---

127. Jewett, *Thessalonian Correspondence*, 63-67, claims to adopt an approach that uses classical Graeco-Roman rhetoric and contemporary rhetorical theory, as well as recent linguistic research. He does so with a specific view to reconstructing the audience of 1 Thessalonians and the sociohistorical situation they experienced at the time the letter was written. This is very different from the view of Wuellner, who wishes to use rhetoric to break the "dual hegemony of traditional science and traditional philosophy" (Wilhelm Wuellner, "Where Is Rhetorical Criticism Taking Us?" *CBQ* 49 [1987]: 462). He, incidentally, specifically rejects Jewett's proposed reconstruction, as well as those of others, on the grounds that such attempts divert attention from the real significance of the general principle addressed by Paul regarding Christian suffering (Wuellner, "Rhetorical Structure," 120-21).

128. Wuellner, "Rhetorical Criticism," 463.

than others in analyzing the rhetorical situation and the rhetorical strategies adopted in the text.[129] One of the dangers inherent in the use of Graeco-Roman rhetoric as a formal system of analysis for Paul's letters is to attempt to explain too much with it. Paul was an heir not only to Hellenistic culture but also to Jewish culture. For example, some of Paul's arguments may owe more to Jewish styles of argumentation than to Graeco-Roman ones. In spite of such limitations, over time rhetorical analysis should, as Kennedy has noted,[130] make clear the power of a document like 1 Thessalonians as a "unitary" message that sought to persuade and inspire the Christians of Thessalonica and that, as Wuellner recognizes, can still have such power.

7. Concluding Remarks: Is a Synthesis Possible?

In considering rhetorical analysis in comparison with formal literary analysis and the closely related thematic analysis, several key differences emerge. In the first place, we know that instruction in rhetoric was central to formal education in the Graeco-Roman world. Even a person of Jewish origins like Paul could not have remained untouched by the influence of rhetoric on all forms of public discourse. This means that rhetorical analysis based on at least Aristotelian, if not the wider tradition of Graeco-Roman, rhetoric has the intrinsic advantage of approaching the writings of someone like Paul from a theoretical framework that undoubtedly had considerable influence on him and his letter-writing practices. By way of contrast, formal literary analysis, and particularly thematic analysis, as applied to Paul's letters, are largely attempts to apply categories that have been discovered inductively because there was no formal theory governing

---

129. For example, Lambrecht, "Structural Analysis," responding to Jewett's analysis, has acknowledged that the thanksgiving of 1:1-10 could be labeled an *exordium* and the material in 2:1-12 and 2:17–3:8 could be termed a *narratio*, but he claims that 4:1–5:22 can hardly be called a *probatio*. He appears to believe that Jewett has forced the "text into the straitjacket of a so-called common pattern" (174). As I indicate in my commentary, *Thessalonians*, 146-47, there are good reasons for seeing 4:1–5:22 as a *probatio* since the material is a "proof" that "the Thessalonians know how to behave and to please God so they must continue to live as they have been instructed by Paul, but with renewed fervor" (*Thessalonians*, 146).

130. Kennedy, *Rhetorical Criticism*, 158-59.

the practices that these approaches have sought to uncover. White has recently acknowledged that formal literary analysis, at least as he has practiced it, has been overly formalistic and the comparative basis of that activity has been too narrowly focused in the past on the nonliterary papyrus letters.[131] This has led to limited success in the analysis of Paul's letters because the approach is inherently unable to deal with the issues of intention and meaning, the very areas that rhetorical analysis has so much potential to explore.

A second difference is noteworthy. Unlike formal literary analysis, which tends to fragment texts like 1 Thessalonians into a series of small formal units without addressing the text as a whole, rhetorical analysis has the potential to look at the smaller units of meaning as well as the text as a whole in terms of their total persuasive effect. Another way of saying this is that formal literary analysis as it has been practiced in relation to 1 Thessalonians has offered little or no help in understanding *why* the text has been constructed in the way in which it has, or even what strategies were used in the construction of the text in terms of the author's intentionality in the particular historical and rhetorical situation. This results from the fact that formal literary analysis is theoretically not interested in the purpose or meaning of the text but only in uncovering formal features.

The way in which the issue of the thanksgiving (or thanksgivings) of 1 Thessalonians is dealt with is instructive. Formal literary analysis has recognized that a thanksgiving period exists in almost all of Paul's letters and therefore sees it as a formal structure. 1 Thessalonians has proved exceptionally difficult with regard to this issue because Paul expresses three different reasons for giving thanks to God at three different points in the text. This does not fit the formal pattern of thanksgivings in Paul's letters. The problem has been to come up with a formal explanation for the deviance of 1 Thessalonians; for example, the thanksgiving constitutes the body of the letter in this instance. The problem is that as a method formal literary analysis is unable to treat the reason(s) why Paul regularly introduces a thanksgiving period into his letters as part of his overall persuasive strategy nor what the significance is of the deviation in the pattern found in 1 Thessalonians. The moment one makes an attempt to talk about the

---

131. White, "Apostolic Mission," 158-59.

purpose or function of a formal literary structure, one begins to move toward the domain of rhetorical analysis.

Is a synthesis possible? Two recent writers have attempted to show us that it is. White, in an essay to which I have referred earlier,[132] applies epistolary analysis to the opening and closing conventions of Paul's letters and to the introductory and concluding conventions of the body-middle (the main content section) of his letters. He then shows the relevance of analyzing the body-middle of Paul's letters in terms of rhetorical style[133] and rhetorical argumentation.[134] Unfortunately, his essay is brief and his application of rhetorical analysis is very limited. What is important about his essay, however, is his recognition that epistolary analysis, of which he is one of the foremost practitioners, has significant limitations and must be supplemented with rhetorical analysis of the body-middle of the letter if we are to have a full appreciation of Paul's letter-writing practices and his communication goals.[135]

Duane Watson has recently presented an integrated epistolary and rhetorical analysis of Paul's letter to the Philippians.[136] This is not the place to discuss the details of his presentation, but his conclusions are particularly relevant. He observes that epistolary analysis has trouble in evaluating the significance of a variety of epistolary formulas and transitional components, as well as in delineating the function of the individual parts of a letter, particularly the body-middle, within its totality. He also notes that epistolary analysis is problematic because it has not engaged in a detailed comparison of literary letters of antiquity with New Testament letters, the problem that caused White to add rhetorical analysis to epistolary analysis when examining Paul's letters.[137] On the other hand, he sees rhe-

---

132. White, "Apostolic Mission," 146-53.

133. White, "Apostolic Mission," 153-57, highlights the importance of chiastic patterns, an aspect of rhetorical style, for understanding Paul's letters.

134. White, "Apostolic Mission," 157-61. His concern is exclusively with Aristotle's three types of argumentation: forensic, deliberative, and epideictic.

135. See the discussion of White above, and especially the quotation from "Apostolic Mission," 146-47, which explains the reason for White's attempt to synthesize epistolary and rhetorical forms of analysis.

136. Duane F. Watson, "The Integration of Epistolary and Rhetorical Analysis of Philippians," in *The Rhetorical Analysis of Scripture: Essays from the 1995 London Conference* (ed. Stanley E. Porter and Thomas H. Olbricht; JSNTSup 146; Sheffield: JSOT Press, 1997), 398-426.

137. See White, "Apostolic Mission," 148-49.

torical analysis as particularly useful for establishing the significance and function of the parts of a letter within the whole. It also has the advantage of treating New Testament letters more appropriately as literary productions. He acknowledges, however, that "rhetorical analysis can be accused of arbitrary demarcation of units and identification of their function."[138] For this reason rhetorical analysis "is more convincing when it can be shown to have a corresponding epistolary analysis."[139]

I agree with him, but I would hasten to add that it is a marriage of unequal partners. Rhetorical analysis, both of the ancient and the modern varieties, takes us far closer to the issues that really matter: meaning and significance, intention and strategy.

138. Watson, "Integration," 426.
139. Watson, "Integration," 426.

1 Thessalonians: Rhetorical Flourishes and Formal Constraints[1]

Edgar Krentz

Both the formal and the rhetorical analysis of 1 Thessalonians have received great attention in recent years. One unresolved question is whether or how they intersect, conflict, or supplement each other. Here I will review and evaluate the recent use of rhetoric in the interpretation of 1 Thessalonians and then examine the letter using the modes of persuasion suggested by Aristotle in his *Ars rhetorica* and, to a far lesser degree, in *Rhetorica ad Alexandrum.*[2]

Some recent scholarship seeks the rhetorical situation under the categories exigence, audience, and constraints, terms not drawn from classical rhetoric but from modern theoreticians.[3] New Testament scholarship of-

---

1. I began this paper intending to urge the use of rhetorical analysis in terms of ancient rhetoric. To my own surprise, I ended by taking an ambiguous stance, recognizing the great value of Aristotle's discussion of proofs for analysis of Paul's letters, wishing that I had had more time to work through the *topoi* he listed and to evaluate the use of ornamentation and figures of thought, but quite disenchanted with the value of analyzing the structure of 1 Thessalonians rhetorically. I did not find any advance over nonrhetorical analysis, and as much disparity in the rhetorical disposition as in the older formal and literary analysis.

2. In his essay in *TD* (pp. 194-240) Frank Hughes examines the form-critical and rhetorical analysis of 1 Thessalonians to see how 1 Thessalonians fits into "the rhetoric of letters." In other words, he understands his "task to be that of, from the rhetorical critical side, trying (again) to synthesize what rhetorical criticism and form criticism of letters tell us about 1 Thessalonians."

3. The terms do not occur in Richard A. Lanham, *A Handlist of Rhetorical Terms* (2nd

ten vacillates between the use of classical rhetorical theory and modern rhetorical analysis, often termed the "new rhetoric"[4] — an appellation drawn from the title of the work by Perelman and Olbrechts-Tyteca.[5] Basing their work on Aristotle's definition of rhetoric as the "art of persuasion," they "were relentless in their definition of and discussion of rhetorical strategies as argumentation."[6] Their work has had immense influence in the study of literature, including New Testament texts.[7]

Other scholars stress a more historical application of ancient rhetorical theory to New Testament texts, an approach widely practiced from the seventeenth to the nineteenth centuries. In recent years Hans-Dieter Betz's use of this approach in his commentaries on Galatians and 2 Corinthians 8–9 has recalled scholarship to its values.[8] George A. Kennedy, the premier American interpreter of ancient classical rhetoric, gave a significant push forward to rhetorical criticism in his monograph *New Testament Interpretation through Rhetorical Criticism,* which illustrated its value for New Testament interpretation.[9] American scholars especially greeted this new mode of analysis and applied it to whole letters or to selected portions of them.

---

ed.; Berkeley, Los Angeles, and Oxford: University of California Press, 1991), or in Kathleen E. Welch, *The Contemporary Reception of Classical Rhetoric: Appropriations of Ancient Discourse* (Hillsdale: Lawrence Erlbaum Associates, 1990).

4. See the survey in Burton L. Mack, *Rhetoric and the New Testament* (GBS; Minneapolis: Fortress, 1990), 1-24.

5. C. Perelman and L. Olbrechts-Tyteca, *The New Rhetoric: A Treatise on Argumentation* (Notre Dame and London: University of Notre Dame Press, 1969).

6. Mack, *Rhetoric,* 15.

7. See David Cohen, "Classical Rhetoric and Modern Theories of Discourse," in *Persuasion: Greek Rhetoric in Action* (ed. Ian Worthington; London and New York: Routledge, 1994), 69-82. For an evaluation of seminal figures in this modern application of ancient rhetoric, see Welch, *Contemporary Reception of Classical Rhetoric.*

8. Hans-Dieter Betz, *Galatians: A Commentary on Paul's Letter to the Churches in Galatia* (Hermeneia; Philadelphia: Fortress, 1979), and *2 Corinthians 8 and 9: A Commentary on Two Administrative Letters* (Hermeneia; Philadelphia: Fortress, 1985).

9. *New Testament Interpretation through Rhetorical Criticism* (Chapel Hill and London: University of North Carolina Press, 1984).

1. Critical Voices

Only recently have critical voices been raised. The seventeen essays in the George A. Kennedy Festschrift, published in 1991, contain no articles evaluating the rhetorical approach.[10] But the essays from the Heidelberg Conference of 1992 contain three that critique rhetorical criticism.[11] These articles summarize the concerns. Stanley Porter raises basic questions in "The Theoretical Justification for Application of Rhetorical Categories to Pauline Epistolary Literature."[12] He points to major problems: 1. ". . . no model has allowed a smooth harmonizing of ancient epistolary and rhetorical categories." Betz's category "apologetic letter" is "based on literature that is hardly germane" (Plato's Seventh Letter, Demosthenes' *De Corona,* Cicero's *Brutus,* and Libanius's *Oratio* 1), while, *pace* Kennedy, it is "difficult to establish what and how much Paul could have known on a conscious or formal basis." Thus the usual references to the ubiquity of rhetoric in Roman education, based on Clarke and Bonner,[13] are called into question.[14]

Porter also stresses the difficulty of defining the rhetoric to use in studying New Testament letters. The ancient rhetorical handbooks do not apply the categories of discourse genres or the categories of rhetorical organization to letters, thus providing no ancient theoretical justification for doing so now. Malherbe's statement that epistolary theory "is absent from

---

10. *Persuasive Artistry: Studies in New Testament Rhetoric in Honor of George A. Kennedy* (ed. Duane F. Watson; JSNTSup 50; Sheffield: Sheffield Academic Press, 1991).

11. *Rhetoric and the New Testament: Essays from the 1992 Heidelberg Conference* (ed. Stanley E. Porter and Thomas H. Olbricht; JSNTSup 90; Sheffield: Sheffield Academic Press, 1993). Julius Victor is not a major author; he is not even mentioned in Albrecht Dihle, *Greek and Latin Literature of the Roman Empire from Augustus to Justinian* (London and New York: Routledge, 1994), and receives two lines in George A. Kennedy, *Classical Rhetoric and Its Christian and Secular Tradition from Ancient to Modern Times* (Chapel Hill: University of North Carolina Press, 1980), 105.

12. Stanley Porter, "The Theoretical Justification for Application of Rhetorical Categories to Pauline Epistolary Literature," in Mack, *Rhetoric and the New Testament*, 100-122.

13. Donald Lemen Clark, *Rhetoric in Greco-Roman Education* (New York: Columbia University Press, 1957); Stanley F. Bonner, *Education in Ancient Rome from the Elder Cato to the Younger Pliny* (Berkeley and Los Angeles: University of California Press, 1977), 65-89, 250-327. Clark's only discussion of letter-writing is a summation of Pseudo-Demetrius, *On Style* 223-36 (105-6).

14. Porter, "The Theoretical Justification," 100-105.

the earliest extant rhetorical handbooks . . . and only gradually made its way into the genre" is justified fully.[15] The handbooks do discuss questions of style (λέξις).[16] The first discussion is in Pseudo-Demetrius's *On Style*,[17] a work whose date is a matter of debate. Grube dates it to the Hellenistic period (late third to second century B.C.E.),[18] Leske to the first century C.E.,[19] while Malherbe suggests that its sources "go back perhaps to the second century, and at the latest, to the first century BC."[20] Demetrius says that the style should be plain (ἰσχνός, 223),[21] somewhat free in its structure (ἐν τῇ συντάξει μέντοι λελύσθω μᾶλλον, 229), that is, avoiding elaborate periods and not using ellipses. It differs from oral speech (224), it may resemble a treatise if it is too long (σύγγραμμα, 229), but it should show the writer's character (τὸ ἠθικόν, 227). Cicero, Seneca, Quintilian, and Philostratus also show that "with regard to epistles only matters of style were discussed in any significant way, virtually always with epistles mentioned in contrast to oratory." Porter concludes that we must analyze stylistic features "in terms of their coordinated use within an entire passage, or even an entire book,"[22] and thus questions the theoretical basis for using rhetorical categories to analyze letters in the New Testament.

15. Porter, "The Theoretical Justification," 110.

16. Porter, "The Theoretical Justification," 106-17; he points out that Julius Victor (fourth century C.E.) is the only writer of a rhetorical handbook to include a discussion of letter-writing (in an appendix to his *Ars Rhetorica*), 114.

17. Pseudo-Demetrius, *On Style* 223-36. The standard text is Demetrius, *On Style* [in the same volume as Aristotle, *Ars poetica* and "Longinus," *On the Sublime*] (ed. and trans. Doreen C. Innes, based on W. Rhys Roberts; LCL; London: William Heinemann; Cambridge: Harvard, 1995), a reworking of his 1927 LCL edition. His still earlier edition, *Demetrius: On Style* (Cambridge: At the University Press, 1902), has extensive notes and a glossary of technical terms not reprinted in either LCL edition.

18. G. M. A. Grube, *The Greek and Roman Critics* (Canadian University Paperbooks; Toronto: University of Toronto Press, 1968), 110.

19. Albin Lesky, *A History of Greek Literature* (trans. James Willis and Cornelis de Heer; New York: Thomas Y. Crowell, 1966), 689.

20. Abraham J. Malherbe, "Ancient Epistolary Theorists," *OJRS* 5 (1977): 5. Reprinted with slight modifications as *Ancient Epistolary Theorists* (SBLSBS 19; Atlanta: Scholars Press, 1988), 4. I cite this later edition.

21. Pseudo-Demetrius, *On Style* 36-37, identifies four styles (χαρακτῆρες τῆς ἑρμηνείας), which he then discusses at length: elevated (μεγαλοπρεπής, 38-127), elegant (γλαφυρός, 128-89), plain (ἰσχνός, 190-235), and forcible (δεινός, 240-304).

22. Citations from Porter, "The Theoretical Justification," 115 and 117.

Joachim Classen raises questions arising from the publications of Hans-Dieter Betz and George A. Kennedy.[23] They include the following:

> Are rhetoric and epistolography meant to be taken together as one art or discipline or are they regarded as two separate ones, each of them separately being of service to the interpretation of the New Testament?

What exactly is the aim of applying the ancient categories?

> Is it only to demonstrate to what extent Paul was familiar with them, with rhetoric and/or epistolography, and with theory and/or practice (as [Betz's] second sentence seems to indicate) or,
> Is it in order to arrive at a more thorough understanding of the letter(s)? . . .

If, however, the aim is a more adequate appreciation of Paul himself, at least three further groups of problems come up:

> When, where, and how is Paul likely to have become familiar with ancient rhetoric and epistolography?
> Exactly which form or which aspect of rhetoric and epistolography is meant at which phase of their history (provided it is possible to distinguish clearly several phases of the development)?
> Did he deliberately draw on such knowledge of rhetorical theory and employ its categories, or not?

Classen argues that Betz did not pay enough attention to the distinction between rhetoric and epistolography. Rhetoric proposed a "standard structure and content," while allowing room for flexibility. Epistolography did not. He concludes that rhetoric is useful within a limited sphere, only in argumentation *(inventio)* and style *(elocution)*, where rhetoric overlaps epistolography.[24] He also argues, based on an analysis of Melanchthon's

---

23. C. Joachim Classen, "St Paul's Epistles and Ancient Greek and Roman Rhetoric," in *Rhetoric and the New Testament: Essays from the 1992 Heidelberg Conference*, 263-91. He published an earlier version of this paper as "Paulus und die antike Rhetorik," *ZNW* 82 (1991): 1-33. I omit some of his questions.

24. Classen, "St Paul's Epistles and Ancient Greek and Roman Rhetoric," 289.

use of rhetoric, that one may go beyond ancient rhetoric in the analysis of letters. Classen sums up the situation as follows:

> However, as the enthusiasm for this new instrument for the interpretation of biblical texts is not shared in all quarters and some scholars prefer simply to ignore it or to suspend judgment, while others, clearly, feel uneasy about their uncertainty or even ask for advice or assistance from classicists, a new assessment seems to be called for.[25]

Jeffrey Reed questions the use of ancient rhetorical categories as tools to analyze Paul's letters. He sharply separates rhetorical and epistolary analysis by showing that the subgenres used in rhetoric (judicial, deliberative, and epideictic) differ from epistolary genres.[26] "Paul could conceptualize a letter in terms of 'praise or blame' and 'expediency or non-expediency.' Paul's use of epideictic-like and deliberative-like argumentation, however, does not necessarily indicate a direct parallel with the systems of rhetoric found in the rhetorical schools." Of the five traditional rhetorical processes used in oratory, two (memory [μνήμη, memoria] and delivery [ὑπόκρισις, pronunciatio]) are irrelevant for epistolary analysis, while invention (εὕρησις, inventio), arrangement (τάξις, dispositio), and style (λέξις, elocutio) may play a role in letter-writing. Invention is not unique to rhetoric. Pseudo-Demetrius 230 already notes that proverbs (παροιμίαι) and proof by logic (ἀποδείξεις) are appropriate topics for letters.[27] Rhetorical arrangement, Reed argues, is foreign to letters. Epistolary structure corresponds somewhat, since the letter-opening shows the close tie of writer and readers, demonstrates the *ethos* of the writer, and introduces the subject matter; it is thus close to the *exordium*. The letter-closing is close to the conclusion of oratory. Style, however, shows some similarity. But he concludes that though "Paul skillfully adapted epistolary tradition, he stayed within the bounds of its categories."[28] Only invention and composition are relevant to epistolary analysis.

---

25. Classen, "St Paul's Epistles and Ancient Greek and Roman Rhetoric," 155-67.

26. Jeffrey T. Reed, "Using Ancient Rhetorical Categories to Interpret Paul's Letters: A Question of Genre," 292-324, especially 297-301 (in *Rhetoric and the New Testament*).

27. Reed, "Using Ancient Rhetorical Categories to Interpret Paul's Letters," 301-4. Aristotle holds that these two are especially applicable in deliberative oratory.

28. Reed, "Using Ancient Rhetorical Categories to Interpret Paul's Letters," 324.

R. Dean Anderson, in an essay published after the writing of this paper, argues that one should not use Aristotle's *Ars rhetorica* in analyzing Pauline letters, since rhetorical theory after him developed along quite different lines.[29] Rather, one should use later Peripatetic Rhetoric (of which little remains),[30] as reflected in Cicero's *Topica* and Demetrius's *De elocutione*, Academic Rhetoric (Cicero, *Partitiones oratoriae*), the Epicurean Philodemus, and the following treatises that he classifies as "Hellenistic Rhetoric": Cicero, *De inventione*, the *Rhetorica ad Herennium*, P. Rutilius Lupus's *Schemata dianoias et lexeos*, Theon's *Progymnasmata*, Dionysius of Halicarnassus's *De antiquis oratoribus* and *De compositione verborum*, Pseudo-Longinus's *De sublimitate*, Cicero's *De oratore* and *Orator*, and Quintilian's *Institutio oratoria*, representing relevant Roman rhetoric.

Anderson questions the applicability of the three structural categories (bouleutic, dikastic, and epideictic) to Paul's letters. However, he supports the contention that Paul's letters "have been influenced by rhetorical methods of style and argumentation more generally."[31] He tests his position by evaluating modern rhetorical analyses of Gal 1:1–5:12, Romans 1–11, and 1 Corinthians. He concludes that Paul often breaks the demand for clarity (σαφήνεια), that his style is more paratactic than periodic, and that he makes extensive use of wordplay (σχήματα λέξεως) of the kind that rhetoricians opposed. In short, the rhetorical analysis of Paul is ultimately not productive.

One way to check these conclusions is to analyze 1 Thessalonians using rhetorical categories that antedate Paul, which Paul, a speaker of Greek, might have known. I will use Aristotle's *Ars rhetorica* as the best resource for doing that.[32] In the process I shall make some evaluation of current

29. R. Dean Anderson, Jr., *Ancient Rhetorical Theory and Paul* (Contributions to Biblical Exegesis and Theology 18; Kampen: Pharos, 1996), 30. I do not discuss Anderson's work in detail, since it postdates the writing of this paper. It deserves careful attention.

30. F. Solmsen, "The Aristotelean Tradition in Ancient Rhetoric," *AJP* 62 (1941): 35-50, 169-90. *Peripatetic Rhetoric after Aristotle* (ed. William W. Ffortenbaukgh and David C. Mirhady; Rutgers University Studies in Classical Humanities VI; New Brunswick and London: Transaction Publishers, 1994) is a series of useful articles on the later use of Aristotle's rhetorical work.

31. Anderson, *Ancient Rhetorical Theory and Paul,* 100-109.

32. I cite Aristotle from *Ars rhetorica* (ed. Adolph Roemer; 2nd ed.; Leipzig: B. G. Teubner, 1898). I also use Aristotle, *The "Art" of Rhetoric* (trans. John Henry Freese; LCL; Cambridge and London: Harvard University Press, 1991 = 1926).

practices of rhetorical criticism and evaluate the relationships of rhetorical and formal approaches to the letters.[33]

2. Aristotle's *Ars rhetorica* and Paul's First Letter to Thessalonica

Aristotle analyzes rhetoric in a logical and coherent fashion as a general art with universal application to discourse, thus implying that it is not restricted to oratory.[34] Its function is to discover that which persuades or appears to persuade.[35] Aristotle lists three means of persuasion early in his *Ars rhetorica:* the disposition of the speaker (ἦθος), disposing the hearer in a certain way (πάθος), and rational argument (λόγος).[36] I will use these three in analyzing 1 Thessalonians in detail later in this paper.

Aristotle created the taxonomy of speeches, dividing them into three genres (εἴδη, γένη): the deliberative (συμβουλευτικόν), the forensic or dikastic (δικανικόν), and the epideictic (ἐπιδεικτικόν).[37] He bases his distinction on what the hearer is asked to do, the subject matter, and the speaker.[38] Deliberative speeches either urge an action on the hearers (προτροπή) or seek to dissuade from an action (ἀποτροπή), whether addressed to a private individual or to a group.[39] They deal with future actions.[40] Forensic speeches are either accusations (κατηγορία) or defenses (ἀπολογία), that is, they ask the hearer to decide about the legality or rectitude of past actions.[41]

---

33. Thomas H. Olbricht, "An Aristotelian Rhetorical Analysis of 1 Thessalonians," in *Greeks, Romans, and Christians: Essays in Honor of Abraham J. Malherbe* (ed. David L. Balch, Everett Ferguson, and Wayne A. Meeks; Minneapolis: Fortress, 1990), 216-36, used Aristotle earlier in an analysis of 1 Thessalonians. I became aware of his essay only as I worked on this paper.

34. It does not apply to a specific field of knowledge (οὐδεμίας ἐπιστήμης ἀφωρισμένης), as medicine does (*Ars rhetorica* 1.1.14).

35. *Ars rhetorica* 1.1.14.

36. *Ars rhetorica* 1.2.3.

37. *Ars rhetorica* 1.3.3. The three terms in 1.3.3.

38. *Ars rhetorica* 1.3.3.

39. *Ars rhetorica* 1.3.3. While Aristotle does not explicitly say so, clearly forensic and epideictic speeches can also address either individuals or groups.

40. *Ars rhetorica* 1.3.4. Later, in 1.8.1 he implies that present events can also be the subject of deliberative speeches.

41. *Ars rhetorica* 1.3.4.

Epideictic oratory deals with praise (ἔπαινος) or blame (ψόγος) of persons, groups, or actions in the present.[42] Deliberative oratory (δημιουργική) is superior (καλλίονος καὶ πολιτικωτέρας οὔσης) to forensic, which is limited to private matters between individuals. Forensic oratory is more likely to bring in extraneous material and engage in wrong or false argumentation.[43] Kennedy sums up well:

> The species is judicial when the author is seeking to persuade the audience to make a judgment about events occurring in the past; it is deliberative when he seeks to persuade them to take some action in the future; it is epideictic when he seeks to persuade them to hold or reaffirm some point of view in the present, as when he celebrates or denounces some person or some quality.[44]

A single speech may use more than one species of oratory, its mixed character thus defying easy classification; yet one species will usually be dominant, indicating the writer's major purpose in writing.

3. Epistolary Form or Rhetorical Genre?[45]

a. 1 Thessalonians: A Deliberative Speech?

Rhetorical critics have given special attention to Aristotle's taxonomy in discussing Paul's letters. How does 1 Thessalonians fare at the hands of rhetorical critics? To what genre do they ascribe it? George Kennedy claims that 1 Thessalonians "is basically deliberative, an exhortation to stand fast in the Lord (3:8) with specific advice for the Christian life, given in chapters 4–5." Let me resume briefly Kennedy's argument. The presence of narrative (1 Thessalonians 2–3) is not enough to insure that it belongs to the forensic genre. Rather, the narrative supports the establishment of Paul's *ethos*. Criticism arising in Thessalonica, caused in part by his absence, de-

---

42. *Ars rhetorica* 1.3.3.
43. *Ars rhetorica* 1.1.10.
44. Kennedy, *Classical Rhetoric,* 19.
45. Raymond F. Collins summarizes recent rhetorical analysis in *The Birth of the New Testament: The Origin and Development of the First Christian Generation* (New York: Crossroad, 1993), 132-37.

termines the rhetorical situation. Paul meets this "by identifying himself with the church and by stressing the continuity in their relationship, as 1 Thess 1:2 makes clear." (The *topos* returns in 3:10.)

"The proem (1:3-12) seeks the goodwill of the audience, but more than that. Paul attempts to convert reciprocal goodwill into a basis of self-confidence on the part of the Thessalonians." 2:1-8 (a *narratio*) refutes the charges against Paul, important for Paul's *ethos* building. 2:9–3:13 (also part of the *narratio*) "recast the materials in striking ethical and pathetical terms." The order is chronological. Urging steadfastness on the readers (3:2-3), Paul moves to a remarkable περιπέτεια in 3:8 when he says ὅτι νῦν ζῶμεν ἐὰν ὑμεῖς στήκετε ἐν κυρίῳ (3:8).[46]

"The headings (4:1–5:22) open with a proposition in general terms (4:1), supported by the authority of Jesus (4:2)."[47] Paul divides this section into an injunction to chastity (4:3-8), love of the neighbor (4:9-11), questions raised in Thessalonica (the dead in 4:13-18; end-time chronology in 5:1-11), with a chiastic return to other injunctions (5:12-22). The epilogue (5:12-24) is a prayer, followed by the closure (5:25-28). Kennedy's discussion is extremely brief. As it stands, Kennedy's position is more assertion than argument, not compelling, though deserving of attention.[48] Kennedy does not detail vocabulary that would be peculiar to this rhetoric, nor list figures of thought peculiar to it.

b. Thessalonians: An Epideictic Letter?

A series of scholars have recently claimed that 1 Thessalonians is epideictic in character. Robert Jewett suggests that "the first step in determining the rhetorical genre of epistolary materials is to identify the epistolary type."[49] He points out that Pseudo-Demetrius identifies a "praising letter" (ἐπαινετικὸς τύπος) and a "thanking letter" (ἀπευχαριστικὸς τύπος),[50] but

---

46. Kennedy, *Classical Rhetoric,* 142-44.

47. Kennedy, *Classical Rhetoric,* 143.

48. I have not had access to B. C. Johanson, *To All the Brethren: A Text-Linguistic and Rhetorical Approach to 1 Thessalonians* (ConBNT 16; Lund: Almqvist & Wiksell, 1987), who also argues that 1 Thessalonians is deliberative.

49. Robert Jewett, *The Thessalonian Correspondence: Pauline Rhetoric and Millenarian Piety* (FFNT; Philadelphia: Fortress Press, 1986), 71.

50. Pseudo-Demetrius, *On Style* 10 and 21 (Malherbe, *Ancient Epistolary Theorists,*

does not mention the "advisory type" (συμβουλευτικὸς τύπος).[51] Jewett then suggests that though Kennedy classifies 1 Thessalonians as deliberative in genre, it "seems more likely . . . that the rhetorical genre most closely associated with 1 Thessalonians is demonstrative/epideictic because it *concentrates on praise and blame* with a prominent traditional subject being *thanksgiving to the gods*" (my italics).[52] He also points out that this matches the evaluation in most major commentaries — in my opinion, a weak statement. Then, too, he presents a detailed rhetorical outline of the letter as epideictic.

Other scholars followed Jewett in this analysis. Frank Hughes gave the most detailed, balanced, and persuasive argument for 1 Thessalonians as epideictic rhetoric in a carefully worked-out analysis of the letter.[53] 1:1-10 functions as the *exordium*, 2:1–3:10 as the *narratio*, while 3:11-13 is the *partitio*, the statement of three themes that require demonstration via three proofs in 4:1–5:3, the *probatio*.[54] The *peroratio* (5:4-11) follows, succeeded by an exhortation (5:12-22) and "final matters" (5:23-28). Hughes notes that this final exhortation "is not mandated in the Graeco-Roman rhetorical handbooks." Exhortation does come at the end of some speeches and "is evidently a standard part of letters"[55] — though Hughes does not discuss how this insight affects his epideictic classification. A detailed rhetorical outline of 1 Thessalonians clarifies his earlier verbal description. He documents his analysis from rhetorical handbooks ranging from Aristotle to Menander Rhetor. This use of a wide chronological range

---

30-31, 40-41). Malherbe reproduces the critical text of Valentin Weichert, *Demetrii et Libanii qui feruntur ΤΥΠΟΙ ΕΠΙΣΤΟΛΙΚΟΙ et ΕΠΙΣΤΟΛΙΜΑΙΟΙ ΧΑΡΑΚΤΗΡΕΣ* (Bibliotheca Teubneriana; Leipzig: B. G. Teubner, 1910).

51. Pseudo-Demetrius, *On Style* 11 (Malherbe, *Ancient Epistolary Theorists*, 36-37). Malherbe translates as follows: "It is the advisory type when, by offering our own judgment, we exhort (someone to) something or dissuade (him) from something."

52. Jewett, *The Thessalonian Correspondence*, 71.

53. Frank W. Hughes, "The Rhetoric of 1 Thessalonians," in *The Thessalonian Correspondence* (ed. Raymond F. Collins; BETL 87; Leuven: Leuven University Press–Peeters, 1990), 94-116.

54. Hughes, "The Rhetoric of 1 Thessalonians," 104-5.

55. Hughes, "The Rhetoric of 1 Thessalonians," 106, with a detailed rhetorical outline on pp. 109-16. He refers to Klaus Berger, *Formgeschichte des Neuen Testaments* (Heidelberg: Quelle & Meyer, 1984), §§42-43; "Hellenistische Gattungen im Neuen Testament," 1031-1432, 1831-85 in *ANRW* II.25.2 (Berlin & New York: Walter de Gruyter, 1984), 1348-50. Berger shows that this is a normal epistolary convention both in the New Testament and in ancient letters.

of texts, many dating after Paul, and extensive texts in Latin is one of the weaker parts of the analysis. On the other hand, the detailed analysis of the text of 1 Thessalonians contains insights into Paul's language and thought that do not depend on the rhetorical genre and disposition.

Charles Wanamaker, following Jewett, also identifies 1 Thessalonians as a "demonstrative/epideictic" letter "because such letters are devoted to praise (or blame) of people's behavior."[56] He rejects the attribution of the deliberative genre by Kennedy because "it is clear that 1 Thessalonians is filled with praise for the readers because of their exemplary behavior (see 1:2-3, 6-10; 2:13-14, 19-20; 3:6-9; 4:1-2, 9-10)." And Karl P. Donfried, following Hughes, argues that 1 Thessalonians is epideictic in genre: ". . . recognizing 1 Thessalonians as belonging to the epideictic *genus* of rhetoric — that is, one emphasizing praise and, to a lesser degree, blame — allows us to see that the Thessalonian Christians have become the objects of Paul's praise."[57] The "allows us to see" in this sentence surprises me a bit, since commentators recognized Paul's positive attitude long before the rhetorical genre epideictic was ever applied to the letter. Donfried later develops this praise motif to conclude that "1 Thessalonians has thus much in common with a *logos paramythetikos,* a word of consolation and encouragement to a Christian church suffering the effects of persecution."[58] In terms of rhetoric one can ask whether a *logos paramythetikos* does not fit into the deliberative genre, since παραμυθητικός can mean encourage as well as console. Or, to put the question in terms of epistolary theory, are not the categories of commendatory and consolatory letters adequate to account for these features?[59] These

---

56. Charles A. Wanamaker, *The Epistle to the Thessalonians: A Commentary on the Greek Text* (NIGTC: Grand Rapids: Eerdmans; Exeter: Paternoster, 1990), 47.

57. Karl P. Donfried, "The Theology of 1 Thessalonians," in *The Theology of the Shorter Pauline Letters* (New Testament Theology; Cambridge: Cambridge University Press, 1993), 1-79, here 4, with a citation from an unpublished paper by Frank W. Hughes.

58. Donfried, "The Theology of 1 Thessalonians," 24-26; he, like others, does not take up the epistolary taxonomy of Stanley Stowers, who puts such encouraging letters under the category "Letters of Exhortation and Advice." See *Letter Writing in Greco-Roman Antiquity* (LEC 5; Philadelphia: Westminster Press, 1986), 91-152, especially 91-94. Stowers comments: "In this discussion I will use *protreptic* in reference to literature that calls the audience to a new and different way of life and *parenesis* for advice and exhortation to continue in a certain way of life" (92). The application to 1 Thessalonians is clear.

59. Pseudo-Demetrius, *On Style* 2 and 5 (Weichert, *Demetrii et Libanii,* 3-5; Malherbe, *Ancient Epistolary Theorists,* 32-35).

scholars also do not discuss vocabulary, style, or ornamentation appropriate to this genre.

c. A Fourth Genre for 1 Thessalonians?

Two scholars propose new genres or modifications of Aristotle's classification. Wuellner stresses rhetorical analysis as a key to the letter. The *exordium* is an *insinuatio*, used when the credibility of a case is paradoxical.[60] Thus the letter is an *enkomion paradoxon*,[61] characterized by the rhetorical figures irony, paradox, oxymoron, and the like.[62] Wuellner finds this particularly appropriate when "the tribulations and griefs experienced and expected [in Thessalonica] are clearly in conflict with, and have a low degree of credibility, and little advocatability, when presented as allegedly compatible with the calling, namely, the life and hope of a religious or cultural community."[63] The *enkomion paradoxon* is especially appropriate for dealing with "the doubly paradoxical nature of their (Paul, Thessalonians, 'all the brethren') respective commitments." The *quaestio infinita* involves two related issues: "(1) everyone's faith commitment in the face of the 'commonplace' topic "we [are] bound to suffer tribulations (1 Thess 3,4), and (2) everyone's commitment to living a God-pleasing life more and more thoroughly (4,1) while facing the constitutive and not accidental dual paradox: the hardships, and the parousia fulfillment."[64] In his analysis of the rhetorical structure of the letter he identifies 1:8-10 as "the full statement of the letter's thesis" at

---

60. Wilhelm Wuellner, "The Argumentative Structure of 1 Thessalonians as Paradoxical Encomium," in *The Thessalonian Correspondence*, 117-36, here 118.

61. Wuellner, "The Argumentative Structure," 126. The transliteration does not make clear whether it should be read as παραδόξων ἐγκώμιον or παράδοξον ἐγκώμιον.

62. Wuellner, "The Argumentative Structure," 127, refers to the longer list of rhetorical figures in H. Lausberg, *Elemente der literarischen Rhetoric* (8th ed.; Munich: Max Huber Verlag, 1984), §37, 1. Lausberg lists irony, emphasis, litotes, hyperbole, various forms of periphrasis, oxymoron, zeugma, chiasm, and related forms of artificial order. Wuellner also cites with approbation Karl A. Plank, *Paul and the Irony of Affliction* (SBLSS; Atlanta: Scholars Press, 1987).

63. Wuellner, "The Argumentative Structure," 122. Wuellner, 121, thus approves Malherbe's pointing to the pastoral purpose of Paul's writing. See Abraham J. Malherbe, *Paul and the Thessalonians* (Philadelphia: Fortress, 1987).

64. Wuellner, "The Argumentative Structure," 126-27.

the end of the *exordium*.[65] The "Main Argument" is 1 Thess 2:1–5:22, in which 2:1–3:13 offers "admirable and vituperative models for the case to be argued," while 4:1–5:22 explicates the "paradoxical commitment" they share. The peroration (5:23-28) includes a recapitulation and a final appeal. Wuellner is unusual in arguing for a general rhetorical situation as opposed to one determined by the historical situation, which the letter uses in the form of a *quaestio infinita*. Thus he regards 1 Thessalonians as a letter to Macedonia in general, in spite of the letter-introduction.[66] Wuellner thus seems to disregard letter form in favor of a rhetorical genre analysis. Nevertheless, he has many fruitful insights into the genre of the letter — as do all of these scholars.

Thomas H. Olbricht points out that recent rhetorical criticism has placed "emphasis . . . on arrangement or structure"[67] — a development he deplores. He argues that a sound method will restrict itself to Greek rhetoric (as opposed to Roman), to rhetorical treatises written before Paul. Functionally that means we are restricted to Aristotle's *Rhetoric*. Aristotle did not claim to exhaust the discipline, but left room for others to build on "his foundations and methodologies,"[68] thus leaving room not only for later Greek rhetoricians but also for us to add categories and strategies to his. Olbricht concludes that modern scholars have applied the three Aristotelian genres too rigidly, none of which fits 1 Thessalonians. Though some features are close to deliberative oratory, the use of praise motifs suggests epideictic, as Jewett and others following him aver. He argues that the Christian assembly is a new setting for discourse that leads to a new genre, "church rhetoric," based on the Christian vision, in which the world is "the arena in which God (through God's Son and the Spirit) carries out divine purposes among humans."[69] Olbricht holds that Paul's purpose in 1 Thessalonians is

to do precisely what he said he did when he was there, "encouraging [παρακαλέω], comforting [παραμυθέομαι] and urging [μαρτύρομαι]

---

65. Wuellner, "The Argumentative Structure," 128-35.

66. Wuellner, "The Argumentative Structure," 119: "Though addressed to the Thessalonians, this letter may deserve to be called more appropriately a letter to the Macedonians!" The discussion of the rhetorical situation is on pp. 124-26.

67. Olbricht, "An Aristotelian Rhetorical Analysis of 1 Thessalonians," 216.

68. Olbricht, "An Aristotelian Rhetorical Analysis of 1 Thessalonians," 223 cites George A. Kennedy, *Classical Rhetoric*, 61, as support for this view.

69. Olbricht, "An Aristotelian Rhetorical Analysis of 1 Thessalonians," 226.

you to lead lives worthy of God" (1 Thess 2:12), which was likewise the reason he sent Timothy "to strengthen [στηρίζω] and encourage [παρακαλέω] you" (3:2), and the reason behind the charge to the Thessalonians: "Therefore encourage [παρακαλέω] one another and build each other up [οἰκοδομέω], just as in fact you are doing" (5:11).[70]

Olbricht titles this reconfirmational church rhetoric, though he allows that Malherbe's "more classical 'exhortation' or 'parenesis'" also fits.[71]

The second half of Olbricht's essay is an investigation of Aristotelian proofs, style, and arrangement in 1 Thessalonians. His analysis of arrangement is simple: Prescript (1:1), *Exordium* (1:2-3), Statement (1:4-10), Proof (2:1–5:11), Epilogue (5:12-24), and Postscript (5:25-28). Prescript and Postscript are epistolary conventions. The four sections framed by them follow Aristotle's suggestions — recognizing that Aristotle warns against the multiplication of divisions.[72] His comments on proofs and arrangement will be taken up later. He concludes with a useful statement:

> Aristotle himself maintained that rhetoric is an art and must follow the conventions of the time, the nature of audiences, the purposes of the speaker, and perhaps chiefly the contours of the subject matter. To address all these facets, we must employ *The Rhetoric* as a fountainhead of insight rather than as a leveed, controlled stream. We need to draw upon whatever conventions and later rhetorical insights may be of help. In my judgment, however, we must steer clear of esoteric modern criticism that obfuscates rather than clarifies.[73]

d. An Evaluation

Which of these rhetorical genres best fits 1 Thessalonians? The survey suggests that no one classifies the letter as dikastic or forensic. One way to

---

70. Olbricht, "An Aristotelian Rhetorical Analysis of 1 Thessalonians," 227.

71. Olbricht, "An Aristotelian Rhetorical Analysis of 1 Thessalonians," 227. He cites Abraham A. Malherbe, "Exhortation in First Thessalonians," *NovT* 25 (1983): 238, now reprinted as "Exhortation in 1 Thessalonians," in *Paul and the Popular Philosophers* (Minneapolis: Fortress, 1989), 49-66; here 49.

72. Olbricht, "An Aristotelian Rhetorical Analysis of 1 Thessalonians," 227-36; *Ars rhetorica* 3.13.3-5.

73. Olbricht, "An Aristotelian Rhetorical Analysis of 1 Thessalonians," 236.

make this evaluation is to ask what the necessary component elements for each genre are. And here we immediately face a problem. Just what rhetorical theory from antiquity should we use? How many of the works included in Leonhard Spengel's three-volume collection[74] dare we employ? The question is more important than may at first appear.

Aristotle says that only two elements are necessary for deliberative (bouleutic) rhetoric, to state the subject (πρόθεσις) and then to prove one's position (πίστις).[75] A narrative (διήγησις) properly belongs to forensic oratory; deliberative and epideictic oratory really have no need of it.[76] But to reject the forensic category immediately implies, in Aristotelian rhetoric, that we need an adequate description of 1 Thess 1:4–3:13 that does not use the sub-category διήγησις *(narratio)*. I suggest that it belongs in the proof, as some analyses suggest.

Whose analysis best correlates with Aristotle's views? Or, to put it differently, whose analysis best correlates with the letter itself, since a conclusion about the letter's rhetorical genre depends on a decision as to the purpose of the letter (that is the decision that its hearers [readers] are asked to make), the argument advanced in it (its λόγος), and the time frame involved? And that also asks for a consideration of its rhetorical structure.

Paul addresses the ἐκκλησία of the Thessalonians. This is the earliest evidence for a name used by Christians to denote their community or assembly. We customarily translate this as "church," using a term that has become so ecclesial in nature for us that it prevents us from hearing first-century associations.[77] The term denotes the legislative and deliberative body of a Greek πόλις. Does Paul select this term here *ab ovo*, or is he appropriating an earlier term in Christian usage? No answer is possible. But the choice suggests, at least, some sort of parallel between the Christian assembly and the assembly in Greek Thessalonica. Is that what necessitates the discussion of life in the public arena in 4:9-12?

What is the subject matter of 1 Thessalonians? At one time I thought that Paul might be producing an apology for his absence from Thessalo-

---

74. L. Spengel, ed., *Rhetores Graeci* (3 vols.; Bibliotheca Teubneriana; Leipzig: B. G. Teubner, 1853-56).

75. *Ars rhetorica* 3.13.1: ἔστι δὲ τοῦ λόγου δύο μέρη: ἀναγκαῖον γὰρ τό τε πρᾶγμα εἰπεῖν περὶ οὗ, καὶ ταῦτ᾽ ἀποδεῖξαι.

76. *Ars rhetorica* 3.13.3.

77. The German term *Gemeinde* is much better, since it can refer to a political as well as an ecclesial entity.

nica. I no longer do. Rather, Paul is urging them to consider and take action in the immediate future. The occurrences of the verb παρακαλῶ and the noun παράκλησις, to which Malherbe and Olbricht point, strongly support this proposal.[78] The only two occurrences of παραμυθέομαι in Paul (2:12; 5:14)[79] and the role of Timothy described in 3:2-3 (εἰς τὸ στηρίξαι ὑμᾶς καὶ παρακαλέσαι ὑπὲρ τῆς πίστεως ὑμῶν τὸ μηδένα σαίνεσθαι ἐν ταῖς θλίψεσιν ταύταις) suggest that this letter is parenetic, its goal being to urge the hearers to make a correct choice about serving God in Thessalonica in the face of opposition. There is no doubt that this opposition is part of the context for the parenesis. 1:6 (δεξάμενοι τὸν λόγον ἐν θλίψει πολλῇ), 2:2 (προπαθόντες καὶ ὑβρισθέντες, καθὼς οἴδατε, ἐν Φιλίπποις ἐπαρρησιασάμεθα ἐν τῷ θεῷ), 2:14 (τὰ αὐτὰ ἐπάθετε καὶ ὑμεῖς), 2:18 (καὶ ἐνέκοψεν ἡμᾶς ὁ Σατανᾶς), 3:3 (ἐν ταῖς θλίψεσιν ταύταις), 3:8 (ὅτι νῦν ζῶμεν ἐὰν ὑμεῖς στήκετε ἐν κυρίῳ). The stress on the action of God in Thessalonians (2:13) supports this. The heading for 4:1–5:24 is "how you must live and please God . . . and abound more" (4:1; τὸ πῶς δεῖ ὑμᾶς περιπατεῖν καὶ ἀρέσκειν θεῷ, καθὼς καὶ περιπατεῖτε, ἵνα περισσεύητε μᾶλλον). The reference to the will of God (4:3) supports this suggestion.

But the overarching theme, in my opinion, goes beyond this. 1 Thess 1:3 mentions a familiar Pauline triad (faith, hope, and love) in an unfamiliar way: work of faith, labor of love, and endurance of hope (μνημονεύοντες ὑμῶν τοῦ ἔργου τῆς πίστεως καὶ τοῦ κόπου τῆς ἀγάπης καὶ τῆς ὑπομονῆς τῆς ἐλπίδος τοῦ κυρίου ἡμῶν Ἰησοῦ Χριστοῦ ἔμπροσθεν τοῦ θεοῦ καὶ πατρὸς ἡμῶν). These three correlate with 1 Thess 1:8-10: the labor of faith is reflected in their resounding the word of the Lord (the account of a true and living God), the labor of love in serving the true and living God, and the endurance of hope in expectant waiting for the Son.

1 Thess 3:1-5 is a key passage for the letter's purpose, the urging of fidelity in the face of social pressure. This correlates well with Paul's description of his initial proclamation, done in spite of opposition, a form of proclamation he describes in terms reminiscent of the philosophic missionary.[80] Paul is not in any sense asking them to pass judgment on his past

78. παρακαλέω, 2:12; 3:2, [7]; 4:1, 10, 18; 5:11, 14; παράκλησις, 2:3.

79. παρακαλοῦντες ὑμᾶς καὶ παραμυθούμενοι καὶ μαρτυρόμενοι εἰς τὸ περιπατεῖν ὑμᾶς ἀξίως τοῦ θεοῦ τοῦ καλοῦντος ὑμᾶς εἰς τὴν ἑαυτοῦ βασιλείαν καὶ δόξαν.

80. See Abraham A. Malherbe, "'Gentle as a Nurse': The Cynic Background to 1 Thessalonians 2," in *Paul and the Popular Philosophers* (Minneapolis; Fortress, 1989), 35-48.

actions. Nor is his major purpose to praise the Thessalonians — though there are expressions of praise in the letter. Thus, in my opinion, urging epideictic as the rhetorical genre for this letter is mistaken — though it will, clearly, not convince many. It is not enough to simply use praise as a key to the genre. If one is to assign the letter to one of Aristotle's three types, it is clearly a deliberative letter, as Kennedy proposes.[81] But Olbricht's proposal, in the light of Aristotle, is also possible.

e. Rhetorical Genre and Epistolary Analysis

Robert Jewett argues that epistolary analysis "should be kept separate from the question of rhetorical genre in the strict sense of that term,"[82] though I do not understand why this is necessary. He cites Malherbe's correct observation that "Epistolary theory in antiquity belonged to the domain of the rhetoricians, but it was not originally part of their theoretical system."[83] That is only partially true. One could argue that the absence of a discussion of epistolography in the early rhetoricians might imply that they felt that rhetoric did not apply directly to letter-writing. As far as analyzing genre is concerned, the two cohere in 1 Thessalonians. In fact, form-critical analysis of 1 Thess 1:9-10 as a pre-Pauline formula supports my suggestion that these verses are a statement of the theme, illuminated by 1:3.

4. The Organization of 1 Thessalonians in the Light of Aristotelian Rhetoric

Scholars, concentrating on analyzing Paul's letters in terms of oratorical genre and the corresponding structure (τάξις), tend to find the full structure of an oration in 1 Thessalonians, often without considering whether epistolary theory collides with that analysis. Recently Margaret Mitchell

81. Kennedy, *Classical Rhetoric,* 143: "First Thessalonians is basically deliberative, an exhortation to stand fast in the Lord (3:8) with specific advice for the Christian life, given in chapters 4–5."

82. Jewett, *The Thessalonian Correspondence: Pauline Rhetoric and Millenarian Piety,* 67.

83. Jewett, *The Thessalonian Correspondence,* 67, citing Malherbe, *Ancient Epistolary Theorists,* 2.

called for a more nuanced application of ancient rhetoric, controlled less by ancient handbooks and more by the investigation of actual ancient speeches.[84] Thus she argues that Jewett's identification of 1:6–3:13, "fully half the letter," as *narratio*, despite the fact that epideictic orations use it rarely, is a mistake. *Narratio* properly belongs to forensic oratory. Her pages deserve careful reading by all who engage in rhetorical criticism.

Aristotle suggests that an oration needs only four sections — (1) προοίμιον *(exordium)*, (2) διήγησις *(narratio)*, (3) πίστις (proof), and (4) ἐπίλογος *(peroratio)* — and warns against over-subtle subdivisions. He argues that deliberative and epideictic speeches, *stricte dicta*, do not use refutation of an opponent, and that they therefore have little use for a narration, while deliberative speeches have no need of an epilogue, whose function is to summarize the argument. Subsequent rhetorical theory multiplied Aristotle's categories into a variety of subforms. Aristotle suggests that simpler rhetorical analysis is better, that only the statement of the issue and its proof are absolutely necessary. Beginning the analysis with the hidden assumption that all parts of an oration will be present may be a Procrustean bed for a sermon or a letter. However, the detailed rhetorical analysis of a letter may be helpful as a guide to the unfolding thought of the letter.

a. Aristotle's Three Means of Persuasion[85]

Aristotle does not begin his discussion of rhetoric with an analysis of oratorical genre, leaving that to the third book. He closes the second book of his τέχνη ῥητορική with a summarizing comment:

> Since there are in fact three things that should be systematically worked out in the discussion of speech, let us regard what has been said as enough about paradigms and maxims and enthymemes and in general about the thought and the sources of argument and how we should re-

---

84. Margaret Mitchell, *Paul and the Rhetoric of Reconciliation* (Louisville: Westminster/John Knox, 1993), 1-19.

85. *Essays on Aristotle's Rhetoric* (ed. Amélie Oksenberg Rorty; Berkeley, Los Angeles, and London: University of California Press, 1996) contains useful essays on Aristotle's theory of means of persuasion, including (399-416) the reprinting of Christopher Carey, "Rhetorical Means of Persuasion," in *Persuasion: Greek Rhetoric in Action* (ed. Ian Worthington; London and New York: Routledge, 1994), 26-45.

fute them. It remains to go through the subject of style and arrangement.[86]

What is the role of rhetoric in relation to thought in Aristotle? Invention (εὕρεσις) is the rhetorical faculty concerned with discoverying the means of persuasion,[87] and persuasion comes from πίστεις (proofs).[88] The term πίστις means more than evidence, covering anything that will lend credibility to the speaker. Proofs are of two kinds, nonartistic and artistic (ἄτεχνοι, ἔντεχνοι). Nonartistic proofs (such as witnesses, tortures,[89] or contracts[90]) do not require rhetoric; artistic proofs do since they are produced by method, through human invention.[91]

Aristotle identifies three forms of proof by which a speaker persuades his hearers: the character of the speaker (ἦθος τοῦ λέγοντος), the disposition created in the hearer (ἐν τῷ τὸν ἀκροατὴν διαθεῖναί πως, πάθος), and argument (λόγος, ἐν αὐτῷ τῷ λόγῳ) which uses proofs.[92] He treats all three extensively. A speech's persuasion depends on three factors: the speaker, the audience addressed, and the argument itself.[93] They are

---

86. *Ars rhetorica* 2.265: ἐπεὶ δὲ τρία ἐστὶν ἃ δεῖ πραγματευθῆναι περὶ τὸν λόγον, <u>ὑπὲρ μὲν παραδειγμάτων καὶ γνῶμων καὶ ἐνθυμημάτων καὶ ὅλως τῶν περὶ τὴν διάνοιαν, ὅθεν εὐπορήσομεν καὶ ὡς αὐτὰ λύσομεν</u>, εἰρήσθω ἡμῖν τοσαῦτα, λοιπὸν δὲ διελθεῖν περὶ λέξεως καὶ τάξεως (my underscore). The translation is Kennedy's, closer to the original than Freese's in the LCL, from Aristotle, *On Rhetoric, Newly Translated with Introduction, Notes and Appendixes* by George A. Kennedy (New York and Oxford: Oxford University Press, 1991).

87. ἔστω δὲ ῥητορικὴ δύναμις περὶ ἕκαστον τοῦ θεωρῆσαι τὸ ἐνδεχόμενον πιθανόν, *Ars rhetorica* 1.2.1.

88. πίστις is a polyvalent term. The normal Christian translation "faith" sometimes blinds us to its broader significance. It can mean proof, as above, or evidence, or trust. It encompasses "the related qualities of trust, trustworthiness, credence and credibility, and extends to objects and means used to secure trust or belief" (Carey, "Rhetorical Means," in *Persuasion*, 26; Rorty, *Essays on Aristotle's Rhetoric*, 399).

89. Slaves regularly gave their testimony under torture. Kennedy even translates "testimony of slaves taken under torture." See Kennedy in Aristotle, *On Rhetoric*, 37 for the translation and n. 38.

90. That is, documents.

91. *Ars rhetorica* 1.2.2.

92. *Ars rhetorica* 1.2.3. I owe a large debt to Carey, "Rhetorical Means of Persuasion." Jewett, *The Thessalonian Correspondence*, 65, points out that these three provide a link between ancient rhetoric and modern communication theory, yet he makes almost no use of them in his analysis of 1 Thessalonians.

93. *Ars rhetorica* 1.2.3.

not, however, equally appropriate to all three forms of speech. Speeches are concerned with making a judgment (ἕνεκα κρίσεώς ἐστιν ἡ ῥητορική), both in deliberative and forensic speeches, but *ethos* is more important in deliberative speeches, *pathos* in forensic.

> ... for it makes much difference in regard to persuasion (especially in deliberations, but also in trials) that the speaker seem to be a certain kind of person and that his hearers suppose him to be disposed toward them in a certain way and in addition if they, too, happen to be disposed in a certain way [favorably or unfavorably to him]. 4. For the speaker to seem to have certain qualities is more useful in deliberation; for the audience to be disposed in a certain way [is more useful] in lawsuits.[94]

While there are common modes of argumentation for the three types of discourse, each is individually more appropriate to one type of discourse than another:

> In general, among the classes of things common to all speeches, amplification is most at home in those that are epideictic; for these take up actions that are agreed upon, so that what remains is to clothe the actions with greatness and with beauty. But paradigms are best in deliberative speeches; for we judge future things by predicting them from past ones; and enthymemes are best in judicial speeches, for what has happened in some unclear way is best given a cause and demonstration [by enthymematic argument].[95]

It is not surprising that amplification is close to paradigms, since Aristotle also holds that "Praise and deliberations are part of a common species (εἶδος) in that what one might propose in deliberation becomes encomia when the form of expression is changed."[96]

Of course, these three means of persuasion do not appear in neatly

---

94. *Ars rhetorica* 2.1.3-4 (Kennedy's translation, p. 120). The key sentence is τὸ μὲν οὖν ποιόν τινα φαίνεσθαι τὸν λέγοντα χρησιμώτερον εἰς τὰς συμβουλάς ἐστιν, τὸ δὲ δικιακεῖσθαί πως τὸν ἀκροατὴν εἰς τὰς δίκας.

95. *Ars rhetorica* 1.9.40. As Kennedy, *On Rhetoric*, 87, n. 181 points out, amplification (αὔξησις) for Aristotle is not a *topos* (2.26.1), but rather "a *koinon* and form of *pistis* (2.18.5), a technique of persuasion, analogous to — though logically weaker than — *paradeigmata* and *enthyumema*. . . ."

96. *Ars rhetorica* 1.9.35: ἔχει δὲ κοινὸν εἶδος ὁ ἔπαιονος καὶ αἱ συμβουλαί.

separated sections of a discourse, but are intermixed more or less artistically by a good speaker or writer. Identifying and describing these three forms of persuasion is the most important contribution Aristotle makes to the analysis of rhetoric, far outweighing the classification of rhetorical genres.

b. Paul's Ethos (ἦθος) in 1 Thessalonians[97]

All speakers or writers need to obtain the goodwill of their audiences. Aristotle says that a speaker persuades "whenever the speech is spoken in such a way as to make the speaker worthy of credence."[98] The speaker's personal moral character is the most magisterial proof of all (κυριωτάτη πίστις, 1.2.4.1356a13). Hearers trust three interrelated qualities in a speaker "other than logical demonstration" (ἀποδείξεις): practical wisdom (φρό-νησις), moral character (ἀρετή), and goodwill (εὔνοια).[99] Nothing else is necessary to show one's ἦθος. One appeals to the emotions of the audience by claiming qualities the audience will prize or by stressing the disadvantages one experiences to gain their sympathy. ἦθος provides strong proof. It is especially proper to use in deliberative oratory.

Paul establishes his character in many ways.[100] He shows his moral character through his mode of preaching the gospel of God. He preached to them in spite of extreme difficulty in Philippi (2:3, προπαθόντες καὶ ὑβρισθέντες, καθὼς οἴδατε, ἐν Φιλίπποις). ὕβρις is a strong term, implying acting beyond what one's status in life allows.[101] Paul stands in strong contrast to the false philosophers whom Dio Chrysostom describes in his Ora-

97. Mario DiCicco has helpful discussions of Aristotle's three methods of proof in *Paul's Use of Ethos, Pathos, and Logos in 2 Corinthians 10–13* (Lewiston, N.Y.: Mellon Biblical Press, 1994); he discusses ἦθος on 36-63 and illustrates it from ancient sources contemporary with Paul on 64-76.

98. *Ars rhetorica* 1.2.4 (ὅταν οὕτω λεχθῇ ὁ λόγος, ἔστε ἀξιόπιστον ποιῆσαι τὸν λέγοντα), translation from Kennedy, 38. He points out that Aristotle is thinking of content and thought, not style or delivery, i.e., διὰ τὸν λόγον.

99. *Ars rhetorica* 2.1.5-6.

100. Three scholars have given attention to this: Hughes, "The Rhetoric of 1 Thessalonians," 97-103, though without calling it Aristotle's proof; Olbricht, "An Aristotelian Rhetorical Analysis of 1 Thessalonians," 228-30; and Collins, *Birth*, 136.

101. Recall Herodotus's schema for interpreting history (κόρος, ὕβρις, ἄτη) and how he applied it to Xerxes' ordering his soldiers to whip the Hellespont.

tion to the Alexandrians.[102] They work for monetary profit and personal reputation, not the benefit of the hearers (κέρδους ἕνεκεν καὶ δόξης τῆς ἑαυτῶν, οὐ τῆς ὑμετέρας ὠφελείας). Since such wandering Cynic philosophers were well known, Paul uses an implied comparison (σύγκρισις) to his advantage. In such well-known cases, one does not need to make the comparison explicit, as is the case in 1 Thess 2:5-12, a marvelous example of rhetorical self-presentation.

Paul shows his virtue by not accepting money or seeking glory (though their glory is a goal, 2:12), and his practical wisdom by his maternal and paternal attitude toward them, and sums it up in three significant adverbs (2:10, ὡς ὁσίως καὶ δικαίως καὶ ἀμέμπτως ὑμῖν τοῖς πιστεύουσιν ἐγενήθημεν). He reinforces his self-presentation with two summons to God to serve as his witness (2:5, 10) and also calls them his witnesses (2:10). His reference to labor and toil to avoid putting a burden on them is also striking, a demonstration of goodwill (εὔνοια).

He also demonstrates εὔνοια in his efforts to come to them (2:17-20) and his sending of Timothy as his *alter ego* (τὸν ἀδελφὸν ἡμῶν καὶ συνεργὸν τοῦ θεοῦ ἐν τῷ εὐαγγελίῳ τοῦ Χριστοῦ, 3:2).[103] Throughout Paul avoids sounding proud in this self-praise. His language fits well with what Plutarch recommends in his treatise *On Inoffensive Self-Praise*. One may praise one's self if one is defending one's good name or has been wronged (see 1 Thess 2:2-3).[104] Paul reminds them that he did not use an authoritarian approach. Plutarch also advises one "to most harmoniously" blend

---

102. Dio Chrysostom, *Orationes* 32: *To the People of Alexandria* 10. See *Dio Chrysostom in Five Volumes* (ed. J. W. Cohoon and H. Lamar Crosby; LCL; Cambridge: Harvard University Press; London: William Heinemann, 1961 =1940), 3.180-81. C. P. Jones, *The Roman World of Dio Chrysostom* (Cambridge and London: Harvard University Press, 1978), 36-44, has a good discussion of the oration. See also Hans von Arnim, *Leben und Werke des Dio von Prusa mit einer Einleitung: Sophistik, Rhetorik, Philosophie in ihrem Kampf um die Jugendbildung* (Berlin: Weidmann, 1898), 435-63, and Malherbe, "Gentle as a Nurse."

103. See Hughes's ("The Rhetoric of 1 Thessalonians") description of the *narratio* (his term for 2:1–3:10), which Paul uses to "underscore the good relationship he enjoys with the Thessalonians" (100) and to "show the consistency of his past behavior with his present behavior" (101).

104. Plutarch, *Moralia* 40: *De laude ipsius* 4.540E and 6.541C. The standard critical text is *Plutarchi Moralia* III (ed. W. R. Paton, M. Pohlenz, and W. Sieveking; Bibliotheca Teubneriana; Leipzig: B. G. Teubner, 1972), 371-93; the standard English translation is *Plutarch's Moralia* VII (ed. and trans. Phillip H. De Lacy and Benedict Einarson; LCL: Cambridge: Harvard University Press; London: William Heinemann, 1959), 114-67.

"the praises of his audience with his own" (9.542B) — which Paul does at length, as every commentator notes. Thus the combination of imitation and praise serves to establish Paul's identity with the Thessalonians.

Paul stresses his suffering and the difficulties he experienced as he tried to come to Thessalonica (2:2, 18), comparing it to the suffering that the Thessalonians are experiencing: δεξάμενοι τὸν λόγον ἐν θλίψει πολλῇ (1:6); προπαθόντες καὶ ὑβρισθέντες, καθὼς οἴδατε, ἐν Φιλίπποις (2:2); ἐν πολλῷ ἀγῶνι (2:2). Comparing the Thessalonians' suffering to that of the Christians in Judea stresses the hostility between them and the non-Christian Thessalonians, while calling attention to the effect: preventing Paul from speaking the gospel (2:16).[105] Paul's language is masterful in a manner Aristotle especially commends for deliberative speech and, secondarily, also for epideictic.

c. Paul's Use of Pathos (πάθος)

πάθος, according to Aristotle, is what creates a certain [positive] disposition [toward the speaker] in the hearer.[106] "For it makes much difference in regard to persuasion (especially in deliberation but also in trials) that ... his hearers ... happen to be disposed in a certain way [favorably or unfavorably to him]."[107] Ethos and pathos often overlap, since a speaker's self-presentation will affect the hearer's response. Pathos is especially at home in forensic oratory, but is also important in deliberative oratory.[108] There-

---

105. 2:14-16 thus serves a rhetorical purpose in the letter. One must take this into account in evaluating its authenticity.

106. Proofs are . . . αἱ δὲ ἐν τῷ τὸν ἀκροατὴν διαθεῖναί πως, 1.2.3.

107. 2.1.3. Translated by Kennedy, On Rhetoric, 120. Carey, "Rhetorical Means," 27 (400 in Rorty, Essays on Aristotle's Rhetoric) lists pre-Aristotelian testimonia to the value of such emotional appeal. There is a series of valuable articles on the emotions in Aristotle's Rhetoric in Rorty's collection: Stephen R. Leighton, "Aristotle and the Emotions" (206-37); John M. Cooper, "An Aristotelian Theory of the Emotions" (238-57); Dorothea Frede, "Mixed Feelings in Aristotle's Rhetoric" (258-85); Gisela Striker, "Emotions in Context: Aristotle's Treatment of the Passions in the Rhetoric and His Moral Psychology" (286-302); Martha Nussbaum, "Aristotle on Emotions and Rational Persuasion" (303-23).

108. Carey, "Rhetorical Means," 33 (405 in Rorty's Essays on Aristotle's Rhetoric). He adds: "It is important for the modern reader to bear in mind that the neat divisions in classical rhetoric are the product of schematizations by theorists rather than oratorical practice." Ethos and pathos dealt with some of the same topics: expediency, honor, and justice. They argue in similar fashion.

fore the *prooemium* plays a role in *pathos*. A speaker "will lay claim to qualities which the audience will respect or stress the disadvantages of his situation as a claim to sympathy."[109] One needs to fend off any hostility the audience might have against the speaker and secure its goodwill. One way to do that is to arouse hostility against someone else. One needs to ward off the feeling that the speaker is meddling in what is not his affair (πολυπραγμοσύνη) and show εὔνοια to the audience, that is, demonstrate that one acts on its behalf. It should be clear from this that *pathos* is the reverse of the coin named *ethos*, and that the same passages will produce both.[110] Paul uses *prooemium* very well in 1:2-10. Here rhetorical analysis and epistolary theory come together. The letter-writer is to show a friendly disposition (φιλοφρόνησις), a concept that correlates well with *ethos* and *pathos*. Collins points to Paul's expression of love in 2:8 and 3:12, the longing expressed in 2:17, and the familial imagery of 2:7 and 12 as evidence of Paul's φιλοφρόνησις.

Since Hughes and Olbricht discuss *pathos* in 1 Thessalonians, I will not rehearse their analyses here. But some details are worth stressing. Paul reminds his readers that their praiseworthy reception of the word of God imitated him and the Lord, thus presenting himself as a model worthy of emulation. His reference to speaking boldly at Thessalonica in spite of the mistreatment in Philippi calls forth sympathy, as do his familial similes.[111] The paragraph 4:9-12 is a good example of Paul's use of *pathos*. Since αὐτοὶ γὰρ ὑμεῖς [the Thessalonians] θεοδίδακτοί ἐστε εἰς τὸ ἀγαπᾶν ἀλλήλους, he has no need to instruct them about brotherly love, which they are already showing widely (though he proceeds to do so, an elleipsis).

Scholars who argue that 1 Thessalonians is epideictic point to the fact that Paul praises the Thessalonians highly. While praise (or blame) is the primary characteristic of epideictic, not all praise is epideictic. Here

---

109. Carey, "Rhetorical Means," 27 (Rorty, *Essays on Aristotle's Rhetoric*, 400).

110. Carey, "Rhetorical Means," 39, comments that "there is often an overlap between *ethos* and *pathos*. . . ."

111. James M. May recently pointed out that Cicero presented himself as "a gentle, understanding, and forgiving father figure" in his oration *Pro caelio*. This prosopopoeia enabled him to gain the court's sympathy by establishing a bond with a client who otherwise might have quite unsympathetic. See "Patron and Client, Father and Son in Cicero's *Pro Caelio*," *CJ* 90, no. 4 (April-May 1995): 434-36. Paul uses a familiar *topos* in appealing to the Thessalonians.

praise is combined with moral instruction about life in the *polis*. The Thessalonians are urged to be good citizens, but not to participate in public life (καὶ φιλοτιμεῖσθαι ἡσυχάζειν καὶ πράσσειν τὰ ἴδια, not τὰ κοινά, 4:11).[112] Paul does this to show that he is not a busybody engaging in πολυπραγμοσύνη, interfering in other people's affairs. Plato had much earlier set πράττειν τὰ ἴδια in antithesis to πολυπραγμοσύνη, that is, to πολιτικὴ πρᾶξις. "Love of the brothers" is expressed in avoidance of participation in political activity out of concern for the survival of the Christian community in the environment of the *polis*. Paul expresses it by using an old antithetical *topos*.

d. Paul's Logos (λόγος) in 1 Thessalonians

"Persuasion occurs through the arguments [*logoi*] when we show the truth or the apparent truth from whatever is persuasive in each case."[113] Proof, Aristotle posits, is available in two forms: enthymemes and examples (παραδείγματα), that is through either deductive or inductive reasoning.[114] Rhetorical reasoning is a faculty (δύναμις), thus part of a τέχνη, that leads to πίστις, not ἐπιστήμη. Paul uses both types of proof in 1 Thessalonians.

1. Examples[115]

Aristotle does not, strictly speaking, define the παράδειγμα, but the *Rhetorica ad Alexandrum* does: "Examples are actions that have occurred previously and are similar to, or the opposite of, those we are now dis-

---

112. Paul reflects an old idea, that ἡσυχία is achieved by πράττειν τὰ ἴδια. See Plato, *Respublica* 6.496D. Herodotus opposes τὰ ἴδια and τὰ δημόσια (Her. 5.63). Thucydides (1.82, 141) uses τὰ οἰκεῖα πράττειν as the antithesis to τὰ κοινὰ πράττειν.

113. *Ars rhetorica* 1.2.6: διὰ δὲ τοῦ λόγου πιστεύουσιν, ὅταν ἀληθὲς ἢ φαινόμενον δείξωμεν ἐκ τῶν περὶ ἕκαστα πιθανῶν.

114. Aristotle seems to add a third form of λόγος at the end of book 2, maxims (γνῶμαι). But one might regard maxims as generalized examples drawn from folk wisdom. In *Ars rhetorica* 1.2.8 Aristotle describes them as deductive and inductive reasoning.

115. There is a good discussion of examples in ancient rhetorical theory in Richard Volkmann, *Die Rhetorik der Griechen und Römer in systematischer Übersicht* (2nd ed.; Leipzig: B. G. Teubner, 1885) §23, pp. 233-39. For additional bibliography see DiCicco, *Paul's Use of Ethos, Pathos, and Logos*, 190, n. 290.

cussing."[116] Aristotle holds that examples are especially important for deliberative rhetoric, since we make decisions about the future on the basis of the past, while enthymemes are for forensic and amplification (αὔξησις) for epideictic.[117] Examples are of two kinds: "for to speak of things that have happened before is one species of paradigm and to make up [an illustration] is another."[118] Such fabricated examples may be comparisons or stories (παραβολαί, λόγοι). Yet, "Although it is easier to provide illustrations through fables, examples from history are more useful in deliberation; for generally, future events will be like those of the past" (2.20.8.1394a5-7).

Paul uses real, not fictive examples that are close in time to the Thessalonians, as [Anaximenes] suggests one should do,[119] and certainly well known to his audience.[120] He provides a positive example as he reminds them that they imitated both him and the Lord, when they received the word with joy in a time of great affliction (1:6). His reference to his taking courage after insult fills out the reference to imitation (2:2). Just as he had "taken courage to use freedom of speech to proclaim the gospel to them in a great struggle," so the word had echoed forth from them, not only in Macedonia but in all Achaia (1:7-8). By imitating him and the Lord they became models for others in their response to the word (1:7). His appeal to their memory of him in 3:6 reinforces his example of faith and endurance in suffering. In this connection it is useful to note Carey's comment on the "potential of narrative as proof,"[121] based on Aristotle's discussion of narrative and on exempla gathered from Demosthenes.[122]

Paul uses a form of σύγκρισις to give both a positive and a negative

---

116. [Anaximenes], *Rhetorica ad Alexandrum* 8.1429a21-23: παραδείγματα ἐστὶ πράξεις ὅμοιοι γεγενημέναι καὶ ἐναντίαι τοῖς νῦν ὑφ' ἡμῶν λεγομένοις. I cite from Aristotle, *Problems II. Books XXII-XXXVIII* (trans. W. S. Hett; ed. H. Rackham; *Rhetorica ad Alexandrum*; LCL; rev. ed.; Cambridge, Mass.: Harvard University Press; London: William Heinemann, 1983 =1957). Most likely, it dates from the fourth century B.C.E.; see George F. Kennedy, *The Art of Persuasion in Greece* (Princeton: Princeton University Press, 1963), 114-15.

117. *Ars rhetorica* 1.9.40.

118. *Ars rhetorica* 2.20.2.

119. [Anaximenes], *Rhetorica ad Alexandrum* 8.1430a7-9.

120. [Anaximenes], *Rhetorica ad Alexandrum* 32.1439a1-5.

121. Carey, "Rhetorical Means," 38-39.

122. *Ars rhetorica* 3.14.16a.

example in 2:14-16. When the Thessalonian Christians suffered at the hands of their Thessalonian neighbors, they imitated the churches in Judea, who remained faithful under persecution from the Jews. The mention of the Lord Jesus reminds one of 1:6 ("imitators of us and of the Lord"), while his reference to the eschatological wrath reinforces his repeated reference to the future in this letter (future wrath, 1:10; 2:16; 5:1-3; παρουσία, 2:19; 3:13; 4:13-18; 5:23). The example of Jesus combines suffering with resurrection and Lordship. The example of Paul and the churches of Judea combines suffering with fidelity in the face of the *parousia* as a basis for exhortation.

2. Enthymemes in 1 Thessalonians

How does Paul use enthymemes? Kennedy argues that Paul's reference to the Thessalonians' faith, hope, and love in 1:3 "takes the form of an enthymeme, whose proof is the presence of the Spirit."[123] Olbricht decodes the enthymemes that underlie Paul's argument about the *parousia* in 4:13–5:11.[124] Collins calls attention to the use of the particle γάρ in 2:3, 5, 9 and 4:14, 15; 5:2, 5, 7 as an indication of enthymemes that one must decode to understand Paul. One can similarly decode enthymemes in 4:1-9 and 4:9-12 that have as their basic premise "Christians live in a manner to please God" (4:2).[125] Paul uses that premise to describe sexual morality and life in a Greek *polis*. It is clear that he uses both example and enthymeme with telling effect.

3. And What of εὖ λέγειν? Style Is the Man!

Aristotle devotes the third book of his rhetoric to two topics: style (λέξις) and arrangement (τάξις).[126] "Mere rhetoric" is a put-down phrase designed to dismiss the art of rhetoric as the deceptive cloak put over falsehood to make it appear as truth. One recalls Aristophanes putting the two *logoi* on the stage in his *Nubes*, describing the one as "making the worse case appear the better." Or one recalls the debate between rhetoric (read

---

123. Kennedy, *Classical Rhetoric*, 142.
124. Olbricht, "An Aristotelian Rhetorical Analysis of 1 Thessalonians," 230-33.
125. Collins, *Birth*, 137.
126. *Ars rhetorica* 3.1.1.

sophistry) and philosophy as to which was the true teacher of Greece. The Gorgianic "figures of speech" (σχήματα λέξεως), which appear to many moderns as mere show, seemed to put the "figures of thought" (σχήματα διανοίας) aside.

New Testament scholarship often too quickly disregards this aspect of ancient rhetoric, which held that "to speak well" was also necessary to persuade. Little has been done since Johannes Weiss published his study of Paul's rhetoric back in 1897.[127] Olbricht devotes slightly more than two pages to a discussion of Paul's style. Aristotle lists the marks of good style (ἀρεταὶ λέξεως) as "perspicuity (σαφηνεία), purity (τὸ ἑλληνίζειν), elevation (ὄγκον τῆς λέξεως), and propriety (τὸ πρέπον)."[128] Paul's language is clear, not elevated but correct, fitting to the subject. He seems to avoid hiatus in 1 Thessalonians. I have not had the time to work at his clausulae — a subject once in vogue, now largely forgotten. There are no truly classical periods in 1 Thessalonians.

Paul uses some rhetorical figures. In 1 Thessalonians he more than once uses ἔλλειψις *(praeteriteo)*, for example in 1:8,[129] 4:9, and 5:1. He introduces the discussion of the *parousia* in 4:13 by a form of λιτότης *(litotes)*, a mild form of ironic expression to stress a point.[130] Weiss stresses his use of parallelism. Olbricht calls attention to Milligan's detection of *meiosis* in 2:15 and *chiasmus* in 5:6. The *polysyndeton* in 4:11 is probably natural (like that in 1:3), not artistic. Compare Paul to Demosthenes and Lysias or to Dio Chrysostom and Aelius Aristides, and one would not suspect him of having studied advanced — or even secondary — rhetorical education.

---

127. Johannes Weiss, "Beiträge zur Paulinischen Rhetorik," in *Theologische Studien* (Festschrift Bernhard Weiss; Göttingen: Vandenhoeck und Ruprecht, 1897), 163-247; also published separately with an index of places and different pagination.

128. Olbricht, "An Aristotelian Rhetorical Analysis of 1 Thessalonians," 233-35. These stylistic characteristics from Aristotle, *Ars rhetorica* 3.2.1-12.6.

129. Wuellner, "The Argumentative Structure," 128, stresses this *praeteriteo* as a key to the rhetorical situation. Collins, *Birth,* 157-58 discusses them as examples of passages that a thematic analysis often disregards, but a rhetorical analysis underscores.

130. For the definition see H. Lausberg, *Handbuch,* 304, §586.

5. Is Rhetorical Criticism Applicable to Letters?

Kennedy says that "The structure of a Greco-Roman letter resembles a speech, framed by a salutation and complimentary closure."[131] Scholars in recent years focused their research on rhetorical genre and oratorical structure as keys to the rhetorical analysis of Paul's letters. One should take note of a number of things about this research. One is that scholars make constant use of Latin rhetorical categories rather than Greek. This is not just a matter of linguistic *Spitzfindigkeit*. The language conceals a hidden assumption, that one can draw on the entire rhetorical tradition of Greece and Rome in New Testament rhetorical analysis. I question that assumption for a number of reasons. (a) The writing of handbooks often is a sign of the death of a discipline. Aristotle's life span saw the end of political oratory in Athens, while Cicero wrote his rhetorical treatises after his public life was over. Quintilian and most of the Greek rhetorical handbooks in Spengel's three volumes postdate both Paul and the practice of oratory, except for epideictic purposes. (b) Did Paul know any Latin? One should not take refuge in the assumption of some sort of generic school rhetoric. Rather than constantly refer to the handbooks, one might better cite actual examples of ancient oratory, for example, the Greek orators from Antiphon to Aeschines or the Latin Seneca Rhetor's *Controversiae* or *Suasoriae*.

In concluding his description of rhetorical means of proof Carey comments: "A persistent theme in this discussion has been the flexibility of oratorical procedure of the classical period in comparison with rhetorical theory."[132] The narrative is far more flexible than the handbooks lead one to expect. One should guard against making rhetorical theory a Procrustean bed to which, willy-nilly, texts must conform. Rhetorical criticism is most fruitful when it does not overpress its claims. That applies especially to the use of the divisions of an oration, when applied to a nonoratorical genre. I am not convinced that the *partitiones orationis* are as useful as some think, and feel that their application without attention to Aristotle's three modes of proof is not productive. We need to pay more attention to affective language and the ἀρεταὶ λέξεως as we interpret Paul. An oral society listened, even when it read, and so was more receptive to the σχήματα λέξεως and the σχήματα διανοίας.

131. Kennedy, *Classical Rhetoric*, 141.
132. Carey, "Rhetorical Means," 43.

Therefore, I agree with Thomas Olbricht's comment: "If Paul was affected by rhetoric, it was Greek rather than Roman."[133] The implication is that we have only two relevant treatises on rhetoric: Aristotle's *Ars rhetorica* and [Anaximenes'] *Rhetorica ad Alexandrum*. Everything else is too late or linguistically out of consideration. In addition, we have the surviving oratorical tradition in Greek, some earlier than Paul and some roughly contemporary. We should be looking to the ten-orator canon of classical antiquity and to such speakers as Dio Chrysostom[134] and Aelius Aristides, and such writers as Plutarch and Lucian, for texts to illustrate rhetorical practice. We tend to overrely on ancient textbooks without adequate attention to the actual speakers and writers of the language.

Wanamaker comments that thematic approaches tend "to fragment the letters into sequences of themes without sufficient attention to the unity of their argumentation and the rationale for their overall structure. [They] also ignore the literary reasons for the inclusion of individual themes and their relationship to one another."[135] Methinks he doth protest too much. Epistolary forms do not mandate fragmentation of thought in letter analysis any more than Aristotle's long list of τόποι in the *Ars rhetorica* does.

Reed cites the conclusion of "a distinguished classical scholar, W. Rhys Roberts," on Paul's rhetorical style:

> It is well thus briefly to remind ourselves that, among the early Christians, there were many writers, including Paul himself, who knew and appreciated ancient Greek literature, though concerning themselves little with formal rhetoric and literary criticism.[136]

---

133. Olbricht, "An Aristotelian Rhetorical Analysis of 1 Thessalonians," 221.

134. D. A. Russell, a distinguished interpreter of ancient Greek style and oratory, comments on Dio Chrysostom: "We have to remember both Dio's fame as an improviser, and his self-representation as a mere talker, an ἀδολέσχης, because that is what philosophers in the Socratic tradition were supposed to be. The rigid limits and structures imposed by the law courts and the rhetoricians were alien both to his talents and to his professed stance and technique" (*Dio Chrysostom: Orations VII, XII, and XXXVI*, ed. D. A. Russell [Cambridge: Cambridge University Press, 1992], 12). *Mutatis mutandis*, one should say the same about Paul.

135. Wanamaker, *The Epistle to the Thessalonians*, 45, referring approvingly to Jewett, *The Thessalonian Correspondence*, 68, who says that such approaches also allow "uncontrolled 'theological biases.'"

136. W. Rhys Roberts, *Greek Rhetoric and Literary Criticism* (New York: Longmans,

Norden agrees.[137] And these two great classicists of the first half of this century, both experts in Greek prose style and rhetoric, remind us of the value of rhetorical analysis and the need to use it with care and precision. For when we do, we do not press New Testament texts into categories not designed for them, nor act as though Paul does not write Greek as one at home in the culture of the early Roman Empire.

Green, and Co., 1928), as cited by Reed, "Using Ancient Rhetorical Categories to Interpret Paul's Letters," 322. See the comments by Russell on Dio in n. 134 above.

137. Eduard Norden, *Die antike Kunstprosa* (3rd printing; Leipzig and Berlin: B. G. Teubner, 1918), 2.493-94, argues against G. Heinrici, who finds much Hellenistic influence in Paul: "Gegen die Methode, mit der in diesem Werk die hellenische Literatur, vor allem die Redner und Philosophen, herangezogen werden, muß ich laut Protest erheben. Ich bitte denjenigen, der etwas von der antiken Rhetorik versteht — der Verfasser scheint seine wesentliche Kenntnis aus Volkmann zu schöpfen — die Kapitel 10–12 der zweiten Korintherbriefs zu lesen und sich zu fragen, ob er darin 'die bewährten Mittel der griechischen Verteidigungsrede' (493) erkennt: gewiß, insofern jeder Mensch, der sich zu verantworten hat, verwandte Töne anschlägt, aber muß er die von anderen erlernen?" . . . "Paulus ist ein Schriftsteller, den wenigstens ich nur sehr schwer verstehe; das erklärt sich mir aus zwei Gründen: einmal ist seine Art zu argumentieren fremdartig, und zweitens ist auch sein Stil, als Ganzes betrachtet, unhellenisch" (499).

"I Command That This Letter Be Read": Writing as a Manner of Speaking

Raymond F. Collins

Is it possible to synthesize an epistolary analysis of 1 Thessalonians with a rhetorical analysis of that same letter, presumably the first of Paul's epistolary compositions? This question goes beyond the more simple question of asking whether it is possible to glean some useful insights into 1 Thessalonians from first applying one type of analysis to the text and then the other. Thereafter one might ask which of the two analyses yielded the most fruitful insights, thereby coming to a conclusion that one or the other deserves to enjoy some sort of priority in the analysis of the text.

My question is not that of the successive application of the two competing analytical methods to Paul's letter; it is rather that of the simultaneous application of the two methods to a single analysis of the Pauline text. Would not a rhetorical-epistolary analysis of Paul's missive be more fruitful than a rhetorical analysis, an epistolary analysis, or a rhetorical and an epistolary analysis of the text? Is not a synthetic analysis of the text preferable to two separated and separable readings of the text? On any response to these questions, I would argue that one must begin with a historical-critical analysis of the text itself. From this point of departure, a reading of Paul's first letter to the Thessalonians suggests that his text ought to be read from a rhetorical-epistolary point of view.

1. 1 Thessalonians: A Speech Act

Twice in his letter Paul mentions his own writing to the Thessalonians. "You do not need to have anything written to you,"[1] he writes in 4:9 and 5:1 (NRSV). What Paul did not have to write about was, in the first instance, the love of the members of the community for one another, and, in the second instance, the times and the seasons. Each of these topics is identified by a textual marker, "now concerning" (περὶ δέ). Despite his professed disavowal of a need to write about mutual love and significant times, Paul does write about each of these topics. 1 Thess 4:9-13 is an isolable *topos* on (fictive) sibling love; 1 Thess 5:1-11 is a unit of *paraenesis* on the attitude that the recipients of Paul's letter should take to the impending eschaton.

a. Epistolary Preterition

In each instance Paul says what he is not going to do but goes ahead and does it. By identifying a topic not-to-be-treated and then treating it, Paul identifies and emphasizes the topic at hand. Paul's technique is a classic example of *praeteritio,* a rhetorical device well known to the ancient rhetoricians and used by them for the sake of emphasis. In each instance Paul offers a reason, introduced by the explanatory γάρ, as to why he does not have to write to the Thessalonians. In the first instance the alleged reason is that the Thessalonians have been God-taught to love one another and that they, in fact, do so (4:9b-10a). In the second instance the alleged reason is that the Thessalonians know full well that the Day of the Lord will come as unexpectedly as a thief in the night, as inevitably as the labor pains of a pregnant woman (5:1b-3).

In each of these cases the reason for the alleged omission is followed by an extended *paraenesis* on the topic at hand (4:11-13; 5:4-11). Paul's exhortation begins with a formula of direct address, "brothers and sisters," and is linked to the immediately preceding material by the connective conjunction δέ and a pronoun in the second person plural. Thus we have (1) the identification of a topic by means of the περὶ δέ formula, (2) a for-

---

1. See E. S. Malbon, "'No Need to Have Any One Write'?" A Structural Exegesis of 1 Thessalonians" (ed. Paul J. Achtemeier; SBLSP 19; Chico, Calif.: Scholars Press, 1980), 301-35; revised in *Semeia* 26 (1983): 57-83.

mula of omission, (3) a warrant for the omission, (4) the connective δε, together with a formula of direct address and a pronoun in the second person plural, and (5) an exhortation.

b. Rhetorical Preterition

1 Thessalonians contains yet a third instance of *praeteritio*, in 1:8c, where Paul says that "we have no need to speak about it." What there is no need of speaking about is the faith of the Thessalonians in God (1:8b). As in 4:9 and 5:1, the topic is identified, albeit without the directive "now concerning," before the preteritional formula is used. Similar to the way in which he will write in 4:9 and 5:1, Paul gives a reason as to why he has no need to speak to the Thessalonians about their faith. The reason, introduced by the explanatory γάρ, is that people throughout Macedonia and Achaia have been reporting on how the Thessalonians had turned to God from idols, with a resultant change in their behavioral attitude (1:9-10).

As in the two previous cases, the preterition is employed for the sake of emphasis. Paul's use of preterition to laud the faith of the Thessalonians may well serve to bolster the contention of those who identify the rhetorical genre of 1 Thessalonians as epideictic.[2] Characteristic of the genre is giving praise where praise is due and placing blame where blame is due. The most cursory reading of 1 Thessalonians quickly reveals that Paul considers the faith of the Thessalonians worthy of praise.

The three formulae of omission in 1 Thessalonians are linguistically similar to one another with one significant difference. The verb "to write" appears in 4:9 and 5:1; the verb "to speak" appears in 1:8. There appears to be functional similarity between these two verbs. This suggests that Paul considers his letter to the Thessalonians to be a speech act, in effect, an exercise of a rhetorical act. Although Paul uses "to write" only in 4:9 and 5:1, he uses "to speak" on three other occasions in his letter (2:2, 4, 16).

---

2. See R. Jewett, *The Thessalonian Correspondence: Pauline Rhetoric and Millenarian Piety* (FFNT; Philadelphia: Fortress, 1986), 71; G. Lyons, *Pauline Autobiography: Toward a New Understanding* (SBLDS 73; Atlanta: Scholars Press, 1985), 219-21; F. W. Hughes, "The Rhetoric of 1 Thessalonians," in *The Thessalonian Correspondence* (ed. R. F. Collins; BETL 87; Leuven: Leuven University Press–Peeters, 1990), 94-116; C. A. Wanamaker, *The Epistles to the Thessalonians: A Commentary on the Greek Text* (NIGTC; Grand Rapids: Eerdmans, 1990), 47.

c. Paul's Speech

In 2:16, which I deem to be authentic, Paul writes about the attempts that had been made to prevent him from speaking to Gentiles. In 2:1-4, however, he writes about his visit to the Thessalonians. In the course of that description he writes about his courage to speak out the good news in spite of great opposition (2:2). The verb that he uses (λαλεῖν) is the same verb that appears in the preteritional formula of 1:8, just three verses earlier.

In 2:2 Paul's describes his speaking out the gospel to the Thessalonians in terms that clearly identify it as a rhetorical exercise. Paul writes of his courage (ἐπαρρησιασάμεθα) in proclaiming the gospel. In both classical and Hellenistic Greek, courage bespeaks the orator's freedom, candor, and courage.[3] Demosthenes proclaimed, "I am going to speak to you openly" (μετὰ παρρησία; *2 Philip.* 6.31),[4] and Philo declared, "The man of worth has such courage of speech (παρρησία), that he is bold not only to speak and cry aloud, but actually to make an outcry of reproach, wrung from him by real conviction, and expressing true emotion" (*Heres*, 19).[5] The philosophers contrast the orator's boldness not only with timidity but also with flattery.[6]

Paul has reminded the Thessalonians that he spoke out among them in the face of great opposition (ἐν πολλῷ ἀγῶνι), a description that evokes the *agon* motif. It serves to compare Paul's appeal to the Thessalonians to the moral discourse of Cynics and Stoics, as they struggled on behalf of the truth and to exhort their followers to right conduct.[7] When Paul describes the purpose of his speaking out the gospel to the Thessalonians, he uses the rhetorical device of antithesis to emphasize that he spoke as he did, not to please his audience, but the God who had commissioned him to speak on his behalf. Indeed, the epistolary unit in which Paul writes about his

---

3. See W. C. van Unnik, "The Christian's Freedom of Speech in the New Testament," in *Sparsa Collecta* 2 (NovTSup 30; Leiden: Brill, 1980): 269-89; C. Spicq, *Theological Lexicon of the New Testament* (3 vols.; Peabody, Mass.: Hendrickson, 1994), 3.56-62.

4. See further *1 Philip.* 4.51; *4 Philip.* 10.53-54; *C. Aristoc.* 23.204; *C. Pant.* 37.55.

5. See further *Heres* 5, 6, 14, 21, 27, 29; *Sac.* 12; *Jos.* 73; *Plant.* 8; *Ebr.* 149; *Conf.* 165; *Praem.* 151; *Prob.* 95, 125, 152; *Spec.* 1.321; 3.138; 4.74; *Gaius* 41; etc.; see Wis 5:1; *T. Reub.* 4.2; Josephus, *Ant.* 15.37; 16.377.

6. See Dio Chrysostom, *Orationes* 32.26-27.

7. See V. C. Pfitzner, *Paul and the Agon Motif: Traditional Athletic Imagery in the Pauline Literature* (NovTSup 16; Leiden: Brill, 1967), especially pp. 23-37, 111-15, 126-29.

speaking (2:1-16), following almost immediately upon 1:8, is one that has manifest similarities with the discourse of his younger contemporary, Dio Chrysostom.[8]

d. Paul's Letter as Speech Act

A further indication that Paul "writes" as if his letter were a speech act is to be found in 4:15. 4:13-18 is the heart of Paul's letter insofar as it is in precisely this epistolary unit that Paul attempts to respond to the lacunae in the faith of the Thessalonians (3:10). In explaining[9] the implications of his argument that the early Christian creed pertaining to the death and resurrection of Jesus is such that the Thessalonians ought not to grieve like those outsiders who have no faith, Paul evokes an enigmatic word of the Lord (4:15-17). The origin of this apocalyptic utterance need not detain us here. What is pertinent to the present study is that Paul introduces the word of the Lord with this striking lemma, "for this we declare to you (ὑμῖν λέγομεν) by the word of the Lord." It is obvious that Paul is not speaking directly to the Thessalonians, yet he claims that he is speaking to them by means of his letter. Through his written word, he speaks. Once again, as in the case of the varying preteritional formulae, Paul writes as if his epistolary communication is a rhetorical act.

The point is not so much that Paul makes use of rhetorical devices, specifically preterition and apostrophe, and that his linguistic usage is to be clarified by an examination of the use of similar expressions by the ancient rhetoricians, as it is to affirm that the parallelism between 1:8 and 4:9; 5:1 and the way in which he writes in 4:15 suggest that Paul considers his writing to be a speech act. 2:1-4 suggests, in turn, that Paul understands his speech acts to be rhetorical exercises.

---

8. *Discourse* 32.11-12. See A. J. Malherbe, "'Gentle as a Nurse': The Cynic Background to 1 Thessalonians 2," *NovT* 12 (1970), 203-17; *Popular Philosophers* (Minneapolis: Fortress, 1989), 35-38, 45-46; *Paul and the Thessalonians: The Philosophic Tradition of Pastoral Care* (Philadelphia: Fortress, 1987), 3-4.

9. Note the explanatory γάρ in 4:15.

2. The Letter

What Paul wrote to the Thessalonians was a letter. The περὶ δέ formula found in the epistolary preteritions, but in no other place in the letter, suggests to some that Paul's letter to the Thessalonians might have been a letter written in response to a letter that the Thessalonians had written and that Timothy had brought with him on his return to Paul's side.[10] To be sure, the περὶ δέ formula is an epistolary convention, but it may simply be a handy formula for listing items that one wants to treat in sequence, rather than a specific indication that one is about to treat issues that had been raised in some correspondence that the author had previously received from those to whom he is writing.[11]

At the end of his letter Paul explicitly directed that his letter be read to all the brothers and sisters (5:27), that is, the entire Christian family in Thessalonica. In the Hellenistic world, as today, an author's use of the epistolary genre was most readily identified by the structure of the written text. Letters were identifiable because of the epistolary salutation and the closing conventions, which encompassed the body of the letter. The body of the letter, which sometimes began with a thanksgiving to one or another deity, contained the letter's main message.

a. Its Opening and Its Closing

Like other Hellenistic letters, Paul's letter to the Thessalonians has an epistolary salutation (1:1) and is brought to a close with various closing conventions (5:23-28). The body of the letter bespeaks the warm relationship that existed between Paul and the Thessalonians. Paul reminisces fondly about his visit to the Thessalonians and what he has heard about the results of that visit. Paul thanks God for those fond memories and for what happened as a result of his visit (1:2–2:16). He writes passionately about his desire to visit the Thessalonians a second time and the anguish that was

10. See C. E. Faw, "On the Writing of First Thessalonians," *JBL* 71 (1952): 217-25; A. J. Malherbe, "Did the Thessalonians Write to Paul?" in *The Conversation Continues: Studies in Paul and John. In Honor of J. Louis Martyn* (ed. R. T. Fortna and B. R. Gaventa; Nashville: Abingdon, 1990), 246-57.

11. See M. M. Mitchell, "Concerning *peri de* in 1 Corinthians," *NovT* 31 (1989): 229-56.

his when he was unable to visit the Thessalonians (2:17–3:5). He shares with the Thessalonians his prayer that God and the Lord Jesus will enable him to visit the Thessalonians once again (3:10-11). News about the Thessalonians was encouraging to Paul and brought him joy,[12] even in the midst of the difficulties that he was experiencing (3:6-9).

Expressions that bespeak the close relationship between Paul and the Thessalonians abound throughout the letter. None is more striking than his use of kinship language to bespeak the bonds that tie him to his beloved Thessalonians. Fourteen times he addresses them as his brothers and sisters (ἀδελφοί).[13] The repeated refrain represents a density of usage unparalleled in the extant Pauline correspondence. The first time that Paul addresses the Thessalonians as his siblings, he describes them as beloved by God (1:4). As he brings his letter to a close, he refers to the Thessalonians as his siblings, not once or twice, but three times (5:25, 26, 27).

Paul uses maternal (2:7) and paternal (2:11) imagery to speak of his own relationship with the Thessalonians. He speaks of them as if they were his own children. Developing the first image, he writes of his care for the Thessalonians[14] and his willingness to give part of his life for them (2:8). Lest he be burdensome to them, he worked night and day (2:9). In turn the Thessalonians were very dear to Paul (2:8). When Paul was separated from them, he felt abandoned, almost as if he were an orphan (2:17). He could hardly bear the separation (3:5). Knowing what kind of people Paul and his companions were (1:5; 2:10), the Thessalonians patterned their lives after the example of Paul (1:6).

b. A Friendly Letter

To one reading language such as this in Paul's letter to the Thessalonians, it would appear that what Paul wrote was a friendly letter. It was "written as to a friend," to use the words of the manual attributed to Pseudo-Demetrius. As a textbook example of the friendly letter, the handbook offers the following model:

---

12. See 2:20.
13. 1:4; 2:1, 9, 14, 17; 3:7; 4:1, 10, 13; 5:1, 4, 12, 14, 25.
14. See, however, N. Baumert, "'Ομειρόμενοι in 1 Thess 2,8," *Bib* 68 (1987): 552-63.

Even though I have been separated from you for a long time, I suffer this in body only. For I can never forget you or the impeccable way we were raised together from childhood up. Knowing that I myself am genuinely concerned about your affairs, and that I have worked unstintingly for what is most advantageous to you, I have assumed that you, too, have the same opinion of me, and will refuse me in nothing. You will do well, therefore, to give close attention to the members of my household lest they need anything, to assist them in whatever they might need, and to write us about whatever you should choose.[15]

Paul appears to have followed scrupulously Pseudo-Demetrius's model even though it is highly unlikely that he had ever read the manual, which, in any case, may not have been composed until some decades after Paul's death.

The model proposed by Pseudo-Demetrius suggests that, even in the friendly letter, close attention should be paid to needs (χρεία). Having spoken of the bonds that link the letter-writer to the addressee, the author of the friendly letter is encouraged to urge the recipient to care for the members of the author's household. The preteritional formulae of 4:9 and 5:1 speak of needs (χρεία) that do not have to be met. Paul, nonetheless, pays considerable attention to these needs in the exhortations of 4:9-12 and 5:1-11. Paul's letter speaks of another kind of need experienced by the Thessalonians, namely, what is lacking (τὰ ὑστερήματα) in their faith (3:10). Paul vicariously experiences this lack to such a degree that he expresses a constant prayer that he might be able to visit the Thessalonians so as to compensate for what is lacking in their faith. What is lacking are "needs rather than deficiencies."[16] Although Paul expresses a strong wish and a prayer that he might be enabled to visit, face to face, with the Thessalonians so as to compensate for this lack, Paul must accommodate to the situation at hand. His letter to the Thessalonians takes the place of a personal visit; its principal concern was to satisfy the faith needs of the Thessalonians.[17]

As far as taking care of members of the household, Pseudo-Demetrius's τοὺς ἐν οἴκῳ, Paul urges the Thessalonians to build one an-

15. Pseudo-Demetrius, *Epistolary Types*, 1.

16. C. Spicq, *Theological Lexicon*, 3.427-31, p. 431.

17. R. F. Collins, *The Birth of the New Testament: The Origin and Development of the First Christian Generation* (New York: Crossroad, 1993), 150-60.

other up (οἰκοδομεῖτε εἰς τὸν ἕνα, 5:11). This general exhortation is fleshed out when immediately thereafter he urges his siblings (5:12, 14) to have respect and love for those who lead the household, to have peace among themselves and do good to one another, and to be especially solicitous for the disorderly, the fainthearted, and the weak among them.

c. Echoes of Orality

While Paul's letter to the Thessalonians clearly corresponds to the type of personal letter outlined by Pseudo-Demetrius, his letter is most clearly recognized as a letter in the structural component of its form, that is, its opening and closing conventions. In 1 Thessalonians each of these epistolary units bears the echo of orality. It is commonly observed that the typical opening salutation in a Hellenistic letter was "rejoice" (χαίρειν) and that the final farewell took the form of a good-by (ἔρρωσο, ἐρρῶσθαι), frequently accompanied by a reference to the recipient, usually in the vocative case.[18] Paul's closing has a reference to the recipients in the vocative case, his constant ἀδελφοί (5:25), but his farewell wish is not "be strong"; rather, it is "the grace of our Lord Jesus Christ be with you" (5:28). The formula forms a literary *inclusio* with the opening salutation, ". . . to the church of the Thessalonians in God the Father and the Lord Jesus Christ, grace to you and peace."[19]

For the simple and common epistolary greeting of his day, Paul has substituted — apparently for the first time in the extant literature — a complex and theologically compact wish. The wish has a formulaic character and has some redundancy with the previous expression of direct address (note the two datives, ἐκκλησίᾳ, ὑμῖν). Each of these qualities suggests that Paul's greeting had an independent existence prior to its incorporation into Paul's first letter. Its "grace and peace" suggest that it may have been a liturgical formula, originating in some bicultural Christian community,[20] which Paul has

18. See J. A. D. Weima, *Neglected Endings: The Significance of the Pauline Letter Closings* (JSNTSup 101; Sheffield: JSOT, 1994), 28-34.

19. One might observe that the opening salutation's references to God and to peace are echoed in the formulaic expression "God of peace," with which Paul begins his final wish-prayer (5:23).

20. See B. Rigaux, *Saint Paul. Les Épitres aux Thessaloniciens* (EtB; Paris: Gabalda; Gembloux: Duculot, 1956), 354-55; Collins, *The Birth of the New Testament*, 148-49.

taken over as an expression of his wish for the Christian assembly in Thessalonica and which he has substituted for the commonplace salutation of Hellenistic letters in this first of his letters, an experiment in Christian writing.[21]

The pronouns in both the opening and closing salutation are in the second person plural (ὑμῖν, ὑμῶν). The first pronoun echoes the "church of the Thessalonians" of 1:1b, the second the "all the brothers and sisters" of 5:27. What is first echoed is a collective noun; the second echo is that of a collective expression. Obviously Paul intends to greet more than one person. In a society in which literacy was limited,[22] Paul's greetings to a group of persons addressed in the second person plural suggest that his letter is to be read to them. Their experience of those to whom the letter was addressed was not visual; it was auditory.

That this was indeed the case is confirmed by the unusually strong exhortation[23] of 5:27, "I solemnly command you by the Lord that this letter be read to all the brothers and sisters." As a closing exhortation it is without parallel in the New Testament.[24] Its presence in 1 Thessalonians may well reflect the experimental character of Paul's first letter. Paul intended that his letter be read to the assembly of Christians at Thessalonica.[25] His injunction serves as a reminder that he was self-consciously aware that his message to the Thessalonians would be conveyed to them in oral fashion and that he intended that this be so. Essentially he was urging that the letter would serve as the medium by which his communication would be conveyed to the Thessalonians, even though they and he were physically at a distance from each other.

Paul's use of a verb in the first person singular, "I solemnly command you," is striking. Among the Pauline letters 1 Thessalonians is singular in

21. See H. Koester, "I Thessalonians — Experiment in Christian Writing" in *Continuity and Discontinuity in Church History* (Festschrift G. H. Williams; SHCT 19; Leiden: Brill, 1979), 33-44.

22. Some studies suggest that the rate of literacy was a mere 5 percent.

23. The emphatic compound ἐνορκίζω is a hapax in the New Testament. Κύριος is a title that implies authority. A command uttered in the name of the Lord is one that demands a positive response. Paul frequently adopts the Κύριος vocabulary so as to give weight to his *paraenesis*.

24. See Col 4:16, but the Paulinist uses only the verb ἀναγινώσκω.

25. See 1 Thess 1:1. Also R. F. Collins, "'. . . that this letter be read to all the brethren,'" *LS* 9 (1982-83): 122-27; reprinted in *Studies on the First Letter to the Thessalonians* (BETL 66; Leuven: Leuven University Press–Peeters, 1984), 365-70.

the consistency of its use of the first person plural. Paul has associated Silvanus and Timothy with himself in the letter's *homilia,* its message. Prior to 5:27, a verb in the first person singular appears in 1 Thessalonians only in 3:5 (ἔπεμψα, "I sent"). Pronouns in the first person singular appear only in 3:5 and 2:18, two passages in which Paul speaks of his personal desire to be with the Thessalonians once again.

In the Hellenistic era it was not unusual for letter-writers to append a personal greeting to their letters when these letters were written by scribes.[26] The papyri offer many examples in which the handwriting of the final greeting is quite distinct from the calligraphy of the body of the letter. The body was written by a scribe; the final greeting by the author of the letter himself. Paul is known to have used scribes (Rom 16:22). Sometimes he added personal greetings to his correspondence, in the large letters of his own hand (1 Cor 16:21; Gal 6:11; Philem 19).[27] Given this situation, it is quite likely that the first person singular conjugation of 5:27 is an indication that Paul had employed a scribe for the physical production of 1 Thess 1:1–5:26 and that 5:27-28 are a personal exhortation and greeting to the gathering of Christians in Thessalonica.[28]

3. An Oral Communication

On the likelihood that 1 Thessalonians represents a dictated composition, is it possible to find traces of orality in the letter itself? Paul was a letter-writer. By his own admission he acknowledges that he is a letter-writer.[29] Paul, the letter-writer, was a significant *Paulusbild* in the early church, one to which the extant deutero-Pauline literature bears ample witness.[30] But

26. The practice was not unlike that of many contemporaries who add to a computer-produced business letter a personal note in their own hand.

27. See Col 4:18; 2 Thess 3:17.

28. See R. F. Collins, "Paul, as seen through his own eyes," *LS* 8 (1980-81): 348-81, especially 353-55; reprinted in *Studies on the First Letter,* 175-208, especially 178-80; E. R. Richards, *The Secretary in the Letters of Paul* (WUNT 2/42; Tübingen: Mohr, 1991), especially 189, n. 281; J. Murphy-O'Connor, *Paul the Letter-Writer: His World, His Options, His Skills* (GNS 41; Collegeville, Minn.: Liturgical Press, 1995), 7.

29. 5:27; 1 Cor 5:9; 2 Cor 3:1; 7:8, 12; 10:9-11.

30. See especially 2 Thess 2:2, 15; 3:14, 17. See R. F. Collins, *Letters That Paul Did Not Write: The Epistle to the Hebrews and the Pauline Pseudepigrapha* (GNS 28; Wilmington, Del.: Glazier, 1988), 237.

Paul was also an orator. His rehearsal of his visit to the Thessalonians is one in which he dwells on the nature and quality of his oratory (2:1-12). That Paul was an orator, that is, a preacher, was a most important *Paulusbild* in the early church, one to which the Acts of the Apostles bears witness.

The reality of an orator who is a letter-writer suggests the likelihood that some evidence of oratory is to be found in the letters dictated by the orator.[31] The letters of Cicero are a case in point. How about Paul? Does 1 Thessalonians show evidence of Paul's oratorical skills? Does it provide evidence of being an oral composition? *Praeteritio* is, as has been noted, a common rhetorical device. It is used by Paul in 1:8; 4:9; 5:1. The rhetorical force of antithesis was noted by Aristotle and other ancient rhetoricians. As a rhetorical device, *praeteritio* is a subtle form of contrast. Paul is explicit in the use of contrast for emphasis's sake when he employs the rhetorical device of antithesis. The entire letter is characterized by Paul's antithetical expression of his thought (1:5, 8; 2:3-4, 5-8, 13, 17; 4:4-5, 7, 8; 5:9, 15).

There are yet other indications of an orator at work in the composition of 1 Thessalonians. Among the most obvious are Paul's use of apostrophe and *repetitio*. The former is the rhetorical device whereby the rhetor directly appeals to his audience. The fourteen occurrences of "brothers and sisters" (ἀδελφοί, in the vocative)[32] that punctuate the letter are one indication of Paul's use of apostrophe. Apart from an expression of direct address in the closing of the letter, formulae of direct address are generally not to be found in the bodies of Hellenistic letters. Paul's use of an apostrophaic ἀδελφοί is a feature of 1 Thessalonians. Paul's preferred formula of direct and familiar address is found in this letter in a rare concentration.

Paul's use of a disclosure formula in 4:13 is another example of Paul's direct appeal to his audience, the rhetorical device of apostrophe.[33] Yet another indication of Paul's use of this device is the recall motif found in 1:5; 2:1, 9; and 4:1. Another well-known rhetorical device used by Paul is *repetitio*. A particularly effective use of *repetitio* is to be found in some of

---

31. That this is to be expected was confirmed for me by Dr. Peter Judge, a former student, who told me that on reading one of my books he could hear my voice in class.

32. 1 Thess 1:4; 2:1, 9, 14, 17; 3:7; 4:1, 10, 13; 5:1, 4, 12, 14, 25.

33. See 2:10.

his triadic expressions,[34] where the repetition of virtual synonyms does not so much advance or qualify the thought as it uses redundancy for the sake of emphasis. This kind of rhetorical repetition is found in 1:5; 2:3, 10, 11; 5:12; and perhaps 5:23.

A more subtle, although rhetorically effective form of Paul's appeal to the Thessalonians is his use of the first person plural in the two apocalyptic disclosure pericopes that embody the letter's particular message. In 4:13-18, Paul uses an emphatic "we" (ἡμεῖς) on two occasions and twice uses a verb in the first person plural so as to affirm the solidarity that exists between himself and the Thessalonians. In 5:1-11, a hortatory "we" characterizes Paul's exhortation and the shared conviction that he and the Thessalonians are awaiting salvation through the Lord Jesus Christ (5:6-10).

Sure evidence of the orality of 1 Thessalonians is to be found in the staccato *paraenesis*[35] (5:16-22) which precedes Paul's final wish prayer. The repeated sound of "p" punctuates the entire paraenetic unit: πάντοτε . . . προσεύχεσθε . . . παντὶ . . . πνεῦμα . . . προφητείας . . . πάντα . . . παντὸς εἴδους πονηροῦ. The alliteration, lost in English translation, "always . . . pray . . . all . . . spirit . . . prophets . . . everything . . . every form of evil," has a rhetorical force that it would not have in a merely literal composition.

As a final indication of the orality of 1 Thessalonians, one might cite the mild oaths found in 2:5 and 2:10. The latter is also an example of Paul's direct appeal to his audience. The oaths themselves are rhetorical asides that Paul used to impart emphasis to the appeal that he was making to the Thessalonians. In a letter as friendly as 1 Thessalonians Paul hardly had need of an oath to affirm the truth of his utterance.

1 Thess 5:27 clearly directs that Paul's letter was to be read to the

---

34. Abraham Smith accurately notes that the readers and listeners of 1 Thessalonians would have noted an overall immanent structure which emphasized a love for threes." See A. Smith, "The Social and Ethical Implications of the Pauline Rhetoric in I Thessalonians" (Unpubl. Vanderbilt Ph.D. diss., 1989), 93.

35. Calvin Roetzel describes Paul's exhortation as "shotgun *paraenesis*" and comments that, ". . . one senses that the end of the conversation is near. The stoccado imperatives quicken the pace. The hasty speech, however, resembles neither animated conversation nor heated argument but the dialogue of an eager and earnest conversation partner bent on completing important business before he bids farewell." See C. J. Roetzel, "I Thess. 5:12-28: A Case Study," *SBLSP* (ed. Lane C. McGaughy; 2 vols.; N.P.: Society of Biblical Literature, 1972), 2.367-83, 375.

Thessalonians. Its use of a verb in the first person singular suggests that Paul had dictated his letter to the Thessalonians. His letter was, in the circumstances of his absence from the Thessalonians, the way in which his oral communication was in fact communicated to them. It was "written" by someone who was speaking. It was read to a gathering of Thessalonians who heard it. It was, in fact, an oral communication, from speaker to hearer. In this respect Paul's letter to the Thessalonians, whose epistolary aspects are in so many respects similar to the letters of today, is quite different from letters written at the end of the twentieth century. We write letters without benefit of the pronunciation of their words; we expect that they will be read by one's eyes rather than that the message of the letter will be grasped as a result of an auditory experience.

Paul wrote letters to overcome the distance between the speaker and his audience. His letter was a means for long-distance oral communication. Were we to attempt to do something similar today we would probably employ the telephone, or perhaps the television, a video recording, or a tape recording. Obviously, such technological troves were unavailable to Paul almost two millennia ago. Hence, he could employ only the written word to serve as the means whereby his oral communication would be conveyed to his beloved Thessalonians in oral fashion. The echoes of orality found in the traces of the written word confirm the mode of communication of the letter, which is itself an act of communication.

4. The Epistolary Function of the Thanksgiving and of the Peace Blessing

The structural elements of its salutation and its particular collection of closing conventions are the most distinctive features of the Hellenistic letter. In Paul's letter to the Thessalonians, what comes between the epistolary opening and the epistolary closing is a fairly long composition that begins with a lengthy thanksgiving (1:2–2:12) and concludes with a wishprayer (5:23-24). These elements are characteristic of 1 Thessalonians as the first of Paul's apostolic letters.

The thanksgiving periods of Paul's letters are, as Schubert noted,[36]

---

36. See P. Schubert, *Form and Function of the Pauline Thanksgivings* (BZNW 20; Berlin: Töpelmann, 1939), 173.

examples of a definite and widely used Hellenistic epistolographic pattern. Even if an epistolary thanksgiving is not to be found in every extant Hellenistic letter, the thanksgiving is a typical feature of the Hellenistic epistolary genre. Accordingly, any epistolary analysis of Paul's Letter to the Thessalonians must pay due attention to Paul's opening thanksgiving. It is, in fact, not so much a thanksgiving as it is a report on Paul's thanksgiving.[37] The thanksgiving is addressed to God, not in the second person, but in the third person.

As a report on his thanksgiving, which he addresses to God because of the remembrance that he has of the Thessalonians, Paul's initial thanksgiving functions within his letter as a kind of *captatio benevolentiae*. The quality of the Thessalonians' life in faith and love, noted throughout the entire area, is what has moved Paul to give thanks. The very mention of the reason for Paul's thanksgiving lauds the Thessalonians. According to Wiles's epistolary analysis of Paul's thanksgiving, 1:3 announces the main subject matter of Paul's letter.[38] It anticipates the train of thought that Paul is about to unfold in the letter.

The peace blessing of 5:23, as those of other Pauline letters, marks the beginning of Paul's letter-closing.[39] In this respect the peace blessing is a feature of the Pauline letter, but such a wish-prayer, at the conclusion of a letter, is not characteristic of the Hellenistic letter genre. It does not find its counterpart in extant Hellenistic letters. The presence of the peace blessing at the conclusion of the Pauline letter may reflect the apostle's expectation that his letter be read to the assembly and his desire to impart a final blessing on the community. In terms of its form, it resembles that of the Jewish homiletic benediction.[40]

The peace blessing is a structural element of the Pauline letter. Like the opening thanksgiving, it is an expression of performative language, but one might nonetheless ask what is the function of the peace blessing with respect to the letter's own function as the conveyor of a message. Struc-

37. From the standpoint of modern linguistic analysis, the prayer report can be cited as an example of performative language.

38. See G. Wiles, *Paul's Intercessory Prayers: The Significance of the Intercessory Prayer Passages in the Letters of St. Paul* (SNTSMS 24; Cambridge: Cambridge University Press, 1974), 175.

39. See Weima, *Neglected Endings*, 184.

40. See R. Jewett, "The Form and Function of the Homiletic Benediction," *ATR* 51 (1969): 18-34.

turally the final wish-prayer begins the closing of the letter. What does it tell the community of the Thessalonians in addition to being an expression of Paul's pastoral concern for them? Essentially the peace blessing recapitulates the letter by echoing its major themes and concerns. Despite its manifest semitisms, the peace blessing appears to be a Pauline composition insofar as much of its vocabulary represents the language of the letter itself. The blessing incorporates many of the major motifs of the body of the letter, for example, the sanctification of the community and the *parousia,* and serves to reinforce Paul's encouragement of the community.[41] From the standpoint of those who heard the reading of the peace blessings, its words echoed and summed up the principal elements of the letter's message.

5. Rhetoric

If, as Wanamaker has suggested, 1 Thess 5:23 sums up the dominant theme of the whole letter, that is, *paraenesis* for Christian living,[42] the letter has as its essential purpose to urge the Thessalonians to live as Christians ought to live. Rhetoric, says Aristotle, "may be defined as the faculty of discovering the possible means of persuasion in reference to any subject whatever."[43] If the purpose of Paul's letter is to encourage and exhort the Christians of Thessalonica to live as Christians ought to live, even if they are doing so already (4:1), then it is reasonable to presume that Paul would have attempted to find a way to persuade the Thessalonians in this regard. Such an attempt is of the very essence of rhetoric.

Attempts to impose the rigid format of the *taxis (dispositio)* as taught in schools of rhetoric particularly with respect to the composition of a forensic speech sometimes lead to an analysis of Paul's letters that some may find artificial and restrictive.[44] Nonetheless, some of the functional aspects of the elements of the *taxis* appear to be present in Paul's letter to the

---

41. See P.-E. Langevin, "L'intervention de Dieu selon I Thes 5,23-24," in *The Thessalonian Correspondence,* 236-56, especially 254-55. See further R. Jewett, "Form and Function," 24; Wiles, *Intercessory Prayers,* 68; Weima, *Neglected Endings,* 92-95, 177, 183-84.

42. Wanamaker, *The Epistles to Thessalonians,* 207.

43. *Ars rhetorica* 1.2.1.

44. See, e.g., E. J. Richard, *First and Second Thessalonians* (SP 11; Collegeville, Minn.: Liturgical Press/Michael Glazier, 1995), 14, n. 22.

Thessalonians. Paul's opening thanksgiving offers a double rehearsal of the events attendant on his visit to the Thessalonians, that is, the impact of the gospel on the life of the Thessalonians (1:2-10) and the preaching of the gospel from the standpoint of those who preached it (2:1-12). The lengthy thanksgiving served Paul's communication as a kind of *captatio benevolentiae* and provided him and his audience with a common form of reference on the basis of which Paul would develop the later message of his letter. These two functions of Paul's epistolary thanksgiving are, however, the function of the *proemium (exordium)* and the *diegesis (narratio)* in classical rhetorical theory. Describing the *exordium* of a speech, Aristotle noted that, "the object of an appeal to the hearer is to make him well disposed or to arouse his indignation, and sometimes to engage his attention or the opposite."[45] Paul's letter, as the good speech, reached out to his audience and established the perspective on the basis of which further communication could be developed.

Aristotle described the rhetorical epilogue as being "composed of four parts: to dispose the hearer favorably towards oneself and unfavorably towards the adversary; to amplify and depreciate; to excite the emotions of the hearer; to recapitulate."[46] The philosopher concluded his treatise on rhetoric with this remark: "To the conclusion of the speech the most appropriate style is that which has no connecting particles, in order that it may be a peroration, but not an oration: 'I have spoken; you have heard; you know the facts; now give your decision.'"[47]

These characteristics of the rhetorical closing are so many appropriate descriptions of the epistolary closing of 1 Thessalonians. The peace blessing of 5:23 not only serves to summarize the main themes of Paul's letter; it also — as part of a communication to the Thessalonians, as distinct from a communication addressed to God on their behalf — serves to capture the goodwill of the Thessalonians. Paul prays for them (v 23) as he urges them to pray for him (v 25). Indeed, the final wish, presumably in his own hand, is a prayer for them.

Even Aristotle's remark about the appropriate lack of connective particles in the closing of a speech is apropos to Paul's way of bringing to a close his letter to the Thessalonians. Although the connective particle δέ

45. *Ars rhetorica* 3.14.7.
46. *Ars rhetorica* 3.19.1.
47. *Ars rhetorica* 3.19.6.

links the peace blessing with the staccato *paraenesis* of 5:16-22, the closing verses of the letter are strikingly devoid of particles. Apart from the particle δέ in verse 23, the only connective particles found in the final thirteen verses of 1 Thessalonians are an explanatory γάρ in verse 18 and a connective δέ in verse 21.[48]

Other features of the good speech, according to Aristotle's understanding of good rhetoric, are also to be found in Paul's letter to the Thessalonians. Aristotle speaks of the rhetorical device of antithesis, noting that, "This kind of style is pleasing, because contraries are easily understood and even more so when placed side by side, and also because antithesis resembles a syllogism."[49] He observes that antithesis contributes to "popularity of form."[50] As for metaphor, "most smart sayings are derived from metaphor,"[51] and again, "smart sayings are derived from proportional metaphor and expressions which set things before the eyes."[52] Metaphor is not as prevalent in 1 Thessalonians as it is in some of Paul's later letters, especially his first letter to the Corinthians, but 1 Thessalonians is hardly devoid of metaphor. It employs similes[53] (2:7, 11; 5:2, 3, 4) and simple metaphors (1:9; 2:2, 17; 4:4, 13 [14, 15], 16; 5:5, 8, 10, 19). Putting things before the eyes of the audience is what Aristotle calls "actuality" (ἐνέργεια).[54] "We ought therefore to aim at three things — metaphor, antithesis, actuality."[55] Paul may not have read Aristotle, but in the composition of 1 Thessalonians he certainly took aim at the three stylistic features highlighted by the philosopher. His imaginative language, which extends beyond the apocalyptic periods of 4:13-18 and 5:1-11, is an example of what the philosopher would describe as actuality.

Paul's letter begins in classic Hellenistic epistolary style, with the names of himself, Silvanus, and Timothy as the senders of the letter. The

48. The particle was omitted by the *prima manus* of Sinaiticus and is not found in A and several other ancient manuscripts.

49. *Ars rhetorica* 3.9.8.

50. *Ars rhetorica* 3.10.5.

51. *Ars rhetorica* 3.11.6. On metaphor, see further *Ars rhetorica* 3.10-11.

52. *Ars rhetorica* 3.11.1.

53. The simile, says Aristotle, "is a metaphor; for there is very little difference. . . . the simile is also useful in prose, but should be less frequently used, for there is something poetical about it" (*Ars rhetorica* 3.4.1-2; see 3.10.3; 3.11.11). The difference, he notes in 3.10.3, is the addition of a word.

54. *Ars rhetorica* 3.11.2.

55. *Ars rhetorica* 3.10.6.

three names are given without further qualification. In this first of his letters Paul does not make use of an epistolary *intitulatio*, as he customarily does in his late letters. "Apostle" is the epithet that he would choose for himself as he wrote Romans, 1-2 Corinthians, and Galatians. Paul's use of this epistolary *intitulatio* was so remarkable that it was taken over by the Paulinists who wrote Ephesians, Colossians, and each of the Pastorals. The designation occurs just once in 1 Thessalonians, where it is buried away in 2:7 as an appropriate description of Paul and his two companions.

Although his letter lacks an epistolary *intitulatio*, Paul does remind the Thessalonians of who he was for them in his rehearsal of his visit to them in 1:5b–2:13. 2:1-12, so similar in form and content to the words of Dio Chrysostom (see above), sets clearly in the eye of the Thessalonians' memory who Paul was for them. He and his companions were men of integrity, men on a mission, men concerned for the Thessalonians themselves.

Reading what Paul has to say about the kind of persons he and his companions were reminds us that, for Aristotle, the first kind of proof in a speech is that which depends on "the moral character of the speaker."[56] "The orator persuades by moral character (ἦθος)," he says, "when his speech is delivered in such a manner as to render him worthy of confidence; for we feel confidence in a greater degree and more readily in persons of worth in regard to everything in general, but where there is no certainty and there is room for doubt, our confidence is absolute. But this confidence must be due to the speech itself, not to any preconceived idea of the speaker's character."[57] Paul's rehearsal of his visit to the Thessalonians, a kind reminiscence at the beginning of his letter (2:1-12), enables him to set before the Thessalonians the moral character of himself and his companions. Having witnessed to his own integrity, he can later urge the Thessalonians to love one another as he has loved them (3:12).

6. Paul's Letter, an Exercise in Rhetoric

In sum, Paul's letter to the Thessalonians gives ample evidence that the apostle's manner of composing his letter was analogous to the way in

56. *Ars rhetorica* 1.2.3.
57. *Ars rhetorica* 1.2.4.

which Hellenistic rhetors composed their speeches. The vocabulary, style, and postscript of the letter indicate that Paul "wrote" it as a speech-act. In historical retrospect this is not surprising. Cicero (106-43 B.C.E.), the earliest Latin author to reflect self-consciously on letter-writing, writes about letter-writing as a speech-act *(iocari, colloqui)*.[58]

In the Hellenistic world, letter-writing was taught in the schools of rhetoric. The first rule of epistolary style is classic. It was borrowed from Artemon, Aristotle's commentator, by Demetrius, who wrote: "It is necessary to write letters in the same manner as a dialogue, for a letter is like the other half of a dialogue (τὸν ἕτερον μέρος τοῦ διαλογοῦ)."[59] In a similar vein, Pseudo-Libanius wrote, "A letter is a kind of written conversation (ὁμιλία τις ἐγγράμματος) with someone from whom one is separated, and it fulfills a definite need. One will speak in it as though one were in the company of the absent person."[60] Demetrius, nevertheless, offered a qualifying reflection. "There is," he wrote, "perhaps some truth in what he [Artemon] says, but not the whole truth. The letter should be a little more studied than the dialogue, since the latter reproduces an extemporary utterance, while the former is committed to writing and is sent as a kind of gift."[61] In analogous fashion, Pseudo-Libanius said that the letter-writer should "adorn the letter with excellence of style, and use the Attic style with moderation."[62] In turn, Philostratus of Lemnos (third century C.E.) would comment that a letter should adopt a form of speech more formal than that of common communication. It should, he noted, be characterized by a kind of language appropriate to public speech with appropriate elegance.[63]

The historian is well aware that the real letters of the Hellenistic world did not correspond to the textbook examples of the rhetorical man-

---

58. See K. Thraede, *Grundzüge griechisch-römisch Brieftopik* (*Zet* 48; Munich: Beck, 1970), 46; M. Bünker, *Briefformular und rhetorische Disposition im 1.Korintherbrief* (GTA 28; Göttingen: Vandenhoeck und Ruprecht, 1983), 24. Bünker adds that Seneca, Ovid, and Pliny stand in this same tradition.

59. *De elocutione* 223.

60. *Epistolary Styles* 2.

61. *De elocutione* 224.

62. *Epistolary Styles* 46.

63. *De epistulis* (ed. C. L. Kayser; *Flavii Philostrati Opera* [BSGRT; 2 vols., Leipzig: Teubner, 1870-1871; repr. Hildesheim, 1964], 258); Eng. trans. in *Ancient Epistolary Theorists* (ed. A. J. Malherbe; SBLSBS 19; Atlanta: Scholars Press, 1988), 43.

uals. The norms that are expressed in these works are somewhat artificial. They are an abstract induction from actual epistolary practice. A real letter did not correspond exactly to the textbook example nor did it perfectly conform to the norms set out in the manuals. In this respect the writers of ancient letters were similar to modern letter-writers, whose letters do not perfectly conform to what is taught in school. The ancient masters of epistolary technique were well aware of this. Demetrius himself commented that there should be "a certain degree of freedom in the structure of a letter. . . . labored letter writing is not merely absurd; it does not even obey the laws of friends."[64]

One can hardly claim that Paul had read Aristotle, that he was familiar with Cicero, or that he had formally studied rhetoric and/or letter-writing in one of the rhetorical schools of his day. It is, however, very clear that Paul knew what a letter was and that he knew how to write a letter.[65] Most likely he learned letter-recognition and letter-writing from the cultural situation in which he lived.

What Paul has to say in 1 Thessalonians about his way of communicating with them lends support to the rhetorical theory that a letter is a form of dialogue, that is, one part of a dialogue. Paul's letter was part of an ongoing conversation with the Thessalonians. Hence, the historical-critical exegesis of a letter demands that it be analyzed with the help of both epistolary criticism and rhetorical criticism. It was a first-century Hellenistic composition, written in a world in which letter-writing was considered to be an exercise in rhetoric. It was written in words that suggest that it was an oral composition. It contains an exhortation that demands that an audience have an opportunity to listen to it. Its text is one that is the result of an oral production. To study 1 Thessalonians as a letter without examining its rhetoric would be like studying one of the Synoptic Gospels without an examination of its *formgeschichte*.

---

64. *De elocutione* 229.
65. See 1 Cor 5:9; 16:3; 2 Cor 3:1-3; 7:8; 10:9-11.

Bibliography

Adinolfi, M., *La prima lettera ai Tessalonicesi nel mondo greco-romano* (BPAA 31; Roma: Editrice 'Antonianum,' 1990).

Aletti, J., "Paul et la rhétorique. Etat de la question et propositions," *Paul de Tarse* (ed. J. Schlosser; LD 165; Paris: Cerf, 1996), 27-50.

Anderson, R. Dean, Jr., *Ancient Rhetorical Theory and Paul* (Contributions to Biblical Exegesis and Theology 18; Kampen: Pharos, 1996).

Arnim, Hans von, *Leben und Werke des Dio von Prusa mit einer Einleitung: Sophistik, Rhetorik, Philosophie in ihrem Kampf um die Jugendbildung* (Berlin: Weidmann, 1898).

Arzt, P., "The 'Epistolary Introductory Thanksgiving' in the Papyri and in Paul," *NovT* 36 (1994): 29-46.

Aune, David E., *The New Testament in Its Literary Environment* (LEC 8; Philadelphia: Westminster, 1987).

Balz, H. R., "παρρησία," *EDNT* 3.105-12.

Barclay, J. M. G., "Mirror-Reading a Polemical Letter: Galatians as a Test Case," *JSNT* 31 (1987): 73-93.

Baumert, N., "Ὁμειρόμενοι in 1 Thess 2,8," *Bib* 68 (1987): 552-63.

Beck, I., "Untersuchungen zur Theorie des Genos Symbuleutikon" (Unpub. D.Phil. diss.; University of Hamburg, 1970).

Becker, J., *Annäherungen: Zur urchristlichen Theologiegeschichte und zum Umgang mit ihren Quellen* (BZNW 76; Berlin and New York: Walter de Gruyter, 1995), 79-98.

Berger, Klaus, "Apostelbrief und apostolische Rede/Zum Formular frühchristlicher Briefe," *ZNW* 65 (1974): 190-231.

————, *Einführung in die Formgeschichte* (Tübingen: Francke Verlag, 1987).

————, "Die Erwählung der Völker durch das Evangelium: Theologie-geschichtliche Erwägungen zum 1 Thessalonikerbrief," in *Studien zum Text und zur Ethik des Neuen Testaments* (Festschrift H. Greeven; ed. W. Schrage; BZNW 47; Berlin and New York: Walter de Gruyter, 1986), 82-101.

————, *Formgeschichte des Neuen Testaments* (Heidelberg: Quelle & Meyer, 1984).

————, "Hellenistische Gattungen im Neuen Testament," in *ANRW* II.25.2 (Berlin and New York: de Gruyter, 1984), 1031-1432.

————, *Paulus: Der Apostel der Völker* (Tübingen: Mohr, 1989).

Best, E., *A Commentary on the First and Second Epistles to the Thessalonians* (BNTC; London, Black, 1972).

Betz, H. D., *Der Apostel Paulus und die sokratische Tradition. Eine exegetische Untersuchung zu seiner "Apologie" 2 Kor 10–13* (BHT 45; Tübingen: Mohr-Siebeck, 1972).

————, *Galatians: A Commentary on Paul's Letter to the Churches in Galatia* (Hermeneia; Philadelphia: Fortress, 1979).

————, "The Literary Composition and Function of Paul's Letter to the Galatians," *NTS* 21 (1975): 353-79.

————, *2 Corinthians 8 and 9: A Commentary on Two Administrative Letters of the Apostle Paul* (Hermeneia; Philadelphia: Fortress, 1985).

————, "The Problem of Rhetoric and Theology according to the Apostle Paul," in *L'apôtre Paul: Personnalité, style et conception du ministère* (BETL 73; ed. A. Vanhoye; Leuven: Leuven University Press, 1986), 16-48.

Binder, H., "Paulus und die Thessalonicherbriefe," in *The Thessalonian Corre-spondence* (ed. R. F. Collins; BETL 87; Leuven: Leuven University Press–Peeters, 1990), 87-93.

Bitzer, L. F., "The Rhetorical Situation," *Philosophy and Rhetoric* 1 (1968): 1-14.

Bjerkelund, C. J., *Parakalô. Form, Funktion und Sinn der parakalô-Sätze in den paulinischen Briefen* (BTN 1; Oslo: Universitetsforlaget, 1967).

————, "'Vergeblich' als Missionsergebnis bei Paulus," in *God's Christ and His People* (Festschrift N. A. Dahl; ed. J. Jervell and W. A. Meeks; Oslo: Universitetsforlaget, 1977).

Black, E., *Rhetorical Criticism: A Study in Method* (New York: Macmillan, 1965; repr. Madison: University of Wisconsin Press, 1978).

Blass, F., and A. Debrunner, *Grammatik des neutestamentlichen Griechisch* (rev. F. Rehkopf; 14th ed.; Göttingen: Vandenhoeck & Ruprecht, 1976).

Boers, H., "The Form-Critical Study of Paul's Letters: I Thessalonians as a Case Study," *NTS* 22 (1975-76): 140-58.

Bolkestein, M. H., *De brieven aan de Tessalonicenzen* (De prediking van het NT; Nijkerk: Callenbach, 1974).

Bonner, Stanley F., *Education in Ancient Rome: From the Elder Cato to the Younger Pliny* (Berkeley and Los Angeles: University of California Press, 1977).

Bornemann, W., *Die Thessalonicherbriefe* (KEK X; Göttingen: Vandenhoeck & Ruprecht, 1894).

Bornkamm, G., *Paulus* (UB 119D; Stuttgart: Kohlhammer, 1969).

Brodie, Thomas L., "Greco-Roman Imitation of Texts as a Partial Guide to Luke's Use of Sources," in *Luke-Acts: New Perspectives from the Society of Biblical Literature Seminar* (ed. Charles H. Talbert; New York: Crossroad, 1988).

Bruce, F. F., *1 and 2 Thessalonians* (WBC 45; Waco, Tex.: Word, 1982).

Bullmore, Michael A., *St. Paul's Theology of Rhetorical Style: An Examination of 1 Corinthians 2:1-5 in the Light of First-Century Graeco-Roman Culture* (San Francisco: International Scholars Publications, 1995).

Bultmann, R., *Der Stil der paulinischen Predigt und die kynisch-stoische Diatribe* (FRLANT 13; Göttingen: Vandenhoeck & Ruprecht, 1910; repr. 1984).

Bünker, M., *Briefformular und rhetorische Disposition im 1. Korintherbrief* (GTA 28; Göttingen: Vandenhoeck & Ruprecht, 1984).

Carey, Christopher, "Rhetorical Means of Persuasion," in *Persuasion: Greek Rhetoric in Action* (ed. Ian Worthington; London and New York: Routledge, 1994), 26-45.

Chapa, J., "Consolatory Patterns? 1 Thes 4,13.18; 5,11," in *The Thessalonian Correspondence* (ed. R. F. Collins; BETL 87; Leuven: Leuven University Press–Peeters, 1990), 220-28.

―――, "Is First Thessalonians a Letter of Consolation?" *NTS* 40 (1994): 150-60.

Christ, W. von, W. Schmid, and O. Stählin., *Geschichte der griechischen Literatur* (ed. Wilhelm Schmid and Otto Stahlin; 6th ed.; 5 vols.; HAW 7; Munich: Beck, 1924).

Clark, Donald Lemen, *Rhetoric in Greco-Roman Education* (New York: Columbia University Press, 1957).

Classen, C. J., "Paulus und die antike Rhetorik," *ZNW* 82 (1991): 1-33.

————, *Recht-Rhetorik-Politik. Untersuchungen zu Ciceros rhetorischer Strategie* (Darmstadt: Wissenschaftliche Buchgesellschaft, 1985).

————, "St Paul's Epistles and Ancient Greek and Roman Rhetoric," in *Rhetoric and the New Testament: Essays from the 1992 Heidelberg Conference* (ed. Stanley E. Porter and Thomas H. Olbricht; JSNTSup 90; Sheffield: JSOT, 1993), 263-91.

Clines, D. J. A., D. M. Gunn, and A. J. Hauser, ed., *Art and Meaning: Rhetoric in Biblical Literature* (JSOTSup 19; Sheffield: JSOT Press, 1982).

Cohen, David, "Classical Rhetoric and Modern Theories of Discourse," in *Persuasion: Greek Rhetoric in Action* (ed. Ian Worthington; London and New York: Routledge, 1994).

Collins, R. F., "Apropos the Integrity of I Thes," *ETL* 65 (1979): 67-106. Reprinted in R. F. Collins, *Studies on the First Letter to the Thessalonians* (BETL 66; Leuven: Leuven University Press–Peeters, 1984), 96-135.

————, *The Birth of the New Testament: The Origin and Development of the First Christian Generation* (New York: Crossroad, 1993).

————, *Letters That Paul Did Not Write: The Epistle to the Hebrews and the Pauline Pseudepigrapha* (GNS 28; Wilmington, Del.: Glazier, 1988).

————, "Paul as seen through his own eyes," *LS* 8 (1980-81): 348-81. Reprinted in R. F. Collins, *Studies on the First Letter to the Thessalonians* (BETL 66; Leuven: Leuven University Press–Peeters, 1984), 175-208.

————, "Paul at Prayer," *Emmanuel* 88 (1982): 412-19. Reprinted in R. F. Collins, *Studies on the First Letter to the Thessalonians* (BETL 66; Leuven: Leuven University Press–Peeters, 1984), 356-64.

————, "'. . . that this letter be read to all the brethren,'" *LS* 9 (1982-83): 122-27. Reprinted in R. F. Collins, *Studies on the First Letter to the Thessalonians* (BETL 66; Leuven: Leuven University Press–Peeters, 1984), 365-70.

————, ed., *The Thessalonian Correspondence* (BETL 87; Leuven: Leuven University Press–Peeters, 1990).

Cooper, John M., "An Aristotelian Theory of the Emotions," in *Essays on Aristotle's Rhetoric* (ed. Amélie Oksenberg Rorty; Berkeley, Los Angeles, and London: University of California Press, 1996), 238-57.

Dautzenberg, G., "ἀγών," *EWNT* (Stuttgart: Kohlhammer, 1980), 1.25-27.

Davies, W. D., "Galatians: A Commentary on Paul's Letter to the Churches in Galatia," *RSRev* 7 (1981): 310-18. Reprinted in W. D. Davies, *Jewish and Pauline Studies* (Philadelphia: Fortress Press, 1984), 172-88.

Deissmann, A., *Bible Studies: Contributions Chiefly from Papyri and Inscriptions to the History of the Language, the Literature and the Religion of Hel-*

lenistic Judaism and Primitive Christianity (Edinburgh: T. & T. Clark, 1901).

———, *Licht von Osten* (Tübingen: Mohr, 1923). English translation, *Light from the Ancient East* (Grand Rapids: Baker, 1978).

Delobel, J., "The Fate of the Dead according to 1 Thessalonians 4 and 1 Corinthians 15," in *The Thessalonian Correspondence* (ed. R. F. Collins; BETL 87; Leuven: Leuven University Press–Peeters, 1990), 340-47.

Demke, C., "Theologie und Literaturkritik im 1. Thessalonicherbrief," in *Festschrift für Ernst Fuchs* (ed. G. Ebeling, E. Jüngel, and G. Schunack; Tübingen: Mohr, 1973), 103-24.

Denis, A.-M., *Concordance Grecque des Pseudépigraphes d'Ancien Testament* (Louvain-la-Neuve: Université Catholique de Louvain, 1987).

———, "L'Apôtre Paul, prophète 'messianique' des Gentils. Étude thématique de 1. Thess II,1-6," *ETL* 33 (1957): 245-318.

Dibelius, M., *An die Thessalonicher I und II, An die Philipper* (HNT 11; 3rd ed.; Tübingen: Mohr, 1937).

———, *Die Briefe des Apostels Paulus. II. Die Neuen Kleinen Briefe* (HNT; Tübingen: Mohr, 1913).

———, *Geschichte der urchristlichen Literatur II. Apostolisches und Nachapostolisches* (Leipzig: Teubner, 1926).

———, *"Zur Formgeschichte des neuen Testaments (ausserhalb der Evangelien),"* *ThR* 3 (1931): 207-42.

DiCicco, Mario, *Paul's Use of Ethos, Pathos, and Logos in 2 Corinthians 10–13* (Lewiston, N.Y.: Mellen Biblical Press, 1994).

Dihle, Albrecht, *Greek and Latin Literature of the Roman Empire from Augustus to Justinian* (London and New York: Routledge, 1994).

Dobschütz, E. von, *Die Thessalonicher-Briefe* (KEK X; Göttingen: Vandenhoeck & Ruprecht, [1909] repr. 1974).

Dobson, J. F., *The Greek Orators* (London: Methuen, 1918; repr. Chicago: Area, 1974).

Donfried, Karl P., "The Assembly of the Thessalonians: Reflections on the Ecclesiology of the Earliest Christian Letter," in *Ekklesiologie des Neuen Testaments* (Festschrift Karl Kertelge; ed. R. Kampling and T. Söding; Freiburg, Basel, and Wien: Herder, 1996), 390-408.

———, "The Cults of Thessalonica and the Thessalonian Correspondence," *NTS* 31 (1985): 336-56.

———, *The Dynamic Word: New Testament Insights for Contemporary Christians* (San Francisco: Harper & Row, 1981).

————, "False Presuppositions in the Study of Romans," in *The Romans Debate* (ed. K. P. Donfried; rev. ed.; Minneapolis: Augsburg, 1991).

————, "1 Thessalonians, Acts and Early Paul," in *The Thessalonian Correspondence* (ed. R. F. Collins; BETL 87; Leuven: Leuven University Press–Peeters, 1990), 3-26.

————, "The Kingdom of God in Paul," in *The Kingdom of God in 20th Century Interpretation* (ed. W. Willis; Peabody, Mass.: Hendrickson, 1987).

————, "The Theology of 1 Thessalonians," in *The Theology of the Shorter Pauline Letters* (ed. K. P. Donfried and I. H. Marshall; New Testament Theology; Cambridge: Cambridge University Press, 1993).

————, "The Theology of 1 Thessalonians as a Reflection of Its Purpose," in *To Touch the Text* (Festschrift J. A. Fitzmyer; ed. M. P. Horgan and P. J. Kobelski; New York: Crossroad, 1989), 243-60.

————, and I. Howard Marshall, *The Theology of the Shorter Pauline Letters* (New Testament Theology; Cambridge: Cambridge University Press, 1993),

Doty, W. G., *Letters in Primitive Christianity* (Philadelphia: Fortress, 1973).

Eadie, John, *Commentary on the Greek Text of the Epistles of Paul to the Thessalonians* (New York: Macmillan, 1877).

Exler, F. X. J., *The Form of the Ancient Letter: A Study in Greek Epistolography* (Washington: Catholic University of America, 1923).

Faw, C. E., "On the Writing of First Thessalonians," *JBL* 71 (1952): 217-25.

Fee, Gordon D., *The First Epistle to the Corinthians* (NICNT; Grand Rapids: Eerdmans, 1987).

Ffortenbaukgh, William W., and David C. Mirhady, ed., *Peripatetic Rhetoric after Aristotle* (Rutgers University Studies in Classical Humanities VI; New Brunswick and London: Transaction Publishers, 1994).

Focant, C., "Les fils du Jour (1 Thes 5,5)," in *The Thessalonian Correspondence* (ed. R. F. Collins; BETL 87; Leuven: Leuven University Press–Peeters, 1990), 348-55.

Forbes, C., "Comparison, Self-Praise, and Irony: Paul's Boasting and the Conventions of Hellenistic Rhetoric," *NTS* 32 (1986): 1-30.

Frame, James E., *A Critical and Exegetical Commentary on the Epistles of St. Paul to the Thessalonians* (ICC; New York: Scribner's, 1912).

Francis, F. O., "The Form and Function of the Opening and Closing Paragraphs of James and I John," *ZNW* 61 (1970): 110-26.

Frede, Dorothea, "Mixed Feelings in Aristotle's *Rhetoric*," in *Essays on Aristotle's Rhetoric* (ed. Amélie Oksenberg Rorty; Berkeley, Los Angeles, and London: University of California Press, 1996), 258-85.

Fridrichsen, Anton, *The Apostle and His Message* (Uppsala: Almqvist-Wiksell, 1947).

Friedrich, Gerhard, "1-2 Thessalonians," in *Die Briefe an die Galater, Epheser, Philipper, Kolosser, Thessalonicher und Philemon* (ed. J. Becker, H. Conzelmann, and G. Friedrich; NTD; Göttingen: Vandenhoeck & Ruprecht, 1981).

Funk, R. W., "The Apostolic 'Parousia': Form and Significance," in *Christian History and Interpretation* (Festschrift J. Knox; ed. W. R. Farmer, C. F. D. Moule, and R. R. Niebuhr; Cambridge: Cambridge University Press, 1967), 249-68.

————, *Language, Hermeneutic, and Word of God. The Problem of Language in the New Testament and Contemporary Theology* (New York, Evanston, and London: Harper & Row, 1966).

Furnish, Victor Paul, "Pauline Studies," in *The New Testament and Its Modern Interpreters* (ed. Eldon J. Epp and George W. MacRae; The Bible and Its Modern Interpreters 3; Philadelphia: Fortress and Atlanta: Scholars Press, 1989).

————, *II Corinthians* (AB 32A; Garden City, N.Y.: Doubleday, 1984).

Gaventa, Beverly R., *First and Second Thessalonians* (IBC; Louisville: John Knox, 1998).

Gebauer, R., *Paulus als Seelsorger: Ein exegetischer Beitrag zur praktischen Theologie* (CThM.BW 18; Stuttgart: Calwer Verlag, 1997).

Gillman, John, "Paul's Εἴσοδος: The Proclaimed and the Proclaimer (1 Thess 2,8)," in *The Thessalonian Correspondence* (ed. R. F. Collins; BETL 87; Leuven: Leuven University Press–Peeters, 1990), 62-70.

Goldstein, Jonathan A., *The Letters of Demosthenes* (New York and London: Columbia University Press, 1968).

Goulder, Michael, "Silas in Thessalonica," *JSNT* 48 (1992): 87-106.

Grimaldi, W. M. A., *Aristotle, Rhetoric I: A Commentary* (New York: Fordham University Press, 1980).

Grube, G. M. A., *The Greek and Roman Critics* (Canadian University Paperbooks; Toronto: University of Toronto Press, 1968).

Hadorn, W., "Die Abfassung der Thessalonicherbriefe auf der dritten Missionsreise des Paulus," *BFChTh* 24 (1919): 157-284.

————, "Die Abfassung der Thessalonicherbriefe auf der dritten Missionsreise und der Kanons des Marcion," *ZNW* 19 (1919-20): 67-72.

Hahn, F., "Gibt es eine Entwicklung in den Aussagen über die Rechtfertigung bei Paulus?" *EvTh* 53 (1993): 342-64.

Hall, R. G., "Arguing like an Apocalypse: Galatians and an Ancient Topos outside the Greco-Roman Rhetorical Tradition," *NTS* 42 (1996): 434-53.

Haufe, G., "Reich Gottes bei Paulus und in der Jesustradition," *NTS* 31 (1985): 467-72.

Heinrici, F. G., *Der zweite Brief an die Korinther, mit einem Anhang: Zum Hellenismus des Paulus* (MeyerK 6; 8th ed.; Göttingen: Vandenhoeck & Ruprecht, 1900).

Hellwig, A., *Untersuchungen zur Theorie der Rhetorik bei Platon und Aristoteles* (Hyp 38; Göttingen: Vandenhoeck & Ruprecht, 1973).

Hendriksen, William, *Thessalonians, Timothy and Titus* (Grand Rapids: Baker, 1955).

Hengel, Martin, *The Pre-Christian Paul* (London: SCM, 1991).

————, and A. M. Schwemer, ed., *Königsherrschaft Gottes und himmlischer Kult im Judentum, Urchristentum und in der hellenistischen Welt* (WUNT 55; Tübingen: Mohr, 1991).

Henneken, Bartholomäus, *Verkündigung und Prophetie im 1. Thessalonicherbrief* (SBS 29; Stuttgart: Katholisches Bibelwerk, 1969).

Hill, J. L., "Establishing the Church in Thessalonica" (Unpub. Ph.D. diss.; Duke University Press, 1990).

Hinks, D. A. G., "Tria genera causarum," *CQ* 30 (1936): 170-76.

Hock, R. F., *The Social Context of Paul's Ministry: Tentmaking and Apostleship* (Philadelphia: Fortress, 1980).

————, "The Workshop as a Social Setting for Paul's Missionary Preaching," *CBQ* 41 (1979): 438-50.

Holladay, William L., *Jeremiah 1* (Hermeneia; Philadelphia: Fortress, 1986).

Holland, Glenn S., *The Traditions That You Received from Us: 2 Thessalonians in the Pauline Tradition* (HUTh 24; Tübingen: Mohr-Siebeck, 1986).

Holtz, T., "Der Apostel des Christus: Die paulinische 'Apologie' 1. Thess. 2,1-12," in *Als Boten des gekreuzigten Herrn* (Festschrift W. Krusche; ed. H. Falcke, M. Omnasch, and H. Schultze; Berlin: Evangelische Verlagsanstalt, 1982), 101-16.

————, "Die Bedeutung des Apostelkonzils für Paulus," in *Geschichte und Theologie des Urchristentums* (ed. E. Reinmuth and C. Wolff; Gesammelte Aufsätze T. Holtz; WUNT 57; Tübingen: Mohr, 1991), 140-70.

————, *Der erste Brief an die Thessalonicher* (2nd ed.; EKK XIII; Zürich: Benziger and Neukirchen-Vluyn: Neukirchener Verlag, 1990).

————, "Paulus, Jerusalem und die Wahrheit des Evangeliums. Beobachtungen zu Gal 1 und 2," in *Nach den Anfängen Fragen* (Festschrift

G. Dautzenberg; ed. C. Mayer, K. Müller, and G. Schmalenberg; GSThR 8; Gießen: Selbstverlag des Fachbereichs Evangelische Theologie und Katholische Theologie und deren Didaktik, 1994), 327-40.

Horbury, W., "I Thessalonians ii.3 as Rebutting the Charge of False Prophecy," *JTS* 33 (1982): 492-508.

Hübner, H., *Biblische Theologie des Neuen Testaments. Die Theologie des Paulus* (Göttingen: Vandenhoeck & Ruprecht, 1993), 2.41-56.

Hughes, Frank W., *Early Christian Rhetoric and 2 Thessalonians* (JSNTSup 30; Sheffield: JSOT, 1989).

————, "New Testament Rhetorical Criticism and Its Methodology" (Unpublished paper presented at the Rhetorical Criticism section of the Society of Biblical Literature Annual Meeting, November, 1986, in Atlanta, Georgia).

————, "The Parable of the Rich Man and Lazarus (Luke 16.19-31) and Graeco-Roman Rhetoric," in *Rhetoric and the New Testament: Essays from the 1992 Heidelberg Conference* (ed. Stanley E. Porter and Thomas H. Olbricht; JSNTSup 90; Sheffield: JSOT, 1993), 29-41.

————, "The Rhetoric of 1 Thessalonians," in *The Thessalonian Correspondence* (ed. Raymond F. Collins; BETL 87; Leuven: Leuven University Press–Peeters, 1990), 94-116.

————, "Rhetorical Criticism," in the *Mercer Dictionary of the Bible* (ed. Watson E. Mills; Macon: Mercer University Press, 1990), 763-64.

————, "The Social World of 2 Thessalonians," *Listening: Journal of Religion and Culture* 31 (1996): 105-16.

Hurd, John C., Jr., "Thessalonians, First Letter to the," in *Interpreter's Dictionary of the Bible* (ed. K. Crim; Nashville: Abingdon, 1976), 4.900.

Jaspert, B., *Sachgemässe Exegese. Die Protokolle aus Rudolf Bultmanns Neutestamentlichen Seminaren 1921-1951* (MThS 43; Marburg: Elwert, 1996).

Jennrich, W. A., "Classical Rhetoric in the New Testament," *CJ* 44 (1948-49): 30-32.

Jervis, L. Ann, *The Purpose of Romans: A Comparative Letter Structure Investigation* (JSNTSup 55; Sheffield: JSOT Press, 1991).

Jewett, R., "The Form and Function of the Homiletic Benediction," *ATR* 51 (1969): 18-34.

————, "Romans as an Ambassadorial Letter," *Int* 36 (1982): 5-20.

————, *The Thessalonian Correspondence: Pauline Rhetoric and Millenarian Piety* (FFNT; Philadelphia: Fortress, 1986).

Johanson, B. C., *To All the Brethren: A Text-Linguistic and Rhetorical Approach to I Thessalonians* (ConBNT 16; Stockholm: Almqvist & Wiksell, 1987).

Jones, C. P., *The Roman World of Dio Chrysostom* (Cambridge and London: Harvard University Press, 1978).

Judge, E. A., "Cultural Conformity and Innovation in Paul: Some Clues from Contemporary Documents," *TynB* 35 (1984): 3-24.

———, "The Early Christians as a Scholastic Community," *JRH* 1 (1960-61): 4-15 and 125-37.

———, "Paul's Boasting in Relation to Contemporary Professional Practice," *AusBR* 16 (1968), 37-50.

Kennedy, George A., *The Art of Persuasion in Greece* (Princeton: Princeton University Press, 1963).

———, *The Art of Rhetoric in the Roman World* (Princeton: Princeton University Press, 1972).

———, *Classical Rhetoric and Its Christian and Secular Tradition from Ancient to Modern Times* (Chapel Hill: University of North Carolina Press, 1980).

———, "Focusing of Arguments in Greek Deliberative Oratory," *TAPA* 90 (1959): 131-38.

———, *Greek Rhetoric under Christian Emperors* (Princeton: Princeton University Press, 1983).

———, *New Testament Interpretation through Rhetorical Criticism* (Studies in Religion; Chapel Hill: University of North Carolina Press, 1984).

Kieffer, R., "L'eschatologie en 1 Thessaloniciens dans une perspective rhétorique," in *The Thessalonian Correspondence* (ed. R. F. Collins; BETL 87; Leuven: Leuven University Press–Peeters, 1990), 206-18.

Klauck, H. J., "Hellenistische Rhetorik im Diasporajudentum. Das Exordium des vierten Makkabäerbuches (4 Makk 1,1-12)," *NTS* 35 (1989): 451-65.

Kloppenborg, J. S., "ΦΙΛΑΔΕΛΠΗΙΑ, ΘΕΟΔΙΔΑΚΤΟΣ and the Dioscuri: Rhetorical Engagement in 1 Thessalonians 4.9-12," *NTS* 39 (1993): 265-89.

Knorr, D. E., "The Rhetorical Consensus: A Proposed Methodology for the Study of Paul's Use of the Old Testament" (Unpublished paper presented at the Midwest regional meeting of the Society of Biblical Literature, February 20, 1986, at Andrews University).

Koester, H., "Apostel und Gemeinde in den Briefen an die Thessaloni-cher," in *Kirche* (Festschrift G. Bornkamm; ed. D. Lührmann and G. Strecker; Tübingen: Mohr, 1980), 287-98.

———, "Archäologie und Paulus in Thessalonike," in *Religious Propaganda and Missionary Competition in the New Testament World: Essays Honoring Dieter Georgi* (ed. L. Bormann, K. Del Tredici, and A. Standhartinger; NovTSup 74; Leiden: Brill, 1994), 393-424.

————, "I Thessalonians — Experiment in Christian Writing," in *Continuity and Discontinuity in Church History* (Festschrift G. H. Williams; SHCT 19; Leiden: Brill, 1979), 33-44.

Koskenniemi, H., "Cicero über die Briefanen (genera epistularum)," *Arctos* 1 (1954): 97-102.

————, *Studien zur Idee und Phraseologie des griechischen Briefes bis 400 n. Chr.* (AASF, B102/2; Helsinki: Suomalaien Tiedakatemie, & Wiesbaden: Otto Harrassowitz, 1956).

Kraus, W., *Das Volk Gottes. Zur Grundlegung der Ekklesiologie bei Paulus* (WUNT 85; Tübingen: Mohr, 1996).

Krentz, E., *The Historical-Critical Method* (GBS; Philadelphia: Fortress, 1975).

Kuhn, H.-W., "Die Bedeutung der Qumrantexte für das Verständnis des Ersten Thessalonicherbriefes. Vorstellung des Münchener Projekts: Qumran und das Neue Testament. — The Impact of the Qumran Scrolls on the Understanding of Paul's First Letter to the Thessalonians. Presentation of the Munich Project on Qumran and the New Testament," in *The Madrid Qumran Congress: Proceedings of the International Congress on the Dead Sea Scrolls (Madrid, 18-21 March 1991)* (ed. Julio Trebolle Barrera and Luis Vegas Montaner; StTDJ XI.1; Leiden: Brill, 1992), 1.339-53.

————, *Enderwartung und gegenwärtiges Heil. Untersuchungen zu den Gemeindeliedern von Qumran, mit einem Anhang über Eschatologie und Gegenwart in der Verkündigung Jesu* (StUNT 4; Göttingen: Vandenhoeck & Ruprecht, 1966).

Kümmel, W. G., *Introduction to the New Testament* (Nashville: Abingdon, 1986).

Kuß, O., *Paulus. Die Rolle des Apostels in der theologischen Entwicklung der Urkirche* (Regensburg: Pustet, 1971).

Lambrecht, J. "A Call to Witness by All. Evangelisation in 1 Thessalonians," in J. Lambrecht, *Pauline Studies* (BETL 115; Leuven: Leuven University Press–Peeters, 1994), 343-59.

————, *Pauline Studies* (BETL 115; Leuven: Leuven University Press–Peeters, 1994).

————, "Rhetorical Criticism and the New Testament," *BPTF* 50 (1989): 239-53.

————, "Structure and Line of Thought in 2 Cor 2,14–4,6," *Bib* 64 (1983): 344-80.

————, "Thanksgivings in 1 Thessalonians 1–3," in *The Thessalonian Correspondence* (ed. R. F. Collins; BETL 87; Leuven: Leuven University Press–Peeters, 1990), 183-205.

Langevin, P.-E., "L'intervention de Dieu selon I Thes 5,23-24," in *The Thessalonian Correspondence* (ed. R. F. Collins; BETL 87; Leuven: Leuven University Press–Peeters, 1990), 236-56.

Lanham, Richard A., *A Handlist of Rhetorical Terms* (2nd ed.; Berkeley, Los Angeles, and Oxford: University of California Press, 1991).

Lausberg, H., *Elemente der literarischen Rhetoric* (8th ed.; Munich: Max Huber Verlag, 1984).

Lee, Ki-Seong, "Die Basileia Gottes bei Paulus" (Unpub. Theol. Mag. thesis; Erlangen, 1993).

Leeman, A. D., *Orationis Ratio: The Stylistic Theories and Practice of the Roman Orators, Historians, and Philosophers* (2 vols.; Amsterdam: Adolf M. Hakkert, 1963).

Leighton, Stephen R., "Aristotle and the Emotions," in *Essays on Aristotle's Rhetoric* (ed. Amélie Oksenberg Rorty; Berkeley, Los Angeles, and London: University of California Press, 1996), 206-37.

Lesky, Albin, *A History of Greek Literature* (trans. James Willis and Cornelis de Heer; New York: Thomas Y. Crowell, 1966).

Litfin, Duane, *St. Paul's Theology of Proclamation: 1 Corinthians 1–4 and Greco-Roman Rhetoric* (SNTSMS 79; Cambridge: Cambridge University Press, 1994).

Lipsius, Richard Adelbert, "Über Zweck und Veranlassung des ersten Thessalonicherbrief," *ThStKr* 27 (1854): 905-34.

Longenecker, Richard N., *Galatians* (WBC; Dallas: Word, 1990).

Lüdemann, Gerd, *Paul, Apostle to the Gentiles: Studies in Chronology* (Philadelphia: Fortress, 1984).

Lührmann, D., "The Beginnings of the Church at Thessalonica," in *Greeks, Romans and Christians* (Festschrift Abraham J. Malherbe; ed. D. L. Balch, E. Ferguson, and W. A. Meeks; Minneapolis: Fortress Press, 1990), 237-49.

Lütgert, W., "Die Volkommenen im Philipperbrief und die Enthusiasten in Thessalonich," *BFChTh* 13 (1909): 547-654.

Lyons, George, *Pauline Autobiography: Toward a New Understanding* (SBLDS 73; Atlanta: Scholars Press, 1985).

Mack, Burton L., ed., *Rhetoric and the New Testament* (GBSNT; Minneapolis: Fortress, 1990).

Mack, Burton L., and Vernon K. Robbins, *Patterns of Persuasion in the Gospels*

(Foundations and Facets: Literary Facets; Sonoma, Calif.: Polebridge, 1989).

Malbon, E. S., "'No Need to Have Any One Write'? A Structural Exegesis of 1 Thessalonians," *SBLSP* (ed. Paul J. Achtemeier; Chico, Calif.: Scholars Press, 1980), 301-35. Revised and republished in *Semeia* 26 (1983): 57-83.

Malherbe, A. J. "Ancient Epistolary Theorists," *OJRS* 5 (1977), 3-77. Reprinted with slight modifications as *Ancient Epistolary Theorists* (SBLSBS 19; Atlanta: Scholars Press, 1988).

———, "Did the Thessalonians Write to Paul?" in *The Conversation Continues: Studies in Paul and John. In Honor of J. Louis Martyn* (ed. R. T. Fortna and B. R. Gaventa; Nashville: Abingdon, 1990), 246-57.

———, "Exhortation in First Thessalonians," *NovT* 25 (1983): 238-56. Reprinted in Abraham Malherbe, *Paul and the Popular Philosophers* (Minneapolis: Fortress, 1989), 49-66.

———, "'Gentle as a Nurse': The Cynic Background to 1 Thess ii," *NovT* 12 (1970): 203-17. Reprinted in Abraham Malherbe, *Paul and the Popular Philosophers* (Minneapolis: Fortress, 1989), 35-48.

———, "Hellenistic Moralists and the New Testament," in *ANRW* 2.26.1, 267-333.

———, *Moral Exhortation: A Graeco-Roman Sourcebook* (Philadelphia: Fortress, 1986).

———, *Paul and the Popular Philosophers* (Minneapolis: Fortress, 1989).

———, *Paul and the Thessalonians: The Philosophic Tradition of Pastoral Care* (2nd ed.; Philadelphia: Fortress, 1988).

Marshall, I. H., *1 and 2 Thessalonians* (NCBC; Grand Rapids: Eerdmans, 1983).

Marxsen, W., *Der erste Brief des Paulus an die Thessalonicher* (ZBK.NT 11.1; Zürich: Theologischer Verlag, 1979).

May, James M., "Patron and Client, Father and Son in Cicero's *Pro Caelio*," *CJ* 90 (April-May 1995): 434-36.

Meeks, W. A., *The First Urban Christians: The Social World of the Apostle Paul* (New Haven: Yale University Press, 1983).

———, *The Moral World of the First Christians* (Philadelphia: Fortress, 1986).

Merk, O., *Handeln aus Glauben. Die Motivierungen der paulinischen Ethik* (MThS 5; Marburg: Elwert, 1968).

———, "Miteinander: Zur Sorge um den Menschen im Ersten Thessalonicherbrief," in *"Daß allen Menschen geholfen werde . . ."* (Festschrift

M. Seitz; ed. R. Landau and G. R. Schmidt; Stuttgart: Calwer Verlag, 1993), 125-33.

———, "Nachahmung Christi: Zu ethischen Perspektiven in der paulinischen Theologie," in *Neues Testament und Ethik* (Festschrift Rudolf Schnackenburg; ed. H. Merklein; Freiburg, Basel, and Wien: Herder, 1989), 172-206.

———, "Überlegungen zu 2 Thess 2,13-17," in *Nach den Anfängen Fragen* (Festschrift G. Dautzenberg; ed. C. Mayer, K. Müller, and G. Schmalenberg; GSThR 8; Gießen: Selbstverlag des Fachbereichs Evangelische Theologie und Katholische Theologie und deren Didaktik, 1994), 405-14.

———, "Zu Rudolf Bultmanns Auslegung des 1. Thessalonicherbriefes," in *Glaube und Eschatologie* (Festschrift W. G. Kümmel; Tübingen: Mohr, 1985).

Merklein, Helmut, "Der Theologe als Prophet: zur Funktion prophetischen Redens im theologischen Diskurs," *NTS* 38 (1992): 402-29.

Mesner, David E., "The Rhetoric of Citations: Paul's Use of Scripture in Romans 9" (Unpubl. Ph.D. diss.; Northwestern University/Garrett-Evangelical Theological Seminary, 1991).

Milligan, George, *St Paul's Epistles to the Thessalonians* (London: Macmillan, 1908).

Mitchell, M. M., "Concerning *peri de* in 1 Corinthians," *NovT* 31 (1989): 229-56.

———, *Paul and the Rhetoric of Reconciliation* (Louisville: Westminster/John Knox, 1993).

Moffatt, James, *The First and Second Epistles to the Thessalonians* (London: Hodder & Stoughton, 1910).

Morris, Leon, *The First and Second Epistles to the Thessalonians* (NICNT; Grand Rapids: Eerdmans, 1959).

Muilenburg, J., "Form Criticism and Beyond," *JBL* 88 (1969): 1-18.

Mullins, T. Y., "Disclosure: A Literary Form in the New Testament," *NovT* 7 (1964): 44-50.

Murphy, J. J., *Rhetoric in the Middle Ages: A History of Rhetorical Theory from Saint Augustine to the Renaissance* (Berkeley: University of California Press, 1974).

Murphy-O'Connor, J., *Paul the Letter-Writer: His World, His Options, His Skills* (GNS 41; Collegeville, Minn.: Liturgical Press, 1995).

Neil, William, *The Epistle of Paul to the Thessalonians* (Naperville: Allenson, 1957).

Nestle, E., and K. Aland, *Novum Testamentum graece* (25th ed.; Stuttgart: Deutsche Bibelgesellschaft, 1963).

Nestle, E., and K. Aland, *Novum Testamentum graece* (26th ed.; Stuttgart: Deutsche Bibelgesellschaft, 1979).

Nestle, E., and K. Aland, *Novum Testamentum graece* (27th ed.; Stuttgart: Deutsche Bibelgesellschaft, 1993).

Norden, E., *Die antike Kunstprosa vom VI. Jahrhunderts vor Christus in die Zeit der Renaissance* (2 vols.; Leipzig and Berlin: B. G. Teubner, 1898; unaltered 3rd ed., Darmstadt: Wissenschaftliche Buchgesellschaft, 1958).

Nussbaum, Martha, "Aristotle on Emotions and Rational Persuasion," in *Essays on Aristotle's Rhetoric* (ed. Amélie Oksenberg Rorty; Berkeley, Los Angeles, and London: University of California Press, 1996), 303-23.

O'Brien, P. T., *Introductory Thanksgivings in the Letters of Paul* (NovTSup 49; Leiden: Brill, 1977).

Oepke, Albrecht, *Die Briefe an die Thessalonicher* (NTD 8; repr. of 1933 ed.; Göttingen: Vandenhoeck & Ruprecht, 1970).

Olbricht, Thomas H., "An Aristotelian Rhetorical Analysis of 1 Thessalonians," in *Greeks, Romans, and Christians* (Festschrift A. Malherbe; ed. David L. Balch, Everett Ferguson, and Wayne A. Meeks; Minneapolis: Fortress, 1990), 216-36.

Parks, E. Patrick, *The Roman Rhetorical Schools as a Preparation for the Courts under the Early Empire* (Johns Hopkins University Studies in Historical and Political Science 63/2; Baltimore: Johns Hopkins, 1945).

Patte, D., *Paul's Faith and the Power of the Gospel: A Structural Introduction to the Pauline Letters* (Philadelphia: Fortress, 1983).

Pearson, Birger A., "1 Thessalonians 2:13-16: A Deutero-Pauline Interpolation," *HTR* 64 (1971): 79-94.

Pearson, L., *The Art of Demosthenes* (American Philological Association Special Publications, 4; Chico, Calif.: Scholars Press, 1981).

Perelman, C., and L. Olbrechts-Tyteca, *The New Rhetoric: A Treatise on Argumentation* (Notre Dame and London: University of Notre Dame Press, 1969).

Perkins, P., "1 Thessalonians and Hellenistic Religious Practices," in *To Touch the Text* (Festschrift J. A. Fitzmyer; ed. M. P. Horgan and P. J. Kobelski; New York: Crossroad, 1989), 325-34.

Pesch, R., *Die Apostelgeschichte* (EKK V 1/2; Zürich: Benziger and Neukirchen: Neukirchener Verlag, 1986).

Peter, H. *Der Brief in der römischen Literatur: Literargeschichtliche Unter-*

suchungen und Zusammenfassungen (ASGW.PH 20/3; Leipzig: B. G. Teubner, 1901; repr. Hildesheim: Georg Olms, 1965).

Pfitzner, V. C., *Paul and the Agon Motif: Traditional Athletic Imagery in the Pauline Literature* (NovTSup 16; Leiden: Brill, 1967).

Philipps, Gerald M., "The Place of Rhetoric in the Babylonian Talmud," *Quarterly Journal of Speech* 43 (1957): 390-93.

―――, "The Practice of Rhetoric at the Talmudic Academies," *Speech Monographs* 26 (1959): 37-46.

Plank, Karl A., *Paul and the Irony of Affliction* (SBLSS; Atlanta: Scholars Press, 1987).

Pobee, J. S., *Persecution and Martyrdom in the Theology of Paul* (JSNTSup 6; Sheffield: JSOT Press, 1985).

Pogoloff, Steven M., *Logos and Sophia: The Rhetorical Situation of 1 Corinthians* (SBLDS 134; Atlanta: Scholars Press, 1992).

Porter, Stanley, "The Theoretical Justification for Application of Rhetorical Categories to Pauline Epistolary Literature," in *Rhetoric and the New Testament* (JSNTSup 90; ed. Stanley E. Porter and Thomas H. Olbricht; Sheffield: JSOT, 1993), 100-122.

Prill, P., "Cicero in Theory and Practice: The Securing of Good Will in the *Exordia* of Five Forensic Speeches," *Rhetorica* 4 (1986): 93-109.

Rabe, H., "Aus Rhetoren-Handschriften: 9. Griechische Briefsteller," *RMP* 64 (1909): 284-309.

Radermacher, L., ed., *Artium Scriptores: Reste der voraristotelischen Rhetorik* (Sitzungsberichte der österreichischen Akademie der Wissenschaften, philosophisch-historische Klasse 227/3; Wien: Rudolf M. Rohrer, 1951).

Radl, W., "Alle Mühe umsonst? Paulus und der Gottesknecht," *L'apôtre Paul. Personnalité, style et conception du Ministère* (ed. A. Vanhoye; BETL 73; Leuven: Peeters, 1986), 144-49.

Reck, R., *Kommunikation und Gemeindeaufbau. Eine Studie zur Entstehung, Leben und Wachstum paulinischer Gemeinden in den Kommunikationsstrukturen der Antike* (SBS 22; Stuttgart: Katholisches Bibelwerk, 1991).

Reed, Jeffrey T., "Using Ancient Rhetorical Categories to Interpret Paul's Letters: A Question of Genre," in Burton L. Mack, *Rhetoric and the New Testament* (GBSNT; Minneapolis: Fortress, 1990), 292-304.

Reicke, Bo, "Thessalonicherbriefe," in *RGG*[3], 6.851-53.

Reinmuth, E., "'Nicht vergeblich' bei Paulus und Pseudo-Philo, Liber Antiquitatum Biblicarum," *NovT* 33 (1991): 97-123.

Richard, Earl J., *First and Second Thessalonians* (SP 11; Collegeville, Minn.: Liturgical Press/Michael Glazier, 1995).

Richards, E. R., *The Secretary in the Letters of Paul* (WUNT 2/42; Tübingen: Mohr, 1991).

Riesner, R., *Die Frühzeit des Apostels Paulus. Studien zur Chronologie, Missionsstrategie und Theologie* (WUNT 71; Tübingen: Mohr, 1994).

Rigaux, B., *Saint Paul. Les Épîtres aux Thessaloniciens* (EtB; Paris: Gabalda and Gembloux: Duculot, 1956).

————, *Saint Paul et ses lettres. État de la question* (SN.S 2; Paris-Bruges: Desclée de Brouwer, 1962).

————, "Vocabulaire chrétien antérieur à la première épître aux Thessaloniciens," in *Sacra Pagina II* (ed. J. Coppens et al.; BETL 13; Gembloux: Duculot, 1959), 380-89.

Robbins, V. K., and J. H. Patton, "Rhetoric and Biblical Criticism," *Quarterly Journal of Speech* 66 (1980): 327-50.

Roberts, J. H., "Transitional Techniques to the Letter Body in the 'corpus Paulinum,'" in *A South African Perspective on the New Testament* (Festschrift B. M. Metzger; ed. J. H. Petzer and P. J. Hartin; Leiden: Brill, 1986), 187-201.

Roberts, W. Rhys, *Greek Rhetoric and Literary Criticism* (New York: Longmans, Green, and Co., 1928).

Robinson, J. M., "Die hodajot-Formel in Gebet und Hymnus des Frühchristentums," in *Apophoreta* (Festschrift E. Haenchen; ed. W. Eltester and F. H. Kettler; BZNW 30; Berlin: Töpelmann, 1964), 194-235.

Rockinger, L., *Über Briefsteller und Formelbücher in Deutschland während des Mittelalters* (Munich: J. G. Weiss, 1861).

Roetzel, C. J., "I Thess. 5:12-28: A Case Study," *SBLSP* (ed. Lane C. McGaughy; 2 vols.; N.P.: Society of Biblical Literature, 1972), 2.367-83.

————, *The Letters of Paul: Conversations in Context* (Atlanta: John Knox, 1975).

Roller, O., *Das Formular der paulinischen Briefe. Ein Beitrag zur Lehre vom antiken Briefe* (BWANT 4.6; Stuttgart: Kohlhammer, 1933).

Roloff, J., *Die Apostelgeschichte* (NTD 5; Göttingen: Vandenhoeck & Ruprecht, 1981).

Rorty, Amélie Oksenberg, ed., *Essays on Aristotle's Rhetoric* (Berkeley, Los Angeles, and London: University of California Press, 1996).

Roth, W., *Hebrew Gospel: Cracking the Code of Mark* (Oak Park, Ill.: Meyer-Stone, 1988).

————, "Scriptural Coding in the Fourth Gospel," *BR* 32 (1987): 6-29.

Sanders, J. T., "The Transition from Opening Epistolary Thanksgiving to Body in the Letter of the Pauline Corpus," *JBL* 81 (1962): 348-62.

Sandnes, K. O., *Paul — One of the Prophets?* (WUNT 2/43; Tübingen: Mohr, 1991).

Schade, Hans-Heinrich, *Apokalyptische Christologie bei Paulus* (GTA 18; Göttingen: Vandenhoeck & Ruprecht, 1981).

Schanz, M., and C. Hosius, *Geschichte der Römischen Literatur bis zum Gesetzgebungswerk des Kaisers Justinian, 1. Teil: Die Römische Literatur in der Zeit der Republik* (4th ed.; Munich: Beck, 1927).

Schlier, H., "Auslegung des 1. Thessalonicherbriefes," *BiLe* 3 (1962): 89-97.

————, *Der Apostel und seine Gemeinde. Auslegung des Ersten Briefes an die Thessalonicher* (Freiburg, Basel, and Wien: Herder, 1972).

————, "παρρησία," *TDNT* 5.871-86.

Schmithals, W., *Die Briefe des Paulus in ihrer ursprünglichen Form* (ZWKB; Zürich: Theologischer Verlag, 1984).

————, "The Historical Situation of the Thessalonian Epistles," in *Paul and the Gnostics* (Nashville: Abingdon, 1972), 128-318.

————, "Methodische Erwägungen zur Literarkritik der Paulusbriefe," *ZNW* 87 (1996): 51-82.

————, *Paulus und die Gnostiker* (ThF 35; Hamburg-Bergstedt: Reich, 1965). English translation, *Paul and the Gnostics* (Nashville: Abingdon, 1972).

————, "Die Thessalonischerbriefe als Briefkompositionen," in *Zeit und Geschichte* (Festschrift R. Bultmann; ed. E. Dinkler; Tübingen: Mohr-Siebeck, 1964), 295-314.

Schneider, G., *Die Apostelgeschichte* (HThK V 1/2; Freiburg, Basel, and Wien: Herder, 1980/1982).

Schnelle, U., *Einleitung in das Neue Testament* (UTB 1830; 2nd ed.; Göttingen: Vandenhoeck & Ruprecht, 1996).

————, "Die Ethik des 1. Thessalonicherbriefes," in *The Thessalonian Correspondence* (ed. R. F. Collins; BETL 87; Leuven: Leuven University Press–Peeters, 1990), 295-305.

Schnider, F., and W. Stenger, *Studien zum neutestamentlichen Briefformular* (NTTS 11; Leiden: E. J. Brill, 1987).

Schoon-Janßen, J., *Umstrittene "Apologien" in den Paulusbriefen. Studien zur rhetorischen Situation des 1. Thessalonicherbriefes, des Galaterbriefes und des Philipperbriefes* (GTA 45; Göttingen: Vandenhoeck & Ruprecht 1991).

Schrage, Wolfgang, *Der erste Brief an die Korinther* (EKK VII 1/2; Zürich: Benziger, 1991/1995).

Schreiber, S., *Paulus als Wundertäter. Redaktionsgeschichtliche Untersuchungen zur Apostelgeschichte und den authentischen Paulusbriefen* (BZNW 79; Berlin and New York: Walter de Gruyter, 1996).

Schubert, P., *Form and Function of the Pauline Thanksgivings* (BZNW 20; Berlin: Alfred Töpelmann, 1939).

Schunack, G., "δοκιμάζω," *EDNT* 1.341-43.

Schüssler Fiorenza, E., "Rhetorical Situation and Historical Reconstruction in 1 Corinthians," *NTS* 33 (1987): 386-403.

Schwemer, A. M., "Gott als König und seine Königsherrschaft in den Sabbatliedern aus Qumran," in *Königsherrschaft Gottes und himmlischer Kult im Judentum, Urchristentum und in der hellenistischen Welt* (ed. M. Hengel and A. M. Schwemer; WUNT 55; Tübingen: Mohr, 1991), 45-118.

Seesemann, O., "ὀρφανός," *TDNT* 5.486-88.

Siegert, F., *Argumentation bei Paulus gezeigt an Röm 9–11* (WUNT 34; Tübingen: J. C. B. Mohr, 1985).

Silva, Moisés, *Explorations in Exegetical Method: Galatians as a Test Case* (Grand Rapids: Baker, 1996).

Smith, Abraham, *Comfort One Another: Reconstructing the Rhetoric and Audience of 1 Thessalonians* (Literary Currents in Biblical Interpretation; Louisville: Westminster/John Knox, 1995).

————, "The Social and Ethical Implications of the Pauline Rhetoric in I Thessalonians" (Unpub. Ph.D. diss.; Vanderbilt University, 1989).

Söding, T., "Der Erste Thessalonicherbrief und die frühe paulinische Evangeliumsverkündigung. Zur Frage einer Entwicklung der paulinischen Theologie," *BZ* 35 (1991): 180-203.

Solmsen, F., "The Aristotelean Tradition in Ancient Rhetoric," *AJP* 62 (1941): 35-50, 169-90.

Spicq, C., *Theological Lexicon of the New Testament* (3 vols.; Peabody, Mass.: Hendrickson, 1994).

Stamps, Dennis L., "Rhetorical Criticism of the New Testament: Ancient and Modern Evaluations of Argumentation," in *Approaches to New Testament Study* (ed. Stanley E. Porter and David Tombs; JSNTSup 120; Sheffield: Sheffield Academic Press, 1995), 129-69.

Stegemann, W., "Anlaß und Hintergrund der Abfassung von 1 Th 2,1-12," *Theologische Brosamen für Lothar Steiger* (ed. G. Freund and E. Stegemann; DBAT 5; Heidelberg: Esprint, 1985), 397-416.

Steinmetz, F.-A., *Die Freundschaftslehre des Panaitios* (Wiesbaden: Steiner, 1967).

Stowers, Stanley K., *Letter-Writing in Greco-Roman Antiquity* (LEC 5; Philadelphia: Westminster, 1986).

———, *A Rereading of Romans: Justice, Jews, and Gentiles* (New Haven: Yale University Press, 1995).

———, "Social Typification and the Classification of Ancient Letters," in *The Social World of Formative Christianity and Judaism* (Festschrift H. Kee; ed. Jacob Neusner, Ernest S. Frerichs, Peder Borgen, and Richard Horsley; Philadelphia: Fortress, 1988), 78-90.

Strecker, G., and Schnelle, U., ed., *Neuer Wettstein: Texte zum Neuen Testament aus Griechentum und Hellenismus, Vol. 2: Texte zur Briefliteratur und zur Johannesapokalypse* (Berlin and New York: Walter de Gruyter, 1996).

Strelan, J. G., "Burden-Bearing and the Law of Christ: A Re-Examination of Galatians 6:2," *JBL* 94 (1975): 266-76.

Striker, Gisela, "Emotions in Context: Aristotle's Treatment of the Passions in the *Rhetoric* and His Moral Psychology," in *Essays on Aristotle's Rhetoric* (ed. Amélie Oksenberg Rorty; Berkeley, Los Angeles, and London: University of California Press, 1996), 286-302.

Thomas, Johannes, "παρακαλέω," *EDNT* 3.23-27.

Thraede, K., *Grundzüge griechisch-römischer Brieftopik* (*Zet* 48; Munich: Beck, 1970).

———, *Umstrittene "Apologien" in den Paulusbriefen* (GTA 45; Göttingen, 1991).

Thrall, M. E., "A Second Thanksgiving Period in II Corinthians," *JSNT* 16 (1982): 101-24.

Trilling, W., *Der Zweite Brief an die Thessalonicher* (EKK XIV; Zürich, Einsiedeln, and Köln: Benziger and Neukirchen: Neukirchener Verlag, 1980).

Unnik, W. C. van, "The Christian's Freedom of Speech in the New Testament," in *Sparsa Collecta* 2 (Leiden: Brill, 1980), 269-89.

Vanhoye, A., "La composition de 1 Thessaloniciens," in *The Thessalonian Correspondence* (ed. R. F. Collins; BETL 87; Leuven: Leuven University Press–Peeters, 1990), 73-86.

Verhoef, Eduard, *Tessalonicenzen* (Kampen: Kok, 1995).

Vielhauer, P., *Geschichte der urchristlichen Literatur* (Berlin/New York: de Gruyter, 1975).

Volkmann, Richard, *Die Rhetorik der Griechen und Römer in systematischer Übersicht* (2nd ed.; Leipzig: B. G. Teubner, 1885).

Walter, N., "Die Philipper und das Leiden," in *Die Kirche des Anfangs*

(Festschrift H. Schürmann; ed. R. Schnackenburg et al.; Leipzig: St. Benno, 1977), 417-34.

Walton, S., "What Has Aristotle to Do with Paul? Rhetorical Criticism and 1 Thessalonians," *TynB* 46 (1995): 229-50.

Wanamaker, Charles A., *The Epistle to the Thessalonians: A Commentary on the Greek Text* (NIGTC; Grand Rapids: Eerdmans; Exeter, U.K.: Paternoster, 1990).

Watson, Duane, "The Integration of Epistolary and Rhetorical Analysis of Philippians," in *The Rhetorical Analysis of Scripture: Essays from the 1995 London Conference* (ed. Stanley E. Porter and Thomas H. Olbricht; JSNTSup 146; Sheffield: JSOT Press, 1997), 398-426.

————, ed., *Persuasive Artistry: Studies in New Testament Rhetoric in Honor of George A. Kennedy* (JSNTSup 90; Sheffield: Sheffield Academic Press, 1993).

————, and Alan J. Houser, *Rhetorical Criticism of the Bible: A Comprehensive Bibliography with Notes on History and Method* (Biblical Interpretation Series, 4; Leiden: E. J. Brill, 1994).

Weichert, V., *Demetrii et Libanii qui feruntur Typoi epistolikoi et Epistolimaioi charakteres* (Leipzig: Teubner, 1910).

Weima, Jeffrey A. D., "An Apology for the Apologetic Function of 1 Thessalonians 2:1-12," *JSNT* 68 (1997): 73-99.

————, *Neglected Endings: The Significance of the Pauline Letter Closings* (JSNTSup 101; Sheffield: JSOT, 1994).

————, "The Pauline Letter Closings: Analysis and Hermeneutical Significance," *BulBR* 5 (1995): 177-97.

Weima, Jeffrey A. D., and Stanley Porter, *An Annotated Bibliography of 1 and 2 Thessalonians* (NTTS 26; Leiden: Brill, 1998).

Weische, A., *Ciceros Nachahmung der attischen Redner* (BKAW 2/45; Heidelberg: Winter, 1972).

Weiss, J., "Beiträge zur Paulinischen Rhetorik," in *Theologische Studien* (Festschrift B. Weiss; Göttingen: Vandenhoeck & Ruprecht, 1897), 165-274.

Welch, Kathleen E., *The Contemporary Reception of Classical Rhetoric: Appropriations of Ancient Discourse* (Hillsdale: Lawrence Erlbaum Associates, 1990).

Welles, C. B., ed., *Royal Correspondence in the Hellenistic Period: A Study in Greek Epigraphy* (New Haven: Yale University Press, 1934).

Wendland, P., *Die Hellenistisch-römische Kultur in ihren Beziehungen zu Judentum und Christentum* (HNT I/2; Tübingen: Mohr/Siebeck, 1908).

————, *Die urchristlichen Literaturformen* (Tübingen: Mohr/Siebeck, 1912).

White, John L., "Ancient Greek Letters," in *Graeco-Roman Literature and the New Testament* (ed. David E. Aune; SBLSBS 21; Atlanta: Scholars Press, 1988).

————, "Apostolic Mission and Apostolic Message: Congruence in Paul's Epistolary Rhetoric, Structure and Imagery," in *Origins and Method: Towards a New Understanding of Judaism and Christianity* (Festschrift J. C. Hurd; ed. Bradley H. McLean; JSNTSup 86; Sheffield: JSOT, 1993), 145-61.

————, *The Form and Function of the Body of the Greek Letter: A Study of the Letter-Body in the Non-Literary Papyri and in Paul the Apostle* (2nd ed. corrected; SBLDS 2; Missoula: Scholars Press, 1972).

————, "Greek Documentary Letter Tradition Third Century B.C.E. to Third Century C.E.," *Semeia* 22 (1982): 89-106.

————, "Introductory Formulae in the Body of the Pauline Letter," *JBL* 90 (1971): 91-97.

————, *Light from Ancient Letters* (FFNT; Philadelphia: Fortress, 1986).

————, "New Testament Epistolary Literature in the Framework of Ancient Epistolography," in *ANRW* II.25.2 (Berlin and New York: Walter de Gruyter, 1984), 1730-56.

————, "Saint Paul and the Apostolic Letter Tradition," *CBQ* 45 (1983): 433-44.

Wilamowitz-Moellendorff, U. von. *Die Griechische Literatur des Altertums* (2nd ed.; Berlin and Leipzig: Teubner, 1907).

Wiles, G., *Paul's Intercessory Prayers: The Significance of the Intercessory Prayer Passages in the Letters of St. Paul* (SNTSMS 24; Cambridge: Cambridge University Press, 1974).

Wilke, C. G., *Die neutestamentliche Rhetorik: Ein Seitenstück zur Grammatik des neutestamentlichen Sprachidioms* (Dresden & Leipzig: Arnold, 1843).

Winter, Bruce, "The Entries and Ethics of Orators and Paul (1 Thessalonians 2:1-12)," *TynB* 44 (1993): 55-74.

————, "Is Paul among the Sophists?" *RTR* 53 (1994): 28-38.

Wolff, P., "Die frühe nachösterliche Verkündigung des Reiches Gottes" (Unpub. Theol. diss.; Greifswald, 1987).

Wooten, C. W., *Cicero's Philippics and Their Demosthenic Model: The Rhetoric of Crisis* (Chapel Hill: University of North Carolina Press, 1983).

Wuellner, Wilhelm, "The Argumentative Structure of 1 Thessalonians as a Paradoxical Encomium," in *The Thessalonian Correspondence* (ed. R. F.

Collins; BETL 87; Leuven: Leuven University Press–Peeters, 1990), 117-36.

————, "Greek Rhetoric and Pauline Argumentation," in *Early Christian Literature and the Classical Intellectual Tradition* (Festschrift Robert M. Grant; ed. William R. Schoedel and Robert L. Wilken; ThH 54; Paris: Beauchesne, 1979), 177-88.

————, "Paul's Rhetoric of Argumentation in Romans: An Alternative to the Donfried-Karris Debate over Romans," *CBQ* 38 (1976): 332-51. Reprinted in *The Romans Debate* (ed. K. P. Donfried; rev. ed.; Peabody, Mass.: Hendrickson, 1991), 128-46.

————, "Toposforschung und Torahinterpretation bei Paulus und Jesus," *NTS* 24 (1978): 463-86.

————, "Where Is Rhetorical Criticism Taking Us?" *CBQ* 49 (1987): 448-63.

Zimmer, F., "I Thess. 2,3-8 erklärt," in *Theologische Studien* (Festschrift Bernhard Weiss; ed. C. R. Gregory; Göttingen: Vandenhoeck & Ruprecht, 1897), 248-73.

Contributors

Johannes Beutler is Professor of New Testament in the Faculty of Theology, Pontifical Gregorian University, Rome, Italy.

Raymond F. Collins is Professor of New Testament in the Department of Theology at The Catholic University of America, Washington, DC.

Karl P. Donfried is Professor of New Testament in the Department of Religion and Biblical Literature at Smith College, Northampton, MA.

Traugott Holtz served as Professor of New Testament in the Theological Faculty of the Ernst Moritz Arndt University, Greifswald, and at the Martin Luther University, Halle-Wittenberg.

Rudolf Hoppe is Professor of Biblical Introduction and Biblical World in the Catholic Theological Faculty, University of Passau, Germany.

Frank W. Hughes is Lecturer in New Testament Studies at Codrington College, St. John, Barbados, West Indies.

Edgar Krentz is Christ Seminary-Seminex Professor Emeritus of New Testament in the Lutheran School of Theology at Chicago.

CONTRIBUTORS

Jan Lambrecht is Professor Emeritus of New Testament at the Catholic University of Leuven and now guest professor at the Pontifical Biblical Institute of Rome.

Otto Merk is Professor of New Testament Studies in the Theological Faculty, Friedrich Alexander University of Erlangen-Nürnberg, Erlangen, Germany.

Johannes Schoon-Janßen is Pastor in the Lutheran St. Urbani Congregation of Münster/Oertze, Münster, Germany.

Johan S. Vos is Assistant Professor in the Theological Faculty of the Free University, Amsterdam, The Netherlands.

Charles A. Wanamaker is Associate Professor of New Testament and Early Christian Studies in the Department of Religious Studies at the University of Cape Town, Cape Town, South Africa.

Jeffrey A. D. Weima is Professor of New Testament at Calvin Theological Seminary, Grand Rapids, MI.

Index of Modern Authors

Index of Ancient Texts